*The Dawn of the Warrior Age*

# THE DAWN *of the* WARRIOR AGE

War Tales from Medieval Japan

Translated by

ROYALL TYLER

COLUMBIA UNIVERSITY PRESS *NEW YORK*

Columbia University Press wishes to express its appreciation for assistance given by the Wm. Theodore de Bary Fund in the publication of this book.

Columbia University Press
*Publishers Since 1893*
New York Chichester, West Sussex
cup.columbia.edu



Library of Congress Cataloging-in-Publication Data
Names: Tyler, Royall, translator.
Title: The dawn of the Warrior Age : war tales from medieval Japan / translated by Royall Tyler.
Other titles: Hōgen monogatari. English.
Description: New York : Columbia University Press, [2024]
Identifiers: LCCN 2023033293 (print) | LCCN 2023033294 (ebook) | ISBN 9780231214667 (hardback) | ISBN 9780231214674 (trade paperback) | ISBN 9780231560405 (ebook)
Subjects: LCSH: Historical fiction, Japanese—Translations into English. | Japan—History—Hōgen and Heiji Insurrections, 1156–1159—Fiction. | Japan—History—Jōkyū Revolt, 1221—Fiction.
Classification: LCC PL782.E8 D39 2024 (print) | LCC PL782.E8 (ebook) | DDC 895.63/08108022—dc23/eng/20231010
LC record available at https://lccn.loc.gov/2023033293
LC ebook record available at https://lccn.loc.gov/2023033294

Cover design: Julia Kushnirsky
Cover image: *Night Attack on the Sanjō Palace*, from the Illustrated Scrolls of the Events of the Heiji Era. © Museum of Fine Arts, Boston.

# Contents

# Introduction

## The Dawn of the Warrior Age

In 1156 effective power in Japan began to slip away from the imperial court in Kyoto. The founding of the Kamakura shogunate in 1192 confirmed the change, and in 1221 the shogunate's victory over an imperial attempt to overthrow it left no doubt about the outcome. The works in this book illustrate the early and final stages of this shift. *The Tale of the Hōgen Years* (*Hōgen monogatari*; hereafter *Hōgen*) covers a deposed emperor's attempt in 1156 to regain the throne, thus provoking in the capital violence unknown there since the city's founding in 794. *The Tale of the Heiji Years* (*Heiji monogatari*; hereafter *Heiji*) narrates an equally fierce conflict in 1159, again in the capital, between rival courtier factions. And *An Account of the Jōkyū Years* (*Jōkyūki*) records Kamakura's victory over the court in 1221. The famous *Tale of the Heike* (*Heike monogatari*; hereafter *Heike*)[1] fits between the first two and the last. The medieval scholar and man of letters Jien (1155–1225) wrote in *Gukanshō*, his history of Japan completed in 1219, that the Hōgen conflict had initiated *musa no yo*, "the warrior age."[2]

## The Warriors

The deposed emperor had the support of one faction among the Fujiwara, the nonimperial nobility who dominated the court, and was opposed by another. These factions, in turn, relied on the members of two great military lineages: the Minamoto (also Genji) and the Taira (also Heike).[3] The chief function of both had long been to serve and protect the interests of the aristocracy, imperial or nonimperial, in the capital.

Fujiwara no Kamatari (614–669) had founded the Fujiwara aristocracy in the seventh century. The most powerful Fujiwara line held the highest civil offices and even claimed divine authority for serving as regent. The Taira (Heike) looked back to Emperor Kanmu (739–806), since their line had been founded by Kanmu's son Kazurahara (786–853). They therefore became known as the "Kanmu Heiji." In 825 the emperor of the time had granted Kazurahara's sons the surname Taira (an emperor or recognized imperial child has none) and so removed them from the imperial line. This action gave them the greater freedom enjoyed by commoners but also reduced their prestige: the upper Fujiwara nobility far outranked the most prominent among them. As for the Minamoto, Emperor Saga (r. 809–823) first awarded this surname to his children in 814, and ten of his successors each started a new Genji line. One was Seiwa (r. 858–876), who gave the surname to five of his children and all of his grandchildren. The Minamoto prominent in this book are all "Seiwa Genji."

Some Taira and Minamoto men became active in the capital, but most settled in the provinces. The Heike came typically, although not inevitably, to inhabit the province of Ise in central Japan. The Genji were especially numerous in the eastern provinces (the Kanto) and further north. Genji figures stand out in *Hōgen* and *Heiji*, but in the second half of the twelfth century their world was dominated by the Heike under Taira no Kiyomori (1118–1181).

The Genji and Heike were rivals. In *Hōgen*, the larger-than-life hero and rebel Minamoto no Tametomo (1138–1170?) boasts to a Taira opponent: "We Genji all descend from Emperor Seiwa. My generation, the ninth after him, is also the seventh after Rokusonnō, the sixth after Manjū, and the fourth after Yoriyoshi. I am the eighth among the sons of Tameyoshi, the fourth son of Hachimantarō Yoshiie." Indeed, a grandson of Seiwa by his son Prince Sadazumi (?–916) had become, by the process described, Minamoto no Tsunemoto (?–961). Down the generations Tsunemoto acquired the name Rokusonnō because Sadazumi was Seiwa's "sixth" (*roku*) son and because he, Tsunemoto, was also Seiwa's grandson (*son*). The ō in "Rokusonnō" further emphasizes the line's imperial origins.[4]

The Manjū mentioned by Tametomo is Tsunemoto's son Mitsunaka (912–997). It is he who, in 969, denounced Minamoto no Takaakira (914–982) to the chief Fujiwara nobles of the day, accusing him of plotting against the heir apparent. This incident consolidated Fujiwara power and won Mitsunaka great favor. In medieval legend, Takaakira's ensuing exile inspired Murasaki Shikibu to begin writing *The Tale of Genji*. Later on Mitsunaka became known as Manjū (another reading of the characters for his name).

Tametomo might also have mentioned Mitsunaka's son Yorinobu (968–1048), who founded the Kawachi (a province name) branch of the Seiwa Genji and whose line passed through his son Yoshiie to produce, in time, Yoritomo, the Kamakura founder. Yorinobu was a retainer of Murasaki Shikibu's patron, Fujiwara no Michinaga (966–1027). He governed several provinces, served as Chinjufu Shogun (Kyoto's military commander in the north), and played a major role in consolidating Genji power in the Kanto.

Yorinobu's eldest son, Yoriyoshi (988–1075), asserted further leadership over the eastern warriors. After clashing in 1056 with the locally powerful Abe family, in 1051 he too was appointed governor of Mutsu (the far north of Honshu) and Chinjufu Shogun. In 1063 he triumphed over the rebellious Abe brothers, Sadatō and Munetō—names that occur repeatedly in the Genji roster of victorious ancestors. Also in 1063, he founded the predecessor to the great Tsurugaoka Hachiman shrine in Kamakura.

Yoshiie (1039–1106), Yoriyoshi's son, came to be known as Hachimantarō, "First Son of [the Minamoto ancestral deity] Hachiman." He, too, governed Mutsu and served as Chinjufu Shogun. In 1087 he won, still in the north, a war against Kiyowara Takehira and Iehira—two more names for the Genji list of conquered foes. Yoshiie was a turbulent figure, and his son Yoshichika was violent. As governor of Tsushima, Yoshichika murdered and plundered, and he ignored an order, issued through his father, to return to the capital. In 1102 the court formally banished him to the island of Oki, but he ignored that order, too.

Such is the lineage proudly claimed by the Genji warriors. With Tameyoshi (1096–1156) it enters the *Hōgen* present. Tameyoshi, Yoshichika's natural son, was adopted by Yoshiie, only to be adopted again, because of his unruliness, by Yoshiie's heir Yoshitada. In 1109 Yoshitada was assassinated, and Tameyoshi succeeded him as the head of the Kawachi Genji. He also became an officer in the capital's police and in a corps of palace guards. Unfortunately, he and his men often behaved so badly that for ten years he held no post at all. In 1143, in search of support, he formally declared himself a retainer of the powerful Fujiwara no Yorinaga, and in 1146 he was reappointed to office. In 1154 he was dismissed again because of the reckless ways of Tametomo, his eighth son.

## The Hōgen Conflict

In 1156 (Hōgen 1/7/2) Retired Emperor Toba (1103–1156; r. 1107–1123) died. Violence broke out within days.

Upon abdicating, Emperor Shirakawa (1053–1129, r. 1072–1086), a predecessor of Toba, had instituted the practice of *insei*: rule by the *in*, the retired emperor. A retired emperor could enthrone or depose a reigning one at will. In 1123 Toba abdicated in favor of Sutoku (1119–1164, r. 1123–1141), but in 1141 his empress, Bifukumon-in, persuaded him to depose this son by another mother in favor her own, Emperor Konoe (1139–1155, r. 1141–1155). Sutoku was furious. Konoe died young, and Bifukumon-in believed that Sutoku and his allies had cursed him to death.

Sutoku, like everyone else, had expected his father to enthrone either himself or his son Prince Shigehito. Instead, Toba enthroned Go-Shirakawa (1127–1192, r. 1155–1158), another, younger son. When Toba died, Sutoku therefore moved swiftly to regain the throne. His faction, which he led along with Fujiwara no Yorinaga (1120–1156), was supported by men under Minamoto no Yoshitomo. Go-Shirakawa and Fujiwara no Tadamichi (1097–1164), Yorinaga's elder brother, led the opposition. They were supported by warriors under Minamoto no Tameyoshi.

The conflict's explosive force arose from bitter rivalry between the closely related leaders. Not only were Sutoku and Go-Shirakawa half-brothers but Yorinaga and Tadamichi were brothers as well. Their father Tadazane (1078–1162), a former regent, strongly favored Yorinaga. In 1150 he dismissed Tadamichi as head of the Fujiwara house (*uji no chōja*) and, with the support of Tameyoshi and Tameyoshi's sons, awarded the position to Yorinaga. He then ordered Tadamichi to cede the office of regent, too, to Yorinaga. Tadamichi refused. Tadazane retaliated by recommending Yorinaga, who already occupied the lofty post of left minister,[5] for imperial appointment as *nairan* ("private inspector"). In early 1151 Retired Emperor Toba complied.[6] Yorinaga was now the de facto regent, although Tadamichi still held the title. Yorinaga wanted the title, too. Sutoku's attempt to wrest the throne from Go-Shirakawa allowed him to make a move of his own.

On the Minamoto side, Tameyoshi (Tadamichi and Go-Shirakawa) and Yoshitomo (Yorinaga and Sutoku) were father and son. A failure in his official career, Tameyoshi had sworn fealty to Tadazane, the brothers' father, and then to Yorinaga. Unfortunately, Tametomo's lawlessness had then frustrated him again.

Genji-Heike rivalry amplified these personal tensions. Taira no Kiyomori, unlike some of his relatives, supported Tadamichi and Go-Shirakawa. This support made him an opponent of Tameyoshi but, briefly, an ally of Yoshitomo. Once the battle was over, he therefore neutralized Yoshitomo by making him execute his own father and brothers. Kiyomori's large family continued to flourish, but Yoshitomo survived almost alone as the senior Genji. In 1159 (the Heiji conflict) he moved disastrously to regain the advantage.

The tensions between the Genji and Heike leaders could not have turned to open conflict unless prompted by discord, at a level above them, between the senior Fujiwara. Nor could this discord between Fujiwara nobles have declared itself so publicly without prompting from the imperial succession dispute. Only two and a half years later, however, trouble broke out again, sparked by a Fujiwara lord's frivolous ambitions. When fighting erupted for a third time in the early 1180s (*The Tale of the Heike*), imperial and Fujiwara interests hardly mattered anymore. The Genji simply set out on their own to settle scores with the Heike. By 1221 (the Jōkyū conflict), sixty-five years after Hōgen, the Kamakura warriors could openly mock the pretensions of Retired Emperor Go-Toba and pack him off in exile to a remote island.

## Editions Consulted and the Question of Performance

Like many medieval and earlier works, including *The Tale of the Heike*, these texts have no original or fixed form. They survive in variant versions, some older or more recent; some complete, some incomplete; some sober, others more ornamented or discursive. They do not necessarily vary widely in content, although some certainly include material not present in others. This variation is to be expected for works that circulated only in manuscript, that could be reproduced only by copying, and that remained of interest to readers over a long period of time. The texts translated are those published in Tochigi Yoshitada, Kusaka Tsutomu, et al., eds., *Hōgen monogatari, Heiji monogatari, Jōkyūki*, Shin Nihon koten bungaku taikei 43 (Tokyo: Iwanami, 1992) (hereafter, SNKBT). The editors deemed these closest to the now-lost earliest state of the work. I also consulted the *Hōgen* and *Heiji* texts published in Yanase Kiyoshi, Yashiro Kazuo, et al., eds., *Shōmonki, Mutsuwaki, Hōgen monogatari, Heiji monogatari*, Shin Nihon koten bungaku zenshū 41 (Tokyo: Shogakukan, 2002) (hereafter, SNKBZ).[7]

The Kakuichi-bon text of *Heike*, the one translated several times into English, was written down in 1371 by the head of a guild of itinerant bards who sang and declaimed the tale throughout Japan. Did any of the works in this book circulate in this way? Slender evidence suggests that at least *Heiji* and perhaps *Hōgen* may have done so for a time. The word *monogatari* ("tale") in both titles suggests possible oral performance. Over time, however, with the spread of literacy and the written word, both *monogatari* in Japanese and "tale" in English came to be associated above all with works for personal reading. In this regard nothing is known of *Jōkyū*, but the *ki* of its title ("record," "written account") is unrelated to speech or song.

## Names

In most premodern Japanese prose works, names and other personal appellations, including official titles in lieu of names, challenge anyone wishing to make the work accessible in another language. Readers may expect a single, consistent name for each person, possibly with a title attached (Lady This, Doctor That, Colonel So-and-So), but in the original there are many ways to refer to an individual, according to various aspects of context.

Fortunately, a single appellation is usually possible, even if it is out of keeping with the original. A man bears a given name of record, one used only rarely in daily life and speech, and this name, if known, allows identification and alphabetization. Japanese scholars use it when compiling a genealogy (centuries ago or now) or a glossary. Without it, a title or office must do. A woman's personal name was rarely entered in genealogical records or even known outside her immediate family, unless she was of exceptionally high rank, and even then she was normally referred to not by name but by personal title. Examples here are Go-Toba's empress, Bifukumon-in, or Taira no Kiyomori's stepmother, Ike-no-zenni.

# *The Dawn of the Warrior Age*

# The Tale of the Hōgen Years

# Summary and Note on the Text

## Book 1

Emperor Toba abdicates in favor of Sutoku, his eldest son. Years later his empress, Bifukumon-in (not Sutoku's mother), bears a son who soon becomes Toba's favorite. Toba deposes Sutoku and in the boy's third year enthrones him as Emperor Konoe. Konoe dies in his seventeenth year. Opinion favors restoring Sutoku to the throne, but Bifukumon-in believes that he and his allies cursed Konoe to death. Toba therefore bypasses Sutoku and enthrones another son of Bifukumon-in as Emperor Go-Shirakawa. Sutoku is outraged.

In the winter of Kyūju 2 (1155), Toba visits the great shrine of Kumano, where an oracle predicts his death and the ensuing chaos. The next year he dies. Sutoku's anger explodes. The senior minister Fujiwara no Yorinaga, already in bitter rivalry with his elder brother, the regent Tadamichi, gathers troops to support Sutoku. Tadamichi supports Go-Shirakawa. Warriors on Sutoku and Yorinaga's side are, among others, Minamoto no Tameyoshi; his sons Yoshikata and Tametomo; and Taira no Tadamasa, the uncle of the leading Taira warrior, Kiyomori. However, Kiyomori rallies to Go-Shirakawa and Tadamichi, together with such Minamoto figures as Yoshitomo and Yorimasa.

## Book 2

Go-Shirakawa's forces attack Sutoku's residence, the Shirakawa Mansion. Tametomo's defense efforts fail, and Yoshitomo sets it on fire. Sutoku renounces the world at the great temple of Ninnaji. Yorinaga, struck by a stray arrow, flees toward Nara but dies on the way. Kiyomori beheads Tadamasa and his son (among others) and forces Yoshitomo to execute Tameyoshi, his own father.

## Book 3

Tameyoshi's five youngest sons are executed. His wife drowns herself in the Katsura River. Sutoku is exiled to the province of Sanuki on Shikoku, where he copies the sutras in blood and dies cursing the realm. Tametomo, who for a time evaded capture, is exiled to the Izu peninsula, where he eventually kills himself.

## Note on the Text

Some fifty *Hōgen monogatari* manuscripts exist. The *Nakarai-bon*, the one translated, is of uncertain date but seems to preserve the earliest surviving form of the work. The *Bunpō-bon*, dated 1318, is the oldest, but only the second of its three books survives. It includes notes and variants clearly drawn from earlier ones now lost. Scholars have proposed 1223 as the earliest possible date for the origins of the extant manuscript lines.

The different versions of *Hōgen*, including an "old movable type edition" (*kokatsuji-bon*) published around 1600, tend toward increasing elaboration and ornamentation. The oldest dated *complete* manuscript, the *Hōtoku-bon* (1451, chosen for SNKBZ), reveals this trend. Its text is almost the same as that of the *Kotohira-bon*, the one best known from the seventeenth century into recent times.

The subheadings are those given in the original manuscript.

# Book 1

## 1. The Accession of Emperor Go-Shirakawa

Lately there lived a sovereign known to the world as Retired Emperor Toba. His generation was the forty-sixth after the Great Sun Goddess, and of emperors since Jinmu he was the seventy-fourth. He was Emperor Horikawa's eldest son. The Posthumous Grand Empress bore him; her father was the grand counselor Sanesue, a grandson of the Kan-in chancellor Kinsue. Born on the 16th of the 1st month of Kōwa 5 [1103], Toba rose to heir apparent on the 17th of the 8th month of that year. Emperor Horikawa then passed away on the 9th of the 7th month of Kashō 2 [1107], and Toba assumed the imperial dignity on the 19th, in his fifth year. During his sixteen-year reign, peace prevailed within the Four Seas and calm pervaded the realm. Wind and rain honored their proper times, nor did cold or heat ever transgress its proper season.

In his twenty-first year, on the 28th of the 1st month of Hōan 4 [1123], Toba ceded the throne to his own first son, Emperor Sutoku, known later in exile as the Sanuki Retired Emperor.[1] Retired Emperor Shirakawa's passing, on the 7th of the 7th month of Daiji 4 [1129], then left Toba governing authority over the realm. He prized loyalty and followed the ways of the sage emperors of the past; he forgave the evildoer and cultivated divine compassion. The land prospered, and the people felt secure. So shone his kindly light that the entire realm enjoyed comfort and ease.

In due course, on the 18th of the 5th month of Hōen 5 [1139], Bifukumon-in, then still a consort,[2] bore him the future emperor Konoe. Delighted, Toba appointed the new prince heir apparent on the 17th of the 8th month of that year, and on the 7th of the 12th month of Eiji 1 [1141], in his third year, this prince assumed the imperial dignity. His predecessor, Retired Emperor Sutoku, was then known as the Junior Eminence, and his father, Retired Emperor Toba, as the Senior.

Nothing significant had ever marred the reign of the heir apparent's predecessor, and his deposition therefore came as a shock. Sutoku must have resented it because there seems to have been thereafter no love lost between him and his father. He presumably aspired to regain the throne, having ceded it only against his will; and no doubt he also wished to ensure the succession for his eldest son, Prince Shigehito. However, his precise intentions remain unfathomable. Retired Emperor Toba, then in his thirty-ninth year and still in full possession of his powers, renounced the world on the 10th of the 7th month of Eiji 1. It is wonderful indeed that he should have so visibly fulfilled, while still in perfect health, the promise of excellent inner karma amassed in past lives by setting out to follow the true way.

On the 23rd of the 7th month of Kyūju 2 [1155], Emperor Konoe unexpectedly passed away. This was a terrible blow. Needless to say, Toba and Bifukumon-in were shattered. Sutoku assumed that at least his son, Prince Shigehito, would now accede to the throne, even if he did not regain it himself, and people at large shared his assumption. However, under wholly unforeseen pressure from Bifukumon-in, Toba instead appointed his hitherto relatively unknown Fourth Prince as Emperor Go-Shirakawa. High and low attributed Bifukumon-in's pressure to the gulf between a mother and the son of another wife. Sutoku was of course the Fourth Prince's full brother, but apparently Bifukumon-in nonetheless maneuvered in the latter's favor and privately advanced to Toba compelling arguments to that end.[3] Naturally, this outcome only deepened Sutoku's outrage.

## 2. Retired Emperor Toba's Pilgrimage to Kumano *and* The Oracle Delivered There

In the winter of Kyūju 2, Retired Emperor Toba made a pilgrimage to Kumano and spent the night there in vigil before the Shōjōden. At midnight the sanctuary doors opened, and a little left hand came forth, lovely and white. The hand turned palm up, then down, three times. Toba wondered what this could mean. It was a sacred dream.

In great astonishment Toba summoned his appointed guide and asked for an accomplished medium. "Send her to me," he commanded. "I wish her to call down the divinity."

Peerless among the mediums of Kumano was Iwaka-no-ita, originally from the province of Mimasaka. Toba had her approach. "There is something that I do not understand," he explained. "You must discover what it means."

She began calling down the deity at the hour of the tiger [4 A.M.]. Midday passed without any response. Those present watched in wide-eyed consternation until at last the deity descended. The medium then delivered an oracle in the form of a poem:

| *te ni musubu* | Cupped so in the hand, |
|---|---|
| *mizu ni yadoreru* | water harbors in its depths |
| *tsukikage wa* | the face of a moon |
| *aru ka naki ka no* | real perhaps, perhaps unreal: |
| *yo ni wa narikeru* | just so are the lives of men. |

She raised her left hand and turned the palm over three times. Initially taken aback, Toba then grasped that the oracle was genuine. In haste he stepped down from his mat, pressed his palms together in an attitude of prayer, and said, "My question is this: What does the future hold?"

"You will die next year," came the reply. "The world will then turn over like the palm of a hand."

Toba wept, and every senior noble and privy gentleman with him. "But at what time next year?" he asked.

The medium promptly replied:

| *natsu hatsuru* | A fan at summer's end, |
|---|---|
| *ōgi to aki no* | or the gleaming drop of dew |
| *shiratsuyu to* | that heralds autumn: |
| *izure ka saki ni* | which of these, as time goes by, |
| *okimasarubeki* | will be the first to fall? |

"The last days of summer, then, or early autumn," Toba said.

"Can nothing be done to spare His Eminence this calamity and prolong his life?" the weeping nobles inquired.

"Such is his fixed karma. I can do nothing for him." With these words the divinity ascended.

Toba was stunned. He returned to the capital in a mournful mood.

## 3. The Death of Retired Emperor Toba

In the spring and summer of Hōgen 1 [1156], Retired Emperor Toba became chronically indisposed. He was no longer himself, spiritually or physically, and sickness overcame him. Those who had accompanied him to Kumano remembered what had happened there. Those who had not attributed his condition to deep sorrow over the loss of Emperor Konoe. In fact, however, his final illness was one fated by karma.

In the summer of that year, on the 12th of the 6th month, Bifukumon-in became a nun at her Jōbodai-in residence and donned the habit of renunciation. It was understood that she had done so because of overwhelming grief caused by Emperor Konoe's passing and by the failure of Toba's condition to improve. All this was very sad. Kankū of Mitaki was the master who administered the precepts.

Hope for Toba dwindled day by day. Those around him lamented loudly, "The greatest and most secret rites have no effect, and the physicians' art achieves nothing! Oh, what is to become of him?" On the 2nd of the 7th month he finally passed away, in his fifty-fourth year. It is a great pity that he never reached even his sixtieth, but that is hardly to be wondered at, for this conditioned existence is so uncertain that the old may live on while the young depart.

All regretted, nonetheless, that his venerable years had not grown to number a thousand. The heavens seemed to have gone dark; it was as though the sun and moon no longer shone. The people grieved as though torn from father and mother. When the Buddha Shakyamuni announced his own passing under the twinned sal trees, to demonstrate the truth that all born must die, men and angels mourned; and when on the 15th day of the 2nd month he entered nirvana, no fewer than fifty-two kinds of beings gathered there in visible grief. Every denizen of the palace, high or low, did the same when Retired Emperor Toba passed away on the second day of autumn. Even insentient grasses and trees made their sorrow plain. How much more deeply, then, did they mourn, those men and women who for long years had given him intimate service!

The Mothers of the Realm[4] and their attendant ladies, from whom no brocade curtain had ever screened him, saw him no more; the senior nobles and privy gentlemen privileged to approach his presence no longer heard him speak.[5] Bifukumon-in's mourning seemed especially intense. Where once she had contemplated the dragon visage with jeweled blinds raised high, or sat beside the jade presence on the clean-swept, golden floor, there lay now only empty bedding.[6] His tears of longing for times past had pooled beneath his pillow, but under the nearby lamp no sign of him remained. The only sound, cricket song from below the fence outside, grated somehow on her ears. She glanced at the flowers in the southern garden, but they had lost their fragrance now that he and she no longer lay sleeve to sleeve; she lent an ear to the insects in the garden to the north, but their singing was not what it had been when his pillow and hers stood side by side. The nights only seemed very, very long, and so too the days. Emperor Konoe's passing the year before had been a bitter blow, and that of His Eminence defied description. Both sovereigns had looked forward to a thousand, nay, ten thousand years, but transience affects all, high or low. Impermanence touches nobleman and commoner alike. The supremely enlightened Tathāgata still betrays the workings of cause and effect; the Shrāvaka, great in wisdom, reveals nonetheless the cost of earlier karma.[7]

As things stood, Sutoku's intentions now gave reason for concern.

## 4. Sutoku Moves to Rebel

So it was that clamor filled the palace and whispers the residence of Retired Emperor Sutoku. "Now that Toba is gone," people told one another, "there will be trouble between Sutoku and Bifukumon-in. There is certain to be strife."

Retired Emperor Toba passed away on the 2nd. The 3rd had not even dawned when warriors attached to Sutoku occupied Tōsanjō.[8] They gathered there that night and plotted rebellion. At daylight they climbed trees and hillocks to spy on Takamatsu House, at the crossing of Ane-no-kōji and Nishi-no-tōin, where Emperor Go-Shirakawa resided.[9]

At the news His Majesty summoned Minamoto no Yoshitomo, the governor of Shimotsuke. He commanded Yoshitomo to detain Fujiwara no Mitsuzane, the official then responsible for Tōsanjō, together with a few of his men, and to question him on what was going on. There had apparently been rumors of rebellion during Toba's last illness, and lately warriors had been entering the capital from far and wide. Horses and carts laden with the accoutrements of war had been pouring in. Armed men had gathered that night at Tōsanjō, although by daylight they kept out of sight.

For some time Sutoku had been saying to himself, "When a father's throne passes to one of his sons, the choice depends less on the seniority of the mother than on the candidate's ability and on the distinction of his commoner father-in-law. In my case, I lost the throne to Konoe solely because his mother was my father's current favorite, and I have suffered from that injury ever since. After Konoe's death the succession should have passed to Prince Shigehito, but no, in the teeth of all good sense Shigehito lost out to the Fourth Prince. It is too much." Those close to him discerned the direction of his thoughts and often debated what to do.

There was a gentleman known as the Uji left minister Yorinaga, the second son of the Chisoku-in regent Fujiwara no Tadazane.[10] His father favored him beyond his other sons. Irreproachable in character, Yorinaga had mastered both Japanese and Chinese formal usage, and he knew the records of other houses as well as he did those of his own. He excelled at scholarship and had plumbed the depths of every worthy pursuit. Such a treasure of the realm promised well as a future regent.

Yorinaga's elder brother was Tadamichi. Yorinaga had no praise for Tadamichi's skill at poetry or for the quality of his calligraphy. "No," he said, "poetry is an idle pastime useless for the conduct of essential court functions. Calligraphy, too, is a passing amusement. The wise man does not waste time on them." For his part, he applied himself to the Chinese classics; upheld the virtues of benevolence, propriety, right conduct, wisdom, and good faith; and pondered matters of reward, punishment, and meritorious service. He saw penetratingly into government affairs and strove to correct the errors of the people. For this reason he was dubbed the "Haughty Left Minister" and correspondingly feared. In fact, however, he was scrupulously correct and fair. When an attendant or an oxherd who had incurred his wrath sought to justify himself, he listened carefully and felt remorse if the man had not actually been at fault. If, while deliberating affairs of state in council at the palace, he saw fit to reprimand a secretary or some other junior official, and the man then defended himself convincingly, he humbly acknowledged his error on the spot and wrote a letter of apology. Should the official be too awestruck to accept it, he would insist as follows: "I wrote this letter of my own free will. Accept it, then. Will you not honor your household by showing off to its every member a letter of apology from your highest superior?" They say that the official would then deferentially comply. Yorinaga accurately distinguished right from wrong and good from evil, and for this he garnered the world's praise.

Yorinaga's father Tadazane, too, thought highly of him. On the 26th of the 9th month of Kyūan 6 [1150] Tadazane made Yorinaga the head of the Fujiwara house; and on the 19th of the 1st month of Kyūan 7 an imperial decree named Yorinaga private inspector, thus giving him practical authority over the affairs of the realm.[11] No minister had held this office before, and the appointment provoked some criticism. However, his father's wish assured his position, and the emperor and his officials gave the appointment their approval.

Lord Tadamichi was regent in name only. Nowhere did he intervene; he merely looked on. He often said, "If under our present emperor the world is to return to warm simplicity,[12] then there are only two possibilities: His Majesty must accept his regent's resignation, or his regent must receive appointment as private inspector and head of the Fujiwara house." The regent and the left minister were certainly brothers, and an arrangement made by their father had bound them to each other in another way as well.[13] They therefore treated each other with great respect. Over time, however, their relationship seems to have soured.

Yorinaga reflected, "Once I have secured Prince Shigehito the succession and given his father sovereignty over the realm, I will be able to govern as I please." He spent the night in consultation with Sutoku at the latter's residence. One wondered what they might be plotting.

Sutoku addressed Yorinaga at length. "Consider the present in the light of the past," he said. "Tenchi, Emperor Jomei's heir apparent, was Jomei's son. Jomei had several other sons, but it was Tenchi who succeeded to the throne. Ninmyō, Emperor Saga's son, did so over the many sons of Emperor Junna. Kazan preceded Ichijō, and Sanjō reigned before Go-Suzaku. There are many such examples. Personally, I lack any particular merit, but fidelity to the ten precepts nonetheless won me birth as my father's heir apparent, and, all unworthy, and despite the degeneracy of the times, I rose to reign over the realm. For me fully to deserve the exalted title of Retired Emperor, Shigehito would have to have received his due; but no, on the contrary, he was passed over in favor of the Fourth Prince, who has no merit in either letters or war. Neither my son nor I could quell an outrage that each passing month and day of my late father's final two years made more unbearable. Now that his smoke has risen to the heavens, I see no need to stifle this outrage any longer. It could hardly violate the will of the gods or contravene the wishes of men if I were now to challenge the world as it stands."

Yorinaga had grasped that he would undoubtedly be regent if Sutoku were to succeed. "You are quite right," he apparently replied. "It is time to act."

Having long been disposed to do just that, Sutoku now resolved to leave the Tanaka Pavilion at Toba.[14] Meanwhile, all sorts of rumors were circulating about what might follow. No one, high or low, actually knew anything, but anxiety pervaded the capital. Households closed their gates, and the clatter of horses and carts carrying the goods of rich and poor in all directions, to hide them, rang out everywhere. "What on earth is going on?" people groaned. "Sutoku may indeed mean to usurp power, but he could hardly move to do so a mere ten days after his father's passing. It is not for mere mortals to divine the will of the great imperial deities.[15] None of this would be happening if Toba were still alive. Under his reign the stars above kept quietly each to its place, and one heard only the barest murmur from the ocean waves;[16] yet suddenly, alas, turmoil is rife!"

## 5. The Emperor's Forces Fan Out *and* Chikaharu and His Men Are Taken Alive

Toba passed away on the 2nd of the month. Rebels then began pouring into the capital. Warriors crowded through the streets, their uproar audible even in the palace. On the 5th, the police were ordered to secure all barriers. Officers Taira no Motomori for the Uji Road, Suezane for the Yodo Road, Koreshige for Awataguchi, Taira no Sanetoshi for the Kukume Road, and Minamoto no Suketsune for Ōeyama received this command: "Secure all barriers, detain anyone armed, and deliver him to the palace." The order was issued through the minor counselor Shinzei. The men received it, kneeling, and withdrew.

That night the regent Tadamichi, the grand counselor Koremichi, and the other senior nobles repaired to the palace, where they discussed a range of subjects. In response to reports that rebels were about, a decree required their arrest and banishment. Muneyoshi, the director of the heir apparent's household, then at the Toba Mansion, was summoned to appear. However, he pleaded illness not to come.

On the 6th, Motomori set out with one hundred horse to secure the Uji Road. Near Hosshōji he encountered fourteen or fifteen helmeted warriors on foot, in light armor and with arrows at their backs, and the same number on horseback: thirty in all. They were coming from toward Yamato. Motomori hailed them to ask where they were from and where they were going. "Who are you," he inquired, "and whose forces do you propose to join? I am Motomori. By imperial command I am on my way to secure the bridge at Uji. If you are going to the palace, then please come with me. If you are not, I cannot let you pass."

"My name is Uno Chikaharu," their leader answered, "and by order of Lord Yorinaga, the left minister, I am on my way to lend my strength to Retired Emperor Sutoku."

Motomori replied, "I am the second son of Taira no Kiyomori, the governor of Aki, and I bear an imperial command. Refuse to obey it, and you will not pass."

"The man of bow and arrow does not serve two masters," Chikaharu retorted. "Now learn who I am. I am Uno no Shichirō Chikaharu, a son of Haruhiro, the provisional governor of Shimōsa. I am at once a grandson of Yoriharu, of the Bureau of Central Affairs, and a descendant of Yorichika, the governor of Yamato, who was himself a younger brother of Raikō, the governor of Settsu. Uno county of Yamato has long been my home, and I make bold to claim the profession of arms. A Genji does not serve two lords. No imperial decree can force me to the palace!" Chikaharu passed on by.

Motomori and his hundred men moved to surround and arrest him. Chikaharu and his riders swiftly closed ranks, bridle to bridle, charged the one hundred with fierce battle cries, and broke through. Chikaharu then wheeled, charged again, cut Motomori's force in quarters, and captured one of his men. Motomori fought back fiercely. He must have been clever despite the youth of his nineteenth year, because he raced up to a high place, surveyed the landscape in all directions, and announced, "I see no reinforcements coming! These are all the men he has! Take them alive, every last one!" Three, four, or five riders closed in on each of Chikaharu's, grappled with him, sent him crashing to the ground, and seized him. The sovereign's word brooks no challenge. Emperor Go-Shirakawa ordered Uno Shichirō and his fifteen taken to the west prison when he learned of their capture.

## 6. Sutoku's Rebellion Comes to Light *and* A Move to Suppress It *with* Palace Minister Saneyoshi's Advice

On the 8th, Tadamichi, Koremichi, Muneyoshi, and the other senior nobles gathered in council. They decided to banish Yorinaga to the province of Hizen on the 11th, for the reason that he was now in open rebellion.

Meanwhile, Yorinaga confined a monk within the Tōsanjō compound and had him perform secret rites there. Word spread that he was laying curses on the emperor. Despite repeated summons to present himself to His Majesty, he failed to appear. Yoshitomo was therefore ordered to bring him in. He went to Tōsanjō and knocked on the gate. When it remained closed, he went round to the small gate at the southwest corner of the compound and entered through there. There was no one about. He was passing the Tsunofuri and Hayabusa sanctuaries[17] when he caught sight of a monk performing a ritual at an altar beside the Senkan spring. It was the adept Shōson, of Miidera.

Yoshitomo ordered Shōson to report to the emperor, but he got no reply. Two of his men approached Shōson from left and right and tried to stand him up, but the monk kept his bent arms clamped to his sides like a wrestler. "Then take care of him as the law requires," Yoshitomo commanded. Five men approached Shōson, laid him out, bound him with a white sash, and carried him off to the emperor together with the sacred image from his altar, his liturgical documents, and Yorinaga's written command.

When Masayori, the deputy director of Civil Affairs, learned of the party's arrival, he sent the senior chamberlain Toshinari to find out what was going on. Shōson stated, "I was merely praying, by Lord Yorinaga's order, that harmony should reign once more between him and the regent, his elder brother." He said no more, since Yorinaga's written order was there for all to see. The rites he had been performing were apparently those of Uzusama, Kongō Dōji, and Shōdengu.[18] The rebel plot was obvious.

Taira no Tadamasa, the deputy right equerry, and Minamoto no Yorinori, a chamberlain, turned out to be among the plotters. Masayori was therefore charged with bringing them in. He sent the Council of State secretary Morotsune to do so, but they made excuses and failed to comply. At Yorinaga's behest, these two had apparently undertaken to lead his attack force when the time came.

This was the initial seventh day since Retired Emperor Toba's passing.[19] Morotsune received the order to proceed to the Tanaka Pavilion at Toba and ensure the performance of the suitable rites. Sutoku was there at the time but did not appear, which greatly puzzled everyone. In fact, confidential intelligence had it that he would soon be on his way to the capital.

The Left City commissioner Norinaga admonished Sutoku sternly. "People will simply not understand your absenting yourself during the first forty-nine days after His Late Eminence's death," he said. "Besides, how could you possibly fail to respect the feelings of the invisible powers?" However, Sutoku ignored him and made it obvious that he refused to listen.

At his wits' end, Norinaga went to call on the palace minister, Saneyoshi, and informed him of Sutoku's intentions. Saneyoshi expressed astonishment. "Someone must secretly be putting him up to it," he said. "He is courting disaster. No doubt these are the latter days, but even now it is not for us ordinary beings to comment on the fate of the Son of Heaven. That is up to the Sun Goddess and Hachiman. Our land is a mere scattering of far-flung millet grains, but we have our gods, and our imperial mausolea protect us. Both the present emperor and his predecessor are Retired Emperor Sutoku's younger brothers. However distasteful he may find it, this is hardly the first time an emperor has lost the throne to a younger brother. He should therefore accept the fate meted out to him by Heaven. If it does not please him, he is free to renounce the world and retire into obscurity, there to pray to the gods and buddhas for his first-born son. In any case, I cannot fathom his leaving for the capital while he is still in mourning for his father. You must find a moment to let him know discreetly that he is inviting later regret."

Norinaga returned to Sutoku with this message, explaining that the palace minister had asked him to deliver it. Sutoku heard him out. "No doubt he is right," he said, "but Hyōe, a gentlewoman of mine, has warned me that I run a grave risk if I stay where I am. I am planning to leave only in order to evade that threat."

On the 10th day Morotsune went to Yorinaga's residence, accompanied by a Council of State messenger bearing an imperial decree. Yorinaga gave him this oral reply: "The men you want are Tadamasa and Yorinori."

Yorinaga was to be banished the next day, the 11th. That night Sutoku moved from the Tanaka Pavilion at Toba to the Shirakawa Mansion of the former Kamo Priestess.[20] No one realized who he was, because the Priestess's household had been told to identify the arrival as that of her predecessor. He was accompanied by Norinaga, the Left City commissioner; Sanekiyo, the provisional right equerry; Yorisuke, the former Yamashiro governor; and Taira no Iehiro, an officer of the Left Gate Watch.

## 7. Sutoku Summons Tameyoshi

Thus modestly attended, Sutoku entered the Shirakawa Mansion and that night summoned the police official Minamoto no Tameyoshi. He had done so repeatedly in recent days, and Tameyoshi had agreed to come, only to change his mind at the last minute. Given his manifest indecision, Norinaga went directly to Tameyoshi's home at Rokujō-Horikawa, there to deliver the summons himself.

Tameyoshi said, "In the past I have often been called to serve the sovereign, but only twice before have I been asked actually to fight for him. The first time was in my fourteenth year, when Yoshiakira was killed. My uncle Yoshitsuna, the governor of Mino, had been branded an enemy of the court and had taken refuge at Kōgayama in Ōmi. When ordered to attack him, I promptly did so. His men fled, and his sons killed themselves. Yoshitsuna himself stooped to renouncing the world, and I took him prisoner. The second time was in my eighteenth year, when ten thousand Nara monks rode up to the capital to attack Mount Hiei. Those are the occasions I mean. Otherwise I have sent young warriors to put down trouble arising here or there in the provinces, but I have no experience or knowledge of pitched battle.

"In this land of Japan there always have been, and there are now, many worthy men-at-arms, and my sons are among them. My eldest, Yoshitomo, grew up in the east and has mastered every secret of the warrior's art. His men are all from the Kanto. However, he has been called to serve His Majesty. None of my other sons would be up to commanding a major force, except for the eighth, Tametomo. Tametomo grew up in Kyushu and is skilled at arms. This is now his seventeenth or eighteenth year. He has courage, and he says that he aims to equal Yoshitomo. What makes him a born warrior is that his left, bow arm is four inches longer than his right. His bow is therefore unusually long, hence his arrows as well. He was sent off to Kyushu when he became insubordinate, and he now lives at Otonashi-ga-hara in Bungo under the protection of Ietō, the provisional governor of Owari.

"Tametomo fought his first battle in the tenth month of his thirteenth year, with the aim of subjugating those Kyushu squires who had not yet submitted to him; and he fought more than twenty between then and the third month of his fifteenth year. He is expert at besieging a fortress or destroying an enemy. In three years he subjugated all of Kyushu and appointed himself, when the court failed to do so, constable-general over the island. That was six years ago.

"Tametomo's insubordination recently got me dismissed from my post. No doubt that was just as well. I will direct him in this instance to act on my behalf. By all means summon him and appoint him to command your attack force. If I decline the honor myself, it is above all because I own eight sets of heirloom armor, named Tsukikazu, Hikazu, Genga-ga-usuginu, Usugane, Hizamaru, Hachiryū, Omodaka, and Tatenashi, and because in a prophetic dream I saw the wind scatter them in all directions. That is the reason for my great reluctance."

Norinaga replied, "That is no reason at all. No dream, however vivid, should affect a man after he wakes. Perhaps you did dream that you lost your armor, but that certainly does not mean that you will lose it in waking life. You must go and explain yourself to Retired Emperor Sutoku in person. You cannot possibly respond this way to an imperial summons without even leaving home."

Tameyoshi therefore set out with six of his sons: his fourth, Yorikata; his fifth, Yorinaka; his sixth, Tamemune; his seventh, Tamenari; his eighth, Tametomo; and his ninth, Tamenaka. In their company he repaired to the Shirakawa Mansion. There he received the Aoyagi estate in the province of Mino, the Iba estate in the province of Ōmi, and appointment as an officer of the retired emperor's household. "You will serve in the Upper North Guards,"[21] Sutoku declared, "and your son Yorikata will be a chamberlain." Iehiro's son Yasuhiro also received appointment to office. Ienaga, Moromitsu, and Yorisuke were then in the North Guards.

## 8. Yorinaga Comes Up to the Capital *with* His Arrival

Yorinaga, at Uji, learned that Sutoku had gone to the Shirakawa Mansion, and he sent Fujiwara no Morinori to verify the report. Now, the Shirakawa North Pavilion stands north of Ōi-no-mikado and east of the Kamo River, along the south side of Kasuga-kōji. Sutoku called Morinori there and spoke to him; then Morinori returned to Uji and reported what he had heard. Yorinaga set out from Uji in a palanquin and, traveling via Daigo to escape notice,[22] repaired to the Shirakawa Mansion in person. Sugawara no Morinobu, an Academy official, and Shigetsuna, a former Yamashiro governor, shared his carriage.[23] This was a secret journey, and Yorinaga therefore continued on via the Kohata hills and Rokuhara. His journey recalled Han Gaozu's[24] device of carrying General Ji Xin in his chariot straight past the enemy camp. Morinobu and Shigetsuna, however, seem to have traveled in a different mood. "How terrifying!" they cried as they alighted, trembling and weeping. "We are to be the prey of demons!"

The following men gathered to Sutoku:

The left minister Yorinaga
The Left City commissioner Norinaga
The Ōmi captain Narimasa
The fourth-rank minor counselor Naritaka
The former Yamashiro governor Yoritsuke
The provisional right equerry Sanekiyo
Norichika, of the grand empress's household
The provisional governor of Bingo
The fifth-rank chamberlain Tsunenori
The former Mino governor Yasunari
The deputy equerry Taira no Tadamasa
  His eldest son, the chamberlain Nagamori
  His second son, Masatsuna
  His third son, Tadatsuna
The Rokujō police official Tameyoshi
  His fourth son, Yorikata, of the Left Gate Watch
  His fifth son, Yorinaka, of the Imperial Household Office
  His sixth son, Tamemune

His seventh son, Tamenari
His eighth son, Tametomo
His ninth son, Tamenaka
The Hanazono chamberlain Yoritsuna
The Murakami police official Motokuni
The Shimōsa police official Masahiro
Saemon no Taifu Iehiro
His seventh son, Yasuhiro
His eighth son, Norihiro
The deputy quartermaster Yasuhiro
The Left Gate Watch officer Tokihiro
The Right Gate Watch officer Morihiro

Sutoku had Chikahisa, one of his guardsmen, take a letter to the emperor. The emperor sent an answer. Sutoku wrote again. This time the emperor did not reply.

## 9. The Mustering of the Emperor's Forces

From the Toba Mansion, the right commander Kinnori and the consultant Mitsuyori took Toba's last wishes to Bifukumon-in at Hachijō-Karasumaru. Korekata transmitted them to her orally. No doubt foreseeing discord between Sutoku and the palace, Toba had previously written down in his own hand a list of warriors to summon in case of armed conflict: Yoshitomo, Yoshiyasu, Yorimasa, Shigenari, Suezane, Koreshige, Sanetoshi, Suketsune, Nobukane, and Mitsunobu. In the 6th month he had charged Yoshitomo and Yoshiyasu with guarding the emperor's residence, and they had recently taken care to secure all its gates.[25]

Bifukumon-in sent the emperor these men, since Toba's last wishes had named them explicitly: Taira no Kiyomori, Minamoto no Yorimasa, and Minamoto no Shigenari. Kiyomori took many men with him. He was a likely candidate to command the imperial forces, but Toba, who detested him as a foster brother of Prince Shigehito, Sutoku's eldest son,[26] had left his name off his written list. However, as Bifukumon-in explained through her messenger, his last wishes had indeed included an order to have Kiyomori guard the palace; so Kiyomori went there after all. Others who did the same included the senior chamberlains Suezane, Sanetoshi, and Nobukane; provincial governors; warriors; and officers both senior and junior from the six corps of guards, each of whom presented himself fully armed at the appropriate guard headquarters. Every member of the nobility was there, from the regent, right minister, consultants, and gentlemen of the third rank down to privy gentlemen of the fourth and fifth ranks. All closeted themselves in the palace to discuss the situation.

## 10. The Gates to Sutoku's Residence Are Secured *with* A Debate on Battle Tactics

Sutoku moved to the Ōi Pavilion[27] when his quarters at the Kamo Priestess's Shirakawa Mansion threatened to become too confined. Yorinaga accompanied him in his carriage.

Sutoku then summoned Tadamasa and Iehiro and put them in charge of the gates. Two gates on the front, south side of the compound gave onto the end of Ōi-no-mikado.[28] The one to the east went to Tadamasa and his four sons, together with Yorinori of the Settsu Genji; the force with them numbered no more than a hundred horse. The one to the west went to Tametomo, alone. The west side of the compound faced the river. Tameyoshi and five of his sons secured it with one hundred horse. They should have had more, but Yoshitomo, Tameyoshi's eldest, had taken every man of his to Takamatsu House, where the emperor currently resided. The north gate in the compound's west side, just south of Kasuga-kōji, went to Iehiro, his sons, and his brothers. More junior warriors secured the other, lesser gates. Sutoku had over a thousand men in all, but with so many dispersed to guard the gates, he seemed really to have no one around him.

Tametomo declared, "I refuse to fight beside any brother of mine, younger or older. Why? Because each slip of his would redound to my glory, and each slip of mine would redound to his, so that in the end no one could distinguish one from the other. So send me alone against the mightiest foe, and I will defeat him." However, he had no men with him. Not that he had none in Kyushu, but the call had come so suddenly that he had had to leave them behind. When asked why he was not taking at least a few, he replied, "Rumors that I plan to lead Kyushu men to attack the Kanto have long made me seem disloyal to my father, and now that, for once, I am called up to the capital, I would never be allowed into the city with a large force. Follow me later, then, all of you who wish to do so!"

So he left them there. Although eager to go, the men of Kyushu felt that they had no choice but to stay where they were. Still, a few of his constant companions remained with him. There were twenty-eight, the chief among them being Tametomo's foster brother and arrow-deflector Sudō Kurō Iesue; Iesue's elder brother, the defrocked Hiei monk Hawkeye Akushichi Bettō; Jōhachi Steelfist; Take-'em-alive Yojisaburō; Longrock Kiheiji; Deadshot Genda; Sachūji; Longshaft Shinzaburō; Longshaft Shirō; Misty Gorō; Yoshida no Tarō; and Hyōe no Tarō. Each could face a thousand men.

Sutoku and Yorinaga both wore full armor. "This is not right," Yorinaga objected. "Armor ill becomes you." Sutoku therefore removed his, but not Yorinaga, who had on scarlet-laced armor over a white cotton hunting cloak. Norinaga and Narimasa alone wore body armor over *suikan* robes and *hakama*—not to fight in, but only for fear of stray arrows. Moromitsu, Ienaga, and Yorisuke, from Sutoku's senior corps of guards, wore body armor over hunting cloaks and *hakama*. By Sutoku's order, his junior guardsmen wore helmets and full armor.

Why had Tametomo been singled out from among his brothers to guard an important gate alone? Because he was recognized throughout the realm for his prowess in war. As a boy he had been ungovernable and shown no respect whatever for his brothers. In fact, he was so alarming that Tameyoshi, his father, decided against keeping him in the capital. He sent him down to the provinces instead.

There he became the son-in-law of one Awa no Heishirō Tadakage, who, without court appointment, had styled himself constable-general of Kyushu and set out to subjugate the whole island. However, the Kikuchi, the Harada, and others entrenched themselves here and there against him, in fortresses surrounded by shield walls. Tametomo did not yet have men of his own, but at the head of Tadakage's he attacked and reduced them all and took the title of constable-general himself. The court summoned him when news of his rampage reached the capital, but he never went. Instead Tameyoshi suffered for his son's misbehavior. He was relieved of his post and reduced to the police rank that he had previously held. Tametomo was shocked. "I never even imagined such a thing," he said. "It is appalling that my father should have been punished. Never mind, then, what punishment is to be mine." He went up to the capital as soon as he heard the news.

Tametomo resembled no one else. He was seven feet tall, and his left arm was four inches longer than his right, which made him a born warrior. He shot arrows eighteen handbreadths long with a bow eight and a half feet tall and as thick as a heavy carrying pole. It took three ordinary men to draw it. His arrows, of three-year bamboo,[29] were the color of metal. Lest scrubbing and rubbing weaken them, he smoothed only the joints and polished them with scouring *tokusa* rush. To fletch them, he was satisfied to collect crow, crane, stork, or owl feathers and bind them on with wisteria fiber. His oiled arrowheads—long, sharp, and as pointed as a bird's tongue—fitted back into the shaft for more than half its length. As for the nock, bamboo could not have withstood the impact of the string, so he made it of horn daubed with cinnabar. Humming arrows he fletched with mountain pheasant or white-flecked black goose feathers. He gave each a humming bulb of birdseye magnolia, eight inches long, with nine holes. Each branch of the forked point curved out six inches from an eight-inch inner blade sharpened also along its trailing edge, so that the arrowhead resembled small, crossed halberd blades. The thick plates of his sturdy armor were laced with white Chinese damask, and round lion motifs adorned the metal bosses on its skirts. His three-and-a-half-foot sword, with its guard of hardened leather, hung at his side in a bearskin sheath guard. No god of pestilence would have dared to face him. Whatever his eye lit upon, soaring through the air or running over the earth, he transfixed at will. He outshone Masakado and surpassed Sumitomo.

Sutoku called Tameyoshi into his presence and asked about battle tactics. He had previously consulted Yorinaga, who had advised him also to question the young Tametomo; so he did. Tametomo appeared with his bow under his arm. There was no mistaking him. He looked like the guardian deity Bishamon. His presence was overpowering. He stepped forward to take his father's place—a very great honor for him.

"How should the engagement proceed?" Yorinaga asked.

With great respect Tametomo replied, "I have lived since boyhood in Kyushu, and I have fought there more than twenty major battles. History and experience suggest that the most effective strategy is a night attack. Before dawn I will swoop down on Takamatsu House, set fire to it on three sides, and attack the fourth. Those fleeing the flames, my arrows will stop; those fleeing my arrows, the fire will claim. Only Yoshitomo will mount any serious defense. I will bring him down with an arrow through a gap in his helmet. Kiyomori's feeble little arrows will make no difference. His Majesty will try to move elsewhere, and I will shoot an arrow into the imperial palanquin. When his bearers abandon it and flee, I will have him brought here. I will then see him deposed, Your Eminence, and you yourself enthroned."

Yorinaga replied, "Your proposal is violent and ill-considered, as one would expect of so young a man. A night attack would do well enough for ten or twenty mounted men acting on their own, but it would ill suit a contest for sovereignty between a reigning and a retired emperor. What hope will you have if you charge alone, without backup, into a superior force that then surrounds you? For tonight, just be patient. I will summon the Nara monks. Tomorrow, Shinjitsu and Genjitsu of Kōfukuji will lead them here, together with the men of Yoshino and the far and near reaches of the Totsugawa valley. They will ride here more than a thousand strong. Tonight they will report at Uji to the regent, Lord Tadazane, and they will be here tomorrow at the hour of the dragon [8 A.M.]. First await their arrival, then calmly proceed to Takamatsu House and there decide victory or defeat. I will also summon tomorrow, on pain of death, the senior nobles and privy gentlemen in my service. Once the heads of two or three have fallen, the others will no doubt comply. For tonight, Tametomo, you are to guard this residence closely."

Tametomo withdrew from the presence, muttering as he went, "Presumably he prefers to wait for tomorrow morning to give the enemy a good look at the strength of his forces. How can he possibly do battle then? Yoshitomo is a past master at the art of war. If Yorinaga insists on waiting until tomorrow, then he will insist on waiting for Shinjitsu and Genjitsu. Too bad! If attacked immediately, the emperor's men would all panic and flee."

Pandemonium spread through the city, and no wonder. People high and low loudly warned one another, "There will be a battle tonight! Oh, where will it all end?"

## 11. The General's Barrow Rumbles *and* A Comet Appears

The officials who had served the late Retired Emperor Toba—the left commander Kinnori, the consultant Mitsuyori, the left minor controller Akitoki—gathered at the Toba Mansion. They groaned when news of these developments reached them and spoke severally as follows.

"A comet has been visible in the east since the 8th, and lately the General's Barrow[30] has rumbled constantly. Divination suggests that such prodigies in the heavens and on earth enjoin extreme caution."

"A large warrior force has joined Sutoku's side, and Yorinaga has threatened with death any senior noble or privy gentleman who fails to answer his call. Surely not even we will be spared. Apparently an order has gone out to attack the palace and burn the city."

"That such things should happen only ten days after His Eminence's passing—why, it is horrifying! How could any senior noble or member of his household think of anything but praying for his enlightenment and performing good deeds on his behalf?"

"And yet Tametomo has apparently declared that he will attack Takamatsu House and shoot an arrow into His Majesty's palanquin when His Majesty tries to move elsewhere. So even the emperor cannot move about in safety! What is to become of us all? The Grand Shrine of Ise vowed to guard the Hundred Kings.[31] Twenty-six reigns still remain, but, alas, it is during the current one that the Sovereign's Way is to end!"

"Still, when all is said and done, ours is the land of the gods. The Mimosuso River flows on forever, and the seventy-four reigns of the Sun-Heir likewise continue unbroken. Ever since the sanctuaries of the heavenly and earthly gods were established of old, in the reign of Emperor Sujin, rites to honor them and the land have been performed with care, through thick and thin. Yes, the gods guard our days and nights. How could they fail to protect us? And that is not all, because in Emperor Suiko's reign [592–628, a woman], Prince Shōtoku made his appearance in the world, chastised the rebellious subject Moriya, and spread the Buddha's teaching far and wide. So it is that we still revere the Buddha and honor the sutras. Under Emperors Shirakawa and Toba, devoted reverence for the gods and deep faith in the Buddha's teaching placed the people of half the provinces and counties in service to the gods and gave all cultivated land to the buddhas and monks—an area larger than the sixteen greater and five hundred lesser lands of ancient India. Therefore the gods are resolved to protect our realm. How could the Three Treasures conceivably abandon us? And our great city, then: the capital moved here in the reign of Emperor Kanmu, on the 21st of the 10th month of Enryaku 13 [794]; and it survived unscathed even Former Emperor Heizei's revolt on the night of the 10th of the 9th month of Kōnin 1 [810].[32] Thereafter twenty-seven emperors have reigned over a period of 346 years. During Jōhei [931–938] Masakado raised rebellion; in Tengyō [938–947] Sumitomo did the same; and in Tengi [1053–1058] Sadatō and Munetō waged war in the north. The first two subjugated eight provinces and fought for eight years; the second two conquered the north and warred on for twelve years. However, all this happened in remote regions. There was no turmoil in the capital. Who would wish to destroy this city? What ruffian would disturb our realm? To the south, the Great Bodhisattva Hachiman has manifested himself on Otoko-yama; in the north, the great Kamo deity mounts guard over the imperial seat. In the direction of the demon gate stands Hiyoshi-Sannō.[33] Tenman Tenjin is manifest near the imperial palace. Elsewhere, near and far, stand the shrines of Matsuo, Hirano, Inari, Gion, Sumiyoshi, Kasuga, Hirose, and Tatsuta, which mount guard over the palace turn by turn, day and night. Therefore offerings to them never cease. Divine light fills His Majesty's Sacred Precinct. The most holy gods will not fail to save us from any turmoil that a rebellious subject may provoke!"

So each of them bravely declared.

## 12. The Emperor Proceeds to Tōsanjō *with* A Roster of the Emperor's Forces

When Takamatsu House proved inconveniently small, His Majesty suddenly moved to Tōsanjō on the 11th of the 7th month of Hōgen 1, at the hour of the hare [6 A.M.].[34] He traveled there in a hand-palanquin,[35] wearing court dress with a long train and carrying the Jewel and the Sword.[36] With him went these nobles:

Tadamichi, the regent
Saneyoshi, the palace minister
Motozane, the Left Gate Watch intendant
Kin'yoshi, the Right Gate Watch intendant,
Kinchika, the secretary-captain,
Sanesada, the left captain,
Shinzei, the minor counselor and novice,
Toshinori, the tutor to the heir apparent,
Sadanori, from the Bureau of Justice
Sueie, from the Central Affairs Bureau,

Takashina no Ieyuki, the director of palace staff
Shigeie, the governor of Kazusa
Nobutoshi, the governor of Echigo
Masatoshi, the governor of Etchū
Masayori, a chamberlain from the Bureau of Civil Affairs
Moronari, the chief secretary.

The warriors, high and low, would be impossible to list.

At Tōsanjō, Yoshitomo stood among his men, waving an open red fan bearing a sun disk. "It is a privilege to have been born to see this day!" he cried. "In conflicts involving personal interests, deference to the throne discourages freedom of action. Today, however, an imperial decree directs me to suppress the enemies of the court and promises a reward. This is a great honor for my house. I shall display my skill at the risk of my life, leave a mighty name to future generations, and ensure the prosperity of my descendants." He was very pleased.

Yoshitomo was then called into His Majesty's presence. He came before him wearing a red brocade *hitatare*, an *eboshi* hat,[37] and a right side-guard,[38] with his sword at his side and his bow under his arm. Through Shinzei, the emperor questioned him on his battle strategy.

With deep respect Yoshitomo replied, "There are many ways to pursue a conflict, but to achieve victory, no tactic can compare with a night attack. Now, I understand that, by authority of Lord Yorinaga, the Nara monks Shinjitsu and Genjitsu are to report tonight to Fuke House with over a thousand horse, including the men of Yoshino and the near and far reaches of the Totsugawa valley,[39] and that all of them are heavily armed and equipped with iron-clad shields. Tomorrow, I am told, at the hour of the hare, they will reach the residence of Retired Emperor Sutoku. Tametomo, my brother, is a brave and powerful warrior. The Yoshino and Nara monks will then march on Takamatsu House under his command. A hundred thousand men sent against them, even equipped with iron-clad shields, would be powerless to resist their arrows. Moreover, by tomorrow my men will be tired, and gaps will have opened in their armor. They will be less stalwart in battle. I recommend entrusting the defense of Takamatsu House to Taira no Kiyomori, while I take command of the attack force, set out with it immediately, and decide the conflict before the enemy ever arrives."

Shinzei wore a grey *hitatare* and a sword named Kogitsune ["Little Fox"].[40] From his position on the veranda, before the emperor, he replied, "You are quite right. Court nobles favor poetry and music but know nothing of your calling. Yes, when the issue is skill at arms, yours is undoubtedly the advice to follow. To disregard imperial authority is to defy the will of Heaven. So go now, crush the evildoers and soothe the imperial wrath. Outstanding achievement will undoubtedly win you the palace access to which you aspire."

Yoshitomo retorted, "I may well lose my life on the field of battle. What good will that privilege do me once I am dead? When am I to enjoy access to the palace, if it is not granted me immediately?" He strode up the steps toward Shinzei.

"What is this?" Shinzei exclaimed. "You are out of order!"

His Majesty laughed. He was obviously enjoying this.

Shinzei spoke again. "As the classic states, to move first is to control the foe; to move after him is to fall under his control. Leave not a man at the palace, but take them all with you into battle."

All present listened intently, deeply impressed by both Yoshitomo's speech and Shinzei's reply.

The attack was set for the hour of the tiger on the 11th, that is, before dawn the next day. The warriors burst forth from Tōsanjō, each vying to lead the charge.

No one around Sutoku suspected an imminent assault. Yorinaga had called in Tameyoshi and was absorbed in quiet conversation with him. "How do you see things going from here?" he asked him. "You must carefully consider your battle plan."

Tameyoshi replied, "Surely the warriors at His Eminence's disposal can withstand any attack. I will fight for him without a thought for my life as long as he remains here. Victory or defeat will then be decided. If he flees, I will convey him to Nara, strip the planks from the Uji Bridge, and keep the enemy from him. Should that plan fail, I will take him down to the east, mobilize my hereditary retainers, and return him to the capital." He expressed himself with great confidence.

Yorinaga replied, "You speak well. Our emperor, who descends in the forty-seventh generation from the Sun Goddess, is the eldest son of the late Retired Emperor Toba. Alas, he was passed over for the throne in favor of his father's Fourth Prince, who knows nothing of letters or war and has no skill at any of the arts. Perhaps the gods erred, but at any rate, what happened has frustrated men's hopes. He now has no prospect of coming into his own without concerted action. So you and your men must arouse the courage of Fan Kai, regard life as lighter than a goose feather, and pride yourselves on supreme valor." Tameyoshi and Yorinaga had both spoken nobly.

At Sutoku's residence, Yorinaga and everyone else quietly made their preparations. Yorinaga summoned Chikahisa, a member of his corps of guards. "Go and see what is going on at Takamatsu House," he said. "They may be expecting an attack from here, or perhaps there are signs of an attack from there."

Chikahisa went for a look and came racing back. "They will attack at any moment!" he reported. "The warriors are all mounted. Yoshitomo had his cheek guards on,[41] and he was just mounting a black horse with a black saddle." He had hardly spoken when battle cries rang out on the west side of the compound, toward the river. Within, there was pandemonium. "Tametomo was right!" people protested to one another; but it was now too late.

"This is exactly what I meant!" Tametomo himself exclaimed, but there was nothing he could do. Sutoku ordered Tametomo and Yasuhiro appointed chamberlains, no doubt to fire them with greater zeal. Every gate was firmly secured.

Yoshitomo and Kiyomori commanded the emperor's men. Yoshitomo moved eastward along Nijō. Because the east was blocked on the 11th,[42] and because in any case he was reluctant to shoot arrows into the rising sun, Kiyomori dropped south to Sanjō, crossed the river, and then marched north along its eastern bank. At the level of Nijō he stopped and waited, facing north. Yoshitomo stopped and lay in wait on the west bank of the river, facing east, at the level of Ōi-no-mikado. A small number of warriors also lurked before the residence of the counselor Ienari.

That day Yoshitomo commanded the following men:

Kamada no Jirō Masakiyo and Kawara no Genda, his foster brothers

FROM ŌMI

Sasaki no Saburō Hideyoshi
Yashima no Kanja

## BOOK 1

### FROM MINO

Yoshitarō
Hirano no Heida

### FROM OWARI

Yoshitomo's father-in-law, the chief priest of the Atsuta Shrine, did not come in person but sent his men.

### FROM MIKAWA

The Shitara warriors

### FROM TŌTŌMI

Yokoji
Katsumata
Ino Hachirō

### FROM SURUGA

Irie no Uma-no-jō
Saburō
Ōshū no Jūrō
Okitsu no Shirō

### FROM SAGAMI

Ōba no Heida Kageyoshi
Ōba no Saburō Kagechika
Yamanouchi Sudō Gyōbunojō Toshimichi
Sudō Takiguchi no Toshitsuna, his son
Ebina no Genda Suesada
Hadano no Jirō Yoshimichi

FROM AKI

Anzai
Kanamari
Numa no Heida
Maru no Tarō

FROM KAZUSA

Sukehachirō Hirotsune

FROM SHIMŌSA

Chiba no Suke Tsunetane

FROM MUSASHI

Toshima no Shirō
Adachi no Shirō Tōmitsu
Chūjō no Shingo
Chūjō no Shinroku
Narita no Tarō
Hakoda no Jirō
Kawakami no Tarō
Beppu no Jirō
Nara no Saburō
Tamanoi no Shirō
Nagai no Saitō Bettō Sanemori
Saitō no Saburō

From Yokoyama

Akuji
Hirayama Rokuji
Gen Gojirō
Kumagai no Jirō Naozane
Hanzawa no Rokurō Narikiyo

From Aibara and Inomata

Okabe no Rokurō
Konpeiroku
Kawawa no Saburō
Tebaka no Shichirō

From Kodama

Shō no Tarō
Shō no Jirō

From Murayama

Kaneko no Jūrō Ietada
Senba no Shichirō
Yamaguchi no Rokurō

From Kōke

Kawagoe
Morooka
The Chichibu men

FROM KŌZUKE

Sejimo no Shirō
Monoi no Gorō
Okamoto no Suke
Nawa no Tarō

FROM SHIMOTSUKE

Hatta no Shirō
Ashikaga no Tarō

FROM HITACHI

Chūgū no Saburō
Seki no Jirō Toshihira

FROM KAI

Shiomi no Gorō
Shiomi no Rokurō

FROM SHINANO

The Maita no Kondō men
Kuwabara no Andōji
Kuwabara no Andōzō
Kiso no Chūta
Yachūda
Shimone no I no Daiyata
Nezu no Shinpei
Kamasaka no Shirō
Shizuma no Tarō
Shizuma no Kojirō

Excluding servants and grooms with fresh horses, the principal warriors numbered over 250.

Kiyomori commanded the following:

His younger brothers
 Yorimori, the governor of Hitachi
 Norimori, the governor of Awaji
 Tsunemori, fifth rank without office
Shigemori, his eldest son, of the Bureau of Central Affairs
Motomori, his second son, the Aki police official

and these men of his:

Chikigo no Saemon Iesada
Chikugo no Shinzaemon Sadayoshi

Sudō Kurō Iesue
Yosōbyōe Kageyasu
Satsuma no Uma no Jō
Hyōdō Takiguchi no Kanesue
Hyōdō no Kotarō Kanemichi
Yawata no Mizu Sakon no Shōgen
Yawata no Tarō
Yawata no Jirō
Kawachi Kusaka no Sazuku
Gendayū

FROM ISE

Itō Musha Kagetsuna
Itō Tadakiyo
Itō Rokurō
The men of the Shiroko League

FROM IGA

Yamada no Kosaburo Koreyuki
Shō no Yajirō
Nakashi no Saburō

FROM BIZEN

Nanba no Saburō Tsunefusa
Nanba no Shirō Mitsukane

FROM BITCHŪ

Senoo no Tarō Kaneyasu

The force under Kiyomori numbered over six hundred mounted men.

Minamoto no Yorimasa, the head of the Armory, commanded these men of the Watanabe League:

Habuku no Harima no Jirō
Sazuku no Hyōe, his son
Tsuzuku no Genda
Atō no Uma no Jō
Kiō no Takiguchi
Chōshichi Tonō
Kiyoshi
Susugu

These came to more than a hundred men.

Other commanders included

Mutsu no Shinhōgan Yoshiyasu, with one hundred
Oki no Hōgan Koreshige, with one hundred
Suō no Hōgan Suezane, with one hundred
Heihōgan Sanetoshi, with over seventy
Minamoto no Shigenari, with over sixty
Izumi no Uemon no Jō Nobukane, with seventy-five

In all, the emperor's forces numbered over fifteen hundred mounted men, each eager to lead the charge. Among them, it was Yorimasa who first reached the gate at the end of Kasuga-kōji.

# Book 2

## 13. Yoshitomo's Night Attack on the Shirakawa Mansion

At Sutoku's residence, the cry went up at the hour of the tiger on the 11th of the 7th month of Hōgen 1: "The enemy is coming!" All the gates were secured. Tameyoshi's six sons held the one opening onto the riverbank, and there each vied to lead. Yorikata assured himself, "I am the eldest. The lead is properly mine. If not mine, then whose?" Tametomo reflected, "No warrior here equals me. Who else could possibly lead?" So the argument went.

Tametomo thought again, "Besides, my father considered me a menace, even as a boy, for the way I pushed my brothers aside and behaved as though the world was mine. For a long time he was fed up with me. Fortunately, he then forgave me after all. It would be wrong of me to argue with my brothers in his presence."

He therefore approached his brothers. "Gentlemen," he said, "do not argue among yourselves! Where I am, who among you could possibly lead? But no: by all means lead, all of you. If you weaken, however, I am here, and my strength will be yours. If you are afraid, leave it to me as often as you like. I will take care of things for you." With these words he returned to his assigned gate.

Yorikata let this outrageous speech pass and won the dispute over leadership. With a dozen of his men around him he sallied forth from the gate and shouted toward the west, "Whose force is that, there before me? I myself am Yorikata, the fourth son of Tameyoshi!"

From the west there came the reply, "I am Sudō Takiguchi no Toshitsuna, the eldest son of Yamanouchi Sudō Toshimichi from Sagami, a retainer of Minamoto no Yoshitomo, the governor of Shimotsuke!"

"Then my arrows are not for you," Yorikata replied. He galloped straight across the river, charged into the mass of men, and raced about with such speed that he frustrated every effort to seize him.

Two of Yoshitomo's warriors advanced to challenge him. Yorikata, very quick with his arrows, shot two. Both crashed from their horses and dragged themselves up on the east bank. Yoshitomo did not like what he saw and prepared to charge in person. His foster brother, Kamada Masakiyo, then addressed him. "This is no time for a commander-in-chief to charge," he said. "When a thousand men are reduced to one hundred and the hundred to ten, and when those ten dwindle to five or fewer: that is when he personally enters the fray. I have never heard of one leaving his men to engage the enemy."

Yoshitomo moved to charge nonetheless. Masakiyo summoned eighty fully armed foot soldiers. "Do not let our commander charge," he ordered. "Keep him from going in among the enemy. Seize his bridle to right and left. Hold his mount's chest rope and crupper, and guard him well." So seventy or eighty men surrounded their commander exactly as Fan Kai might have done.

Now, Fan Kai served Emperor Gaozu of Han. Xiang Wang had Gaozu surrounded, in the days when Gaozu was still known as Pei Gong, and Fan Kai heard about it. With one hundred men he thrust the attacked gate open, raised his shield, sent the enemy tumbling head over heels, and protected his lord against Xiang Wang's attack. Every witness stared, wide-eyed. His white hair stuck out like silver needles from beneath his helmet.

"Who are you?" Xiang Wang demanded to know.

"Fan Kai," came the answer, "a man in the service of Pei Gong."

Xiang Wang offered Fan Kai wine accompanied by raw boar flesh. Fan Kai lowered his shield and carved the meat on it as upon a cutting board. When served wine, he easily drank several gallons. Pei Gong, his lord, seized this opportunity to flee. That is the way those eighty men surrounded and guarded Yoshitomo.

Meanwhile, Kiyomori emerged on the Sanjō riverbank, crossed diagonally eastward, and came up the opposite bank to attack. Itō Kagetsuna led the advance with fifty men. "You who guard the gate at the end of Ōi-no-mikado," he said, "who are you? Are you Genji or Heike? Are you from a warrior league or from a great warrior house? Identify yourself! I wish to hear your name. I myself belong to the household of our commander, Lord Kiyomori, the governor of Aki. I am Itō Musha Kagetsuna from Ise. Itō Tadakiyo, Itō Rokurō, and I are the best of the men from Furuichi."

Tametomo replied, "I guard this gate—I, Tametomo. You are no worthy opponent for me. If you are a Taira underling, then withdraw now. Not even your lord, Kiyomori, is worthy of me. No doubt the Heike are of imperial descent, but their ancestor is only the Kazurahara Emperor,[43] who lived much too long ago. We Genji all descend from Emperor Seiwa [r. 858–876]. My generation, the ninth after him, is also the seventh after Rokusonnō, the sixth after Manjū, and the fourth after Yoriyoshi. I am the eighth among the sons of Tameyoshi, the fourth son of Hachimantarō Yoshiie. To draw my bow and loose arrows against your men would be even further beneath me. If you are Kagetsuna, then remove yourself immediately."

Kagetsuna laughed. "The Genji and Heike both serve His Majesty like the two wings of a bird," he answered, "and they wield military power over the realm. Never before has a Heike man shot a Genji, and if none does now, then obviously there will be no clash. Yes, I am Kagetsuna, and I serve my lord, but His Majesty himself has recognized me for having taken alive Ono no Shichirō, the ringleader of the Suzuka-yama bandits. In reward, an imperial decree has appointed me, Kagetsuna, the deputy commander of this force. So what do you say, Tametomo? Will a Heike arrow stick in a Genji hide? Let us see!"

He shot an arrow that harmlessly struck the metal trim on Tametomo's scabbard, with its hardened leather guard. Not one of his fifty men's arrows stuck in its target. Tametomo roared with laughter. "No, you're no opponent for me," he declared. "You're not a man at all! You're nothing! You just spout hot air! Here, try one of mine! Take it, and claim glory in this life and the next!" He fitted to the string a lethal, sharp-tipped arrow, drew to the full, and let fly.

Stationed closest to him, immediately in front of Kagetsuna, were the brothers Itō Tadakiyo and Itō Rokurō. Rokurō, in his seventeenth year, was a fighter to whom death meant nothing. His green armor shaded downward from dark to light, and a triple-plated neckpiece completed his helmet. The arrows in his quiver were fletched with dyed feathers; he carried a laminated, rattan-bound bow;[44] and his bay horse bore a saddle decorated with shell motifs. The arrow first sped through his breastplate, then pierced the left sleeve of Tadakiyo's armor. Rokurō toppled instantly, dead, from his mount.

Tadakiyo turned back, the arrow still in his arm, to present himself before Kiyomori. "Itō Rokurō is dead, and I am wounded," he announced. "Look, sir! Tametomo's bow has colossal power! No ordinary man could do such a thing. This arrow went through Rokurō's breastplate, then through my left armor sleeve. I have never seen anything like it!"

The sight struck Kiyomori and his men dumb with fear. Itō Tadakiyo spoke again. "Of old," he said, "after Yoriyoshi had reduced the Kuriyagawa fortress in his campaign against Sadatō and Munetō, Takenori remarked to Minamoto no Yoshiie, 'I would gladly admire the strength of your bow. Your arrows fell every man they hit, even through armor.' Yoshiie hung three suits of armor, each plated with well-forged steel, on the branch of a tree and shot an arrow through all six layers. 'You are a veritable god!' Takenori exclaimed, deeply impressed. That is how I heard it. Now I have seen the same with my own eyes. It would take four or five layers of armor to survive facing him. We have no choice. Turn back!"

Taira no Shigemori, at the time an officer of the Bureau of Central Affairs, responded, "What are you saying, Tadakiyo? Watch me take an arrow from him!"

Shigemori galloped, alone, straight toward the gate. Kiyomori watched him go. "I received no imperial command to attack the west gate on Ōi-no-mikado," he said. "While advancing I simply had the misfortune to stumble across this gate in the dark. Now, to no purpose, I have lost one of my young men. Do not for a moment take your eyes off Shigemori." His servants surrounded and protected Shigemori.

"Now," he continued, "should I go on to the east gate or the north?"

One of his men replied, "The east gate is nearby. The same fellow is probably guarding it, too."

"Withdraw, then," Kiyomori ordered, "go round by the other side of the river and attack the gate onto Kasuga-kōji." Accordingly they withdrew westward along the end of Sanjō. Of old, as now, reckless bravery has always been mere folly.

Among the least of Kiyomori's men was one from Iga, Yamada no Kosaburō Koreyuki by name. This youth, a fierce fighter, charged straight ahead with never a glance to right or left. A veritable wild boar, he ignored everything but the foe. He now stepped forward. "Young gentlemen," he cried, "I have some words for you all! Halt a moment and watch! I will take an arrow from Tametomo and leave a glorious name to future generations! Not even his bow could shoot straight through two warriors in armor. I am quick to shoot my second arrow, and it is still dark. Two arrows will look like one. He may be able to shoot through two men, but not through me, not when I have on armor that has been in my family for three generations. This armor has seen fifteen battles, and I have worn it in three. Not one of the many arrows it has taken ever pierced it. One may die of an arrow strike through a gap in the armor, as all know who wield the bow; but that is merely a matter of karma. Now, watch, and join me!"

No one moved to do so. Instead, all retreated. Alone and undaunted, Koreyuki stood fast. Despite serving Kiyomori, he owed him no debt of loyalty,[45] and for that reason he had no servant on a fresh horse. He did not even have a groom. Having been accused, justly or unjustly, of crimes of banditry or piracy, he was obliged to Kiyomori only because Kiyomori had pardoned him and taken him into his service. He had no followers and no groom, only a boy to lead his horse.

Koreyuki said to this boy, "The time has come for you to requite my kindly employing you. The tide of passion swept me into addressing Lord Kiyomori as I did. A man does not take back his uttered word. I hardly know what my lord will think of me if I go home without following through on mine; and, above all, fear of my comrades' opinion of me fills me with shame. 'So where was it that Tametomo's arrow got you?' they will ask. 'All right, show us the wound!' And what will I do then? 'Did you mean to go after him only if you had an audience?' That question will end the high renown I have won over the years. Bury my body if I die and tell my wife and children how it happened. If I live, bear witness to my deed. Look, I have no one else to do so!" The boy ignored this flood of eloquence. He simply turned his horse and started toward the gate.

All of Kiyomori's men recognized Koreyuki's warlike prowess. He drew a strong bow and was a fine archer. His arrows were thirteen handbreadths and two fingers long. In his black-laced, somewhat worn armor he wore his helmet, with its *kuwagata* horns, tilted back a little on his head. Eighteen arrows fletched with the black feathers from under an eagle's wing projected high above his head. Carrying his laminated, rattan-bound bow, he rode a bay horse with a black saddle.

He had uttered no empty boast. "One touch of the whip, then," he said to himself, "to see how it goes. No doubt Tametomo wields a mighty bow, but it may be a contest if only I can get my little arrow into him first. There is nothing strange about a warrior dying on the field of battle. What is strange is that he should return home alive."

He moved up to the gate. The boy said, "I have long enjoyed your kindness, and besides, I do not see how a warrior advancing onto the field of battle can rightfully return from it alive. You asked me to witness your deed because I have no rank. I wish you had not, because I mean to stay with you to the last. In any case, even if I were to survive, could a nobody like me really bear effective witness? No, I will first discard my own life." Brandishing his halberd, he charged in among Tametomo's servants, never to be seen again.

The sight further steeled Koreyuki's resolve. He revealed his presence and announced, "I am Koreyuki, a man of no particular standing. You will not have heard of me. Today I appear before you for the first time. I am from the province of Aki and belong to the entourage of Lord Kiyomori. My full name is Yamada no Kosaburō Koreyuki. I am in my twenty-eighth year. Despite my insignificance, my grandfather was Yamada no Shōji Yukisue, who long ago captured the Suzuka-yama bandit Tate-eboshi ["Tallhat"] and presented him to the emperor. I have arrested more pirates, burglars, and robbers than I can count. I have fought three major battles and conducted myself impeccably each time. High or low, old or young, it is a privilege to bear arms; and to display high mettle is to aspire to encounter others similarly famed. For that reason I would gladly set eyes on the great Tametomo and take an arrow from him. If I die of it, in the life to come I will count it a glory to have done so. If I do not, I will count it a glory in this one."

Tametomo listened and summoned Sudō Kurō Iesue, his foster brother. "What should I do?" he asked. "This fellow must be waiting for me with his bow drawn. There must be something to him if he wants to engage me. I suppose he is listening for my voice and will shoot for a gap in my helmet. I think I will leave him the first arrow. He can have his second, too. Then I will shoot him. I just want him to feel my arrow, wherever it may hit. That should do it."

Over a white brocade *hitatare* Tametomo wore armor laced with Chinese damask. It being midday,[46] he wore a helmet adorned with a glittering dragon-head and a gold-trimmed sword. Of his twenty-four arrows, fletched from the tail of the mountain pheasant and wrapped at the joins[47] with wisteria bark, he had already shot one; the others rose high over his head.

Wisteria bark likewise wrapped the joints of his bow, with its thick grip. It was eight and a half feet long and looked very powerful indeed. His pale roan horse, tremendously muscular and with an exceptionally thick tail and mane, stood fourteen hands tall[48] and bore a gold-trimmed saddle. He advanced, halted his mount in a slightly slantwise position, and identified himself. "I have heard of you among Kiyomori's men," he said. "I am Tsukushi no Hachirō, Minamoto no Tametomo."

Koreyuki's bow had been drawn, sure enough, and Tametomo's words were scarcely out before he loosed the arrow. It pierced Tametomo's armor skirts on his left side like a sewing needle. Koreyuki had indeed let fly at the sound of Tametomo's voice. "I knew it!" thought Tametomo. He fitted one of his usual arrows, with its long, sharp point, to the string. "I like the way you talk," he said, "so here's one for you. Once it's yours, you'll be dead. It will make a nice memory for your next life." He let fly in turn.

The arrow smashed through the pommel of Koreyuki's saddle, pierced the many-layered skirts of his armor, went straight through Koreyuki himself, and fixed itself in the cantle. Bitterly disappointed to have missed with his first arrow, Koreyuki had fitted his second to the string and now lifted his bow two or three times, but darkness overcame him. He dropped his bow and crashed to the ground. Supported by the arrow, he then struggled to charge; but the arrow broke, and he fell. This incident perfectly illustrates, one might say, the folly of excessive courage.

## 14. The Fall of the Shirakawa Mansion

Koreyuki's horse went galloping about and ended up on the west bank of the river. Kamada Masakiyo noticed it. "Look at that, my lord!" he exclaimed to Yoshitomo. "Just look at the arrow fixed there in the saddle! It is from Tametomo's bow. I have never heard of such a thing. There must not have been any rider. Considering that the arrow smashed straight through the pommel, it can hardly have passed also through a man in armor. What it has done is frightening enough as it is." He was astounded.

Yoshitomo replied, "No, Tametomo could not have done that, however powerful his bow. It is remarkable enough that his arrow should have broken through the pommel. It is simply impossible that it should then have passed through the rider before planting itself in the cantle. Tametomo thought this up to frighten us. Where in the world is the man capable of shooting straight through a mounted man in full armor? Go and try him yourself then, Masakiyo.

"Very well, sir," Kamada Masakiyo replied. Forthwith he charged the gate with a hundred riders. "You who guard the south gate, here at the end of Ōi-no-mikado," he cried, "are you of the Genji or of the Heike? I who address you am Kamada no Jirō Masakiyo, a foster brother of Lord Yoshitomo!"

"I am Tametomo from Kyushu," came the reply. "Apparently you belong to my house. You are my foe today, no doubt, but you cannot possibly strike your hereditary lord. Withdraw!"

With a derisive laugh Masakiyo retorted, "My erstwhile lord is a rebel guilty of the eight treacheries, and His Majesty has appointed me deputy commander. See, then, whether or not a retainer's arrow can bury itself in this lord of mine! Actually, the arrow comes not from me, but from the Ise Shrine and from Hachiman." Expecting Tametomo to shoot the instant he finished speaking, he loosed his own first arrow. It grazed through the space between Tametomo's nose and cheek guard and planted itself in the swept-back forward edge of his neckplate. The outraged Tametomo wrenched it out and threw it away, but he shot no answering arrow of his own. Instead he roared to his men, "The scoundrel! I won't waste an arrow on him. Get up beside him and take him prisoner with your bare hands!"

Twenty-eight men slipped their bows under their arms and charged forward, shouting, "Get Kamada! Don't let Masakiyo get away!"

Masakiyo wheeled and fled several hundred yards down the river, whip high and stirrups flailing,[49] urging his mount to desperate speed. "How far d'you think you're going to get?" voices shouted behind him.

They pursued him to the west gate of Hōshōgon-in. When Masakiyo still refused to turn and engage them, Tametomo halted. "Young men of mine," he said, "don't keep after him forever. You'll wind your horses. And our gate worries me. It will fall if they cut us off. Lord Tameyoshi is a brave warrior, but he is old now and could never hold it. My older brothers talk big, but they have few men, and they could not stave off a large force. Come, young gentlemen!" He turned around and started back.

Masakiyo had meant to flee westward along Ōi-no-mikado, but he disliked the thought of enticing the enemy into his lord's presence. He therefore fled instead some six hundred yards down the east bank of the river. When he saw his pursuers give up, he raced across and back up the river to

Yoshitomo. There he leaped down from his mount, doffed his helmet and slung it over his shoulders, clasped his bow under his arm, and declared, panting, "I have fought often enough in the eastern provinces, but never in my life have I had such a deafening clatter of hooves after me or encountered so aggressive a foe. I thought I was finished. Just one arrow from me, the first, so enraged him that he came after me to take me alive. He turned around and raced back again when he saw that he could not catch me, but those shouts of 'How far d'you think you're going to get?' and the crash of hooves behind me sounded like thunder. It was terrifying."

"You only imagined all that, Masakiyo," Yoshitomo replied. "Just work out how old Tametomo is—in his eighteenth year, I would say. He can hardly be that strong yet, however many his men. He has probably learned to shoot an arrow far, since he grew up in Kyushu, and no doubt he is good with his sword. On foot he may do well enough, but in hand-to-hand, mounted combat he could hardly equal our young men from Musashi or Sagami. Just try him, gentlemen! You will not be that impressed."

The hot-blooded Musashi and Sagami youths heard him. "Oho!" they whispered among themselves. "So he wants to trick us, does he, into letting Tametomo kill us all? We'd better stick to bows and arrows. He learned swordsmanship from that Higo fellow, the famous Oite no Jirō Noritaka, the best swordsman in all of Kyushu, and apparently he's far better than his teacher. He may not yet be as strong as he will be, but he's probably still too much for the likes of us at full strength. We might get him with an arrow though a chink in his armor, shot from a distance, but we'd better not go up against him with swords."

Yoshitomo saw what was going on and made his choice. "Get after him, my young men from Sagami," he ordered, "get after him!"

Ōba no Heida, Ōba no Saburō, Yamanouchi Sudō and his son, Ebina Suesada, Hadano no Jirō Nobukage, and others set out in pursuit with two hundred mounted men. Tametomo's force turned and engaged them behind Hōshōgon-in, to the west. From the rear Yoshitomo cried, "You who oppose us, are you Genji or Heike? I speak as my men's commander, Yoshitomo, the governor of Shimotsuke!"

"I, too, am a Genji," came the reply: "I am Tametomo from Kyushu!"

"Then you are my much younger brother! The gods have no blessings for the younger brother who draws a bow against his elder! Withdraw! I will show you mercy!"

Tametomo burst into laughter. "All right, Lord Yoshitomo, but if the gods have no blessings for the younger brother who draws a bow against his elder, how do they feel about the man who draws it against his father?" He had a point. There was no reply.

Tametomo rose in his stirrups, steadying himself with his bow, and surveyed the scene. There was Yoshitomo, taller than anyone around him and perfectly placed to take an arrow through a gap in his helmet. Tametomo fitted one of his usual, slender-pointed arrows to the string and peered ahead by the light sifting through the clouds. "Just one, inside his helmet," he said to himself, "and down he goes."

He lifted his bow and drew, then relaxed the string. "Wait!" he said to himself. "Wait a moment! Our two emperors, reigning and retired, are brothers, and Tameyoshi and Yoshitomo are father and son. Yoshitomo has pledged himself to Go-Shirakawa, Tameyoshi to Sutoku. No doubt it is tacitly understood that Go-Shirakawa will look to Yoshitomo if he wins, and I will submit; and that Sutoku will look to me if he wins, and Yoshitomo will be looked after. So if I shoot Yoshitomo off his mount now, I will regret it later. Besides, I have been accused ever since boyhood of wanting to kill all my brothers and survive them alone; and for that I have long been called unfilial. It was rare good fortune that I was allowed up to the capital. I will be considered doubly unfilial, and there is no telling what may happen to me, if I now cruelly shoot an elder brother without sanction from my father." Such were his thoughts, and they changed his mind.

Tametomo removed the arrow from the string. In his heart of hearts he understood kindness and compassion. For a while he kept up the fight, but then he reflected that his men were few against many and that his gate would fall if the enemy came from east or west and cut him off from it. He fell back thirty or forty yards.

"Attack, attack!" shouted Yoshitomo, elated by this victory. "No pause for breath! After them, and die!"

These warriors dismounted and rushed forward to be the first to fight before the gate:

Ōba no Heida
Ōba no Saburō
Yamanouchi Sudō

Ebina Suesada, his son
Hadano Nobukage
Gotōbyōe Sanemoto
Katagiri Kageshige from Shinano.

All these outstanding warriors led the attack.

Kageshige posted himself west of the gate, on the narrow level strip between the compound wall and the ditch, his halberd under his arm. "Ah, he's an old warrior!" the others exclaimed. "He's been through many battles, and now he's afraid. He isn't even going to fight!" In a moment, though, Kageshige dashed forward and made off with the great shield that rested on the ground before Tametomo. "Fight on from behind this, gentlemen!" he cried and threw it out to them. Then he got a good grip on his halberd, swept the enemy from before him, and withdrew.

Hadano Nobukage said, "Kamada Masakiyo was fighting just now, but I don't see him anymore. I don't like that. I'll just go for a word with him. Gentlemen, close behind me." And off he went.

He found Masakiyo behind Yoshitomo, still mounted, leaning on his bow and shaking. "You were fighting just now," Nobukage said. "Are you not going to fight anymore? Lord Kamada, why will you not face the enemy?" Masakiyo did not reply.

Yoshitomo said, "Masakiyo has been suffering lately from attacks of malarial fever. He said he doubted that he would be able to stay on his horse, if he had one. He will recover by-and-by."

Nobukage laughed. "What a shame!" he said. "He certainly is not the man he was when he won that argument over where to stay." Then he left.

The others remarked, laughing, "Nobukage's been seething lately. No doubt he's feeling more cheerful now. At the Hashimoto post station Masakiyo insisted on taking the room that Nobukage had reserved for himself, on the grounds that it was near Lord Yoshitomo's and that he had business to discuss with him. Nobukage didn't like that, so he came over just now to give him a piece of his mind."

Tametomo had his men shoot arrows and fight hand to hand, but he refrained from shooting any of his own as long as no worthy opponent appeared. Then Yoshitomo came up to the gate. "How strong is your bow, Tametomo?" he demanded to know. "They say it's powerful. I'd like to try you."

"Very well," Tametomo replied. He called over Sudō Kurō Iesue, his foster brother. "The way these Kanto warriors are, they just ride straight over a dead father or son and keep fighting. The enemy are many and our arrows few. When we run out of them, it will come to swords. One rider cannot stand against a hundred. This gate is under dire threat, but while they may break through the others, I will not let them past this one. Yoshitomo is pressing forward and ordering an attack, but he will not pass, no, not even if our hundred are reduced to one. So I have a mind to let him feel the breeze from one of my arrows."

Iesue discouraged him. "Your arrow might go astray," he said.

"Do you think my aim is no better than yours?" Tametomo replied. "I'll send it past him at just the right distance to get him to fall back. His men are sure to follow their commander."

Yoshitomo moved not toward Tametomo's gate, but rather toward the chapel gate across the road from it. There he turned around, his back toward the gate's tall, flanking wooden panels, and stood facing northeast, leaning on his bow and issuing orders. Within the mansion compound Tametomo positioned himself facing southeast, two bow lengths from the compound wall. He fitted the best of his battle arrows to the string, drew to the full over the heads of his men, and let fly. With a clang the arrow knocked seven or eight stars off Yoshitomo's helmet, adorned as it was with a dragon-head and *kuwagata* horns, and plunged more than half its length through a flanking panel. Stunned, Yoshitomo nearly fell off his horse but clung to saddle and mane. After feeling over his helmet and finding no arrow, he sat up straight again, collected himself, and affected cool indifference to the blow. "Oh no, Tametomo," he shouted, "you're not as good as they make you out to be! It all depends on your opponent. You're no good against someone like me!"

Tametomo laughed. "You're my older brother," he retorted, "so I left some room between you and that first arrow. I had my reasons. With your permission, my second will answer you more to the point. I wouldn't presume to shoot you in the face, though. Your neck, perhaps? Your breastplate? Belly plate? Shoulder plate? Side-guard? Bowstring guard? Your armor skirts, upper or lower? Tell me where you'd like it. Get those servants around you out of the way!"

Yoshitomo saw Tametomo fit an arrow to the string and must have decided that discretion was the better part of valor, because he dropped back into the shadows against the gate doors. "My young men from Sagami," he cried, "for what golden future are you saving yourselves? Attack! Attack! Get after him!" They rushed to the gate, only to be repulsed by a volley of arrows from within.

Ōba no Heida and his brother Saburō, tired after long combat, called for their horses, mounted them, and together raced through the gate, uttering fierce cries. They halted at a distance from Tametomo and announced, "You must have heard of us. Of old, when Hachimantarō Yoshiie attacked the Kanezawa fort during the Later Three Years War and captured the Tori-no-umi Hall, Gongorō Kagemasa of Kamakura, then in his sixteenth year, took an arrow in his left eye while stationed before the melee. Nonetheless, he shot his answering arrow and brought his enemy down—a feat that earned him everlasting fame. We are his descendants in the fifth generation, Ōba no Heida Kageyoshi and Ōba no Saburō Kagechika, from Sagami."

Tametomo replied, "Yes, I have heard you mentioned. Then you are my retainers from four generations back."

"Yes, we are."

Tametomo summoned Sudō Kurō Iesue. "I have never before shown Kanto men what I can do. My battle arrows and killer arrows will go through anything. This time I might try a humming arrow on those two.[50] What do you think?"

"Sir, by all means do."

Tametomo fletched not even his battle arrows, still less others, with noble feathers, except possibly for the rare ceremonial occasion. Because he was always out hunting, day and night, he daily shot arrows fletched the day before and damaged them. An arrow fletched one day served for the hunt the next, and his shafts and feathers never lasted, since he hunted all the time. For that reason his arrows were fletched with chicken or crow feathers.

On arrival in the capital, Tametomo gathered that there would be fighting and foresaw the need for humming arrows. He had himself made a quiverful of hunting arrows, fashioned from close-jointed, three-year bamboo purposely left unwashed and serviceably fletched as usual with white crane-wing feathers bound on with wisteria bark fiber. He had the humming bulb carved and hollowed from magnolia wood cut just two days earlier. This humming arrow was bigger than anyone else's, having an eight-inch-long bulb pierced by nine holes with beveled edges. The binding that secured the *karimata* tip to the shaft, lacquered just the night before, was not yet quite dry. Each branch of the fork was six inches long. The fork opening gaped six inches across, and its sharpened, inner edge ran eight inches around. The trailing edge, too, was so well sharpened that the tip as a whole resembled two small, crossed halberd blades. The arrow was an awesome eighteen handbreadths long.[51]

Tametomo drew the string all the way up to the bulb and let fly, meaning the arrow to sever the base of Kageyoshi's spine. With a long whine that rang through the mansion grounds, it sped fifty or sixty yards to where Kageyoshi had halted, partially severed his left knee, cut his stirrup leathers, broke two of his mount's ribs, and passed straight on through the belly. The broken bulb fell to the ground on the archer's side. The horse collapsed on the spot. Kageyoshi tried to dismount, but with his damaged knee he could not stand. From further within the compound warriors rushed toward him, shouting, "His head's mine!"

Kagechika, then in his twenty-fifth year, raced to where his older brother lay crushed by his mount, dragged the horse off him, and tried to draw him to his feet; but in vain, since Kageyoshi's knee was shattered. Kagechika therefore slung his brother over his shoulders, carried him out the gate, and followed the riverbank downstream five or six hundred yards before laying him down and glancing back. The enemy had not chased him. There was no servant to be seen.

"I'll go back then and fight on," Kagechika said.

Kageyoshi clung to the sleeve of his armor and begged, "You have brought me this far—please stay with me now!" His younger brother showed him the bulb and *karimata* head of Tametomo's humming arrow. "Without my leg I won't be able to fight back if anyone comes to strip me of my armor," Kageyoshi continued. "They'll steal my armor and take my head, too. Lord Yoshitomo couldn't possibly blame you for absconding. He must have seen you face the arrows and fight. He must have seen me be wounded. Surely he saw you save me by carrying me off on your shoulders. He couldn't possibly accuse you of cowardice."

Kagechika had no answer. He set off toward the city with his brother over his shoulders, meanwhile fearing condemnation as a deserter. In the Shirakawa quarter, where he hoped to find lodging, there was none. He feared that their armor would attract robbers. Since his brother's set was an heirloom, and since he was prepared to guard his own with his life, he wore both.

Desperate to save his brother, he carried him on his shoulders from the riverbank at Ōi-no-mikado, with two pauses to rest, to a Yamashina estate owned by Yoshitomo. From there he turned back and rejoined the day's battle.

Tametomo regretted felling his adversary that way. "Surely no warrior in Japan is more blessed by the gods that Ōba no Heida Kageyoshi. I have shot many men, but against a target on my left side,[52] within easy range, I doubt that an arrow of mine has ever gone that far astray. I assumed that it would pierce his armor wherever it hit, whether his head or elsewhere, and I shot much too low—I believe I hit him in the knee. Judging from the way his horse died, I doubt that he died as well."

A warrior announced himself as "Ebina Suesada, likewise from Sagami!" and charged. Sudō Kurō Iesue shot him where the shin guard failed to protect his left leg. Suesada fell from his horse, and one of his men carried him away. Toshima no Shirō, from Musashi, charged next, only to retreat when shot in the left thigh by Akushichi Bettō. Chūjō no Shingo, Chūjō no Shinroku, Narita no Tarō, and Hakoda no Jirō, all from Musashi, then charged in turn, only to retreat, grievously wounded. Tamanoi no Shirō next took their place. Akushichi Bettō, with his sharp eye for every vulnerable spot, shot his mount in the belly, and Tamanoi crashed to the ground.

The next to charge, his bow over his left shoulder and brandishing a drawn sword, announced, "I am Kaneko no Jūrō Ietada, in my nineteenth year. This is my first battle!"

"He's quite a fellow, this Ietada," Tametomo remarked. "They'll still say it took several men to kill him, even if only one of us does. Go at him, then, anyone with a mind to, and take him down in full view of the enemy."

There were two warriors from Kyushu, brothers named Takama no Saburō and Shirō. Shirō, the younger, charged alone to within a dozen yards of the enemy force and grappled with Ietada. He was a very powerful man in his thirtieth year. Kaneko Ietada, in his nineteenth, was still too young to have filled out. The two crashed to the ground. Ietada got on top and pinned Shirō down by treading on both his sleeves. He had drawn his dagger and was preparing to take Shirō's head when Saburō, Shirō's older brother, joined the fray to keep him from doing so. In hasty response, Ietada gave up taking Shirō's head and attacked Saburō to save his own. Saburō got his hand through the hole at the top of Jūrō's helmet and tried to pull him down, but Ietada's neck was too strong, and he failed. Ietada, his dagger already drawn, lifted the skirt of Saburō's armor on the left side and thrust it in full length three times, hilt and fist. The wound was grave, and Saburō collapsed on his back. Then Ietada took the head of the man whose sleeves he had pinned underfoot.

Yamaguchi no Rokurō and Senba no Shichirō, two other members of the Kaneko League, joined him. From Tametomo's side Kiheiji Taifu, who could throw a stone three hundred yards, and Ōya no Shinzaburō fell upon them. A sword fight ensued. Rokurō slashed Kiheiji's right shoulder, and the man fled without throwing a single stone. Shinzaburō lost his left arm to Senba no Shichirō, who fled without shooting a single arrow.

Kaneko Ietada had wounded one man and, oblivious to life or death, taken another's head. Now he remounted and proclaimed, "In the presence of Lord Tametomo, famous throughout Japan, I have disposed of two able adversaries. Now I shall withdraw. Look to me, warriors of generations to come, as an example to you all!" With this he calmly rode away, and no man there failed to praise him.

Sudō Kurō Iesue drew his bow to shoot the fellow, but Tametomo put his hand in front of the arrow. "Don't shoot, Iesue," he said. "He's worth too much. Let him live. No army could boast a man like him. I've seen many fighters, but never his like. Shooting him could hardly decide victory or defeat. What difference would it make? No engagement will hang on your shooting him or not. Once we have won, and I control the eight provinces of the east, I will call him into my service. Just let him go." Iesue did.

The man of bow and arrow must merit his standing. To die is to leave one's name to future generations and a debt of gratitude to one's descendants. To survive is to outshine all men and to receive rich rewards. Kaneko no Jūrō Ietada was a man of such mettle that the enemy spared him, and he emerged safe and sound from the jaws of the leviathan.

A stiff southerly wind arose and blew the gate doors open. Yoshitomo and his men hastily withdrew to either side, expecting an enemy sortie. Only Seki Toshihira, from Hitachi, stood his ground, a single arrow in hand.[53] "You cowards!" he shouted. "It's just the wind!" Everyone laughed and charged the gate again. Among them, Nakakura no Saburō, another Hitachi man, received a grave wound and withdrew. When Shiomi no Gorō and Rokurō, from Kai, charged bridle to bridle, an arrow from Tametomo's bow went straight through Rokurō's neck and neckplate, and he crashed from his horse. The sight must have convinced Seki Toshihira that the second arrow would be for him, because he brazenly toppled from his mount and crawled off, claiming that his horse had been shot in the belly. Maita no Kondōmusha, Kuwabara no Andōji, and Adachizō, all from Shinano, were wounded and withdrew. Kiso no Chūta and Yachūda likewise sustained grave wounds and left the fray. Nezu no Shinpei and Nenoi no Daiyata, too, were wounded. Shizuma no Kojirō charged, only to crash from his mount, his breastplate pierced by an arrow from the bow of Akushichi Bettō. Fifty-one of Yoshitomo's personal followers faced the adversary's arrows and were struck down. Eighty men were gravely wounded, and the number of lesser casualties was beyond counting.

Having lost so many, Yoshitomo withdrew and attacked the west gate. Tameyoshi commanded the defense with six of his sons. They fought so fiercely that this gate, too, resisted all attempts to take it.

Yoshitomo said to himself, "The compound has many gates, after all. It is bitter indeed to attack the one defended by Tametomo, my brother, and more bitter still to attack the one held by Tameyoshi, my father. To do so is the worst of evil karma. The east gate, defended by Taira no Tadamasa[54] and his four sons, and by Tada no Yorinori, is under attack from Minamoto no Yorimasa and the Watanabe League, but they, too, have failed to break through it. To the north, on the Kasuga-kōji side, Taira no Iehiro's younger brother and sons stand ready to defend their gate against Taira no Kiyomori, who at present still has some way to go before he gets there. The din of humming and whistling arrows never stops at any of these gates, nor do the archers' cries. The more times passes, the more men will die. This battle started at the hour of the tiger [4 A.M.], and now, at the hour of the hare [6 A.M.] there is no sign that either side is weakening. I do not see how we are to reduce the Shirakawa Mansion."

He sent a messenger to Emperor Go-Shirakawa to say, "The enemy is very strong, and there is no easy way to reduce the mansion. I see no chance of success without resort to fire. However, the wind is toward Hosshōji, and fire might destroy the temple as well."

Shinzei responded, "You are a fool, Yoshitomo. Hosshōji could be rebuilt in a day if only His Majesty were to commission the work himself. There is no need even to inform him. Press the attack by burning down the Shirakawa Mansion."

Armed with this authorization, Yoshitomo set fire to the house of Fujiwara no Ienari, immediately north of the residence. The strong west wind then carried the flames to the mansion itself. Smoke choked and blinded the warriors in the compound. Yoshitomo and his men attacked.

## 15. Sutoku and Yorinaga Flee

Retired Emperor Sutoku's defeated forces scattered in all directions. Taira no Iehiro and his son Mitsuhiro galloped out the west gate and on to report to Sutoku, "The Shirakawa Mansion is burning, and our men have fled. Already the enemy is swarming through the buildings. For His Eminence all hope is lost. He cannot remain here."

Sutoku and Yorinaga panicked. Sutoku summoned minor counselor Naritaka, gave him his imperial sword, and said, "My life is in your hands." Then he hastily mounted a horse and set off with the chamberlain Nobuzane riding on the croup behind him, his arms around the sovereign. Yorinaga, too, set off on horseback, with Naritaka on the croup in the same way, his arms around him. They went out through the east gate. Tameyoshi, Tadamasa, Yorinori, Iehiro, and Tokihiro rode before them. Tameyoshi called his six older sons together. "Cover their flight with your arrows," he ordered, then went on with the august party. The six brothers had a little over twenty riders left with them, still accoutered as though in Sutoku's presence. They raced to fight from gate to gate. In the ensuing encounters they killed over thirty riders and wounded more than seventy.

Tametomo had emptied three quivers of arrows during the conflict: one of twenty-four, one of sixteen, and a last one of nine hunting arrows. Only two of these arrows had flown wide: the one that grazed Yoshitomo's helmet and the one that half-severed Ōba no Heida's knee and killed his horse. Every one of the others had hit its target—an extraordinary feat. He had fought as though sufficient alone to hold the gate, but his men had faltered, the enemy had burst in, and he had been unable to stop them. Now his entire side was fleeing. He shot his last humming arrow into the wood of the Shirakawa Mansion main gate, so that it might stand there and feed the talk of generations to come.

Sutoku and Yorinaga fled north with the enemy behind them. To keep them at bay and allow both free passage, their warrior escort turned back and engaged the pursuers. Sutoku was riding ahead, with Yorinaga some way behind him, when a stray arrow sank most shockingly into Yorinaga's neck. Naritaka removed and discarded it.

Now unconscious, Yorinaga could neither hold the reins nor keep his feet in the stirrups. For a time Naritaka held him up. The horse was spirited, however, and Yorinaga was so weak that in the end he fell, streaming blood that reddened his white damask hunting cloak. His condition, which so far had prompted grave concern, now seemed beyond hope. In tears, Morinori and Naritaka rushed to his aid and held him.

Tadamasa galloped past, and Morinori shouted out news of what had happened. Tadamasa dismounted, put his arms around the minister, lifted him up, and tried to set him back on his horse, but he failed. He could only lie him back down again, weeping. The chamberlain then arrived, too, and in tears threw his arms around Yorinaga. One Shōgenmotsu Nobuyori was just then galloping by on his way to Matsugasaki. He dismounted and tried to lift Yorinaga again into the saddle, but Yorinaga made no motion at all. Nobuyori and Tsunenori decided to take him to a nearby house and treat the wound with moxa. Upon inspection, they found that the arrow had passed from the beneath the left ear to the right side of the throat. "It is extraordinary for an arrow to strike a rider on a downward trajectory," they said. "Perhaps the gods shot this one against him from on high."

The arrow may have been one shot high into the air, against a distant target, by Sado no Hyōe Shigetada of the Ōmi Genji. It had probably glanced off the ridgepole of the east gate and fallen from there. Shigetada said to the regent, Lord Tadamichi, "I was aiming at either of the men on those two horses, and I hit the one riding ahead[55]—the plump one in the white hunting cloak."

"That must be Yorinaga, the left minister," Tadamichi replied. "Honor accrues to the man who strikes down an enemy of the court." The imperial forces raced off to Engakuji on Tameyoshi's Kita-Shirakawa estate.

Tsunenori, at his wits' end for what to do, brought up a carriage. He placed Yorinaga in it, took him to Saga, and there went looking for the priest in charge of the graveyard where his own father, Akinori, lay. He failed to find him, however, nor was there anyone nearby. He therefore carried Yorinaga into a little house and passed the night with him there.

## 16. Sutoku's Escape to Mount Nyoi

Tameyoshi, Iehiro, and Sueyoshi—one of the guards assigned to the retired emperor's residence—remained in attendance on Sutoku during his flight to Mount Nyoi.[56] On the mountain, Sutoku dismounted and continued on foot. One could only avert one's eyes from the pitiful spectacle of the

Sovereign Complete in Virtue treading the soiled earth.[57] The warriors dismounted, took him by the hand, and sought to lighten his steps. And there, on the slopes of the mountain, Sutoku suddenly fainted. His panicked escort sought to protect him, hardly knowing any longer what they were doing. In a moment he asked whether anyone was with him. Failing to see the warriors lined up beside him, he imagined that he had no one beside him at all. He seemed to have gone blind. "Present, Your Eminence," "Present, Your Eminence," every man replied, with his name.

"Water, please!" said Retired Emperor Sutoku.

They rushed to the bottom of the ravine, but it was dry. "Oh, what are we to do?" they lamented. Perhaps Sutoku's allotted days were not yet over, however, because a monk then approached, carrying a bucket of water to his temple. Iehiro asked for some and offered it to the retired emperor, who drank it and revived a little. The sight cheered everyone present. However, Sutoku remained utterly prostrate.

Tameyoshi said, "The enemy is surely behind us, Your Eminence. You simply must proceed further."

"I quite agree," Sutoku replied, "but I cannot move. Just leave me here and flee, all of you, wherever you wish to go. Save yourselves."

"How could we, Your Eminence, when our lives are yours already? To what remote shore do you wish us to take you?" So said every man.

"You will fight to protect me if I go with you, and I, too, will be killed. If I am alone when the pursuers come upon me, I will say, 'It is I! Save me!' With palms pressed together I will beg for my life. I can quite well at least stay alive that way, and for that reason I refuse to accompany you. It will go badly for me if you insist on keeping me with you." He repeated this several times.

Tameyoshi and the others, equally loath to stay or go, moistened their armor sleeves with tears. So desperate was their plight that all then fled to the four directions. They left behind Sutoku, whom they had so long revered, and they abandoned Yorinaga, too, to wander away, lost, hardly knowing where they were going. Dawn came. Only a few of Sutoku's closest attendants—Iehiro, Mitsuhiro, Sueyoshi—remained with him.

They carried him to the bottom of the ravine and laid him down. They cut grass to cover him and waited beside him for sunset. Dark indeed were his thoughts and theirs. The imperial forces surrounded a few sections of forest in the Shirakawa area and searched, but they found nothing and eventually left. There on the mountain Sutoku expressed the wish to renounce the world. They told him that at present they had with them neither priest nor razor to make that possible.

## 17. The Burning of the Rebels' Houses

The conflict had begun at the hour of the tiger [4 A.M.] and broken up at the hour of the dragon [8 A.M.]. Yoshitomo, Kiyomori, and their men burned Sutoku's North Pavilion residence at Shirakawa, then set off after him through the Eastern Hills. The imperial forces sought the fleeing rebels but did not know where they had gone. Yoshitomo heard that they had taken refuge in Hosshōji and looked for them there, but the temple was too big, and he never found them. He then sent the emperor this message: "The enemy warriors have taken refuge in Hosshōji, but I cannot locate them. I request authorization to burn the temple down." The reply came: "The presence of a few fugitives at the temple is not sufficient reason to burn it. Authorization is denied." Therefore Yoshitomo did not set fire to Hosshōji.

Yoshitomo burned down Tametomo's Engakuji house. At a stroke, several hundred common people's houses nearby were reduced to ashes. The rebels had vanished, no one knew where. Meanwhile, Tadamasa and Yorinori fled toward Ise.

At the hour of the serpent [10 A.M.] Emperor Go-Shirakawa returned from Tōsanjō to Takamatsu House, escorted by Bettō Tadamasa, the Fujiwara captain Kinchika, the left captain Kin'yasu, the left lieutenant Sanesada, the chamberlain and right minor controller Sukenaga, the chamberlain and Civil Affairs official Masayori, and the chamberlain-lieutenant Tadachika. Victory in the day's battle seemed to have preserved imperial rule from danger and upheld the wishes of the gods. The whole court had prayed with profound fervor. Saiun, the abbot of Mount Hiei, had been entrusted with a supplication written by the emperor himself and addressed to the Hiyoshi Shrine. Saiun had presented it in person to the deity, together with appeals so urgent that the deity had responded; for indeed, despite the desperate battle waged by Tameyoshi, Tadamasa, and their sons in utter disregard of their lives, Sannō's wishes had apparently prevailed, and the enemy had been swiftly quelled.[58]

Divine might had proven itself brilliantly, and imperial authority had displayed its awesome power. Of old, when news came that Masakado had subdued the eight provinces of the east and was now on his way up to attack the capital, the imperial visage had paled and the officials had lapsed into confusion. Prayers to suppress the rebels had then been offered at many temples and shrines, but nothing had any effect until the great abbot Son'i, in compliance with an imperial decree, enshrined Fudō Myōō in the Lecture Hall on Mount Hiei and there, before the altar, performed rites to protect and pacify the realm. Masakado then appeared, fully armed, in the sacred flame, and was soon killed. The prayers of two Enryakuji abbots had safeguarded two reigns—a truly wonderful thing. No wonder people call Sōji-in the sanctum protector of the realm.[59]

## 18. Sutoku Renounces the World

That night, Iehiro and his son Mitsuhiro carried Sutoku down from the mountain on their shoulders; passed behind Hosshōji; near Tōkōji, in the Kita-Shirakawa district, borrowed a palanquin from an acquaintance of Mitsuhiro; placed the retired emperor in it; and asked him where he wished them to take him. "To the home of the gentlewoman Awa-no-tsubone," Sutoku replied.

They followed Nijō westward to Ōmiya and knocked at Awa-no-tsubone's gate. It remained closed, and no sound came from within. "Then to Norinaga's house," Sutoku said. They took him there, but Norinaga, too, had fled the scene of the battle and disappeared, and in his absence his house offered no safe refuge. No one responded to their knock at the gate.

"To Shō-no-naishi's house, then," Sutoku said. However, no one was there, either. The realm had once seemed vast, but every quarter was now closed to him, and he had nowhere to go. "This is a sorry pass," he said. "I now have nowhere even to spend the night." He seemed understandably downcast. The situation was beyond Iehiro's and Mitsuhiro's competence to help, but they took him wherever he wished. "We can still do our best for him during the night," they reflected in intense anguish, but what will day bring?"

They carried him to Chisoku-in and put him down in a monks' lodge unfamiliar to them. He immediately lay down to rest. He had neither eaten nor drunk since the evening, apart from that water on the mountainside, and no wonder he was feeling weak. His escort understood that all too well, and they anxiously did all they could for him. At last they managed to offer him some thin rice gruel, which made him feel a little better.

He then arose and renounced the world. Mitsuhiro cut off his own topknot. Iehiro wanted to do likewise, but Sutoku restrained him, saying, "It would not be right for you to do so, too. Do not cut off your topknot." So Iehiro refrained.

"Where shall we carry your palanquin?" they asked him. "To Ninnaji, where the Fifth Prince is abbot," he replied. "However," he went on, "he will be afraid to accept me if he knows that I am coming. Just take me there without a word to him." The prince-abbot, a younger brother of both Sutoku and Go-Shirakawa, presumably had no personal wish to avoid Sutoku. Having lost the conflict, however, Sutoku assumed that the prince-abbot would now be too frightened to admit him. Actually, the prince-abbot was away at the time, having gone to the Toba Mansion to pray for his father's repose. Iehiro therefore simply deposited Sutoku at Ninnaji and went on to seek refuge in the Northern Hills. There he met an ascetic practitioner and cut off his topknot at last.

## 19. By Imperial Command, Shigenari Guards Sutoku

Meanwhile the prince-abbot of Ninnaji, greatly alarmed by recent events, required Sutoku to leave his personal residence and move to the lodge of Kanpen, his chief administrator. He then informed the emperor, who sent Minamoto no Shigenari to guard Sutoku. Being under warrior guard did not exactly inspire Sutoku to flights of poetry, but he expressed his feelings in these words:

| | |
|---|---|
| *omoiki ya* | No, I never dreamed |
| *mi wa ukikumo ni* | that I would become one day |
| *narihatete* | homeless as a cloud, |
| *arashi no kaze ni* | drifting here and drifting there |
| *makasubeshi to wa* | at the mercy of the wind. |
| *uki koto no* | Life's sorest trial |
| *madoromu hodo wa* | gives way to oblivion |
| *wasurarete* | when one falls asleep |
| *samureba yume no* | and, once wakefulness returns, |
| *kokochi koso sure* | seems perhaps only a dream. |

## 20. The Regent Tadamichi Resumes His Rightful Duties *with* The Warriors' Rewards

The retired regent Fujiwara no Tadazane, dismayed by the news of Sutoku's defeat, had the planks stripped from the Uji Bridge and fled to Nara with Yorinaga's three sons. These were Kanenaga, the right commander; Moronaga, a counselor; and Takanaga, a left captain. Kakukei, a son of Tadamichi and the acting superintendent of Kōfukuji, fled up to the capital because his grandfather, Tadazane, meant to have him assassinated.

Meanwhile Tadazane arranged to defend Nara. From Kōfukuji he summoned Jinpan of Zenjō-in, Sengaku of Tōboku-in, the chief administrator Shinjitsu, the senior temple official Genjitsu, and also their brother Minamoto no Yorinori. He ordered them to assemble the temple's warrior monks, mobilize the warriors of the nearby provinces, and lend him their aid; and he promised to reward generously anyone who gave him outstanding service. They therefore roused themselves, mustered their warriors, and guarded Nara.

People said of this, "What can Lord Tadazane be thinking? His Majesty himself defers to him, and the world at large holds him in high esteem. Lord Tadamichi, his proper successor, has naturally enough followed his father as regent. Otherwise, however, Tadazane has favored Yorinaga, his youngest son, by giving him at Tadamichi's expense two posts normally filled by the regent: that of private inspector and that of head of the Fujiwara house. The world has criticized him for this, but the emperor and his officials have forgiven him so understandable a leaning toward a favorite son. Moreover, his steadfast respect for the ten excellent precepts seems to have saved him from the present disaster. Nonetheless, he now seems to be gathering forces against His Majesty, as though he were intent on repeating his favorite son's utter failure."

In truth it was difficult to see how Tadazane could have harbored rebellious intentions, and yet his favorite son's adherence to Sutoku's cause had plainly inspired in him sympathy for that side. No doubt that is why the fear of being attacked as well had alarmed him and driven him into hiding. Nara was therefore declared in a state of rebellion, and the police official Suezane was dispatched to guard the Uji Bridge.

At the hour of the sheep [2 P.M.], Kiyomori and Yoshitomo went to Sutoku's and Yorinaga's residences and burned them down. When they returned to Takamatsu House, the emperor summoned them from among the other warriors present and proclaimed to them, through Shinzei, "Recently, evil rebels arose and banded together in great numbers, plotting to overthrow the realm and sow chaos throughout the world. However, you swiftly destroyed them, cleansed the land of its shame, and lifted high the names of your houses. I am deeply impressed. Your just reward will endure through all generations to come." The two men humbly touched their foreheads to the ground, withdrew, and announced this proclamation to their men, who listened reverently.

This day Tadamichi, the regent, once more became the head of the Fujiwara house. It was his loss of that title to Yorinaga, during the Kyūan years [1145–1151], that had made him so angry. It was further decreed that, for having supported his predecessor, the Nara monks Jinpan, Senkaku, Shinjitsu, Genjitsu, and others should have their property confiscated. It was decreed, too, that the acting Kōfukuji superintendent Kakukei, whose property the previous head of the Fujiwara house had confiscated, should have it restored.

The rewards for signal service were announced that night. For his deeds Kiyomori, the governor of Aki, was transferred to Harima.[60] Yoshitomo, the governor of Shimotsuke, was appointed acting chief left equerry. He had previously been deputy right equerry. Yoshitomo and Ashikaga Yoshiyasu were for the first time accorded access to the palace. Yoshiyasu came to be known as the police chamberlain.

Yoshitomo said, "No one could complain if I had been inducted for my achievements into the ranks of the senior nobles. The office awarded me was first held by my ancestor Tada no Manjū, and of course I am glad to follow him in it; but to move from deputy right equerry to acting chief left equerry can hardly, to my mind, be called a reward. There is no glory in it. What I have heard is that he who quells an enemy of the court receives half a province, and that his glory lasts forever. I turned against my father and abandoned my brothers to serve His Majesty, and I risked my life to fight for him. An imperial command is no doubt beyond challenge, but for having drawn my bow and shot arrows against my father, I should surely have been rewarded beyond others." He insisted repeatedly on this point, and since there was indeed something to it, Takasue, the chief left equerry, was reassigned to the post of Left City commissioner, and Yoshitomo replaced him. That soothed his anger.

## 21. The Death of Yorinaga *with* Tadazane's Grief

Although still alive on the 12th, Yorinaga could only move his eyes. All he could say was, "I want to see Lord Tadazane before I die." His sorrowing attendants had no idea how to get him to Nara, but they did want to bring Tadazane his dying son. They therefore put Yorinaga in a carriage, as they had done the day before, and left Saga. The monks came forth in large numbers when they reached the Shaka-dō, stopped the carriage, and made various demands. The party then continued on to Umezu, where for the price of a *katabira* robe they hired two small boats, lashed them together, gathered a load of brushwood, put Yorinaga aboard underneath it, and took him on downstream in the guise of woodcutters. At nightfall they stopped where the Kamo River joins the Katsura.

The next day, the 13th, they entered the Kizu River.[61] From Hahaso Wood they sent the librarian Koremune no Toshinari to Tadazane with the message "Your son is here and begs an audience with you. He is dying. You may wish to look upon him in his last moments."

"No, no, I could not possibly do that!" Tadazane replied in a manner that made his feelings all too plain. What he really longed to do was to rush to see his son, but the blow was too heavy. "Why does he want to see me?" he cried. "I have no wish to see him. Tell me, Toshinari, how a figure so considerable as to hold the post of head of the Fujiwara house could have succumbed to a weapon of war? It would ill befit me to enter the presence of so unfortunate a man. Let him vanish where my eyes cannot see him and my ears receive no news of him." He then dissolved in tears. No wonder he felt as he did. It is misery merely to hear the tale.

Toshinari rushed back and reported Tadazane's words. Yorinaga nodded, paled, bit off the tip of his tongue, and spat out the blood. His feelings are beyond imagining. It was a terrifying moment. Those with him had no idea where to take him next. They went looking for the monk Senkaku, but he was away. They then sought Genken of Matsumuro. Once they had found him, they hurried back to Yorinaga, put him in a palanquin, and took him into Nara. Since Genken's lodge was in a corner of the Kōfukuji compound, they discreetly took Yorinaga to a small house nearby and did for him what they could. They offered him thin rice gruel, but he swallowed not a drop. The sight so moved Genken that he approached Yorinaga's pillow and said, "Genken is here, Your Excellency.

Can you see me?" Yorinaga nodded but gave no sign that he recognized the speaker.

They took him to that little house on the 14th of the 7th month, at the hour of the hare [6 A.M.]; and that same day, at the hour of the horse [noon], he died. Genken and everyone else present yielded to grief. Yorinaga could not of course remain where he was, and after nightfall they therefore carried him secretly to the place known as Gozanmai, at Hannya-no;[62] and there, in tears, they buried him. Then they went their ways.

As a last gesture of service to his lord, Tsunenori immediately became a monk. He then called on Tadazane, at Zenjō-in, and described Yorinaga's last moments to him. Tadazane pressed his sleeves to his eyes, dissolved in tears, and for a moment remained silent. Then he asked Tsunenori to approach. "But did he leave no final word with you?" he asked. "Quite apart from his own fate, he must have been desperately worried about his children. Surely he remained deeply attached to this world. Alas, I refused to see him because I imagined that he still had a little longer to live; but then he died after all. He should have died on my lap. I will never see him again. Oh, how I regret what I said! I so looked forward to seeing him become regent and administer the realm. I have lived my long life in vain. To think that I have witnessed such a disaster!" He had not finished before he burst into tears. How indeed could he not have burned with regret?

"The man who risks his life on the field of battle may still come through unscathed," Tadazane continued. "I gather that not one of the principal Genji and Heike figures who fought at the Shirakawa Mansion was killed. Senior nobles, privy gentlemen, and members of the retired emperor's guard had sought refuge there, but which of them, I ask you, was slain? Why should an arrow have struck and killed only Yorinaga? Who shot it? It could have hit so many others! It is heartbreaking that it should have hit precisely him.

"Emperor Gaozu of Han did indeed pacify the realm with his three-foot sword, but a stray arrow struck and killed him when he slew Qing Bu of Huan Nan. Everything that happens follows from past karma. In India and China, ministers beyond counting have been assassinated throughout history, while in our own land of Japan the period between Tsubura and Emi[63] offers already eight examples. No, Yorinaga is not alone in having suffered such a fate. No head of the Fujiwara house, though, has ever been killed by an arrow. Oh, I would have given my life for his gladly, if only that had been possible! Alas! Su Wu went to the land of the Huns but in the end saw again the moon over his emperor's palace, ten thousand leagues away. Ruan Jun entered the grotto of the immortals, yet still returned to the life and ways of the court of Qin. But Yorinaga—now that he is gone, when will he ever return? If told that he was in the east, I would of course whip my mount that way, even to the fens where the Ezo live, or to Tsugaru. If told that he was in the west, I would not hesitate to row my boat in that direction, even to Kikai-ga-shima. If Yorinaga had been sent into permanent, distant exile, at least he would still be alive and might look forward with hope to a general amnesty. I never imagined such agony troubling my old age!"

He spoke at length this way of past and future, amid streaming tears. Everyone in his residence, high or low, wept with him. Chamberlains and controllers hardly knew what to do, now that the left minister Yorinaga was gone, and the world helplessly lamented the imminent ruin of both emperors, reigning and retired. The Kasuga Deity[64] had abandoned him, and the feelings of ordinary mortals hardly mattered any longer.

This left minister had been born into a long line of regents and had received imperial appointment as private inspector. He had outshone all others in brilliance and was famed for his mastery of the arts. What karmic lapse, then, can have brought him to such a pass? Despite having risen to head the Fujiwara house, he had neglected the rites to the buddhas and gods, and had failed to satisfy their wishes. So it is that the Kasuga Deity is said to have declared in an oracle, "I withdraw my presence from him."

# Book 3

## 22. The Capture of the Rebels

On the 15th of the 7th month of Hōgen 1, the following were subjected to interrogation at Tōsanjō:

Norinaga, the Left City commissioner
Narimasa, the Ōmi captain
Naritaka, the fourth-rank minor counselor
Ienaga, the governor of Noto
Tsunenori, the chamberlain-commissioner
Morinori, of the Bureau of Ceremonial.

Shinzei had already announced the province of each man's banishment. All therefore emerged from their hiding places, in monkish guise, trusting that their lives, at least, would be spared.

Tsunenori and Morinori were brothers. They and Hata no Sukeyasu, formerly of the retired emperor's guard, were singled out for torture at the Gate Watch headquarters. The brothers were Yorinaga's maternal relatives, and the interrogators therefore assumed that they knew how the affair had started. Rumor had it that they had laid curses on Emperor Konoe and Bifukumon-in. Another issue concerned the circumstances surrounding the burning of Tokudaiji.[65]

Gate Watch underlings first stripped them naked and tied ropes around their necks. "What have I done? Spare me!" Morinori cried and, weeping, pressed his palms together before them in supplication. Being neither stock nor stone, the witnessing officials could not bear to look. The code of punishments imposed its requirements, however, and the torture was applied seventy-five times. Narimori screamed at first, but then he lost consciousness and seemed dead. It was almost unexampled that the instrument of torture[66] should be used on a gentleman of the fifth rank or above. Something similar had happened of old, however, in the reign of Emperor Seiwa [858–876]. The Ōten Gate burned down on the night of the 10th of the 3rd month of Jōgan 8 [865], and the grand counselor Ban no Yoshio was sent down to the Gate Watch headquarters, to be interrogated under torture on suspicion of arson. The case in question followed that precedent.

## 23. Prince Shigehito Renounces the World

Prince Shigehito, Sutoku's eldest son, had no idea what to do. Men had been searching for him in vain. On the evening of the 15th he boarded a woman's carriage and set out toward Ninnaji, where his father was.

He was passing the Suzaku Gate when the police official Taira no Saneyoshi detected his presence and stopped the carriage. He then reported his find to the emperor. "Ask him where he is going," came the reply. Prince Shigehito answered, "My only wish is now to save myself by renouncing the world, and that is what I am on my way to do."

"Then you may proceed," his captor said and conducted him to the residence of the great prelate Jōgyō at Ninnaji, where he mounted guard over the prince. With the prince were Norimori of the Left Gate Watch and Mitsushige of the Right.

Jōgyō declined several times, but a direct command from His Majesty required him to obey, and he shaved the prince's head. The prince had been expected to succeed as a matter of course either to the throne itself or to the position of heir apparent, and it was this forced renunciation that so saddened Jōgyō that he declined several times to perform it. Prince Shigehito had been brought up by Taira no Tadamori, the former head of the Bureau of Punishments, and he was therefore a foster brother of Kiyomori and Yorimori. Neither had any wish to lose him, but they were at Takamatsu House in attendance on the emperor and were powerless to intervene. Both wept to learn that he had renounced the world. They mourned his plight in tears.

## 24. The Surrender of Tameyoshi

On the 16th, Tameyoshi was reported to be hiding out in Higashi-Sakamoto. On the 17th, imperial forces were dispatched to the spot under Kiyomori, now the governor of Harima. In response to assurances that no such person had turned up there, Kiyomori arrested the local householders and confiscated their property. The monks of Mount Hiei then rose in protest. "Never," they said, "since time immemorial, have such arrests and confiscations been carried out in this place. There is no possible excuse for engaging in such conduct without a word either to the priests of the Hiyoshi Shrine or to the monks of the Mountain."

Cowed, Kiyomori withdrew. Flushed with victory, the monks then seized three of his men. Driven out of Higashi-Sakamoto, Kiyomori burned down houses in the Nishi-no-ura section of Ōtsu. Why? Because word now had it that people from there had helped Tameyoshi to escape northward across the lake. The rumor was false.

Tameyoshi was not where Kiyomori had been looking for him. He was at Sakamoto-mitsukawajiri, at the home of Gorōdayū Kageyoshi. On the 16th he had ridden with fifty men through Miidera land, meaning to head for the provinces of the east. Unfortunately, however, he had then become so ill that he hardly knew where he was. His close attendants secured him on horseback and continued on. The other warriors sought to stop them when they caught up, but they fled when they saw how ill their commander was.

Apart from Tameyoshi's six sons, only four of his retainers and the servant Hanazawa remained with him. They attempted to board a boat at Mino-ura in Ōmi, but twenty enemy horsemen then came down on them. Resistance was out of the question. All fled, including the retainers. The situation was more desperate than ever. Tameyoshi tried to go on toward the east part of Ōmi, but he was gravely ill; and, besides, he gathered that the Suzuka[67] and Fuwa barriers were closed. That made flight toward the east all but impossible. He had no wish to be struck down beside the road, or indeed to die at all, and he recoiled also from the shame of dying as he was. He therefore changed his route. From Mino-ura he returned to Higashi-Sakamoto and from there stole into Kurodani.[68] At the urging of the servant Hanazawa he then climbed Mount Hiei and went to the lodge occupied by the scholar-monk Gachirinbō; and there he renounced the world. Glory had once been his, but alas, he now donned monkish black.

In his fourteenth year Tameyoshi had attacked his uncle Yoshitsuna, the governor of Mino, and for this exploit he was appointed an officer in the Left Gate Watch. In his eighteenth year he had driven the Nara monks back from Kuriko-yama.[69] In his twenty-third he was assigned to the police, apparently in reward for that service. From there he seemed destined to become a provincial governor. When asked which province he preferred, he answered that he wished to succeed his father and grandfather in Mutsu. The court objected that in his case Mutsu would be ill-omened. "Your grandfather Yoriyoshi fought the Twelve-Years War there," he was told, "and your adoptive father Yoshiie fought the Later Three-Years War. That province has caused a lot of trouble. Giving it to you would start another rebellion."

So it was that the court refused to have Tameyoshi succeed there to his forebears. Tameyoshi's response was that no other province interested him. From his twenty-third to his sixty-third year he therefore remained a low-ranking officer in the police, without access to the palace. His many sons caused trouble here and there, resulting in recurrent court displeasure and even dismissal from office. Then, after being dismissed [in 1154] as a result of Tametomo's lawless conduct in Kyushu, he was restored to his post in the police. However, he never governed Mutsu, as he had always hoped to do; and now, quite improbably, he was a monk. He took the religious name Gihōbō.

Six of his sons sought refuge on Mount Hiei. Tametomo, however, said to his father, "Is the Mountain really the place for you? You should go on from here to the Kanto. There, like Masakado, you could appoint Yoshiakira, Hatakeyama Shigeyoshi, and Oyamada Arishige, and so on—the men who did not come up to the capital to take part in this conflict—chancellor, left minister, right minister, and palace minister, and their sons grand counselors, consultants, and privy gentlemen of the third, fourth, and fifth ranks. You could style yourself the 'new emperor' and secure the Nezu barrier.[70] In league with Motohira,[71] in Dewa, you could appoint Yorikata[72] to command the forces of the north; have Yorinaka secure the coastal provinces of the east and Tamenari the mountain provinces behind them; and put me in charge of the Kanto. Then, surely, you would stand above all the world."

Tameyoshi replied, "In the flower of my youth I failed to become the governor of Mutsu, and in my waning years I am an enemy of the court. I see no hope of enjoying any such good fortune now that I have renounced the world. All I want is to be well again and to live. At the moment, I doubt that I can last a day longer. If only I could be myself again, I would wish to set off with my sons toward the eastern provinces and seek refuge there in the wilderness. Tadamasa, Kiyomori's uncle, and his four sons no doubt became monks, but Kiyomori himself is safely alive; and Yoshitomo, in reward for his services, is now the left chief equerry. I cannot help wondering why Yoshitomo's father, too, should not be spared in recognition of all that he has done. So I will seek out Yoshitomo, beg for my life, and live out my natural term. What do you think?"

His other sons approved and replied with one voice, "By all means do so. Things will become increasingly difficult for us if we go on together. We will have no freedom, and we cannot imagine either you or us surviving for long. Your plan may certainly save you, and it could easily help to save us as well."

"Very well, then, Hanazawa," they said, "hurry to the capital, see Yoshitomo, and tell him: 'Tameyoshi, your father, is now on the Mountain. Please send a palanquin for him. He will come to you.' "

Tameyoshi left the Mountain early that night. With six of his sons he passed it, and they accompanied him as far as at the spring below it, knowing that they were doing so for the last time. "The palanquin coming for me will be here soon," he said. "Leave me now."

They agreed to do so but remained nonetheless where they were, for the bonds of love and gratitude are very strong, and they could not bring themselves to go. The tie between parent and child is for this life only, as they knew all too well, and it was clear that they would never see him again.

Each begged him to wait a moment longer. "We have something to tell you!" they cried.

"What is it?" he asked, coming back up the slope toward them. In truth, though, they had nothing to say. Overcome by the distress of parting, they could only cling to his arms and legs, and weep. No wonder they felt as they did, for separation is painful enough when a promise of reunion lies ahead, and this one was indeed final. No, they would never see him again, and their grief was beyond words.

Tameyoshi said, "I fought as hard in the recent battle as my old body would allow, and now I have little time left. Success is beyond my reach, and it was to give all of you some hope of a place in the world that I assumed my present guise. I may soon be drawn deep into fire or down into a watery abyss, but as long as I live, I will do so only to ensure your safety. It is not for myself that I long to remain alive. Once I have gone into hiding in whatever wilderness I find, then by all means come for me. For now, go quickly. Go back up the Mountain."

Despite his brave words, he was overwhelmed when they roused their courage and agreed to do so. "Yorikata! Yorinaka!" he cried. "I have something to tell you!"

His sons came back down the slope at his call. Neither side had anything to say. Sorrow alone had moved them to speak. When Tameyoshi resolutely started down, his sons called him back up again; when they started up, he called them back down. However, this could not go on forever, and at last all went their separate ways. The sons fled each in his direction, shrouded by a pall of dark misery. Unlike ocean billows, their heaving waves of longing knew nothing of return. Where were they to find the aspen road home? The parasol trees know not whither blows the smoke through their branches.[73] No feathered denizens of the air, they yet parted as do parent birds and nestlings; no fellows of the finny tribe, they still suffered the pangs of the hooked fish. Down streamed their tears, while their spirits wandered the empyrean.

No two of the sons journeyed on together. Each followed his solitary way toward Ohara, Shizuhara, Kibune, or the fastness of Kurama. Meanwhile the servant Hanazawa came to Yoshitomo, who heard him out. He then sent Kamada Masakiyo with a hand carriage,[74] in great secrecy, to receive his father, whom he entertained with joy. Tameyoshi felt quite safe. However, the emperor learned of his arrival. All those who had opposed His Majesty in the recent battle were mercilessly detained.

## 25. The Execution of Tadamasa, Iehiro, and Others

Surely the like had never occurred in this realm of ours, whether in ancient or in more recent times. This question was therefore put to the right minister Masasada, to the palace minister Saneyoshi, to the grand counselor Koremichi, to the master of the heir apparent's household Muneyoshi, and to the right controller and consultant Akitoki: "Are these men to be executed, or are they not?"

The gentlemen replied as follows. "The death penalty has lapsed in our realm ever since Fujiwara no Nakanari was executed long ago, during the reign of Emperor Saga [r. 809–823], on the compassionate grounds that the dead do not live again. An example is the case of the palace minister Fujiwara no Korechika, who shot Retired Emperor Kazan with an arrow during the Chōtoku years [996]. Strolling along masquerading as a goblin, Kazan sat down under a garden wall dressed in a red *hakama* divided skirt, with a robe of the same color pulled over his head. Korechika took him for a real goblin and shot him. The legal scholars declared this a capital crime, but the sentence was nonetheless reduced one step, to distant exile. There were no executions after that, either. We cannot revive the practice now. Besides, we are still within the first forty-nine days of mourning for His Late Retired Eminence. All in all, it would be preferable to reduce the level of punishment."

This judgment then came under discussion. Shinzei insisted, "Your Majesty, I believe this opinion to be in error. It is written, 'In exceptional cases, leave judgment entirely to the sovereign.' In other words, when a case is highly unusual, it is the sovereign's command that must be obeyed. In this instance, to banish a large number of rebels to the provinces would invite trouble and undoubtedly provoke disorder. Please, Your Majesty, order them executed." Such was his considered opinion, and the emperor saw its merit. All the rebels were executed, as Shinzei had recommended. Some people objected, but in vain.

On the 25th, seventeen Heike and Genji men were beheaded. Yoshiyasu undertook to execute the first four at Ōeyama. These were Iehiro, Morihiro, Yorihiro, and Yasuhiro. Nobukane executed Norihiro on the riverbank at Rokujō. Sanetoshi likewise executed Mitsuhiro at Funaoka-yama. Suezane took Tokihiro into his custody, with the order to behead him. On the Rokujō riverbank Taira no Kiyomori executed Taira no Tadamasa; Nagamori, Tadamasa's eldest son; Tadatsuna; Masatsuna; and Taira no Michimasa and his four sons. They had looked to Kiyomori, their nephew, to save them and had appealed to him in person, but he beheaded them all. He could easily have requested leave to spare them if he had wished to do so, but, quite apart from the bad blood between him and them, he understood that if he executed his uncles, Yoshitomo would have to execute his father. That fiendish calculation decided him.

## 26. The Death of Tameyoshi

The order requiring the nephew to execute his uncles was followed by one addressed to Yoshitomo: "You are to behead your father." Yoshitomo, who did not grasp Kiyomori's devious intent, summoned his foster brother Masakiyo. "What am I to do?" he asked. By imperial command Kiyomori has already executed his uncles. If I obey this command to behead my father, I will commit one of the five heinous crimes. If I ignore it for fear of the crime, I will be in contempt of the emperor's word."

Masakiyo replied, "The same thing happened, long ago. The Sutra on the Contemplation of Eternal Life mentions it. It says, 'Those who would kill their father in order to usurp the throne and steal the realm number 18,000.' That is the number of princes who would strike down their father for personal gain. However, your case in no way resembles theirs. Your father became an enemy of the court, and you have received an imperial decree requiring you to chastise him. What need could there be for further reflection? I have heard it said, 'The emperor's word is like sweat: once issued, it does not return.' You know now that your father, an enemy of the court, has no escape, and you should execute him here so as not to let him fall by another's hand. If you then pray devoutly for his happier rebirth, who could accuse you of any crime?" He concluded, "You need only behead him."

"I am sorry to hear you say that," Yoshitomo answered. "Very well then, Masakiyo, make whatever arrangements you think necessary to act on this command."

Masakiyo went to Tameyoshi and said, "My lord told me to say to you, 'Kiyomori and I were appointed commanders in the recent battle and crushed the enemies of the court. Both of us therefore deserve equal reward. Kiyomori's entire family takes pride in enjoying such imperial favor that no other can compete with it. In comparison I hardly exist; my plight unfortunately resembles, as they say, that of a spider caught among rocks.' Under these circumstances my lord means to go down to the provinces of the east, cut off the road at Ashigara, and at the cost of his life, if need be, keep it closed for a time. So, go down by boat to Kumano. I will accompany you.

My lord will then join you there via the Tōkaidō. That is what I have come to tell you. I have a hand carriage ready."

Tameyoshi replied, alas, "I am at Yoshitomo's disposal."

Masakiyo helped him into a hand carriage of plain, unfinished wood. The two set off in the middle of the night, accompanied also by Hadano Yoshimichi. They headed not eastward, but west along Shichijō. Sturdy men in monkish guise arrived to move the hand carriage. At the Shichijō-Suzaku intersection they had Tameyoshi move from the hand carriage to a palanquin.

"We will just behead him quietly before he suspects anything," Masakiyo explained to Yoshimichi.

"How can you say that, Masakiyo?" Yoshimichi protested. "What a horribly cruel idea! Hachimantarō Yoshiie stood as the protector of the imperial house, and thanks to him, his son, our lord, was appointed commander in turn and earned imperial gratitude. The father nurtures the son. There is no excuse for striking so foul a blow against a righteous father, whatever the complaint against him. On the other hand, Lord Tameyoshi has no reason to hold our duty against us now that he is an imperial foe. Death is what matters most for us all. If we kill him without a word, he will lose any chance for enlightenment in the life to come. We can show him the compassion that should prevail between father and son, and between lord and retainer, only by telling him what we mean to do and allowing him to call the Name. I recall that our forebears came to serve this house when Yoriyoshi still governed Iyo, and that their service then passed to his son, Hachimantarō Yoshiie. Tameyoshi is Yoshiie's son and therefore our lord in turn; and in the same spirit we look to his son, Yoshitomo. It would be a dire sin not to inform our hereditary lord of the order that we have received. I will tell him and urge the Ten Callings upon him."[75]

"You are right," Masakiyo replied, "and I was wrong. I wanted to proceed without a word to him because I was overly anxious to spare him distress. You are quite right to speak as you have done. By all means tell him."

Yoshimichi grasped one of the shafts of the hand carriage and said with the deepest respect, "Has my lord not yet informed you? He has received an imperial decree. I am to wield the sword when in a moment, between this hand carriage and the palanquin yonder, you are to be beheaded. Please quietly call the Name."

The astonished Tameyoshi had never imagined such a thing. "But why did you two not tell me?" he asked and burst into tears.

At the Shichijō-Suzaku crossing he alighted. They spread a furred animal hide and sat him down on it. He said, "Yoshitomo has done a terrible thing. The man whose arrow struck the sovereign was spared,[76] and surely I should be, too. I was destined to die somewhere in the wilderness, but life is hard to give up, and I thought that if I appealed to Yoshitomo in the hope that he might save me after all, he could certainly claim in reward for his service the privilege of doing so. After triumphing as he has done, he could surely save the father who comes to him begging for his life. The father cares more for the son than the son for the father: that is the way of the world, and even if I am to be killed, I do not wish my son ill.

"I can just imagine how this will make people talk. 'To what glory did he then aspire,' people will say, 'that he should have beheaded his father? What a brute!' Friends and strangers alike will no doubt shun him. Alas, Tametomo warned me repeatedly against going to him! But Yoshitomo is my son, after all, and I trusted him. If only I had known what would happen, I would have ranged those six sons of mine to my left and right, shot every last arrow in my quiver, and then taken my life. That is what I should have done. Instead, I am now to die like a dog.

"However, I have one consolation. If I had fallen, say, to the Heike, my end would have started much talk, whether I died well or ill, and that would have blemished my house and harmed Yoshitomo. I much prefer falling into the hands of my son and having you, my hereditary retainers, take my head. If you wait too long, all sorts of people will gather here, and they will say, 'They made a bad job of that beheading, didn't they! The fellow was too much of a coward to hold his head out properly.' So do it now, before there are witnesses. You are men of experience—no one will think the worse of you for it.'"

This was the moment, and he was ready; yet the very beasts of moor and mountain, the fish of river and stream value their lives, and still more so do humans prize life as the greatest treasure. The criminal who has no wife or children, and who could therefore die without regret, nonetheless begs for one more day, despite his mutilated arms, legs, and body. How could Tameyoshi not long equally to live?

Regrets he had aplenty. He had many children by his various women: forty-six sons and daughters, counting Yoshitomo. His old ambition, however, had been to have sixty-six sons, each of whom he would have govern one of Japan's sixty-six provinces. That hope had never been realized. He had made Yoshitomo, his eldest, the son-in-law of Suenori, the chief priest of the Atsuta Shrine. He had married a daughter to a priest of the Sumiyoshi Shrine. He had married a daughter to the Kumano superintendent. He had wanted this, aspired to that; and now, this very day, his life was over. What bitter disappointment he must have felt!

No doubt he understood that no cry of his, no howl of protest, could sufficiently convey what he felt. Still, he descended in the sixth generation from Rokusonnō and in the fifth from Manjū; he was a grandson of Yoriyoshi and the fourth son of Hachimantarō Yoshiie. Until just yesterday he had been the rebel commander. Although a monk, today he pressed his sleeves to his eyes to conceal any sign of weakness. Nonetheless, the tears spilled over. Their flow surely washed the black of his robe to a light grey.

He turned toward the west, and his last words were deeply felt. "It is strange indeed," he said, "the life of the man of bow and arrow. I had imagined being dragged off by Heike warriors, no doubt to my sons' shame; but instead my captor turned out to be my son, and my executioner Masakiyo, a hereditary retainer. That is astonishing. Still, being executed as an enemy of the court is something in which to take pride. No man of bow and arrow could claim a greater honor."

Masakiyo moved to strike before he even finished, but his vision darkened, his courage failed, and he found himself unable to proceed. He therefore handed his sword to the man beside him, who took it and delivered the blow. Such was the darkness before his eyes, however, that the sword struck Tameyoshi's shoulders instead. Tameyoshi did not flinch, but called the Name two or three times. At the next blow his head fell to the ground. Masakiyo hastily slipped it into a sleeve and threw his arms around it.

Yoshitomo sent Suezane to performed the formal inspection; and on the same spot Suezane executed Tokihiro, Iehiro's younger brother, whom he had taken into his custody for this purpose. He then reported to Yoshitomo. "Tameyoshi's head is not to be hung in the tree before the prison," he reminded Yoshitomo, presenting him with the head. Yoshitomo took it and placed it and the body together in a palanquin, which he accompanied to Engakuji. He built a tomb, erected a stupa, and performed litanies for the repose of his father's spirit. The departed may not have accepted his prayers.

## 27. The Execution of Yoshitomo's Younger Brothers

Another imperial decree arrived. It said, "It appears that many of Yoshitomo's brothers directed arrows against me. Arrest each and bring him to me."

Yoshitomo sent men in various directions to execute this order. Tametomo had apparently been in the hills beyond Ohara, but he broke through and escaped. The other five had gone into hiding on one mountain or in one valley or another beyond Shizuhara, Kurama, Kibune, and so on. Yoshitomo's men came down upon them, seized them, and prepared to execute them at Funaoka-yama. The five dismounted there and stood in a row. Four declined an offer of water. The fifth, Yorinaka, wiped his lips with moistened paper and said, "I have executed many men in my time. What else my own crime might deserve, I have no idea." He cut his helmet cord, swept the helmet aside, and stretched out his neck. The sword fell. The other brothers did the same. Nobutada was sent to inspect the five heads.

On the 17th, thirteen Genji and Heike leaders were beheaded. The report concerning them was made the next day, the 18th. All this occurred during the forty-nine-day mourning for the late Retired Emperor Toba. In consideration for the order that the heads were not to be hung in the tree before the prison gate, an officially appointed messenger was sent to discard them behind the south side of the imperial granary.

## 28. The Execution of Yoshitomo's Child Brothers

Yet another decree came down to Yoshitomo. It said, "It appears that you have many young siblings who are still children. Kill all the boys."

Yoshitomo summoned Hadano Yoshimichi and gave him this cruel order: "It would be pointless to insist on trying to find those whose mothers or nurses have fled with them to distant provinces or into the wilderness. Those presumably still in the capital are the ones who must be killed. As far as I know there are four living in a house at Rokujō-Horikawa. Give them some story or other to keep them from crying on the way, take them to Funaoka-yama, and behead them."

Yoshimichi took fifty mounted men to Tameyoshi's house at Rokujō-Horikawa. The boys' mother was away on a pilgrimage. Otowaka, the eldest, was in his thirteenth year; Kamewaka, the second, was in his eleventh;

Tsuruwaka, the third, was in his ninth; and Naruten'ō, the fourth, was in his seventh. Yoshimichi said to them, "There will probably be another battle today in the capital. Lord Tameyoshi is in hiding on Funaoka-yama and wants me to bring his sons to him there. Please now, quickly, get into these palanquins."

The four had not met their father since the previous clash. Word had reached them that he had renounced the world, but they had never seen him in monkish guise, and the news that he was now calling for them made them very happy. Alas, they raced to board the palanquins. The warriors pitilessly urged the bearers all the way to greater speed. Just as the sheep walks in patient ignorance to slaughter, so, too, these unfortunate boys knew nothing of what awaited them.

On Funaoka-yama the party went not to where the five brothers had been executed the previous day, but to another spot, fresh and clean. There the bearers set the palanquins down. While Yoshimichi wept copiously, Naruten'ō, the youngest, stepped out of his palanquin and asked where his father was. Wiping away his tears, Yoshimichi took the boy on his lap, stroked his hair, and said to them all, "Actually, Lord Yoshitomo had Masakiyo execute Lord Tameyoshi at dawn today, at the Shichijō-Suzaku crossing. Tametomo alone has escaped. Yesterday morning, Lord Yoshitomo likewise had Yorikata, Yorinaka, Tameie, Tamenari, and Tamenaka executed here. Now I have received the order to execute the four of you. Lord Yoshitomo commanded us to keep you from crying on the way, and that is why I spoke to you as I did. If you have any last words, please say them now."

The four boys cried out. Naruten'ō said, "He must have meant, 'Kill the boys old enough to fight.' I am too young—he can't have meant me!"

Tsuruwaka spoke in turn. "I know there is little hope," he said, "but I would like to send Yoshitomo this message: 'Are you sure that you want to kill four allies of yours? We are worth more to you than a hundred retainers.' "

Kamewaka lay face down in his palanquin and wept in silence.

Otowaka restrained his tears and feigned indifference. He emerged from his palanquin and said, "What fools little boys are! How much could a monster capable of killing his father, whose life he should feel obliged to save at all costs, care about his young brothers? Send him any message you like, but nothing will come of it except messengers rushing back and forth all day long. We are already back here in the gloomy mountains—just think how much worse we will feel by nighttime! No, better to let the sword fall now, while the sun is still in the sky. Ah, Yoshitomo is an evil man! No doubt he acts this way because of Kiyomori's slander. He has killed his father, he has killed his brothers, and now he is alone. Alas, the Genji line will soon die out. It will not last more than another two or three years.

"Do not weep, my brothers! Weep you may, but no one will save you. Death is certain for all, and for us the time has come. Dying now can hardly be worse than at seventy or eighty. What is the point of living longer? The father who should have smoothed our way in life has been executed. All the older brothers we could have looked to are dead. Yoshitomo, who should have supported us, is now our enemy. We have not a shred of property. We could only beg our way along the roads. 'Look,' people would say of us, 'there go what is left of Tameyoshi's sons!' Would you want that? If you love our father, dry your tears and quietly pray, 'All hail, Amida Buddha, Lord of the Western Paradise, O come, we beg, to receive us four and our father, too!' Then we will join our father again."

His three brothers stopped crying, bowed their heads, pressed their palms together, and prostrated themselves toward the west; at which the fifty warriors present all moistened their armor sleeves with tears. The hatchling kalavinka already sings more sweetly than any other bird. Young he was, indeed, this warrior's son, but at heart very brave. Hadano Yoshimichi's tears must have washed the color from his red-laced armor sleeves.

Otowaka spoke again. "The boys' hair is all disheveled and hangs down over their faces. They look hot. Tie it up for them, make them feel cool. Wipe the sweat from their heads and necks. Carefully wipe their faces. Once we are dead, Yoshimichi, wash our faces, smooth our hair nicely, and tie it back neatly before you present our heads to Yoshitomo. We must not appear unsightly."

Each of the brothers had a tutor with him: Otowaka's was Genpachi, Kamewaka's Gotōji, Tsuruwaka's Yoshida no Shirō, and Naruten'ō's Heida, the secretary. These now came forward. Each smoothed his charge's hair, bound it high, and wiped the perspiration from the boy's neck. They kept their voices low, to conceal the tears spilling from their eyes. They were visibly overcome.

Otowaka said, "My initial thought was to go first, but then I realized that worrying about my younger brothers would keep my thoughts tied to this earth. I would rather have them go first, so that I can die without regret."

The time to act had come. The weeping Hadano Yoshimichi beheaded the three younger boys one after the other. Otowaka watched impassively. "Well done, Yoshimichi," he said. "I trust that you will do the same for me. But you may imagine that I asked to go last in order to live that much longer, and that thought makes me ashamed. I spoke as I did only because my brothers had stopped crying, and by remaining behind I wanted to be able to keep them from starting again. My idea was then to die in my turn.

"My mother, you see, set off at dawn today on pilgrimage to Yawata.[77] All four of us begged to accompany her on this third day of her retreat, but she pointed out that although we had the palanquins required, all the servants had fled because of the fighting. 'Your mother will look bad enough,' she said, 'on foot and so poorly attended. Quite apart from what onlookers might say along the way, the people of the shrine itself would surely remark, "How quickly poverty has claimed her! To think that Tameyoshi's sons are here on pilgrimage without an escort!" No, by all means follow me to Yawata once we regain our place in the world.' So she stole away while we were asleep and went alone. She is probably starting back now.

"When she learns that we are all dead, she will ask those who stayed behind to mind the house, 'What did Otowaka say? And Kamewaka—what did he say? Did Tsuruwaka and Naruten'ō have no last words?' It will be awful. If we had known we were going to die we might have left some last words for her, but we were told that our father was calling for us, and we were so happy that we raced to board the palanquins. So give her these, to remember us by." He cut sidelocks from his three brothers, then cut his own; wrapped up the four together; drew blood from his finger; wrote the four names, one by one; and said to Yoshimichi, "Give this to my mother. Do not lose it."

He then went to where the three headless bodies lay, made room for himself between the two youngest, sat down very straight, bowed low three times toward the west, and looking very beautiful, called the Name twenty or thirty times. Then he stretched out his neck to let the sword fall. The four tutors lifted the headless bodies in their arms and lamented in unison until the mountain echoes rang.

Heida, Naruten'ō's tutor, undid the cord of his robe and pressed the body to his bosom, skin to skin. "These seven years I have not once been parted from him!" he cried. "Who will there be now to climb onto my lap? To throw his arms around my neck? O when will I ever again hear him say, sweetly, 'One day I will have property of my own, and you will look after it for me'? Who will go with him over the Mountain of Death? Who will ever be mine to look after, once I am home again? Whom will I serve?" So saying, he slit his belly and collapsed. The three others then likewise took their lives.

One of Otowaka's pages, one of Naruten'ō's, and four others died there, too. Hadano Yoshimichi honored Otowaka's last words by washing the blood off, combing the hair, and tying up proper topknots. Then he submitted the four heads to Yoshitomo for inspection and reported on the executions. "Those heads are not to be hung on public view, either," Yoshitomo declared. "Get rid of them." Since the boys had loved their father so much, Yoshimichi sent them to be buried in their father's grave at Engakuji.

## 29. Tameyoshi's Wife Drowns Herself

Hadano Yoshimichi galloped back to the house at Rokujō-Horikawa. The lady was not yet home when he arrived, so he hurried on toward Yawata. He met her on the Akae riverbank. In great haste he dismounted, gripped the shaft of her palanquin and reported the words of her four sons. He then described what had happened and how they had behaved. She thought that she must be dreaming; she could not believe it was true. He gave her the packet containing the four locks of hair. Tears so blinded her that she could not read the names and hardly knew whose each was. Contorted with anguish, she pressed them to her face and breast. She tumbled from the palanquin, lifted her eyes to the heavens, threw herself to the ground. She cried out but made no sound; she wept, but no tears came. She gasped for breath and writhed in agony.

By and by she regained her breath. "I have no idea whether this is real or whether I am dreaming," she said. "Oh, what am I to do? For whom did I go to Yawata? I went only to pray for my husband and my sons. How the demons must be laughing! Why oh why did I go to Yawata rather than to Funaoka-yama? My sons wanted to come too, but I felt that if I took them all, the one or two attendants I had with me would be too few, and I left them behind. If only I had not! If I had taken one or two I would still have *them*, at least for the time being. I cannot go back to Rokujō. There are no sons there to welcome me or to reproach me for not having taken them.

No, I will go now to Funaoka-yama. Their faces will not be there, but I will see their bodies." With these words she started up the east bank of the Katsura River.

On the riverbank beyond the end of Gojō she had her bearers put her palanquin down. "I actually prefer not to go to Funaoka-yama," she said. "By now birds and beasts will have torn the headless bodies apart, and it would be too awful to find fragments here and there—an arm in a thicket, a bone in a ravine—and to find myself thinking, 'Oh, this is Otowaka's leg! This is Kamewaka's arm! These bones are Tsuruwaka's, these Naruten'ō's! I would become a nun at Hōrinji, Ninnaji, or Ohara, but they would ask me there who was my husband, who was my father, and they would insist on the truth. If I gave it to them, they would say, 'So, she's Tameyoshi's wife, is she? What about her looks—is she pretty or not? Her hair—is it long or short? And what about her age? How old is she, anyway?' It would be horribly embarrassing. No, better to have my head shaved by a priest who knows me. Till then, though, I cannot stay just as I am. I would be too ashamed of people's idea of me."

She asked for a dagger, cut her own hair off at the roots, distributed locks of it to those around her, dedicated some to the buddhas and gods, and sank the rest in the river, weighted with stones. She then said, in tears, "It is taught that in a single day and night we humans have 800,004,000 thoughts.[78] Whatever those thoughts may be, there are apparently that many of them. So I do not see how I could possibly forget what has happened, not for as long as I live.

"Now, some people seem to live to seventy or eighty. Lord Tameyoshi was in his sixty-third year, so he clearly might have lived a good many more if they had not killed him. Whenever in the future I might count up how old each of my sons would have been by then, I would feel horror at their execution and bitter anger against the man who ordered it. Seeing some rise high in the world, I would only ache that my sons had never lived to achieve the same success, and so I would heap sin upon sin. I doubt that reading the sutras and calling the Name could help me enough. No, I will simply drown myself."

She had with her three gentlewomen, two or three servant girls, five retainers, twelve sturdy porters in monkish guise, and seven or eight junior male attendants. These said among themselves, "No wonder she grieves so. Such things have always happened, though, in ancient times as well as our own. Children lose their parents, parents lose their children, wives are torn from their husbands—this is a matter of common experience. But for her to throw herself into the river and die—surely that would be taking it a bit far. Lord Yorinaga's wife became a nun after the recent battle, but she did not drown herself. Others were torn each from each while alive, still others were parted by death. Taira no Tadamasa's wife became a nun when she lost her husband and four sons, but she did not drown herself, either. Neither did Iehiro's wife when she lost her husband and three sons. None went further than renouncing the world."

"Do not imagine that I, too, will refrain, just because others have done so," the lady said. "To each her choice." She tied back the sleeves of her robe, gathered stones, and placed them in her robe's front fold. She then faced the west and prayed, "All Hail, Amida Buddha, Lord of the Western Paradise! Come forth, I beg, to greet Tameyoshi, my husband, my four sons, and me, and seat us all on one lotus throne!"

She moved to plunge into the river, but the men and women with her formed a hedge, side by side, to keep her from doing so.

"Yes," she responded, "life *is* precious! I would probably fail to die even if I tried. No, I will instead go back to Rokujō and find out what last words my sons had for me. Besides, I expect that they left their toys scattered about. I will pray for their happier rebirth." With these words she walked toward her palanquin.

"That's better!" her relieved attendants said. They, too, left the water's edge and started toward her palanquin; whereupon she ran back to the river, this time unhindered, and sank into its depths.

A gentlewoman, her foster sister, clung stubbornly to her sleeve, only to be dragged into the river herself. None of the others could really swim. The river was high at the time, and at that spot it was deep. One or two who could swim a little took turns trying to pull her out, but she had stones in her robe. They nearly drowned, holding on to her. Their attempts to lift her out failed. When eventually they succeeded, it was already too late. The hours they spent trying to revive her did no good, so they carried her a little higher up the bank and held a brief funeral service there. Then they went away, sighing that she could never have imagined, when she started out early that morning, where her pilgrimage would end. Alas, they lamented in vain. Such wives have always been rare, in times past as in our own.

## 30. The Inspection of Yorinaga's Body

It was now the 21st of the 7th month. Three Takiguchi guards[79] and an envoy from the Council of State were sent to verify that Yorinaga, the Haughty Left Minister, was really and truly dead. This envoy was Nakahara no Koretoshi, and the guards were Moromitsu, Yoshimori, and Suketoshi. The place was Hannya-no in Kamimura, in the county of Soenokami in Yamato. A hundred yards or so east of the main road, the monks Gen'en and Jissei dug into a recent grave on the east side of the cluster of graves. They found a few bones still linked at the joints, some with a little flesh still on them. It was impossible to identify them, nor was there any question of re-burying them.[80] The guards just left them there and returned to the capital.

The next day, the 22nd, Yorinaga's three sons went together to call on Tadazane. The eldest among them was the right commander Kanenaga, and the next was the counselor-captain Moronaga. Both were in their nineteenth year.[81] The youngest was the left captain Takanaga, in his sixteenth. In tears they said, "You know the situation. Our father is dead, and we do not know where to turn for survival. There is no sign that the penalty for our father's crime is to be lightened in any way. His crime was very grave, and we gather that we are to be executed. Yesterday, apparently, an imperial envoy went to his grave, dug up his body, and left after inspecting it. No son of a father treated that way can ever again look another in the eye. We wish to resign our posts, renounce the world, and, for as long as our dewdrop lives last, enter the True Way and pray for our revered father's enlightenment."

Lord Tadazane replied, "It is indeed impossible to know what tomorrow will bring, but it is a relief to see you here today, still alive. I wonder, though, how great that relief will continue to be if you do as you intend. Whatever fate you may have to suffer for the time being, would you not prefer to follow in your father's footsteps by again serving His Majesty? Deeply attached as he was to this world, his wish even now is undoubtedly that you should do so. Even the man in distant exile may find in time that his fate does not at all resemble what he expected. Emperor Xiaoyang of Han emerged from prison to claim the throne. In our land, the right minister Toyonari[82] was banished to Kyushu as Dazaifu deputy; but then he was pardoned, returned to the capital, and became a minister once more. There are other such examples. Why should you not continue to hope, as long as the Kasuga Deity has not abandoned you?" He wept as he spoke.

Fearing to sin gravely by disappointing him, the three young men refrained from giving up the world.

## 31. Retired Emperor Sutoku Moves to Sanuki

Meanwhile, Sadanaga brought the prince-abbot of Ninnaji[83] a message from the emperor, to the effect that the following day, the 23rd, Sutoku was to be moved to Sanuki. Sutoku had already gathered that he was to be removed from the capital, but the arrival of a messenger bearing that explicit order threw him into utter confusion.

That night Prince Shigehito moved to the residence of the abbot of Kezō-in.[84] At first the abbot declined to accept him, but he had to give in when Prince Shigehito and the imperial messenger arrived at his residence together. He then proceeded to shave the prince's head. The prince was in his seventeenth year. Those who had long served him said, weeping, "Ah, I always took it for granted that he would be named heir apparent and succeed to the throne!" Prince Shigehito had been brought up by Taira no Tadamori, and it is sad indeed that Tadamori's son, Kiyomori, should have turned away from him.

Sutoku left Ninnaji the next day, the 23rd, well before dawn. In the presence of Shigenari's warriors he boarded a carriage belonging to Yasunari, the governor of Mino. The three gentlewomen with him wailed loudly as he did so. He said, "In the past, when a retired emperor traveled in a carriage with eaves,[85] senior nobles and privy gentlemen always attended him, and men from the Palace Guards escorted him. But oh, the louts who brought up this carriage for me! I must be dreaming!"

At the main north gate of the Toba Mansion, he summoned Shigenari. Shigenari approached. "I wish to visit my father's grave and bid him a last farewell," he said.

Shigenari replied, "It is difficult to know how His Majesty might react, should he hear later of your having done so. Besides, your progress would then fall behind the decreed schedule." He would not allow it.

"Very well, I have no choice," Sutoku answered. He ordered the ox unhitched and the carriage drawn on to Retired Emperor Toba's Anrakuju-in grave.[86] Whatever he may have said there, from outside the carriage one heard only his sobs.

"There are other ways to serve the court," Shigenari reflected. "It is too painful to have to accompany him like this and hear such things." He pressed his sleeves to his eyes and wept.[87]

Shigenari had been sent to take Sutoku all the way to Sanuki, but he refused to do so and went no further than Kusatsu.[88] There Sutoku, unaware that Mitsuhiro had been executed on the 11th, said, "You will have Mitsuhiro come to me immediately. As for yourself, I will never forget your kindness to me during these past days."

The Sanuki governor Sueyuki,[89] aided by a few warrior guards, took custody of Sutoku and led him into the boat's cabin. He then locked the cabin from the outside. Once more the three gentlewomen wailed, just as they had in the Ninnaji abbot's carriage. No intrepid warrior, no lowly commoner present failed to shed tears.

Go-Shirakawa issued Sueyuki the following instructions concerning where Sutoku was to live: "Not on the Sanuki mainland, but on the island of Naoshima. The island lies two hundred yards from the mainland.[90] Few people live there. There are no rice fields. You will build a walled enclosure one hundred yards in circumference with a raised base at the center, and on this base you are to build his dwelling. There will be one gate, locked from the outside. Warriors posted outside the gate will mount stern guard. No one is to enter or leave the compound, except for those bringing food and supplies. Any communication from him must be conveyed to the throne through the provincial governor's local representative."

When Retired Emperor Sutoku learned how far he was to go, he stopped eating and wept deep-hued tears.[91] He seemed not long for this world. The sights along the way, harbor by harbor and island by island, might have diverted him if he had been able to see them, but the cabin door, always closed, blocked the light of sun and moon, and he heard as though only from a distance roaring wind and breaking waves.

They told him that he was passing Suma, then Akashi, and he understood that this was where Ariwara no Yukihira, exiled for some misdeed or other, had lamented his fate.[92] "Yonder lies Awaji," they told him, and he recalled all too well the fate of Emperor Junnin,[93] who was banished there and soon died of grief.

The passing days measured his growing distance from the capital. He worried about Prince Shigehito, his eldest son, and also about the gentlewomen whom he had glimpsed, on the day of the battle, fleeing through the smoke of the burning Shirakawa Mansion toward the mountain crossings over into Shiga and toward Miidera. He wondered what could have become of them. They had been in his service so long, and now he would never in this life see them again. Death seemed almost to have claimed them.

A strange rumor arose after Sutoku left Ninnaji on the 23rd of the 7th month. It was widely repeated that Minamoto no Yoshitomo and Taira no Kiyomori would soon meet in battle. Genji and Heike men rushed to them from all sides. People high and low, who by now had retrieved their possessions from hiding in the belief that it was safe to do so, feared that this time the world really was coming to an end. Once more they carried off their goods as though fire had broken out nearby. The dust they raised along the avenues resembled black smoke.

The same rumor reached the emperor. Senior nobles and privy gentlemen rushed in a dense throng to the palace. Shinzei, too, heard the talk. He said to Yoshitomo and Kiyomori, "If you each have a case to make, you should present it to the throne and await His Majesty's august judgment. But no, they say that you mean to fight instead. The streets are full of warriors, as His Majesty has learned to his consternation. Cease your insubordination immediately! What is all this about?"

The two men insisted that there was no truth to the rumor. Perhaps it had all been a tengu trick. It was unfortunate that everyone had been so terribly frightened.

On the evening of that day Tomokane, a clerk from the Chamberlains' Office, inspected two imperial residences that had escaped burning: the one at Sanjō-Karasumaru, and the one at the Naka-no-mikado and Higashi-no-tōin crossing.[94] A book cart left before the one on Sanjō bore a small, sealed chest, obviously with something precious in it. Tomokane took it to Takamatsu House and submitted it for imperial inspection. It contained Sutoku's record of his dreams. He had written down every unusual dream, and these dreams foretold that he would regain the throne. After each one he made many vows to ensure that it should come true.[95]

In the past, Saimei and Shōtoku had indeed recovered the throne,[96] but Suzaku and Shirakawa had not. Suzaku ceded the throne to Emperor Murakami[97] at his mother's urging, but he later regretted having done so and prayed desperately to regain it. He even sent a senior noble as his personal representative to Ise, but his prayers were not answered. Retired Emperor Shirakawa so deeply desired the same thing that even after renouncing the world he delayed for a time taking a religious name. He must have had in mind another monk who assumed the throne. Of old, when under attack from Prince Ōtomo, the future Emperor Tenmu[98] shaved his head and took refuge in the Yoshino mountains; but then he regained power and assumed the imperial dignity. People gathered from Sutoku's repeated dreams of regaining the throne that he longed intensely to do so.

## 32. Yorinaga's Sons and Other Rebels Start into Exile

The counselor-captain Moronaga, Yorinaga's second son, addressed the following appeal to his grandfather, Lord Tadazane:

7TH MONTH, 30TH DAY

> I withdrew the other day from your presence, swallowing tears of parting, and since then my concern for you has only grown. My gratitude surpasses my powers of expression. I am, as it were, a man facing a wall with a pot over his head.[99] In this eighth decade of your life you inhabit the ninefold, flowering capital, while for myself I wish to follow cloud-roads ten thousand leagues, my biwa in hand. When shall I behold again your august countenance? Never, I fear, unless in dream. Tears stream from my eyes at the thought. I shall miss you through all eons to come. My hand trembles, my thoughts wander; I cannot convey my flood of feeling. If I have pursued since boyhood the arts of music, poetry, and writing, it is because I have aspired loyally to uphold the imperial way. Now, however, this misfortune has come upon me, and I have renounced forever that lofty ambition. Although resigned to my fate, I cannot restrain the bitter sobs that choke me. Alas! No paper could record all that I would gladly say. I ask only your wise understanding. To relieve me of worry, please ensure that after vanishing into the clouds and mists I still receive your news. This confused letter does not deserve your perusal. Please glance through it in private and then tear it up. Allow no one else to read it.
>
> With the deepest respect,
> Moronaga
> Sent from hiding in a mountain temple

On the 2nd of the 8th month Yorinaga's four sons were taken to Inayazuma in Yamashiro, and from there each continued on to his place of exile. The death sentence had been lightened for them to distant banishment, but they still trembled to imagine where they might be bound. Kanenaga apparently went to Izumo, Moronaga to Tosa, Takanaga to Izu, and the monk Hanchū to Awa.

The police officials Koreshige and Sukeyoshi escorted them to Yamashiro. All four wore the robes of deep mourning. They rode horses provided by menials in police service, horses so poorly saddled as to be thoroughly degrading. Moronaga, bound for Tosa, knew that he would never see his old home again. He said, looking about him, "How can I hope ever to see you again in this life?" His brothers were too choked with tears to reply.

In addition, Norinaga was banished to Hitachi, Narimasa to Echigo, Naritaka to Awa, Toshimichi to Kazusa, Norichika to Shimotsuke, and Masahiro (Iehiro's father) to Mutsu.

In cruelty nothing, alas, equals ambition. Kiyomori had beheaded Tadamasa, his uncle. Yoshitomo had beheaded Tameyoshi, his father. This was cruelty indeed. After loosing arrows against the imperial forces, Tameyoshi must have known what fate awaited him, but he also looked to his eldest son for safety; and Yoshitomo, for his part, did indeed want at first to save him. However, the court refused to let him do so. Rather than give his father over to another, he therefore had him executed himself.

Some people said, "Why did he not give up his reward in exchange for his father's life?"

Others nodded, saying, "Tameyoshi was Yoriyoshi's grandson, and his father was Yoshiie. He headed a warrior house, and he had recently commanded an attack against the emperor. For him, leniency was out of the question. At the same time, though, he was over sixty years old, he had renounced the world, and he came to Yoshitomo with palms pressed together, begging for mercy. Seen from that perspective he deserved leniency. He could hardly have caused further trouble. Leniency might have been preferable, considering that 'the protection of the Son of Heaven should extend even to foreign lands.' "

Still others remarked, "The son who beheads his father and the father beheaded by his son both suffer from bitter karma and deserve pity. Namu Amida Butsu, Namu Amida Butsu."

At the Toba Mansion, the late Retired Emperor Toba's old officials said, "People claimed that the palace was under serious threat, but it remains unscathed; and the capital, too, is still there. Surely the gods protected both and will continue to do so in generations to come. Retired Emperor Sutoku has been exiled, and fourteen others have been banished to provinces far and wide. They have left the realm of civilization and moved to that of dark ignorance. Wives have been torn from husbands, children from fathers, friends from friends; and lord and follower have gone their separate ways. The grief of parting, the sorrow of remaining behind—each in its way is very painful. Lord Tadazane's burden of suffering is especially heavy. He has lost Yorinaga, whom he esteemed so greatly; and Yorinaga's sons, who were always such a comfort to him, have gone into exile. He has lived this long all in vain."

Still others said, "Sutoku's departure was terrible to see. Not one senior noble or privy gentleman was there, and the boat that he boarded made a distressing sight. In far-off China, He,[100] the king of Changyi, was deposed and returned to his homeland, while Emperor Xuanzong was banished to Shushan.[101] Nearby, in our own land, Emperor Ankō[102] was murdered by his stepson, and Emperor Sushun was killed by a rebellious subject. Sovereigns Complete in Virtue these emperors may have been, but even they could not escape karma from past lives."

## 33. Lord Tadazane's Return to the Capital

His Majesty sent Shinzei to Tadamichi, the regent, with this message: "You will banish Lord Tadazane."

The regent replied, "With him in exile, how could I possibly govern the realm?" In tears Shinzei reported this reply to His Majesty, who had to let the matter drop.

Lord Tadazane announced that he would return to Uji and Fuke House. The senior nobles forbade him to do so. In fear of what Nara might yet do, they decided to move him instead to Chisoku-in. When the party charged with taking him there arrived, he pleaded illness not to go. By way of reply, he submitted only a letter containing this solemn oath: "If I harbor any rebellious intent toward the throne, may the gods of heaven and earth chastise me in this life, and in the next may the buddhas of the three ages withhold their blessings from me." How indeed could he ever forget what he had sworn? The regent was his son, after all. People felt that the matter was settled. Nonetheless, he did in the end move to Chisoku-in.

## 34. The Capture and Exile of Tametomo

On the 10th of the 8th month, the court received confirmation that Sutoku had arrived in Sanuki. "His residence is not yet built," the document said. "He resides in the Matsuyama chapel of Takatō, an official of the province."[103]

Tametomo was hiding out in an isolated mountain temple in Ōmi. Despite meaning to go on down to Kyushu, he had remained in Ōmi to avoid an encounter with Iesada, a Heike retainer who was then establishing the annual tax yield for estates in Higo. Laid up as he was with a serious illness, he had had one of his men become a monk and lived from what the fellow managed to beg.

He was in a bath house nearby, taking a curative bath, when one Shigesada, a Genji and an officer of the Watch with a property at Yashima,[104] received a report from a servant of his: In the bath house nearby a tall, unidentified man with a wound in his forehead was being bathed by a young, healthy one. Shigesada realized that the tall man must be Tametomo. He sent a few servants who knew Tametomo to have a look. They confirmed his suspicion.

Tametomo was in the bath when Shigesada took action. He burst in with thirty men and seized him, despite Tametomo's protests at being caught naked. Shigesada then took him up to the capital. His reward was a post at the same rank in the Right Gate Watch.

On the 26th of the 8th month, Tametomo was delivered to the headquarters of the Watch, at the Sakuhei Gate. He wore a red, unlined robe over a white *hakama*. The wound on his forehead was still there. "Masakiyo shot me there during the battle," he said.

The police official Suezane was assigned to interrogate him. Tametomo said little. They considered beheading him but felt that that would be wrong, since he had survived the battle. If banished unscathed, however, he might in time turn against the court. The order came down to sever both his shoulder joints. Yoshitomo, not Suezane, executed it. He severed Tametomo's shoulder joints. Unable even to hold a fan, Tametomo could no longer hold the reins, either, and therefore he did not ride. Instead they built a sort of cage to be carried like a palanquin, put him in it, and sent him on his way from one post station to the next.

Tametomo said, "You have me in a palanquin, and my shoulder joints are cut. What could I do now? You men probably think I am finished. Well, just watch!" He rocked his body, set the palanquin swaying, and smashed his way out of what had seemed a secure cage. "Whatever my destination," he said, "I inhabit the sovereign's realm, and this how I will travel through it."

On arrival in Izu they considered restraining the banished Tametomo by hanging stones around his waist to weigh him down, but in the end they did not. They took him on to Ōshima by main force.[105]

## 35. Sutoku Copies the Sutras in Blood and Writes a Curse at the End *with* His Death

One can only imagine Retired Emperor Sutoku's feelings upon finding himself, on arrival in Sanuki, lodged in such strange, rustic surroundings. He had no visitors, either official or personal. The few gentlewomen in his service did little but lie prostrate, weeping. His melancholy grew with the lengthening autumn nights. Wind roared through the pines, and cricket song from grassy thickets slowly died away. All too often tears drenched his sleeves as he wept over those bitter days in the capital. Over and over his thoughts returned to the same theme.

"I succeeded in my time to the Sun-Goddess, I assumed the dignity of the Son of Heaven, I received the honored title of Retired Emperor, and I inhabited the Hallowed Abode. While my father lived I wielded no governing power, but I long enjoyed the pleasures of the retired emperor's residence. I have lasting memories of those years. In spring I delighted in the blossoms, and in autumn, under the moon, I gave myself to the festivities of the season. Now I admired the flowers of the golden valley, now I contemplated the moon over the southern tower. Meanwhile, thirty-eight years slipped by. All that past remains with me as though it were yesterday. What have I done to deserve exile to a distant island and life in such a dwelling? Horns on a horse, a white-headed crow—these challenge the bounds of the possible; and so it is that I do not know the year or month of my return. The gloom of this remote place is unbearable. A demon of homesickness: that is what I will be. In the reign of Emperor Saga, long ago, Heizei, his predecessor, raised rebellion at the instigation of Kusuko, his mistress of staff; but he was spared exile because he had renounced the world. As for me, I am blameless. I merely defended myself when a warrior force attacked me. It is shocking that the emperor should have forgotten my good will toward him and charged me with a terrible crime."

In this frame of mind he spent three years personally copying the Five Mahayana Sutras.[106] He then wrote to the prince-abbot of Ninnaji, "For the sake of enlightenment in the life to come, I have to the best of my ability made ink copies of the Five Mahāyana Sutras. I cannot bear to have them remain here in this remote province, where conch and bell are never heard.[107] I should therefore like to send them, if I may, to Yawata, or to Toba, or perhaps to Hase—at any rate, somewhere near the capital." And at the end of the letter he added this poem:

| | |
|---|---|
| *hama chidori* | Plover on the shore, |
| *ato wa miyako ni* | whose footprints reach all the way |
| *kayoedomo* | to the capital, |
| *mi wa matsuyama ni* | I remain here, nonetheless, |
| *ne o nomi zo naku* | at Matsuyama, weeping. |

The prince-abbot consulted the regent on the subject. The regent hastened to recommend a favorable response, but Emperor Go-Shirakawa remained adamant, and, as usual, Shinzei supported him. In the end, therefore, the request was denied. "That is unfortunate," Sutoku said when this news reached him. "Not only in our land, but in India, China, Silla, and Paekche as well, uncles and nephews have fought, brother has warred against brother for the throne or for power over the land, and karma has decided victory or defeat. Uncles have lost, and so have older brothers. The loser has then gone to the victor on bended knee, palms pressed together, to beg forgiveness, and forgiveness has been his. In my case, however, I am not even allowed a place to deposit sutras copied for my enlightenment in the life to come. My brother and I therefore remain enemies into future lives as well. I will now sink all the good gained from copying these sutras into the Three Evil Realms and become the greatest, most evil demon in all Japan."

This he vowed to do. He then bit off the tip of his tongue, and with the blood wrote an oath to that effect at the end of the sutras he had copied.[108] Thereafter he no longer cut his hair or nails, and while still alive he came to resemble a tengu.

On the night of the 9th of the 12th month of Heiji 1 [1159], at the hour of the ox [2 A.M.], Nobuyori, the superintendent of the Right Gate Watch, in collusion with the chief left equerry Yoshitomo, burst into the retired emperor's Sanjō Palace residence, burned it down, destroyed Shinzei, seized both Go-Shirakawa and the reigning Emperor Nijō, installed himself in the imperial palace, and proceeded to announce a roster of official appointments. Shinzei was dug up from underground, far into the mountains, and beheaded. His head was then paraded through the streets and hung in the tree before the prison. This act seemed obvious retribution for his having ordered so many beheadings during the Hōgen conflict and for having had Yorinaga's remains exhumed. The defeated Nobuyori was beheaded on the riverbank at Rokujō. Yoshitomo fled the capital in defeat, only to be struck down at Noma, in Owari, by Osada no Shirō Tadamune. All this happened exactly as Otowaka had predicted it would just a few years earlier.[109]

In the capital, Korenari, the governor of Awaji and a *gagaku* musician greatly favored by Sutoku, became a monk under the religious name Rennyo.[110] He then traveled to Sanuki in the hope of obtaining an audience with Sutoku. The exile's dwelling being excessively dilapidated, he was lodged instead in the provincial government headquarters compound.

Rennyo spent the night playing his flute outside, under an unclouded moon, but got no response. Then the gate opened quietly, not as though anyone within were actually listening, and Rennyo went toward it. A man came forth, apparently a servant. Rennyo said, "I am the musician Korenari, whom His Eminence often favored in the capital, but now I am a monk named Rennyo. I should like His Eminence to have this." He took out a poem and voiced it aloud:

| | |
|---|---|
| *asakura ya* | O Asakura! |
| *ki no marodono ni* | Into that log house I went, |
| *irinagara* | yet my noble lord |
| *kimi ni shirarede* | never knew, and now I leave, |
| *kaeru kanashisa* | my heart heavy with sorrow.[111] |

He received a reply and read it by bright moonlight:

| | |
|---|---|
| *asakura o* | To Asakura |
| *tada itazura ni* | you came and were sent away, |
| *kaesu ni mo* | your journey in vain; |
| *tsuri suru ama no* | and meanwhile this fisherman |
| *ne koso nakarure* | could do little more than weep. |

Rennyo pressed the paper to his face and returned to the capital in tears.

Eight years later, on the 26th of the 8th month of Chōkan 1 [1163], in his forty-fifth year, Sutoku passed away in his Sanuki government headquarters lodging. He was cremated on a pyre on the mountain Shiromine, also in Sanuki. Alas, it seems that the smoke drifted toward the capital.

Rennyo had a dream. Sutoku boarded a square palanquin,[112] and Tameyoshi and five of his sons rode before him. Behind him rode Taira no Tadamasa with his four sons, and Taira no Iehiro with his three. Their procession attempted to enter Go-Shirakawa's residence but was turned back. Tameyoshi then dismounted before the imperial palanquin and explained, "Fudō Myōō and Daiitoku defend Retired Emperor Go-Shirakawa's residence and bar access to it." "Very well," Sutoku replied, "then take me to Kiyomori." His train obediently entered Kiyomori's residence and carried Sutoku in with them. That is what Rennyo dreamed.

Thereafter Kiyomori began to overreach himself. He rose to the office of chancellor, and even his sons and retainers enjoyed unrivaled imperial favor. In his overweening pride he banished or killed Go-Shirakawa's favorite Narichika and his son, beheaded Saikō and his son, packed the regent off to the province of Bizen, and in the end confined Go-Shirakawa to the Toba Mansion. They say that all this stemmed from Sutoku's curse.

Thereafter, Sutoku appeared in one place or another and trampled to death anyone who saw him.

The monk Saigyō[113] traveled to Sanuki. Before the provincial headquarters he made this poem.

| | |
|---|---|
| *matsuyama no* | Tossing on the waves, |
| *nami ni yurarete* | a boat traveled all the way |
| *koshi fune no* | to Matsuyama, |

| | |
|---|---|
| *yagate munashiku* | only in the end, alas, |
| *nari nikeru kana* | to disappear from this world. |

He went to the grave on Shiromine and remained there for some time, absorbed. Then in tears he offered this:

| | |
|---|---|
| *yoshi ya kimi* | You must see, my lord, |
| *mukashi no tama no* | that the life of luxury |
| *yuka totemo* | you prized in those days, |
| *kakaran nochi wa* | now, when all is said and done, |
| *nani ni ka wa sen* | deserved not a moment's thought. |

Surely, they say, this must have calmed the spirit's anger.

## 36. Tametomo Crosses to Devil Island *and* His Death

Tametomo had had his shoulder joints cut because of his role in the Hōgen conflict, and he had been exiled to Ōshima, off the Izu coast.[114] However, in the natural course of things his shoulders healed, and although he could no longer draw a bow as powerfully as before, he still became very good indeed. Also, his arms now stretched two finger-breadths further than before. "I cannot draw as strong a bow as I used to," he said, "but my arrows are longer and penetrate the target even better."

He also said, "It really is too bad. I attacked the enemies of the court by order of my commander, and for that I should have received a province and estates; but no, sure enough, I myself became an enemy of the court and ended up in exile. That is a bitter blow. But at least these islands are mine." He laid claim to the seven islands of Ōshima, Miyakejima, Kōzojima, Hachijō-ga-shima, Mitsuke-no-shima, Oki-no-shima, Niijima, and Mikurajima.[115] They had belonged to Miyanotōsai Mochimitsu, his father-in-law, but he left Mochimitsu not a single one. He appropriated them all.

In fear and trembling, Mochimitsu's representative, Shima no Saburōdayū, sent the islands' tax proceeds to Izu under Mochimitsu's close supervision. Tametomo heard about this. He arrested his father-in-law and cut off all five fingers of his right hand. On the grounds that islanders competent with bow and arrow were enemies, he then began breaking their arms. To escape his wrath they decided to discard their weapons rather than die. On each island the warriors gathered together and burned their bows and arrows. Thereafter, only Tametomo had any.

One dawn Tametomo saw, from Hachijō-ga-shima, a gray and a white heron fly together toward the east. He said, "They must be flying that way because there is another island somewhere out there. Even an eagle cannot fly more than two thousand leagues. A heron is much smaller and could hardly cover one or two hundred. All right, I will go and see."

With impetuous haste he boarded a boat and had the rowers follow the herons. A following wind sprang up, and they continued on for a day and a night. They reached an unknown island, where white waves broke on the rocks. There was nowhere to land. However, they rowed around the island and found to the northwest a spot where a stream emptied into the sea. There they landed their boat. The island's inhabitants, ten feet tall, with long, unkempt hair, each carried a sword at his right side.[116] Their speech was unintelligible, but with patience a degree of communication turned out to be possible.

"Where are you from?" the islanders asked.

"From Japan," Tametomo replied.

"Did you come here on purpose or blown by the wind?"

"We came on purpose."

"How can that be, when no one in the outside world even knows that our island exists? Those blown onto our island in the past never got home again. Their boats were always smashed to pieces on the rocks. We cannot take anyone home because we have no boats on the island and no food for such men as you. That is why, soon, they all died. Hurry, go back where you came from before the food you brought with you runs out."

Tametomo walked up onto the island and looked about him. There were no fields, wet or dry. There were no trees to bear fruit of the kind that we eat in our land. "What food do you live on?" he asked.

"We eat fish and birds."

"How do you catch them? You have no fishing boats or nets."

"What food we need washes up on the shore."

Tametomo saw many large fish caught in the crevices in the rocks, battered by the waves. He and his men took some. Since they could not cook and season them properly, they simply roasted and ate them with their hands.

"How do you catch birds?" Tametomo asked.

"On the mountain there are a great many bulbul-sized birds. Each of us digs a hole, claims his stretch of ground, hides in the hole, and then whistles to call the birds down. When one comes, he grabs it and eats it."

Tametomo's arrows brought those birds down from the sky or caught them perched on branches. After shooting the birds he turned his bow against the islanders. They shook with fear of his arrows. "Submit, or I will kill you all!" he said. So they declared submission to him. Their clothes were of gross silk, rough-woven like a net. They brought out a great quantity of this silk and heaped it before him.

"Does this island have a name?" he asked.

"It is called Onishima, Devil Island."[117]

"So you are devils?"

"Once, yes, we were devils, but that was long ago. We no longer have the devil's cloak of invisibility, the devil's hat of invisibility, his walk-on-water boots, his deep-dive boots, or his magic mallet, and we never leave this island. So we have lost our courage as well."

The islanders were indeed big, tall of body and long of face, but the name "Devil Island" hardly suited them. Tameyoshi dubbed the island Ashijima ["Reed Island"], since thick beds of reeds grew there. And because the next island was Hachijō-ga-shima, he ordered them to pay their tax there. "But how can we," they protested, "when we have no boats?" They were told that a boat would come to receive their tax remittance once every three years.

"And now," Tametomo said, "before our food gives out . . ." They took one of the islanders with them back to Hachijō-ga-shima.

Mochimitsu went up to the capital and submitted this report to Go-Shirakawa, now the retired emperor: "Tametomo's shoulders have healed. He shoots longer arrows than ever. His bow does not have its old power, but his arrows penetrate their target just as well as before. He has appropriated the seven islands that were my property and left me not a single one. Moreover, by following the herons he has discovered one previously unknown. The inhabitants descend from devils. They are ten feet tall, have long, unkempt hair, and carry a sword to their right. They look nothing like humans. Tametomo's ruffians subjugated them, and no doubt they have their eye on Japan as well. I request a retired emperor's decree authorizing me to suppress him."

Retired Emperor Go-Shirakawa indicated his approval and soon issued the decree. It authorized Mochimitsu to attack Tametomo with forces raised from the entire province of Izu or, if they did not suffice, from the eight provinces of the east. For an initial attack Mochimitsu assembled five hundred Izu warriors under Itō, Hōjō, Usami no Heida, Katōda, and Katōji. These sailed to Ōshima in one hundred boats.

No one rallied to Tametomo's support. Children were crying because their fathers had had their fingers cut off or their arms broken. All longed to be rid of Tametomo. The islander he had taken knew nothing of bow or sword, and besides, he, too, had parents and children on the island and longed for home. Tametomo would never have his allegiance. Moreover, rites performed to quell him left him bedridden for thirteen days.

Mochimitsu's fleet attacked on the third day after Tametomo began feeling better. He was not a man to linger at the last over old memories. He shot his usual, slender-tipped arrows nine inches below the waterline of an enemy boat. Being capable of piercing two or even three layers of armor, they went straight through the cryptomeria planks from one side to the other and on into the sea. Water poured in through the holes, and down the boat went. The more heavily armored men on board sank to the bottom, while the lighter ones swam about, to be saved by a grappling hook or a bow tip held out from another boat. Of old, one of Tametomo's arrows could go straight through two men in armor. Now he dispatched men by shooting boats.

Before this spectacle the other boats turned around, rowed out of bowshot, and dropped anchor together. They would clearly get nowhere unless they protected themselves better. So they gathered all the armor layers they could and discussed whether to hang them over the sides of the boats or to cover plank shields with them.

Tametomo watched. "The enemy are swarming like clouds and mists," he said, "and I am alone. My arrows might finish them all, and all of Japan would still come after me. They would wear me down, and then these miserable islanders would do me in. I cannot have that."

He beckoned to his eldest son, then in his ninth year. The boy came straight to him. Tametomo struck off his head and tossed it away. The boy's mother fled to hide her second and third sons, then in their seventh and fifth years. Tametomo next set fire to his house, slit his belly, and fell to the ground. The sight of the burning house drew the boats in closer. The men would gladly have burst in, but fear that Tametomo's suicide might be just a ruse discouraged them from doing so.

Then the ridgepole collapsed. Katōji Kagetaka said, "We cannot send a burned head up to the capital." He gripped his great halberd short, kept his head down and his neckplate forward, and entered. The suicide had been real. Tametomo was dead. Kagetaka sent the head up to the capital, where it was presented to the retired emperor for inspection. Mochimitsu regained his rights over the island.

Someone or other made this poem:

| | |
|---|---|
| *minamoto wa* | The Minamoto, |
| *tae hateniki to* | so I thought, had been wiped out, |
| *omoishi ni* | but I saw this day, |
| *chiyo no tametomo* | there for all eternity, |
| *kyō mitsuru kana* | immortal Tametomo. |

Of old Raikō, supported by the Four Heavenly Kings, stood as a bulwark of the realm.[118] More recently, Hachimantarō Yoshiie twice went down to Mutsu, valiantly conquered Sadatō and Munetō, and subdued Takehira and Iehira. In our own time Tametomo was in his thirteenth year when he went down to Kyushu. Within three years he had seized control of the island and appointed himself constable-general. Six years later, in his eighteenth year, he went up to the capital; loosed arrows against the imperial forces; had his shoulder joints severed; was banished to Ōshima off Izu; and lorded it over the islands as described. In his twenty-eighth year he killed himself to avoid falling into enemy hands. He was the greatest Genji of them all.

During the Hōgen conflict sons beheaded their fathers, nephews beheaded their uncles, younger brothers banished their elders, and women drowned themselves in despair. These were the strangest events ever known in Japan.

# The Tale of the Heiji Years

# Summary and Note on the Text

## Book 1

Emperor Go-Shirakawa, enthroned in 1155, in 1158 abdicated in favor of his son Emperor Nijō and acquired a retired emperor's authority. Close to him were the brilliant Fujiwara no Shinzei (1106–1159) and his favorite, the extravagantly vain Fujiwara no Nobuyori (1133–1159).

The Genji had gained less than the Heike from their role in the Hōgen conflict; hence increased rivalry between the two. Shinzei also disdained Minamoto no Yoshitomo and blocked a promotion that Nobuyori had coveted. The result was an alliance between Nobuyori and Yoshitomo, including their sympathizers Fujiwara no Tsunemune and Korekata.

In the last month of 1159, Taira no Kiyomori goes on pilgrimage to Kumano. Five days later Yoshitomo attacks Go-Shirakawa's Sanjō Palace by night, burns it down, and confines Go-Shirakawa and Nijō in the imperial palace compound. Shinzei flees, but his head is soon paraded through the streets and hung in a tree at the prison gate. The triumphant Nobuyori and his allies distribute rewards.

Kiyomori rushes back to his Rokuhara residence, despite the efforts of Akugenda Yoshihira, a son of Yoshitomo, to intercept him. The Heike at Rokuhara and the Genji in the imperial palace compound each expect the other to attack. Meanwhile, Go-Shirakawa goes to Ninnaji, and Nijō to Rokuhara. The Heike set out for the imperial palace, where a dramatic battle takes place at the Taiken Gate. Other scenes include Nobuyori's display of terror and a fierce clash between Shigemori, Kiyomori's eldest son, and Akugenda Yoshihira. In order to draw the enemy out of the palace, the Heike return to Rokuhara as though in defeat.

## Book 2

Nobuyori flees. Yoshitomo attacks Rokuhara. Minamoto no Yorimasa, a senior Genji, goes over to the Heike, who counterattack. Yoshitomo and his men flee Kyoto, cross over Mount Hiei to Lake Biwa, and then head eastward along the Tōkaidō road. Yoshitomo's son Yoritomo, then in his thirteenth year, flees with them, and after him the badly wounded Tomonaga, another young son of Yoshitomo. Unable to go on, Tomonaga asks his father to behead him.

Nobuyori, captured, pleads in vain for Go-Shirakawa's protection and is beheaded. Yoshitomo gets as far as Noma on the Chita peninsula, but there he and his foster brother Kamada Masakiyo are assassinated. Yoshitomo's head is returned to Kyoto and publicly exposed. Akugenda Yoshihira, too, is captured and beheaded. Yoritomo is found and returned to the capital.

Minamoto no Yoshitomo had had three sons by Tokiwa, once a maid in an empress's service. The last of them, Ushiwaka, born that year, is the future hero Minamoto no Yoshitsune. The story of Tokiwa's flight with her children through the snow to the province of Yamato is a highlight of the tale.

## Book 3

In the capital, Lady Ike, Kiyomori's stepmother, persuades Kiyomori to spare Yoritomo, who is eventually exiled to Izu, in eastern Japan. For the next twenty years he is forgotten.

Eager to find Tokiwa and her children, Kiyomori captures and tortures her old mother. Upon learning this, Tokiwa gives herself up with her children at Rokuhara. Moved by her beauty and distress, Kiyomori gives up the idea of executing Tokiwa's three sons, now that he has spared Yoritomo. (Later, Tokiwa will bear Kiyomori a daughter.)

The tale goes on to cover Yoritomo's journey into exile; Kiyomori's purely nominal renunciation of the world; Akugenda Yoshihira's attack in the form of a thunderbolt; the childhood of Tokiwa's sons, particularly Ushiwaka; Yoshitsune's (Ushiwaka's) eventual journey to northern Japan; and the brothers' path to triumph.

## Note on the Text

Scholars date the origins of *Heiji* to the 1230s or 1240s, roughly the period suggested for *Hōgen* and *Jōkyūki*. The oldest surviving manuscripts are held by Gakūshuin University in Tokyo and Yōmei Bunko in Kyoto, but neither is satisfactory in its entirety. The text of the second book is very similar in both, but the first book of the *Gakūshuin-bon* and the third of the *Yōmei Bunko-bon* both coincide with the much later and significantly different *Kotohira-bon*. As a result, the text translated here is a composite: the *Yōmei Bunko-bon* for the first book, despite various flaws, and the *Gakūshuin-bon* for the second and third.

Fragments of a *Heiji monogatari emaki* ("picture scroll") also survive, scattered among many owners and datable to perhaps the middle or late thirteenth century. By far the most famous fragment depicts the burning of the Sanjō Palace, held by the Boston Museum of Fine Arts.

The subheadings are those given in the original manuscript.

# Book 1

## 1. The Rivalry Between Nobuyori and Shinzei

From antiquity to this day, in both China and Japan, the sovereign has weighed the worth of his subjects against two standards above all: skill in letters and skill at arms. Letters support every aspect of government; arms quell barbarian disorder in the four directions. With respect to ensuring the integrity of the realm and peace in the land, letters stand to the sovereign's left and arms to his right. They resemble a man's two hands. Both are indispensable. In this latter age, especially, men arrogantly flout imperial authority, while the people are proud and harbor rebellious notions. The brave and strong are estimable above all. So it is that Emperor Tai Zong of Tang, posthumously styled Wen Huang, cut off his beard and roasted it into medicine; bestowed this medicine upon meritorious subjects; and sucked his warriors' bleeding wounds to ease their pain. It is said that they therefore served him out of gratitude, and that because he was righteous they made light of their lives. They thought nothing of courting death, for death was what they aspired to achieve. The emperor did not turn his own hand to fighting, no, but because his heart belonged to his men, he had their sole devotion.

Recently there lived a gentleman known as Fujiwara no Nobuyori. He descended in the eighth generation from the regent Fujiwara no Michitaka, himself descended in direct line from Amatsukoyane-no-mikoto.[1]

Nobuyori's grandfather was Suetaka, of the third rank, the governor of Harima; and his father was Nakataka,[2] also of the third rank, the governor of Iyo. Untutored either in letters or at arms, he lacked any accomplishment; nor did he have in any art any skill to commend him. However, he stood so high in the emperor's esteem that promotion never concerned him.

Nobuyori's forebears had spent their careers as provincial governors and in their declining years had barely reached the junior third rank; but in just two or three years he rose through the offices of senior palace guard, head chamberlain, deputy director of the empress's household, consultant-captain, and chief of the police. In his twenty-seventh year he had reached counselor and superintendent of the Gate Watch. A regent's first son can no doubt expect such a rise, but for anyone else it was unheard of. Whatever offices and emoluments he desired were his. He had his eye on the posts of minister and of commander of the Palace Guards, both of which had passed out of his line long ago, and he behaved—be this said with all due respect—with unfailing arrogance. Those who saw him blinked in astonishment; those who heard him could hardly believe their ears. In pride he surpassed Mi Zixia and outdid An Lushan.[3] He did not fear the offense of the half-eaten peach and prided himself only on his glory.

There also lived at that time a gentleman known as Shinzei.[4] He descended in the eighth generation from Lord Fujiwara no Naganori, of the third rank, who had resided at Yamanoi. His grandfather was the Echigo governor Suetsuna and his father the scholar-chamberlain Sanekane. Although born into a line identified with Confucian studies, he had not devoted himself especially to that subject. Instead he was familiar with all areas of learning and knew something about everything. His knowledge covered the Nine Fields and the Hundred Schools. He was the most broadly learned scholar of his generation.

Shinzei's wife was Emperor Go-Shirakawa's nurse, Ki-no-nii. This is why he had administered since Hōgen 1 every affair in the realm, great or small; restored lapsed lineages; revived abandoned paths of learning; established a Records Office according to the precedent set in the Enkyū years [in 1069]; judged lawsuits; and adjudicated right and wrong. Imperial judgments stirred no resentment because they had no personal bias. He returned the world to pure simplicity and led his emperor to the heights of Yao and Shun.[5] In greatness the reign matched Engi and Tenryaku[6] and surpassed the three years' sway of Yoshichika and Koreshige.[7] Palace maintenance had long been neglected. Halls leaned perilously, and towers were falling to ruin. Pasture once grazed by cattle and horses now harbored only pheasants and rabbits. In only a year or two, however, Shinzei put everything to rights, and His Majesty moved back to the palace proper.[8] He immediately restored grace and dignity to the Great Hall of State, the Buraku-in, the many offices of government, the Eight Bureaus, the Academy, the Morning Council Chamber, and so on, giving them elaborately ornamented rafters and roof bracketing. All this was done swiftly, yet without cost to the people or inconvenience to the realm. He revived the long-lapsed Privy Banquet and Sumō Tournament,[9] and he organized poetry and musical gatherings on every appropriate occasion. Palace ceremonies stood favorable comparison with any in the past. At all times protocol followed hallowed precedent.

On the 11th of the 8th month of Hōgen 3 [1158], Emperor Go-Shirakawa abdicated and ceded the throne to his son, who then became Emperor Nijō. However, Shinzei's authority only grew, until birds fell at his wish from the sky, and grasses and trees bent low before him, while Nobuyori rose still further in favor, until none could stand beside him.

At this juncture some devil or other must have got into both men, because there came to be bad blood between them. Shinzei remarked of Nobuyori whenever he saw him, "There goes a man who endangers the realm and threatens to throw the world into turmoil"; and he longed somehow to bring him down. At the time, however, both stood above all others at court. The hearts of men being unfathomable, Shinzei took no one else into his confidence on the subject. He only watched and waited for an occasion to act. Meanwhile Nobuyori, who had his way in everything, suspected Shinzei and laid plans to bring *him* down, should a chance to do so ever present itself.

Retired Emperor Go-Shirakawa told Shinzei that Nobuyori aspired to command a corps of Palace Guards and asked him his opinion. "His lineage does not necessarily encourage him to aim that high," Go-Shirakawa said, "but I gather that his forebears held the post at times."

Shinzei's silent reaction was "Well then, our world is done for." Aloud, however, he replied, "If Nobuyori were to become a Palace Guards commander, who in the world might not aspire to do the same? Selection of appointees to office is the first task of government. Once appointment to rank and office goes awry, those above flout the will of heaven, those below are subjected to censure, and the world lapses into chaos. Such examples abound both in China and in our land. No doubt that is why, when Retired

Emperor Shirakawa considered awarding the post of commander to the Akomaru grand counselor Munemichi, Emperor Horikawa refused to allow it. Retired Emperor Toba wanted to appoint the late Naka-no-mikado counselor Fujiwara no Ienari to the office of grand counselor, but the senior nobles warned him against doing so, saying, 'It is a very long time since a man from a lineage destined normally to rise no higher than the fourth or fifth rank has ever become a grand counselor. For him, the office of counselor is already too much.' Toba therefore gave up the idea. Wishing at least to let the gentleman know how greatly he esteemed him, however, Toba addressed his first official document of the year 'To the new Naka-no-mikado grand counselor.' Apparently Ienari's old eyes streamed tears of emotion at the sight, and he said to himself, 'This is an honor still greater than actual appointment as minister or commander. His kindness utterly overwhelms me.' Of old, the emperor seems to have valued the post of grand counselor very greatly, and his officials undertook to do the same. How much loftier still is the post of commander of the Palace Guards! Even among those who have occupied the three supreme offices,[10] there are some who never held it. It promises a regent's son, or another of such superlative distinction, ultimate success. Nobuyori will scale new heights of arrogance and plot rebellion if he sullies it with his person, and in the end heaven will destroy him. Your Eminence, how could you not regret such an outcome?"

Go-Shirakawa showed no sign of being convinced. Shinzei made a last attempt to persuade him by having painted for him a picture scroll illustrating the arrogance of An Lushan in Tang China. However, His Eminence rejected this warning.

Nobuyori refused to appear at court when he learned of Shinzei's slanderous talk about him. Instead, in collaboration with the Fushimi counselor Minamoto no Moronaka, he confined himself to a place in Fushimi, where he practiced mounted archery, tests of strength, and other martial skills. He did all this with the aim of killing Shinzei.

## 2. Nobuyori Plots to Destroy Shinzei

Nobuyori allied himself with Taira no Kiyomori by marrying his son Nobuchika to a daughter of Kiyomori. He planned to rely on Heike armed might to achieve his goal. However, he then realized not only that Kiyomori was the Dazaifu deputy, but also that he also had been granted many major provinces; that he stood too high in imperial favor to have anything whatever against the court; and that he would never fall in with Nobuyori's plan. In contrast, after the Hōgen conflict Minamoto no Yoshitomo, the chief left equerry, had fallen below Kiyomori in standing and therefore had reason to be discontented. Nobuyori cultivated him and took him into his confidence. "Now that you have me," he said, "I can intercede to get you whatever provinces and estates you want, and rank and office as well. Our sovereign[11] would never question my recommendation."

Yoshitomo replied, "After such kind assurances, I will simply await whatever good news you see fit to give me."

Nobuyori also approached Fujiwara no Tsunemune, a grand counselor. He likewise discussed these matters with Narichika, a captain and the third son of Fujiwara no Ienari, since Go-Shirakawa greatly esteemed him. Nor did he neglect Fujiwara no Korekata, Nobuyori's maternal uncle and another intimate member of Go-Shirakawa's entourage. He also made Nobutoshi, a younger brother whom he trusted implicitly, Korekata's son-in-law. In this way he marshaled a circle of sympathizers and awaited a chance to make his move.

On the 4th of the 12th month of Heiji 1, Kiyomori set off with Shigemori, his eldest son, on a pilgrimage to Kumano, to fulfill a long-standing vow. This was the moment. Nobuyori summoned Yoshitomo. He said, "As Ki-no-nii's husband, Shinzei has full control of every affair in the realm, great or small. A word from him, as he pleases, gives his sons office and promotion. Where I am concerned, he calls fire 'water' and speaks only foul slander. The longer he lives, the more likely he is to destroy the realm and throw the world into chaos. The retired emperor agrees, but for lack of a suitable occasion he has not yet told him so. And you, then—where do you feel *your* future lies? You might give the matter some thought."

Yoshitomo replied, "Seven generations separate me from Rokusonnō. Each has restrained insurgents thanks to skill at arms and crushed the foe by means of masterful tactics. During the recent Hōgen conflict, however, my whole house became an enemy of the court, and its other members were executed. I alone remain. Kiyomori, I am convinced, secretly planned this outcome. In fact, I expected it and am not surprised. However, your trust encourages me to seize this precious opportunity and to attempt to restore the fortunes of my house; for that is my deepest desire."

Very pleased, Nobuyori brought out an impressive sword and presented it to Yoshitomo as an initial expression of his thanks. Yoshitomo was leaving, with every mark of deference, when a white and a black horse, each bearing a mirror saddle,[12] were led before him. It was night, but Nobuyori had torches raised high so that Yoshitomo could see them.

Yoshitomo said, "Nothing counts more in battle than a man's mount. Victory would be certain on either of these two splendid steeds. I urge you also to approach such men as the Suō police official Suezane, the Izumo governor Mitsuyasu, the Iga governor Mitsumoto, and Sado Shikibu-no-tayū Shigenari. I gather that they, too, desire a private word with you." Yoshitomo then withdrew and returned home. Nobuyori sent after him fifty suits of armor that he had had made for such an occasion.

## 3. The Attack on the Sanjō Palace *with* The Burning of Shinzei's House

So it was that Nobuyori watched for the moment to act. On the night of the 9th of the month, at the hour of the ox [2 A.M.], he and Yoshitomo led five hundred horse to Go-Shirakawa's Sanjō Palace.[13] They surrounded the gates on all four sides of the compound. Nobuyori then rode onto the open ground before the palace's south side and declared in a great voice, "In years past I stood supreme in your favor, but now I hear that Shinzei's slander is to result in my execution. To save my worthless life I will therefore go down to the east."

"But who would even dream of killing Nobuyori?" the astonished Go-Shirakawa exclaimed. He had hardly finished speaking when warriors brought up a carriage and urged him roughly to board it. Voices shouted, "Quick, set the fires!" Go-Shirakawa boarded the carriage in desperate haste. His sister Jōsaimon-in, who shared the palace, joined him.

Nobuyori, Yoshitomo, Mitsuyasu, Shigenari, and Suezane surrounded the carriage and led it into the palace compound, where they confined Go-Shirakawa in the imperial library building. Shigenari and Suezane received an order to guard him securely there. During the Hōgen conflict this Shigenari had guarded Retired Emperor Sutoku at Ninnaji, when Sutoku was confined to the quarters of Kanpen, the temple administrator; and he had accompanied Sutoku as far as Toba when Sutoku started into exile. People wondered what karma could have led him to mount guard over *two* sovereigns.

No words can describe the scene at the Sanjō Palace. Warriors surrounded each gate and set fire to the buildings within from every direction. Fierce flames soared aloft, and strong winds swept the smoke higher still. Senior nobles, privy gentlewomen—arrow or sword killed them all, on the assumption that they belonged to Shinzei's family. Those who rushed out to escape the fire were transfixed by arrows; those who sought to escape the arrows burned in the fire. Those terrified of both jumped into the well. The ones underneath drowned in the water, while those on top were buried under embers from buildings burning in the fierce wind. Not one survived. The conflagration at the Afang Palace killed none of the First Emperor's greater and lesser ladies,[14] but, alas, many senior nobles and courtiers died when Go-Shirakawa's palace burned. The attackers skewered the heads of the Gate Watch officers Ōe no Ienaka and Taira no Yasutada on halberd blades and hung them on the Taiken Gate.

That same night, at the hour of the tiger [4 A.M.], they attacked Shinzei's residence at the crossing of Ane-no-kōji and Nishi-no-tōin, and burned it to the ground. In this case, however, the perpetrators were apparently underlings at the beck and call of warriors associated with the imperial palace.

The realm had been at peace now for three or four years. In city and country people no longer bothered to lock their doors. Their lives were cheerful and happy. High and low coexisted in peace. Now, however, these fires alarmed everyone nearby. No one could keep from groaning, "What is the world coming to?"

## 4. Shinzei's Sons Are Stripped of Office

Shinzei's five sons—Toshinori, his eldest; Shigenori, his second son; then Sadanori, Naganori, and Korenori—were dismissed from office. Apparently the Kasan-no-in grand counselor Tadamasa presided over the deciding council of senior nobles, and the chamberlain and right minor controller Nariyori acted as the council secretary. A rumor spread through the capital that, when Nobuyori and Yoshitomo attacked the Sanjō Palace that night and set it ablaze, Go-Shirakawa never emerged from the smoke. Another rumor, however, had it that he had gone to the imperial palace.[15]

Meanwhile the former and current regents, Tadamichi and Motozane, both rushed to the palace. So too, in desperate haste, did the chancellor Morokata, the left minister Koremichi, as well as other senior nobles and privy gentlemen, and the guards assigned to the retired emperor's residence. The clatter and rumble of horses and carriages racing this way and that echoed through the heavens and shook the earth. Panic overcame everyone.

Shigenori was Kiyomori's son-in-law, and on the night of the 10th he therefore took refuge at Rokuhara. When repeated summons from the palace forced him out at last, he was given into police custody. "This would never have happened if Kiyomori had been here," he kept telling himself. "It is my evil luck that he and his party are away on pilgrimage to Kumano." The police official Sakanoue Kaneshige took charge of him on the riverbank at Rokujō and from there proceeded to the palace. There Narichika interrogated him and took him into his own custody.

News arrived that Toshinori had renounced the world. The police official Koremune Nobuzumi found Naganori, informed Fujiwara no Korekata, and received custody of him. Korenori, the governor of Shinano, cut off his topknot and gave himself up to the police official Norimori, who retained custody of him.

## 5. How Shinzei Came to Renounce the World *and* The Matter of the Appointments List

Shinzei, a scholar born into the Southern House of the Fujiwara,[16] had been adopted by Takashina no Tsuneshige. Despite entering so wealthy a house,[17] he never took up an academic post; nor did he become a controller, since that post was not held in the Takashina line. Instead he was called into service by Retired Emperor Toba under the name Hyūga-no-zenji Michinori. One day he expressed in person to Toba the wish to receive appointment as a minor counselor.

Toba reflected, "That office belongs in the regental line and is closed to any lesser man. How could I possibly award it to him?" He hardly knew what to say. Michinori so insisted, however, that at last he gave in.[18] Soon Michinori renounced the world and was known thereafter as the minor counselor and novice Shinzei. Always desperate for high office, he went on to hold simultaneously all three critical posts open to a man of the fifth rank; then he served as head chamberlain. His sons had joined the company of the seven controllers, had become senior nobles, and had then presumed to occupy the offices of middle and minor controller. Yesterday's pleasures and today's sorrows are dream and illusion. That all things pass is plain to see. Good and ill fortune are as though twisted into a single rope, as these examples show.

On the 14th, the Izumo governor Mitsuyasu went to the palace to report that he had discovered Shinzei's whereabouts. Upon receiving the order to execute him, he set off to do so.

Meanwhile, a series of appointments was announced, to reward those who had performed meritoriously on the night of the 9th. The idea was to embolden the warriors who had seized Go-Shirakawa and confined him in the imperial library, as well as those who had discovered the whereabouts of the wanted men. Minamoto no Shigenari became the governor of Shinano; Minamoto no Yorinori, the governor of Settsu; Minamoto no Yoshitomo, the governor of Harima; and Minamoto no Yoritomo,[19] an officer in the Right Watch. Fujiwara no Masaie (formerly Kamada Masakiyo)[20] became an officer in the Left Watch. Minamoto no Kanetsune was appointed an officer in the Left Gate Watch. Yasutada and Tamenaka were appointed to the staff of the chief left equerry. So many men received rewards that Koremichi said, "Why was that well not appointed to office? After all, it killed more people than anyone else." Those who heard him laughed.

## 6. The Inspection of Shinzei's Head *with* His Flight to Nara *and* His Death

On the 16th of the same month, at the hour of the hare [6 A.M.], fire suddenly broke out along Ōi-no-mikado. People cried out in panic that some attacking enemy had set it. That proved not to be so, but the panic was understandable, considering that the fire had broken out in front of the Yūhō Gate.

On the same day, the Izumo governor Mitsuyasu went again to the palace. "Today," he reported, "I have beheaded Shinzei and taken the head to my house on Kagura-oka." Nobuyori and Korekata then shared a carriage to Kagura-oka and inspected the head. The sight dispelled Nobuyori's profound anger.

On the 9th of the month Shinzei had apparently received, in secret, word of an impending night attack and gone to warn Go-Shirakawa. At the time, however, His Eminence was absorbed in music-making. Reluctant to spoil the mood, Shinzei withdrew after telling a gentlewoman what he had heard.

Accompanied by only three or four retainers, he then started down toward Yamato, by way of Uji, and came to Daidōji, an estate of his situated beyond Tahara. Shinzei was a master of astrological lore and read the stars with the greatest of ease, but perhaps his time really had come, because he noticed only that night a celestial portent that had appeared three days earlier. Its meaning was: "Jupiter stands in the house of death; the loyal subject replaces his lord. The strong is weak, the weak strong. The higher is weak, the lower strong."[21] It was then that Shinzei conceived the idea of dying in place of his sovereign.

On the morning of the 10th, Shinzei summoned Narikage, his retainer.[22] "What is going on in the capital?" he asked. "Go and find out for me."

Narikage galloped on his way until in the Kohata hills[23] he encountered a panic-stricken groom of Shinzei's. "What is the matter with you?" he demanded to know. "Has something happened?"

The weeping groom answered, "What do you mean, has something happened? The whole capital is in darkness. Lord Nobuyori and Lord Yoshitomo attacked the Sanjō Palace last night with a large force and burned it down. They say that the retired emperor never emerged from the smoke, although others claim that he went to the palace. Later in the night, at the hour of the tiger, they burned down Lord Shinzei's house. Everyone in the capital is saying that their real object the whole time was to kill Lord Shinzei himself. I am on my way to let him know. Where is he?"

"Servants are so hopeless," Narikage said to himself. "When harshly questioned they will ignore any likely consequences, however grave, only to spare themselves unpleasantness. I had better not tell him." To the groom he said, "It is a good thing you are here. Lord Shinzei is at such-and-such a spot in the hills behind Kasuga-yama. He will be glad to see you. Hurry to him."

Once the groom had vanished into the distance, Narikage galloped back to Daidōji and reported to Shinzei what he had heard. Shinzei's thoughts did not dwell on his own destruction. Instead he grieved for the two emperors, reigning and retired.[24] "Who now will save our sovereign," he said, "if I do not take his place? Hurry, dig me a pit."

They dug a pit, lined it with planks, and placed him in it.[25] "If the enemy discovers me before I die," he said, "I will kill myself. Give me a dagger."

Weeping, Narikage drew his own and gave it to him. Four warriors cut off their topknots and buried them with him. "As a last kindness, my lord," they said, "please give each of us a name in religion. "Very well," Shinzei replied. He named Narikage Saikei, Morozane Saijitsu, Morochika Saishin, and Morokiyo Saisei. Thus each received the *sai* character from Shinzei's name and kept one character from his own lay name.[26] Moromitsu, who had remained in the capital, renounced the world when he heard the news and took the name Saikō.[27]

Shinzei entered the pit on the 11th. On the 14th, one of Mitsuyasu's men, bound for Kohata on an errand, encountered in the hills nearby a young man, apparently a groom, leading a well-saddled stable horse. The groom's tear-stained face stirred his curiosity. "Whose horse is this?" he asked. For a time the groom remained silent. "I'll have your damned head off," the man threatened. In great distress the groom told him that the horse was Shinzei's and that he was leading it up to the capital. Mitsuyasu made the groom lead him to Daidōji, where he found freshly disturbed earth. He dug into it and discovered the body of a man who had stabbed himself to death. He severed the head and presented it to the authorities.

## 7. Shinzei's Head Is Paraded and Hung at the Prison Gate

On the 17th, on the riverbank at Ōi-no-mikado, a police corps under Minamoto no Suetsune took possession of Shinzei's head. They paraded it along the avenues and hung it in the chinaberry tree before the gate of the eastern prison.

Every denizen of the capital, high or low, crowded to see it. Among them was a monk in deep black, apparently long a recluse. At the sight he wept and said, "What can this man have done to deserve such a fate? The great mirror of the realm is broken. Who will now survey the past and weigh the present? Why, hereditary scholars fell silent when he expounded the works of Confucius and Laozi; when he discoursed on the deep truths of the exoteric and esoteric teachings, monks could only bow their heads in awe. If this man had lived, peace would have continued to spread through the land; but no, destroyed by a fawning flatterer, he has now left us no more than the memory of a loyal sage. Atrocious! Who ever heard of displaying the head of a man who was never an enemy of the court? What was his crime? What can he have done in a past life to deserve such retribution in this one?" He carried on, weeping, without fear or shame, and all who heard him wrung the tears from their sleeves.

The feelings of Ki-no-nii are painful to surmise. It was bad enough, not knowing what had happened to her husband, but imagine the agony of learning that his body had been dug up, and that his head had been cut off, paraded through the streets, and hung in a tree before the prison gate! Her sovereign lord, Go-Shirakawa, to whom she looked as to the everlasting mountains and seas, had been shut away from the light of sun and moon. Her twelve sons, clerical and lay, had been arrested, and she did not even know whether they were still alive. "Woman though I am," she cried, prostrate and weeping, "I have no idea what may yet happen even to me!"

## 8. Rokuhara Sends a Courier to Kumano

Kiyomori, then on pilgrimage to Kumano, was staying at the Kirime post station when a courier from Rokuhara caught up with him. "On the night of the 9th, Nobuyori and Yoshitomo attacked the retired emperor's Sanjō Palace and burned it down," the courier reported. "Some claim that Retired Emperor Go-Shirakawa never emerged from the smoke, while according to others he went to the palace. They say that Shinzei's whole family burned to death. The Genji must have been preparing this for some time, because their men are gathering in the capital. More than Shinzei's fate is at stake. People are also whispering doubts about the future of your house."

Kiyomori gathered his family and retainers to discuss the situation. "We have come far," he said, "but with the imperial house in crisis there is no choice but to send our guides[28] on by themselves and return to the capital. We are unarmed, though. What can be done?"

Taira no Iesada, the governor of Chikugo, said, "Actually, I have some equipment on hand." He called for fifty long chests that his men had been carrying all the time somewhat behind the main party, without ever mentioning what was in them. The chests yielded armor, swords, and arrows. The partitions between the joints of the bamboo carrying poles had been pierced, and each of the fifty concealed a bow. Iesada's martial skill and foresight impressed Shigemori deeply.

The Heike had retainers in Kii as in other provinces, and at the news these rushed to Kiyomori's assistance. However, they amounted to no more than a hundred armed men.

A fresh report now arrived. An attack force under Yoshitomo's eldest son, Akugenda Yoshihira, had started toward Kumano and was camped near Tennōji in Settsu, in the pine woods of Abeno. It was waiting there for Kiyomori on his return journey. Kiyomori declared, "With Akugenda and a large force lying in wait, it would take a thoroughly reckless warrior to leave bodies strewn about between Abeno and Tennōji, and never to reach the capital at all. No, I would rather gather boats from every harbor in Kii; cross over to Shikoku; from there mobilize a Kyushu army; and then march on the capital, crush the rebels, and calm the imperial wrath. What do you say, gentlemen?"

Shigemori stepped forward. "Your proposal deserves consideration," he replied. "However, if I may voice my humble opinion, His Eminence is now confined within the palace precincts, and decrees from him and His Majesty[29] must therefore have gone out already to the provinces. The Shikoku and Kyushu warriors will never follow us if we are branded enemies of the court. For the sake of our sovereign and also of Rokuhara, which is currently unoccupied—that is, for reasons of both state and private interest—we cannot afford a moment's delay. Iesada, what do you think?"

Iesada answered, weeping freely, "Not for the first time, my lord, your words strike me as exactly right." Nanba Saburō signified his complete agreement, left the gathering, mounted his horse, and rode away toward the north. Persuaded by the company's mood, Kiyomori did the same.

Shigemori swept his gaze over the mass of men around him. "We will soon face death at Abeno, where, I gather, Akugenda awaits us. Any man inclined to flee will present a sad spectacle on the battlefield. Let him take his leave of us now, then, and remain behind!" The warriors understood that their best reply was to advance. Each raced forward, whip raised high.

They came to Onoyama, on the border between Izumi and Kii. There, a man in light armor and riding a grey horse, bow in hand and arrows at his back, dismounted by the side of the road and bowed low. He identified himself as a messenger from Rokuhara and continued, in response to further questioning, "I left Rokuhara in the middle of last night. Nothing has happened there yet. Despite Lord Kiyomori's absence on pilgrimage, messengers kept arriving from the palace to demand that those left in charge at Rokuhara present themselves there immediately. They got promises of swift compliance, but no one has yet actually gone. Lord Shigenori fled to Rokuhara for refuge on the night of the 10th, but messengers repeatedly demanded his surrender, citing a decree from the retired emperor, and it was impossible not to let them take him."

Shigemori listened attentively. "I knew it!" he exclaimed. "To think that they surrendered Shigenori, after he had so trustingly sought their protection! What an awful thing to do! Now, did you encounter any particular difficulty on your way here?"

"None, my lord. Itō Kagetsuna, Tate Sadayasu, Gohei Shirō, and others are stationed with some men near Tennōji and Abeno. They admit that in principle they should go on, but they do not know what they might find further south, so they prefer to stay put, feed and rest their horses, and prepare to fight where they are. In all they are about three hundred horse. I gathered that more retainers are on their way as fast as possible from Iga and Ise, so that they may be four or five hundred by now." The Heike men understood with relief that these men must be the ones reported to be under the command of Akugenda.

## 9. Lord Mitsuyori Goes to the Palace *with* Kiyomori Returns to Rokuhara

A council of senior nobles, to be held in the privy chamber, was announced for the 19th. Fujiwara no Mitsuyori, the intendant of the Left Gate Watch, arrived attired with exceptional brilliance, bearing a slender, ceremonial sword in a lacquered, gold-sprinkled scabbard and accompanied not by retainers but, rather, by four or five splendidly dressed servants. His retainer Noriyoshi, dressed as a servant, carried a slender sword in the fold of his robe. Mitsuyori had told him, "If something happens, I want *you* to be the one to kill me."

The great assembly observed so strict an order that the senior nobles and privy gentlemen already at the palace joined it somewhat timidly. Mitsuyori, however, swept in through the throng of warriors as though they did not even exist. They lowered their bows and turned their arrows aside to let him by. He then passed along the gallery on the north side of the Shishinden and took a turn around the nearby small court for a good look into the privy chamber. Nobuyori occupied the highest seat, with the senior members of the gathering ranged below him.

Mitsuyori found this very strange. The right grand controller and consultant Akitoki sat in the lowest consultant place. Mitsuyori adjusted his grip on his *shaku*[30] and said with visible annoyance, "This rank-order is all wrong." He then calmly approached Nobuyori and plunked himself down precisely in Nobuyori's place. The humiliated Nobuyori pitched forward, flat on his face. "Oh no!" murmured the horrified gathering of lords.

"It looked as though this gentleman were the senior official present," Mitsuyori explained, rearranging his train and tidying his collar. "And what is the matter that we are here to discuss?" he went on, now seated in perfect formal posture. The assembled senior nobles and privy gentlemen said not a word, still less the lower-ranking gentlemen present.

A moment later Mitsuyori stood up again and calmly walked out. The warriors crowded into the open space outside remarked, "He has guts, all right! A while ago, when they were all coming in for the meeting, not one sat above Nobuyori—not one, that is, until *he* did. You could see when he entered through the gate that he wasn't afraid of anybody, and he's certainly proved it! Yes indeed, I'd like to fight under *him*! He'd do things right, I know he would. Perhaps he's like that because he has the same name as Yorimitsu of old—the two characters are just reversed."[31]

"But Yorimitsu's younger brother was Yorinobu," another objected, "and Yorinobu backwards makes Nobuyori. So why is Lord Nobuyori such a lily-liver?"

"I didn't hear that!" someone else chuckled. "The walls have ears, the stones have mouths!"

Mitsuyori was in no hurry to leave, despite his bold behavior. Before the privy chamber's lattice window he loudly trampled the audience boards.[32] Then he beckoned to Korekata, his younger brother, who stood near the side door, just north of the sliding panel bearing the painting of Kunming Lake.

"A council of senior nobles was announced for today," Mitsuyori said, "so I hastened to present myself for duty. As far as I can tell, though, the council has no agenda. I hear that I am among those condemned to death. Perhaps that is true. The men mentioned to me are our best and most learned, and I count it an honor to be named among them. As for *you*, however, you rode to inspect Shinzei's head, at Kagura-oka, in the rear of Nobuyori's carriage.

You should not have done that. A Palace Guards commander and the chief of the police each has his own weighty office to uphold.[33] No precedent allows a police chief to ride in the back of someone else's carriage. It is humiliating to do so, especially since a head inspection is a particularly solemn matter."

Korekata reddened. "His Majesty wished me to do so," he said.

"What do you mean?" Mitsuyori retorted. "Why should His Majesty's wish keep you from expressing your own view on the subject? Nineteen reigns and eleven generations have passed since our ancestors Fujiwara no Takafuji and Sadakata served the sage Engi emperor, and each governed virtuously. Not one indulged in evil. Our line is not of supreme distinction, but we have always associated ourselves with just officials and shunned those who spout slander and flattery; and for that reason we have never incurred blame. You are the first to have fallen in with a rebellious subject and sullied our line's good name. That is a very great shame. Kiyomori never reached Kumano. Instead he is on his way back up to the capital from the Kirime post station, and I gather than he has a large force with him. The warriors allied with Nobuyori appear to be relatively few. Is there any time to waste, then, when a large Heike force will attack soon? And how would even His Majesty remain impassive if they were to start fires? It would be agony for him to see the palace reduced to ash. And if the worst should happen to him and his officials, the Sovereign's Way would end there and then. I gather that Nobuyori consults you on every matter, great or small. Miss no opportunity, then, to devise a way to ensure His Majesty's safety. Now, where *is* His Majesty?"

"In the Black-Door Chamber."[34]

"And His Eminence?"

"In the imperial library."

"Where is the Sacred Mirror?"

"In the Unmeiden."

"And the Sword and Seal?"

"In His Majesty's sleeping chamber."

"I hear people moving about in the Morning Room, and I see shapes passing back and forth across the half-moon window.[35] Who is in there?"

Korekata replied, "That is where Lord Noriyori lives. You must be catching glimpses of his gentlewomen."

"So this is the world we inhabit now, is it?" Mitsuyori answered. "Noriyori lives in the Morning Room, where His Majesty should be, and His Majesty is relegated to the Black-Door Chamber. No doubt these are the latter days, but the sun and moon have not yet fallen to earth. What did I do in past lives, that I should have been born into such a world, to witness nothing but outrages? In China, yes, subjects have usurped their sovereign's place, but never in our land, as far as I know. What are the Sun Goddess and Hachiman doing to protect the Way of the Sovereign?"

Mitsuyori's unbridled rebuke sent a chill up Korekata's spine. "But people may hear us!" he murmured and wept.

"Long ago," Mitsuyori went on, "Xu You washed his ears with Ying River water when he heard evil talk. The current state of the palace makes me want to wash out my ears and my eyes." At last he left, the sleeves of his outer robe soaked with tears. Dauntless though he had seemed when he seated himself above Nobuyori, now, before the spectacle of the emperor's plight, he could only withdraw, pale and weeping. Nobuyori commonly wore the wide-mouthed red trousers and formal headdress of an emperor, and he behaved exactly like one.

That night Kiyomori returned from his journey toward Kumano. He went first to the Fushimi Inari Shrine, where he broke a sprig from each cryptomeria tree to display on the sleeves of his armor. Then he proceeded to Rokuhara. Those at the palace worried that he might attack from there that very night, and they donned their helmets. Nothing happened, however, and dawn broke at last.

## 10. The Sentence on Shinzei's Sons Is Commuted to Exile

On the 20th a council of senior nobles was to be held in the privy chamber. Tadamichi, the regent Motozane, the chancellor Morokata, the left minister Koremichi, and the other senior nobles and privy gentlemen repaired to the palace without delay. The purpose of the meeting was to pronounce sentence on the twelve sons of Shinzei, clerical and lay. Koremichi's intercession got the death penalty (first class)[36] commuted to distant exile. Apparently this matter had been due to be decided the previous day but was deferred to the 20th because of the disturbance caused by Mitsuyori. Toshinori was banished to Izumo, Shigenori to Shimotsuke, Sadanori to Tosa, Naganori to Oki, Korenori to Sado, the monk Jōken to Awa, the monk Kanbin to Shimōsa, the monk Shōken to Aki, the monk Ken'yō to Mutsu, the monk Gakuken to

Iyo, the monk Myōhen to Echigo, and the monk Chōken to Shinano. So it was that all were banished to widely scattered provinces.

On the 23rd the palace warriors tied on their helmets, expecting a Rokuhara attack, but none came. Rokuhara had been in turmoil since the 10th, expecting an attack from the palace, and the palace had been expecting an attack from Rokuhara. Warriors from both houses, Genji and Heike, with their white banners or red badges, were constantly rushing in all directions through the streets. The year was almost over, but there was no question of observing the practices customary during the first days of the New Year. No one felt safe. People high and low throughout the city lamented, "Ah, if only things would settle down and peace return to the world!"

## 11. Retired Emperor Go-Shirakawa Moves to Ninnaji

Late in the night of the 26th, the chamberlain Nariyori went to the imperial library and there addressed Go-Shirakawa as follows: "Your Eminence may wish to consider what he would prefer to do. Fighting is expected to break out before dawn. Have Tsunemune and Korekata conveyed no warning to you? You must move. Please hurry away, wherever it pleases you to go."

The astonished Go-Shirakawa replied that he would go to Ninnaji. He therefore disguised himself as a privy gentleman and slipped out of the building. Before the Jōsai Gate[37] he prostrated himself toward Kitano, then mounted a horse. Sovereign though he was over the realm, not one senior noble or privy gentleman accompanied him. He let his mount wander as it pleased. The sky had not yet begun to lighten, and the dawn moon was still up. A cold, moaning wind swept down from the Northern Hills, and snow fell from an unbroken expanse of cloud. He hardly knew what route to take. Rustling trees and grasses stirred pangs of fear, evoking as they did pursuing warriors. He remembered how Retired Emperor Sutoku had gone to Mount Nyoi during the Hōgen conflict. Sutoku had had Iehiro with him then, though, and despite being on the losing side he must have felt safe. That is the way it should have been this time, too, but Go-Shirakawa was completely alone and had no one with whom to talk over his plight. He instead made a great many vows. They say that his pilgrimage to the Hiyoshi Shrine, once peace was restored, fulfilled one of them.

Somehow or other he reached Ninnaji, where he explained his predicament. Delighted, the prince-abbot conducted him to a specially prepared room, offered him a meal, and treated him very hospitably. That other year, when Sutoku came to Ninnaji, he was taken to chief administrator Kanpen's quarters and received only a lukewarm welcome. All three were full brothers, but on this occasion Go-Shirakawa was treated very differently.

## 12. Emperor Nijō Proceeds to Rokuhara

Emperor Nijō, for his part, had a carriage brought up to the north gate[38] and dressed as a gentlewoman wearing layered robes. "Bring me Genjō, Suzuka, my chair, my seal and keys, and the slips to announce the hours,"[39] he ordered. All this was too much, however. The Sacred Mirror in its Chinese chest was brought to the wide aisle of the building, but Kamada Masakiyo's men spotted it and allowed it to go no further.

The departure of His Majesty's carriage aroused the warriors' suspicion. "It's just some gentlewomen on their way somewhere," Korekata told them. "There's nothing suspicious about them." However, this did not allay the men's doubts. They approached the carriage, raised a torch, and lifted the blind with the tip of a bow. Emperor Nijō, then in his seventeenth year, had only recently acceded to the throne. His face still had the fresh beauty of youth, and, colorfully dressed as he was, he did indeed resemble a dazzlingly beautiful gentlewoman. They let the carriage pass without further ado.

His empress rode in the carriage with him. Ki-no-nii, although genuinely a woman, so feared what might happen if they found her that she lay hidden under the empress's skirts. Tsunemune and Korekata attended them in plain court dress, the pendant tails of their formal caps rolled and held in place by a wooden clip.[40] Kiyomori's retainer Itō Kagetsuna accompanied them wearing a servant's costume over armor laced with black silk, with a two-foot sword at his waist. Tate Sadayasu followed the carriage in black-leather-laced armor, with a battle dagger at his waist and wearing over it all an oxherd's robe. They went out the Jōtō Gate and started eastward along Tsuchimikado. Shigemori, Yorimori, and Norimori came from Rokuhara with three hundred horse and met the carriage at the crossing of Tsuchimikado and Higashi-no-tōin. His Majesty felt a great deal safer having them with him. He reached Rokuhara without incident. Kiyomori greeted him there with encouraging words, and the warriors supporting His Majesty entered with pleasure into the spirit of the occasion.

Kiyomori had Nariyori announce: "Rokuhara is now the imperial palace. All who wish to avoid being branded enemies of the court are to gather there without delay." Tadamichi, the regent, the chancellor, the left minister, and every other senior noble or privy gentleman came as fast as they could. Soon there was no room for any more horses and carriages before the Rokuhara gate. Some among the colorfully dressed servants wore helmets, and a crowd filled the area between the river and the Rokuhara compound wall. This spectacle inspired the thoroughly satisfied Kiyomori to remark, "All this means glory for our house and honor for the profession of arms."

## 13. The Roster of Nobuyori's Forces

So addicted to pleasure was Lord Nobuyori that that night he was, as usual, dead drunk. He lay there without a thought in his head, ordering the gentlewomen to rub him here or massage him there. At dawn on the 27th Narichika approached him. "How can you lie about this way?" he said. "His Eminence has already left, and for that matter, there is not one senior noble or privy gentleman here. You are finished, as far as I can see."

"Impossible!" Nobuyori replied. He rose in haste and went to the imperial library. Go-Shirakawa was not there. He went to the Black-Door Chamber but found the emperor gone. He rushed back, clapping his hands loudly, and whispered in Narichika's ear, "Whatever you do, make sure that no one finds out!"

Narichika was highly amused. "But Yoshitomo and his men already know," he replied.

"They've done me in!" Nobuyori roared, hopping with rage. Big and heavy as he was, however, he achieved nothing but thunderous pounding on the boards. He hardly got off the ground.

Korekata, long a close associate of Nobuyori, had nonetheless taken Mitsuyori's views so much to heart that he had spirited the emperor out of the palace. Thereafter the people of the capital dubbed him "Superintendent Mid-Small."[41] On this subject Koremichi remarked, "This 'mid' [*chū*] cannot be meant to suggest the position of a go-between [*chūbai*]. No, it must be the *chū* of *chūshin*, 'loyal official.' After all, Mitsuyori's admonition inspired

Korekata to mend his ways and follow the example of the sages by acting loyally. The *chū* of *chūshin* is the one that fits." All agreed that he was right.

On the 27th, news that warriors from Rokuhara were moving against the palace roused the warriors there to don their armor. Nobuyori, their commander, wore purple-laced armor, lighter above and darker below, over a red brocade *hitatare*. On his head, *kuwagata* horns spread from the front of a helmet studded with silver stars, and a gold-trimmed sword hung at his side. And there he sat, on the lintel, in the middle of the south side of the Shishinden, right under the framed plaque bearing the name of the hall. He was a big, handsome man in his twenty-seventh year, superbly accoutered. Whatever his quality at heart, he looked every inch a commander of men. His mount, a black, was one that Motohira, in Mutsu, had presented to the retired emperor as the very best in all the six counties of his province. Fourteen hands tall, the animal bore a gold-trimmed saddle and stood tethered, facing east, under the orange tree at the foot of the Shishinden steps.

Narichika wore light-green-laced armor, darker above and lighter below, over a dark blue *hitatare*. A band of metal roundels displaying a mandarin duck pattern adorned the lower edge of his neckplate, and also of his armor sleeves and skirts. His mount, a pale roan bearing a silver-trimmed saddle, was tethered to the south of Nobuyori's, facing the same way. He was an exceptionally fine-looking man in his twenty-fourth year.

Yoshitomo wore black-laced armor over a red brocade *hitatare*. His helmet, with its *kuwagata* horns, boasted a five-plate neckpiece. In his thirty-seventh year, he stood out in any company. This, one saw at a glance, was a true commander-in-chief. His black horse, bearing a black saddle, stood tethered to the Jikka Gate.[42] The governors of Izumo and Iga had apparently gone over to the other side, and Yoshitomo would have liked very much to kill them. "But no," he told himself, "with a decisive moment looming, a private quarrel would only strengthen the enemy, and that would be unfortunate." He gave up the idea.

## 14. The Battle at the Taiken Gate

The senior nobles gathered in council at Rokuhara. They pronounced themselves as follows: "No weakness afflicts the sovereign, and rebellious subjects are therefore to be chastised without delay. For the imperial house, it would be a catastrophe if the newly rebuilt palace[43] were to suffer the ravages of fire. If the imperial forces, mindful of this threat, feign retreat, the evildoers will advance. Then the imperial forces will surge forward to claim their position, prevent any conflagration, and, thanks to their feint, repel the enemies of the court. They will righteously exterminate them."

Three commanders started from Rokuhara in obedience to this decree. They were Shigemori; Yorimori, the governor of Mikawa; and Norimori, the governor of Hitachi. Their three thousand men rode to the Rokujō riverbank and drew up there, facing west. Shigemori surveyed their ranks. "The battle today will be of unparalleled significance," he declared. "The current year-period is Heiji ["peace and security"], and the capital likewise is Heian-jō ["citadel of peace and tranquility"]. We ourselves are of the Heiji [or Heike, "house of peace"]. These three congruent names suggest that we are sure to prevail." His speech roused the men's spirits and renewed their courage.

The host then proceeded up the bank of the river, turned into the two east-west avenues of Konoe and Naka-no-mikado, and then came to the wall surrounding the greater palace compound. The Yōmei, Taiken, and Yūhō Gates stood open. Peering through, they saw that the Jōmei and Kenrei Gates into the inner palace compound were also open. In the great court before the Shishinden were tethered one hundred saddled horses.

Three battle cries rang out on Ōmiya, and others joined in from the palace grounds. Nobuyori, who had been sitting under the Shishinden plaque, paled, and his manner changed so dramatically that he was now visibly useless. He rose with the others to mount his horse, but his knees were shaking so badly that he could hardly walk, and he only barely got down the Shishinden steps. On reaching his horse he got just one foot in a stirrup before the clattering of the plates of armor skirts started him trembling so violently that he could go no further. A man of his came and lifted him up, only to have his lord lurch straight over the saddle and crash headfirst to the ground on the horse's left side. The man rushed to lift him to his feet. Soil clung to Nobuyori's face and the tip of his nose was broken. He was dripping with blood and clearly dazed with fear. This ghastly moment nonetheless amused some of his men.

Yoshitomo saw at a glance that fear had unmanned Nobuyori, and pity briefly reduced him to silence. Then he could contain himself no longer. "What a coward that man is, and look what he has got us all into!" he murmured. "He started this without ever realizing that he had some devil in him, and now his name will go down in infamy!" Yoshitomo called for his own mount and rode off toward the Nikka Gate.

Yoshitomo's most trusted lieutenants were his eldest son, Akugenda Yoshihira, then in his nineteenth year; his second, Tomonaga, in his sixteenth; his third, Yoritomo, in his twelfth; his younger brothers, Yoshiakira and Yoshimori; his uncle, Yoshitaka; and Hiraga no Shirō Yoshinobu of the Shinano Genji. His immediate circle of men consisted of Kamada Masakiyo; Miura no Suke Yoshizumi; Yamanouchi Yoshimichi; Yoshimichi's son, Takiguchi Toshitsuna; Nagai no Saitō Bettō Sanemori; Katagiri Kageshige, from Shinano; Kazusa-no-suke Hirotsune; and Sasaki no Genzō Hideyoshi from Ōmi. These included, the force under him came to no more than two hundred men.

Lord Nobuyori, undone by the battle cries, nonetheless wiped the blood from his nose, brushed the soil from his face, briefly collected himself, had himself helped into the saddle, and with his three hundred men secured the Taiken Gate. Actually, he looked none too steady. Three hundred more men secured the Yōmei Gate, under the command of Mitsuyasu, the governor of Izumo; Mitsumoto, the governor of Iga; Suetoki, the governor of Sanuki; and Tokimitsu, the governor of Bungo.

Yorimori headed for the Yūhō Gate, secured by Yoshitomo, and Tsunemori for the Yōmei Gate, secured by Mitsuyasu and Mitsumoto. Shigemori went for the Taiken Gate, secured by Nobuyori.

The initial arrow exchange took place halfway through the hour of the serpent [10 A.M.]. Neither side gave way. They fought for two hours. Shigemori divided his thousand men into two corps. He posted one, of five hundred, on Ōmiya, and with the second, fiercely yelling five hundred he broke through the Taiken Gate, overwhelming Nobuyori. Shigemori pursued him to beneath the chinaberry tree in the great court.

Yoshitomo saw it happen and glanced over at his eldest son, Akugenda. "Did you see that, Akugenda?" he said. "That idiot Nobuyori seems to have lost the Yūhō Gate. Get the enemy out of there!"

At his father's order, Akugenda led his seventeen men into the great court, where he approached the enemy and loudly announced his name: "You will have heard of me, and now you see me before your eyes. I am Akugenda Yoshihira from Kamakura, the eldest son of Minamoto no Yoshitomo, in my nineteenth year. In my fifteenth, at the battle of the Ōkura fortress in Musashi, I slew my uncle, Yoshikata, and since then I have never once faltered in battle. The man in the burnt-orange-laced armor, riding the light red roan, is Shigemori, the scion of the Heike and today their senior commander. Get right up to him, men, grapple with him, take him!"

Bridle to bridle, the seventeen riders bore down on Shigemori. The visibly best among them—Miura no Suke Yoshizumi, Shibuya Shōji Shigekuni, Adachi no Shirō Tōmoto, and Hirayama Sueshige—raced around their man, their eyes fixed upon him, as Akugenda had ordered them to do. Side by side with these warriors, each worthy to face a thousand, Akugenda himself mounted a fierce attack. Before these few men's challenge, Shigemori's more than five hundred fell straight back to Ōmiya. The spectacle of Akugenda's daring heartened Yoshitomo, who sent him this message: "Well done, Akugenda! Give him no quarter! Attack! Attack!"

Shigemori retreated to the avenue, where he gave men and horses a moment to catch their breath. Over a red brocade *hitatare* he wore armor with burnt-orange lacing and trimmed at each lower edge with metal roundels displaying a butterfly pattern. His exceptionally powerful mount, a light red roan, stood over fourteen hands tall and bore a gold-trimmed saddle. In his twenty-third year, imposing in build and every inch the accomplished horseman, he so expertly directed the engagement that one recognized at a glance the true successor to the house of Taira, a superb warrior, and a born commander of men.

Shigemori rose in his stirrups and cried, "No doubt the decree that I received commanded a feigned retreat, but effective conduct of war follows circumstance. I have lost face by retreating, as though in defeat, before so small a force. So let us now attack instead, and only then obey the decree!" He and the five hundred posted earlier on the avenue burst once more through the Taiken Gate, uttering fierce cries.

Akugenda Yoshihira and his seventeen, their colors unchanged,[44] had retired to their original position. Akugenda declared when he saw Shigemori charge, "These warriors look new, but Shigemori still commands them. All together, men, get in there, knock him off his horse! Get after him and kill him!" He raced about, issuing orders, while fifty of Shigemori's men—Sadayoshi, Kagetsuna, Sadayasu, Kageyasu, Sanekage, Kagetoshi, and others—surrounded their commander and fought back fiercely. Akugenda never paused or stopped shouting, "Keep them moving! Go for the burnt-orange armor, the light red roan!" Closer and closer came his voice, and he obviously meant to execute his own command. Shigemori fell back once more to the avenue.

Hugely relieved to see Akugenda drive the enemy out yet again, Yoshitomo now attacked from the Yūhō Gate. Nine of his men charged, howling, in one line of drawn swords: Kamada Masakiyo, Gotō Sanemoto, his son Gotō Shinhyōe-no-jō, his second son Takiguchi, Nagai Saitō Bettō Sanemori, Katagiri Kohachirō Tayū, Kazusa-no-suke Hirotsune, and Sasaki Genzō. They stormed straight in among Yorimori's great host of a thousand, and Yoshitomo joined them with his two hundred bellowing riders. Yorimori's force did not stand still. It split into three and withdrew.

By its very nature the palace compound made a superb fortress, one all but impossible to reduce without resort to fire. To draw the enemy out, the imperial forces therefore fell back toward Rokuhara. As they did so, Mitsuyasu, Mitsumoto, Suetoki, and Tokimitsu shifted their allegiance and galloped to join them. Only Yoshitomo and his men, and the craven Nobuyori, remained within the palace walls.

Now, Yoshitomo had a favorite daughter,[45] then in her sixth year. Since her mother lived near the Rokujōbōmon-Karasumaru crossing, she was called Bōmon-no-hime. Gotō Sanemoto was in charge of her upbringing. At a point when the outcome of the engagement was still in doubt, Sanemoto, in full armor, took her in his arms to the field of battle, to give her a last look at her father. Tears sprang to Yoshitomo's eyes when he saw her, but he feigned indifference. "Drop this creature into the well at the Ukon riding ground!" he ordered. Sanemoto thrust the girl into the arms of a groom, one Chūji, and had him flee as fast as he could.

Nobuyori suffered many indignities once the battle cries had undone him, but when Yoshitomo set off to attack Rokuhara he rode after him, looking quite normal. On the way he kept an eye out for a chance to escape. "Where does that avenue go?" he would ask. "Where can I find safety?" He got no answers from his men, who followed him snapping their fingers with contempt. "It's unbelievable," they muttered, "that such a hopeless coward should have set in motion so grand a scheme. Where have they gone, then, all those martial skills that he cultivated for months at Fushimi? Does it unman you then, to train for war? What a miserable character!" Their complaints achieved nothing, however.

Shigemori put up a fight for a while, then withdrew in feigned retreat. Flushed with victory, Akugenda pursued him. His arrows sank into the chest and belly of Shigemori's horse, and the animal reared constantly until at last Shigemori dismounted on a stack of lumber beside the Horikawa brook. Kamada Masakiyo raced across the stream, dismounted in turn, and attacked Shigemori. One of Shigemori's men, Kageyasu, gripped Kamada hard. They rolled over and over until Akugenda arrived, fell on the pair, and took Kageyasu's head. He then pulled Kamada, who had been underneath, to his feet, and he was about to attack Shigemori when another of Shigemori's men, Shindōzaemon, saw from a distance what was happening and galloped, whip and stirrup, to the rescue. He leapt to the ground beside the lumber, got Shigemori up onto his mount, turned the animal's head eastward, and applied the whip, saying, "Flee, my lord!" He then turned and attacked Akugenda. A desperate fight ensued. Felled by a powerful blow to the helmet from Akugenda's sword, Shindōzaemon was struggling to rise again, his sword still in his hand, when Kamada came down on him, pinned him to the ground, and took his head. Shigemori fled far away, while the fight cost his two men their lives.

While Yorimori fell back eastward along Naka-no-mikado, one of Kamada's men, in full body armor and equipped with a grappling hook, pursued what he saw as a thoroughly worthy opponent. He caught Yorimori's helmet with his hook and tugged at it with a mighty shout. Unbowed, Yorimori rose in his stirrups and with his left hand seized the pommel of his saddle. With his right hand he then drew his sword, Nukemaru, and severed the grappling hook handle. The attacker holding the other end tumbled over backwards. Yorimori raced away, the hook still caught in his helmet. Onlookers of every degree exclaimed, "Why, he cut it! Well done!" No one failed to praise him.

Who gathered to defend Yorimori, when he seemed done for? Twenty men, including Yawata, Mikawa no Saemon Suketsuna, Shōkenmotsu Narishige, Hyōdōnai, and his son Tōnai Ietsugu. For some time these fought back to support him. Hyōdōnai ended up on foot when his horse was killed beneath him, and besides, he was old; so he sought refuge from the fray in a small house nearby. Outside, pairs of men were shouting out name and province to one another and joining in mortal combat. Swords flashed like lightning, racing hooves pounded like thunder. Some were dragged off, grievously wounded; others lay dead on the spot. Some stood motionless, their mounts shot in the belly; others, lightly wounded, charged back into the fight. It was a fierce engagement. Tōnai Ietsugu, in his thirty-seventh year, fought with outstanding gallantry. He took the heads of seven or eight outstanding fighters before he was slain in turn, in a clash with another worthy foe. Hyōdōnai, his father, saw it all from inside the house. "Ah," he sighed, "If only I were young, how eagerly I would rush out to fight beside him!" He was too old for that, though, and instead he returned to his lodging in tears. Yorimori's men continued their retreat after Tōnai's death.

Racing, separately, southward down the thoroughfare, Gotō Sanemoto and Hirayama Sueshige saw ahead of them two riders wearing red badges, whom they took to be stragglers from Rokuhara. Now and again the two turned back to fight an attacker. One of them, in armor with scarlet lacing, rode a chestnut; the other, in black-laced armor, rode a light red roan. Gotō and Hirayama gave chase, determined not to let them escape.

When they approached, the rider in scarlet armor turned his horse around, exchanged sword blows with Gotō, and grappled with him. Gotō got on top and had him pinned him down when Hirayama spotted him and exclaimed, "Well done, Gotō!" He then raced off after the rider in black-laced armor.

The man's fast horse got so far ahead that Hirayama fitted a small humming arrow to the string and let fly. It planted itself in the fleeing mount's flank. The rider dismounted in haste from his frantically rearing horse and fled into a roadside chapel. Hirayama, too, dismounted, calmly tethered his horse to a gate post, drew his sword, and stole into the chapel. His foe's sword must have snapped, because the man put an arrow to the string, darted behind a pile of lumber in the chapel yard, and waited with his bow partially drawn. The arrow flew when Hirayama came straight after him. Because he was moving forward, the shaft aimed to strike inside his helmet hit instead the outside of his neckplate. The man dropped his bow, drew his dagger, and stood his ground. When Hirayama's sword struck off his forearm, he rushed Hirayama to grapple with him. Hirayama dropped his sword, seized the man, cut off his head, placed the head on the lumber, and paused, breathing heavily.

Just then Gotō appeared with a head, presumably that of the man in the scarlet-laced armor. "Well, well, Gotō," said Hirayama. "You can drop that head. We have quite enough of them for today. What are you carrying it around for? To present it to someone? Just drop it!"

"The way these men fought," Gotō replied, "they cannot have been rank-and-file. No, let us leave the heads here, get some local to mind them, and come back for them later." So they put both heads on the pile of lumber and warned someone from nearby to take good care of them, on pain of bringing down punishment on the neighborhood. Then they mounted their horses and went thundering off after the men from Rokuhara.

The Heike warriors turned back again and again to engage their pursuers and were struck down here or there. Meanwhile Shigemori and Yorimori reached Rokuhara. People remarked, deeply impressed, "Without Kageyasu and Shindōzaemon, Shigemori would not have survived; and Yorimori would not have stayed alive without Nukemaru. That pair of men and that sword both proved their heirloom worth."

The sword Nukemaru had belonged to Taira no Tadamori. Once Tadamori was napping in the Ike Pavilion at Rokuhara when, as though in a dream, he heard the sword that stood by his pillow slip twice from its sheath. He opened his eyes and saw a great serpent, thirty feet long, rise from the pond nearby and threaten him. It returned to the pond at the sight of the unsheathed sword, which then slid back into its scabbard. The serpent reappeared, and the sword unsheathed itself once more. At last the serpent disappeared for good back into the pond. Tadamori understood that the sword was imbued with spirit power, and he named it Nukemaru ["Slip-Sheath"]. Kiyomori no doubt expected it to pass to him, as Tadamori's eldest son; but Yorimori was Tadamori's favorite by his current wife, and so it was he who received the sword. For that reason there seems to have been discord between the two brothers.

# Book 2

## 15. Yoshitomo Attacks Rokuhara *with* Nobuyori's Flight *and* Yorimasa Backs the Heike

Yoshitomo then moved to attack Rokuhara. The men there broke up the Gojō bridge and erected a double plank-and-shield wall. The areas inside and outside the wall swarmed with warriors. This message went out to every barrier and down every highway: "Rokuhara is the emperor's palace. Those who fail to come to His Majesty's aid will be viewed as enemies of the court. Come, then, to the last man! Do not risk later regrets!"

Nobuyori went in fear and trembling to survey the Rokujō riverbank and reflected when he saw these preparations, "I will never get out alive if that army surrounds me. Better by far to flee elsewhere, anywhere." He fled west along Yamamomo, then north up Kyōgoku.

Yoshitomo's page, Kon'ōmaru, spotted him. "Look, sir!" he cried. "Look over there! Lord Nobuyori is fleeing!"

"Let him go," Yoshitomo answered. "Don't even look at him. He'd be no use to us. He'd only get in the way."

Minamoto no Yorimasa, the head of the Armory, had stationed himself with three hundred men on the riverbank at Gojō. Akugenda saw him. "I can't make out what Yorimasa is up to," he said. "He seems to be weighing us against the Heike, with a view to joining the stronger of the two. I won't let him get away with that." He headed up Kyōgoku and turned east on Gojō.

Yorimasa saw him and said to himself, "If Mitsuyasu and Mitsumoto go to Rokuhara, I'll let them know that I mean to join them."

Meanwhile Akugenda emerged on the riverbank with fifteen men, flying a single banner. Yorimasa looked on in dismay as Akugenda cried in a great voice, "This miserable Yorimasa is a turncoat! How could a famous Genji warrior harbor divided loyalty? No, he will not pass, not while I have my eye on him!" Brandishing his sword, he attacked with fierce cries. He charged Yorimasa fiercely from east, west, north, and south, or in a cross pattern, while before him Yorimasa's three hundred men, clustered in parties of seven or eight, raced here and there to escape.

Yorimasa was not the main enemy, however. Akugenda broke off his attack and went to join Yoshitomo on the Rokujō riverbank. Seven or eight of Yorimasa's men rode after him, shooting a furious volley of arrows, whereupon one of Akugenda's men—Takiguchi Toshitsuna, a son of Yamanouchi Toshimichi—stopped and fought back. He blacked out for a moment when an arrow from the bow of the Shimōsa warrior Shimokawabe Yukiyasu pierced his neck; but, true warrior that he was, he pulled it out, tossed it away, clung to his pommel, rested the front of his helmet against his mount's neck, and caught his breath a moment. Akugenda saw him. "Takiguchi looks badly wounded," he said. "Don't let the enemy take his head! Have one of us take it himself!"

Kamada Masakiyo summoned a servant. "Don't let the enemy take Takiguchi's head," he commanded. "Go and find out how badly he is hurt."

The servant, armed with a halberd, raced up to the wounded man. Takiguchi opened his eyes. "Who are *you*?" he asked. "You seem to be one of ours."

"Yes, sir, I am. I serve Kamada Masakiyo. Lord Akugenda has ordered that if you are very badly wounded, I am not to let your head fall into anyone else's hands but instead take it myself. I have come to find out whether or not that will be necessary."

"The wound is certainly serious," Takiguchi answered. "Yes, the man of bow and arrow does well to serve a worthy commander. Mine even cares enough about my corpse to forbid letting it fall into enemy hands. For that I am truly grateful." He wept. "Take my head, quickly," he then continued, sliding down from his horse. The servant did so.

Takiguchi's father, Yamanouchi Toshimichi, said, "Every warrior goes into battle prepared to die, but I had hoped to be killed first and bequeath true martial glory to my descendants. But now my son, the future of my house, is dead, and this old life of mine, which I would gladly give anyway, no longer means anything to me. I will go with him across the Mountain of Death." He galloped about with wild abandon, but each life has its allotted term. To his chagrin, no sword cut him down, and no arrow struck him.

Distressed to see Akugenda supported in battle by so few, Yoshitomo came down from the Gojō riverbank to join the attack. Yorimasa's three hundred men went over to Rokuhara.

## 16. The Battle of Rokuhara

Akugenda galloped across the river to join his father, and the two made for Rokuhara. These men accompanied Yoshitomo toward what would no doubt be their last battle:

Akugenda Yoshihira
Chūgū Tayū no Shin
Uhyōe no Suke
Saburō Senjō Yoshiakira
Jūrō Kurando Yoshimori
Mutsu no Rokurō Yoshitaka
Hiraga no Shirō Yoshinobu
Kamada Masakiyo
Gotō Hyōe-no-jō Sanemoto
His son Shinhyōe
Miura no Arajirō
Katagiri Kohachirōdayū Kageshige
Kazusa-no-suke Hirotsune
Sasaki no Saburō
Hirayama Mushadokoro
Nagai no Saitō Bettō Sanemori

and others, for a total of just over twenty. These launched their attack, broke through the first and second plank-and-shield walls, and, uttering war cries, engaged there in fierce combat.

Taira no Kiyomori directed the battle from the double doors at the west end of his north wing.[46] A shower of enemy arrows struck the doors.

Enraged, Kiyomori roared, "Obviously not one of my men here has a sense of honor, or the enemy could never have got in this way. Get them out! I'll do it myself!" He tied on his helmet and charged out from the double doors. He had a horse, standing ready outside, brought up to the veranda and leapt into the saddle. That day he wore a *hitatare* of dark blue Shikama cloth under black-laced armor. Eighteen lacquered arrows, fletched with black feathers from under hawk and eagle wings,[47] rode in the quiver strapped to his waist, and in his hand he gripped a lacquered, closely rattan-wound bow. The scabbard and hilt of his sword were lacquered black, and he wore bear-skin boots. His powerful black steed stood almost fourteen hands tall and bore a black saddle. Kiyomori himself was in black from head to foot; only the *kuwagata* horns affixed to his helmet threw off a bright gleam. In this distinctive accoutrement he looked every inch the great commander. Thirty or more foot soldiers in body armor, with swords and halberds, ran before him, behind him, and to his left and right as he burst out the west gate. Shigemori, his eldest son, Motomori, his second, and his third, Munemori,[48] meanwhile led over thirty mounted Heike warriors in a furious charge, each man keen to avoid blocking his commander's arrows.

Shigemori spotted Minamoto no Yorimasa. "Yorimasa," he cried, "you seem to have joined us! Quickly, to the attack!" Yorimasa and his three hundred raced westward down the riverbank. Before this onslaught Yoshitomo retreated to the west bank, where he gave his mount time to catch its breath. "Young men of mine," he said, "this is where we will die. Not one more step in retreat!" Bridle to bridle, his men charged with fierce cries, and Yorimasa's three hundred drew back to the east bank.

For a moment both sides paused, the Genji on one side of the river and the Heike on the other. Yoshitomo shouted, "Listen, Yorimasa! That title of yours, Gen Hyōgo no Kami, means nothing. Why do you now side with the Ise Heiji?[49] Your treachery dishonors the men of our house!"

Yorimasa replied, "Supporting our sovereign, so as not to render null and void the feats of generations of warriors, has nothing to do with treachery! It is our support for Nobuyori, the biggest fool in Japan, that shames our house!" The remark must have struck home, because Yoshitomo said no more.

At this point, Kamada Masakiyo noticed Kagetsuna and Iesada heading north up the east bank with over five hundred men. He said to Yoshitomo, "Look, sir! Look there! The enemy has sent men to surround us! We must pull back and consider the situation."

Yoshitomo replied, "And if we retreated, where would we go? Our only choice is to die in battle."

He was preparing to charge when Kamada leapt to the ground, seized Yoshitomo's bridle, and said, "I spoke as I did because something had occurred to me. Your house is godlike in martial greatness, and the people of the realm are assuring one another that if you have now passed to action, there must a reason for it. It would be terrible if you were to leave your body lying in full view of the Heike, to be trampled by their horses' hooves. I was not suggesting that you should try to save yourself. Never mind how many hundreds of thousands of men the enemy may boast; just find a good stretch of ground to fight on, break through, continue on into the hills of Ohara or Shizuhara, and take your life there. If a chance of escape opens up for you, then go on to the north and east. After all, every man in the eight provinces of the east is your retainer. The commander who aims high but too easily yields his life will find no favor with later generations." Yoshitomo moved to charge nonetheless, but his men seized crupper, martingale, reins, and girth, turned his horse around, and led him off toward the west.

## 17. Yoshitomo's Defeat

The imperial forces raced from Rokuhara after him, shouting, "Now you know why we withdrew from the palace. Why will you not turn and face us?" That Yoshitomo could not do, however, because his men would not let go.

West along Yamamomo he fled, then north up Kyōgoku. The Heike men, flushed with victory, kept after him and showered him with arrows. Only one of Yoshitomo's turned back and proclaimed his name to the foe. Over a dark blue brocade *hitatare* he wore armor with light green lacing; a pink arrow-guard hung at his back, and he rode a pale roan. "Nevertheless," he declared, "you will have heard of me. I am Minamoto no Yoshinobu from Shinano, in my seventeenth year. Anyone with the heart to fight me, let him come! Let him test himself against me!" He fought his challengers fiercely. At the sight another man turned and announced his name: "Katagiri Kageshige, also from Shinano!" Next to turn back and do the same was "Yamanouchi Toshimichi, from Sagami!" and, after him, "Nagai no Saitō Bettō Sanemori, from Musashi!" While these fought without a thought for their lives, Yoshitomo fled into the distance.

Yamanouchi had lost his son at this spot and was reluctant to leave it. Determined to die in battle, he charged in among the enemy, slew three riders, closed with a worthy fourth, pinned the man's head down, and took it. He was about to straighten up again when the foe pounced, surrounded him, and took his. Katagiri Kageshige saw it happen. He charged in among the men who had slain Yamanouchi, picked a worthy opponent and felled him, and then fought on without a glance right or left. Perhaps his fate had run its course, however, because his sword broke in two. He drew his dagger, lowered his head to present his neckplate to the foe, and closed with a worthy opponent. Each stabbed the other to death. While these men died in their rear-guard action, the unfortunate Yoshitomo pursued his flight.

The battle was over. The Rokuhara forces set fire to three houses: Nobuyori's, Yoshitomo's at Rokujō-Horikawa, and Suezane's at the crossing of Horikawa and Ōi-no-mikado. A strong wind then carried the fire to several thousand innocent commoners' houses, and the resulting smoke blanketed the city. Tales of the smoke that rose in great clouds over the Xianyang Palace reach us from long ago in a foreign land, but those who know life's vicissitudes weep nonetheless. How bitterly, then, must anyone thoughtful have lamented the ruin of our land, upon seeing the great city of Heian-kyō reduced to ash!

With only a few remaining men, Yoshitomo fled past West Sakamoto, at the foot of Mount Hiei, and on toward Ohara. He was about to pass Yase when he came across some 150 monks from the West Pagoda of Mount Hiei, lying in wait for him behind a barrier of abatis. The path at this point ran between a cliff on one side and a raging river on the other. The enemy were no doubt behind him, as he well knew, and before him were the monks of the Mountain. What could he do?

At this point Sanemori came galloping up, shooting arrows back at his pursuers. "I will get you through here, sir!" he declared. He went straight on, doffed his helmet and hung it on his wrist, clasped his bow under his arm, went down on bended knee, and began, "You see, reverend sirs, our lord has been killed in battle, and we, his miserable, shameless underlings, are fleeing for our lives to our home provinces, to rejoin our wives and children. For you, it would only be a sin to take our heads. Not one head here could possibly win you any reward. And even if there were one such among us, you are monks, after all, and you would of course show him mercy. What good would it do you to take the heads of menials like us? Take our armor, then, and grant us our poor lives!"

"Then throw your armor over here!" the monks replied. Yoshitomo's men immediately tossed their armor in among the youthful band. Monks and servants alike were fighting over it when one of the monks, having grabbed what he wanted, thrust the rest of them aside and stood up. Sanemori jumped at the chance. He leapt onto his horse, raced up to the man, snatched the helmet, put it on, drew his sword, and declared, "You monks must have heard of me. I am the greatest brave in Japan: Nagai no Saitō Bettō Sanemori! Anyone with the heart to fight me, let him come! Let him test himself against me!" With a crack of his whip he dashed through. Yoshitomo and all the others did the same. Their horses trampled some of the monks, who were on foot; others fell into the river or tumbled into the ravine. It was a dreadful scene.

Sanemori's trick had worked like a charm. They fled on northward, up the bank of the Yase River. A voice hailed them from behind. Yoshitomo glanced back and recognized Nobuyori. He had just been wondering what had become of the man.

"Where are you off to?" Nobuyori shouted. "The provinces of the east? You might as well let me come with you!" Then there he was, beside them.

So distasteful was his presence that Yoshitomo glared at him. "You miserable coward," he said, "you're the one who started this disaster!" He got a good grip on his whip and struck Nobuyori several times on the left cheek. Nobuyori's foster brother, Sukeyoshi, protested. "How dare you insult him like this?" he demanded to know. In reply the enraged Yoshitomo commanded, "Drag that lout down from his horse, men, and split his jaw open!"

"There is a time and place for everything," Kamada Masakiyo warned. "The enemy must have nearly caught up with us by now. We must move on immediately." He was clearly right. The party dropped the matter and hastened on. Nobuyori kept rubbing the mortifying blows to his face. Lacking any idea which way to turn, he fled westward along the base of the Northern Hills.

Saburō Senjō Yoshiakira and Jūrō Kurando Yoshimori said to Yoshitomo, "You *must* go down to the east, sir, one way or another. The Kanto warriors are all your hereditary retainers, and you must have them lead an attack force back up to the capital. That is beyond dispute. Until you do so, we will hide in the mountains and forests and wait for you. You can count on us to be there when the time comes. We are very sorry to have to leave you." They bade him farewell in tears and continued their flight toward the hills of Ohara.

Yoshitomo, too, was sorry to see them go. When he came to Ryūge Pass, he found it blocked by several hundred Yokawa monks intent on stopping the fleeing men. They had laid abatis and, high above, had readied boulders to drop on the path below.[50] "At Yase we got through somehow, but what are we going to do *now*?" Yoshitomo's men wondered.

Gotō Sanemoto spoke up. "I'll get us through here or die in the attempt," he said. He had the abatis cleared away and charged with fierce cries. Yoshitomo and all his men followed and got through. The monks loosed the boulders, but none hit anyone.

Yoshitomo's uncle, Mutsu no Rokurō Yoshitaka, controlled the Mōri estate in Sagami. Some called him Master Mōri. His horse was so exhausted that he fell some way behind, and the monks surrounded him. He kept them at bay with fierce sword cuts and slashes while they rained arrows on him. However, the mountain path was treacherous, and his horse had no room to maneuver. In the end an arrow caught him under his helmet and nearly stunned him. He dismounted and calmly sat down on the root of a tree to catch his breath.

One among the monks of the Mountain was seven feet tall; he wore black-laced body armor, armor sleeves laced likewise in black, and full arm guards; and he wielded a halberd. This figure was coming down on Yoshitaka to dispatch him when Kazusa-no-suke Hirotsune turned back, leapt from his mount, and engaged him. Hirotsune's servant rushed to Yoshitomo to report, "Master Mōri is gravely wounded, and Lord Hirotsune has turned back to fight the enemy, to keep him from taking Master Mōri's head. But he, too, may now be struck down at any moment!"

Yoshitomo turned back on the spot and attacked with fierce cries. Hirayama Mushadokoro and Saitō Bettō Sanemori turned back as well. Yoshitomo put an arrow to the string. "You wretches," he roared, "if that is the way you want it, I will not leave one of you alive!" The monks fled in all directions before his charge. The one who had threatened Master Mōri ran up the mountainside, and Yoshitomo loosed after him the arrow that he had ready. It pierced the back-plate on the man's armor and, traveling at that upward angle, emerged five or six inches beyond the edge of his breastplate. He crashed forward, dead.

After dispersing the enemy Yoshitomo dismounted, went to Master Mōri, and took his hand. "How are you, Master Mōri?" he asked. "How are you feeling? Master Mōri opened his eyes, glanced at Yoshitomo, wept, and died. Yoshitomo could not bear the sight and struggled not to shed tears of his own. He had Hirotsune cut off the head and then continued his flight, carrying the head himself, but not before he had stripped the skin from the whole face lest anyone recognize it. He tied it to a stone and dropped it into a deep pool in the stream. To avoid appearing fainthearted he had swallowed his tears even when he parted from Bōmon-no-hime, his beloved daughter. Now, however, he rode along weeping without shame, mourning the loss of this last son of Hachimantarō Yoshiie.

"If I head for the north," he reflected, "my news will spur an army of men to rush up to the capital. It would be too bad to die a dog's death at the hands of some nameless fighter. No, better now to make for Higashi-Sakamoto. If anyone wonders what we are up to, I will claim that we are hurrying up to the capital in response to the troubles there. Nothing will happen." They passed through East Sakamoto, and no one paid any attention to them. On they went, past Shiga, Karasaki, and the shore at Ōtsu. At Seta there was no bridge, so they crossed the river by boat.[51] Warriors allied with the Heike had apparently closed the Suzuka and Fuwa barriers, but Yoshitomo nonetheless followed the Tōkaidō toward Fuwa. There was no other way.

Gotō Sanemoto was a big man and very fat. His horse was all but exhausted, and on foot he clearly would never keep up. Yoshitomo saw the difficulty. "Stay here, Sanemoto," he said. Sanemoto tried desperately to follow, but he could not. In the end he stayed where he was.

News of the recent conflict brought warriors racing toward the capital, and they cast a suspicious eye on Yoshitomo's party. There would so clearly be trouble if they kept to the normal route that they skirted instead Mikami-yama and Kagami-yama. Along heavily wooded trails, under cover of night, they reached the western base of Mount Ibuki.

## 18. Nobuyori's Surrender *with* His Death

At the foot of the Northern Hills, Nobuyori turned to flee westward. Those war cries had so undone him that he was now exhausted and in a pitiful state. Sukeyoshi put him down beside a stream, soaked dried rice in water, and offered him some. Nobuyori was too dispirited even to glance at it, so Sukeyoshi lifted him up again and rode on, meanwhile striving to keep him from falling. This was the night of the 27th of the 12th month. Deepening snow was falling. Sukeyoshi let the horse wander as it would over hill and dale—he could hardy tell which was which—until at last they emerged on Rendai-no.[52]

By torchlight, fourteen or fifteen monks, a few laymen among them, were walking home from a cremation. Some had bamboo quivers on their backs and bows in their hands; others carried unsheathed halberds. They cried in great excitement when they spotted the pair, "Fugitives! Get them down, seize them, take them to Rokuhara!"

"We are nameless fighters, not men of rank," Sukeyoshi told them. "Seizing us will gain you nothing. Besides, I see that you are monks and that you have just conducted a funeral. If you kill us, your crime will also taint the spirit of the departed. By all means take our arms and armor, but leave us our lives." They removed everything they wore, from head to foot, and gave it to the monks. The monks accepted this splendid equipment and went their way that much richer. Stripped of two *kosode* robes and his heavy silk divided skirts, Nobuyori, just that morning so imposing in his red brocade *hitatare* and three resplendent *kosode*, was now down to a last *kosode* and a white under-robe.

"The last of your luck is gone, then," Sukeyoshi groaned. "Is this even possible?"

Nobuyori offered trite comfort. "Enough!" he said. "Never mind! Everyone feels that way when things go wrong."

Now, Nobuyori knew that Retired Emperor Go-Shirakawa was at Ninnaji with the prince-abbot, and he conceived the hope that salvation might lie in that direction, if only Go-Shirakawa remained well disposed toward him. He went there in desperate haste. Moronaka and Narichika had done the same. These two sent in an assurance that they had joined the emperor only in order to protect him, and that they had done nothing very wrong.

"Why, then," the gentlemen around Go-Shirakawa demanded to know, "were you in armor among the warriors?" The two had nothing to say to that.

A written communication from Go-Shirakawa announced these arrivals to Rokuhara, whereupon Shigemori, Yorimori, and Tsunemori led over three hundred horse to Ninnaji. There they assumed custody of the men and took them back to Rokuhara.

Who, then, repaired to Rokuhara on the 28th of the month? Fujiwara no Tadamichi; the regent Motozane; the chancellor Morosuke; the left minister Koremichi; the grand counselor Tadamasa; the counselor Masamichi; Fujiwara no Chikataka; and Fujiwara no Takasue. All these gentlemen gathered at Rokuhara.

Narichika was delivered there. They sat him down in front of the stables, in his seashore-patterned *hitatare* and straightened fold-over *eboshi* hat.[53] The death sentence had already been pronounced when Shigemori put in an urgent plea on his behalf. "As a reward for my recent services," he said, "I ask to be made responsible for him." The death sentence was therefore waived. This Narichika, a great favorite of Go-Shirakawa, had had full authority over anything affecting the retired emperor's residence, and he had always treated Shigemori with consideration when Shigemori went there to wait upon His Eminence. That now saved him.

"Yes," everyone agreed, "it pays to be nice."

As for Nobuyori, they sat him down on the riverbank near Rokuhara, where Shigemori interrogated him. Nobuyori had nothing to say for himself. "Some devil got into me" was the best he could do. Weeping and quite oblivious to the gravity of his crime, he begged in tears at least to be granted his life. "What good would it do to reduce your sentence?" Shigemori replied. "Besides, that will not happen." Nobuyori merely dissolved in tears.

Since the 10th of the month Nobuyori had made himself at home in the palace, acting and speaking so strangely that court officials had feared the serpent's venom, while the people had lamented the depredations of wolf and tiger. High and low gathered to watch and mock him. "Look at him!" they said to one another. "Any rustic lout deserves more respect! He's lower than a beggar or an outcaste!" The great Bo Juyi rightly wrote, "The left counselor and the right secretary received favor in the morning and in the evening death."

Nobuyori wept to no avail. His cries made no difference. In the end his head fell from his shoulders. He was a big man, very heavy. Once the headless body had slumped forward, they merely kicked dirt over it. It was raining at the time, and the water that collected along the runnel of the spine ran red with blood. The sight was unbearable.

A novice monk in his seventies now broke through the crowd, coughing all the way. He wore a persimmon-dyed *hitatare*, carried a document pouch around his neck, walked in low clogs, and leaned on a forked staff. The onlookers assumed that the poor fellow must be an old servant of Nobuyori, come to witness his master's end. But no. Instead, he glared at the corpse and muttered, "You bastard!" Then he got a good grip on his staff and repeatedly beat the corpse with it. No one had any idea what this was about, but the old man's next words explained it: "You forcibly appropriated my hereditary property, drove off or killed most of my servants, and reduced me and my descendants to the miseries of hunger and cold. Yes, *you*. That was *you!* And your karmic reward is to have your head cut off and to expose your shame before my very eyes. At last I've lived long enough to thrash your corpse! You're dead, though—you don't really know the stick is mine. Imagine it's a hell-fiend's rod, and you'll be right! If you're still hanging around here in spirit, then listen! Shigemori, Lord Kiyomori's eldest son, is known to be a wise man. I'll show him this document, he'll confirm my title to my land, and then I'll give you a good look at it from the grave. No indeed, I'm not finished with you yet!" He gave the body another stiff whack before he left.

Shigemori returned to Rokuhara and reported to the nobles gathered there that Nobuyori's head was off. They all wanted to know about his last moments. Shigemori replied, "Well, you know, it was pathetic and comical all at the same time. He had fallen off his horse on the day of the battle, so the tip of his nose was broken, and a whip blow from Yoshitomo, during his flight, had raised a purple welt on his left cheek."

Koremichi remarked, "They joke that a day of *sarugaku* can lose you your nose.[54] Well, a day of fighting lost this Nobuyori his." The company burst into laughter. His Majesty heard it and asked what it was about. He laughed, too, when Nariyori told him. A *sechie* banquet, an imperial progress, or any weighty council meeting would always elicit some witty crack from Koremichi, and this one so tickled senior nobles and privy gentlemen alike that decorum broke down. Nonetheless, Nobuyori had been immensely learned, skilled at every art, and in fact a model courtier. The sovereign indulged him for that reason, and his officials refrained from condemning him.

## 19. Official Appointments for the Emperor's Men *with* The Rebels Are Stripped of Offices and Honors

Lord Minamoto no Moronaka was asked to explain his actions. "I deserve a reward," he replied. "Why? Because when Nobuyori was scheming to take the Sacred Mirror down to the east, I hid it in the house of my wife, Bōmon-no-tsubone, near the Ane-ga-kōji and Higashi-no-tōin crossing. This proves beyond a doubt that I never meant to join the rebels. Nobuyori's stay at Fushimi, at my invitation, had to do only with fear of his power, which forced me against my will to seek a relationship with him. I ask your understanding in this matter." Suezane, the governor of Kawachi, and his son Suemori, a recently appointed officer in the Left Gate Watch, were both executed.

Meanwhile, the Heike were rewarded for their role in the recent conflict. Kiyomori's eldest son, Shigemori, was appointed to govern Iyo; his second, Motomori, was named governor of Yamato; and Munemori, his third, became governor of Tōtōmi. His younger brother, Yorimori, who governed Mikawa, became the governor of Owari. Itō Kagetsuna became the governor of Ise. The council's presiding senior noble was the grand counselor Tadamasa. Its executive secretary was the chamberlain and left minor consultant Tomokata.

Seventy-three men were dismissed from office. These included[55] Nobuyori's brothers Motoie, Motomichi, and Nobutoshi; Nobuyori's son Nobuchika; Minamoto no Yoshitomo; his sons Tomonaga and Yoritomo; Minamoto no Shigenari; Minamoto no Arifusa; Kamada Masakiyo; and their allies and relatives. Just yesterday these had enjoyed imperial favor, each shedding reflected glory on his whole house; yet today each was sentenced to death, and the wretchedness of it passed to nine generations of each man's descendants. Dreamed pleasures mean waking misery. The moon, brilliant tonight, soon slips behind the shifting clouds of the passions. Morning smiles turn by evening to tears. Fleeting blossoms, quickly gone, demonstrate to every eye the swiftness of passage from glory to ruin. Who among the living is spared these sorrows?

The realm had been at peace during the thirty and more years between Kashō 2 [1107], when Minamoto no Yoshichika was executed during Emperor Horikawa's reign, and Kyūju 2 [1155]. The people took pride in virtue worthy of the Chinese sage kings Yao and Shun. No wave stirred upon the waters, and the land enjoyed the good government that had prevailed in the Engi and Tenryaku eras. Then came the Hōgen conflict, however, and all too quickly the recent armed clashes. "This must be the end of the world," thoughtful people lamented. "The days of the realm are surely over."

Another council of senior nobles was convened on the 29th. It reached this decision: "Recently, evildoers installed themselves in the palace and for many days behaved there in a disorderly manner. It would be improper for His Majesty to return until the palace has been purified." Accordingly, His Majesty proceeded to the residence of Bifukumon-in at Hachijō-Karasumaru. Shigemori accompanied him there with a quiver of arrows at his back.

## 20. The Report to Tokiwa *with* The Exile of Shinzei's Sons

Now, late in life Yoshitomo had had three sons by Tokiwa, a maid in the service of Kujō-in.[56] The eldest, Imawaka, was in his seventh year and the second, Otowaka, in his fifth; the last one, Ushiwaka, had been born that year. Deeply attached to them all, Yoshitomo sent a page named Kon'ōmaru back to the city with this message: "The battle is lost, and I am now fleeing wherever I can go, but my thoughts always return to the capital and to the children. What the future holds I do not know. I will bring you all to any province that gives me refuge. In the meantime, go, hide in some far mountain village, and await further news."

At this, Tokiwa collapsed and lay still with a robe drawn over her head. The boys all cried, in tears, "Where is Father? What has happened to Father?"

Weeping, Tokiwa stood up again. "Where did his lordship say he was going?" she asked.

"He said that he would go to the east—he was going to look for some of his hereditary retainers," Kon'ōmaru replied. "He is so much on my mind that I will leave now, if I may."

He was on his way out when Imawaka caught his sleeve. "This is already my seventh year, you know," he declared, in tears. "Am I not old enough to strike down my father's foe? Put me on your horse, let me ride behind you, take me to my father! There is no safety for me here. If you cannot take me, then I wish that you would kill me yourself rather than leave me to the men of the Heike. Find a way to take me with you!"

Kon'ōmaru could bear neither to look at him nor even forcibly to break his grip. "Your father is hiding in the Eastern Hills," he said soothingly, "and I must rejoin him tonight. Please let go of my robe." The boy did. It was heartbreaking to see happiness shine through his tears. Kon'ōmaru had bade them farewell and was just leaving again when the boy said, "You have given us news of my father, but I will miss you, too, you know! Ah, when will I ever see you again?" It was a sad, tearful moment.

All twelve of Shinzei's sons, clerical and lay, were sentenced to distant exile. Thoughtful people remarked among themselves, "These are the sons of a man who gave his life for his sovereign. Yes, Nobuyori and Yoshitomo banished them, but they should have been recalled and rewarded for their loyalty once these enemies of the court were destroyed. That they should be exiled defies comprehension." Tsunemune and Korekata recommended banishment for fear that, if these men were retained in office, their own actions during their period of collusion with Nobuyori might come to His Majesty's attention; and, in the current, chaotic state of the realm, the sovereign and his ministers misunderstood their motive.

Shinzei's sons excelled in mastery of the inner and outer teachings[57] and were brilliantly accomplished in both Japanese and Chinese learning. Up to the very day when they started into exile, they gathered at one or another's home to compose poetry in Chinese or Japanese and to lament their impending separation. Once the time had come, and they set out toward their various places of banishment, they still sent one another, from their first few stops on the journey, letters expressing concern and affection. Those bound for the western provinces traveled the eightfold tide-lanes of the sea; those bound for the east saw a thousand leagues of mountains and rivers drop behind them. They passed through barrier after barrier and lodged in a new place every night, but they found no solace anywhere. The days passed, the months went by, but their tears flowed on and on.

There are no words to describe the grief of one of them, Shigenori, at having to abandon both his aged mother and his young children for a journey into regions so remote. So desperately did he miss the capital that he stopped frequently on the way and could hardly bear to go on. At Awataguchi he halted his horse to write:

| | |
|---|---|
| *michinobe no* | Here beside the path, |
| *kusa no aoba ni* | on a green, grassy expanse, |
| *koma tomete* | I rein in my steed |
| *nao furusato o* | and upon the home I love |
| *kaerimiru kana* | cast a longing, backward glance. |

Covering in this spirit the great distances of the Tōkaidō, he passed the Shiohi tidal flats along the Narumi coast, then Futamura-yama, Miyaji-yama, Takashi-yama, and the bridge at Hamana. Sayo-no-nakayama and

Uzu-no-yama—once to him, in the capital, no more than names—then followed. Next he contemplated the storied peak of Fuji and crossed over Mount Ashigara, wondering the while where his journey would end, until he reached Musashi and gazed upon the Horikane well.[58] Eventually he came to the capital of Shimotsuke and saw Muro-no-yashima, where he was to live.[59] A thin, forlorn plume of vapor rose there, and in his desperate melancholy he could not help reflecting, in tears:

| | |
|---|---|
| *waga tame ni* | For me, no one else, |
| *arikaeru mono o* | what I see comes into view. |
| *shimotsuke ya* | Ah, Shimotsuke: |
| *muro no yashima ni* | at Muro-no-yashima |
| *taenu omoi wa* | anguished love forever burns. |

He had never even dreamed of one day seeing such a place, and yet this, now, was his home: a hut built of grasses,[60] outlandish beyond the power of simile to convey. Turning past and present over in his mind, he wondered when the year would come, when the day, that his sleeves might at last dry. Nonetheless, life went on. Sun after sun rose and set, but his longing for home never wavered.

## 21. Kon'ōmaru Races Back from Owari to Report Yoshitomo's Death

The brave New Year came on the opening day of Heiji 2 [1160], but the ceremonies proper to the first and third days went forward in only perfunctory fashion. At the palace,[61] the Tengyō precedent[62] was invoked to cancel the morning salutation. The New Year salutation to the retired emperor was canceled as well, since he was at Ninnaji.

On the 5th, Yoshitomo's page Kon'ōmaru turned up secretly at Tokiwa's home. He crumpled, fell from his horse, and for some time remained breathless and silent. Eventually he rose and announced, weeping: "At dawn on the 3rd, at Utsumi in the Noma district of Owari, Lord Yoshitomo came under attack from his hereditary retainer Osada Tadamune and was slain." Tokiwa and every member of her household wailed with bitter grief, and no wonder. His pillow had stood by hers, their sleeves mingled. The blow would have been heavy enough had she been alone, but there were also her three unfortunate children. Imawaka was now in his eighth year, Otowaka in his sixth, and Ushiwaka in his second. All were boys, and she wept that they might be taken from her and suffer a dreadful fate. No words can describe her misery.

Kon'ōmaru gave her an account of the journey. "Once the battle was lost," he said, "Lord Yoshitomo made for Ōhara. At Yase, the Ryūge Pass, and elsewhere, monks from the Mountain engaged him in skirmishes, but he swept them aside and emerged on the western shore of the lake. Pretending to lead a band of warriors racing up to the capital from the northern provinces, he passed West Sakamoto, Tozu, Karasaki, and the Shiga coast. No one paid us any attention. We crossed the river at Seta by boat.

"Once past the Noji post station, we skirted Mikami-yama, vanished into the forests of Kagami-yama, and reached the Echi River. Lord Yoshitomo kept calling out for Master Yoritomo, but he got no answer. 'This is terrible!' he exclaimed. 'He must have fallen behind!' Hiraga Shirō, from Shinano, turned back to look for him and found him. Lord Yoshitomo was very glad, and at the Ono post station he asked Master Yoritomo why he had fallen behind. Yoritomo replied, 'I had whipped my horse along all night, and when morning came I fell asleep in the saddle. On the Shinohara embankment I heard loud voices and opened my eyes. There were forty or fifty men around me. I drew my sword and beheaded the one who had seized my horse's bit. I also cut off another's arm. The sword flash startled my horse, which bolted forward and knocked a few of them down. The rest ran away when they saw two of their number killed or wounded. I broke through them, and here I am.'

"Yoshitomo looked fondly at him. 'You did well,' he said. 'Even a full-grown man would have to be good to do that much, and *you* are still a boy. Well done!' He was full of praise.

"News came that the Fuwa barrier was guarded, so Lord Yoshitomo turned instead into the mountains, along unfamiliar trails. The snow was so deep that we dismounted and got through the steepest, most dangerous spots by hanging onto trees and rushes. Master Yoritomo rode like a grownup but could not keep up on foot. Lord Yoshitomo stopped in the deep snow and called his name repeatedly but got no answer. 'Ah, this is bad!' he said. 'He has dropped behind already. He could end up being captured!' He was weeping freely, like all of us.

"He summoned Akugenda. 'Go down to Kai and Shinano and attack from the Tōsandō,' he said. 'I will go on to the east, then attack by the Tōkaidō.' So Akugenda started out, all alone, along the mountain ridges toward the province of Hida.

"At the Aohaka post station in Mino, a courtesan named Ōi runs the establishment where Lord Yoshitomo normally stays; he has a daughter there by her. He went there, and he and Kamada Masakiyo visited the *imayō* singer Enju. The courtesans were entertaining them when they heard the local people shouting, 'Fugitives! There are fugitives in there! Find them, seize them!'

"Lord Yoshitomo wondered aloud what to do. Shigenari said, 'They shall have my life, sir, instead of yours.' He put on Lord Yoshitomo's brocade *hitatare*, resolutely mounted his horse, and raced from the inn toward the foot of the mountains to the north. The men from the inn caught up with him. Shigenari drew his gold-trimmed sword and drove them back. 'Oh no,' he roared, 'you will not get your hands on me! Who do you think I am? I am the great commander of the Genji, Minamoto no Yoshitomo!' He then took his own life. The men were very pleased with themselves for having put an end to Lord Yoshitomo. They had no idea that Yoshitomo was actually hiding in the storehouse in Ōi's back garden.

"Lord Yoshitomo was leaving the inn that night when it became clear that Tomonaga, who had taken an arrow in the knee during the skirmish at Ryūge Pass, who had ridden a long way from there, and who had then struggled on foot through deep snow, could not walk a step further. His knee was too badly swollen. 'I am too seriously wounded to go with you,' he said. 'Please say goodbye to me here.'

"Lord Yoshitomo urged him very sadly to come anyway, if he possibly could. However, Tomonaga only wept and replied, 'Please be kind enough, if you are willing, to take my head yourself.' He then stretched out his neck. Lord Yoshitomo did as he asked, then drew a robe over the body. 'Tomonaga's leg is very bad,' he said as he left. 'Look after him, please.'

"Kazusa-no-suke Hirotsune took his leave of Lord Yoshitomo, saying, 'You have many men with you, sir, and travel will not be easy with so large a party. I will gather forces and join you when you move on the capital from the east.' He went no further.

"Lord Yoshitomo reached the Kuize River and asked a boat bound downstream to take him aboard. The boatman readily agreed to do so.

He was Genkō of Washi-no-su, the resident priest of Yōrōji. He examined Lord Yoshitomo curiously and said, 'Hide under these rushes if you prefer not to be seen.' Lord Yoshitomo, Kamada, and I did so. The boat was allowed straight past the Kōzu barrier, on the claim that it was only carrying rushes.

"On the 29th of the 12th month of last year, Lord Yoshitomo reached the home of Osada no Shōji Tadamune, at Utsumi in the Noma district of Owari. He naturally trusted this man, a hereditary retainer in the service of Lord Yoshitomo's house and also Kamada Masakiyo's father-in-law. Lord Yoshitomo asked him for horses, arms, and armor because he wanted to move on quickly. Tadamune replied that he, his men, and his sons would go with him. 'But first,' he said, 'stay here and rest a while.'

"Tadamune readied the bath for Lord Yoshitomo and took him there. Then, on the pretext of entertaining Kamada Masakiyo, his son-in-law, he invited him to join him and cut off Yoshitomo's head. Next, he went to the bath with seven or eight men and attacked Lord Yoshitomo. Lord Yoshitomo managed to cry out just once for Kamada, not knowing that he had been killed the evening before. I myself was lying there, holding my lord's sword close against me, but I suppose they must have thought I was too young to bother with, because no one paid me any attention. I drew the sword and killed two of the attackers, then dashed into the house proper to kill Tadamune himself, but he fled into a secure inner room,[63] and I could do no more. I leapt onto a horse that stood saddled and ready outside, and I rode for three days to get here."

Tokiwa wailed, "He spoke of the east as a place of safety, so I always expected more news from him, but now I know that he will never return. I see no hope for myself, either, and nothing more to live for. I only want to drown myself in some watery deep, so as not to live on in this hateful world. But whom could I trust to look after my children, once I was gone? Because of those pathetic keepsakes he left me,[64] I end up clinging after all to this useless life of mine!"

Otowaka looked up in tears at his mother's face. "Mama, mama, don't drown yourself!" he cried. "We would be so unhappy!" Kon'ōmaru only wept the more.

Kon'ōmaru spoke again, "During the whole journey his words made it plain that his greatest concern was his children, and for their sake I have prolonged my worthless life in order to come back to you, fearing that unless the news reached you quickly, you would miss going into hiding and perhaps risk disastrous consequences. I have now rendered my late lord my last service. I will become a monk and pray for his enlightenment." Then he added, "I bid you farewell." So it was that, on the evening of the 5th of the 5th month, in tears, he left them.

"This page was our last link to Lord Yoshitomo!" So lamented Tokiwa and every member of her household. They keened and mourned without shame.

## 22. Tadamune, Yoshitomo's Killer, Hastens to Rokuhara *with* The Parading of Yoshitomo's Head

On the 6th, Go-Shirakawa left the prince-abbot's residence at Ninnaji and proceeded to the house of Fujiwara no Akinaga at Hachijō-Horikawa. This was apparently to be his formal residence, since the Sanjō Palace had burned down.

On the 7th, Osada no Shōji Tadamune and his son Kagemune came up to the capital and announced that they had brought with them the head of Yoshitomo. This Tadamune was a descendant of Heidayū Tomoyori. His grandfather was Kamo Jirō Yukifusa, his father Heisaburō Munefusa. He was both Yoshitomo's hereditary retainer and Kamada Masakiyo's father-in-law. All in the capital who heard the news, high or low, muttered angrily, "I'd like to saw the heads off those two!" Eight officers of the police—among them Kaneyuki, Nobufusa, Norimori, and Tomotada—went to receive the heads. They then paraded them up Nishi-no-tōin avenue, from Sanjō to Konoe, and hung them in the chinaberry tree before the gate of the east prison.[65] Since Yoshitomo had been the governor of Shimotsuke, someone or other worked that into a poem that he posted there on a sign:[66]

| | |
|---|---|
| *shimotsuke wa* | Old Shimotsuke |
| *ki no kami ni koso* | got Kii and found himself |
| *narinikere* | quickly up a tree: |
| *yoshi to mo mienu* | by no means the flattering rise |
| *agetsukasa kana* | he had hoped, Yoshitomo. |

Of old, the sight of Masakado's head hanging at the prison gate drew this from a poet called Tōroku:[67]

| | |
|---|---|
| *masakado wa* | Poor Masakado |
| *komekami yori zo* | got that old noggin of his |
| *kirarekeru* | neatly lifted off |
| *tawara tōda ga* | by a vorpal snicker-snack |
| *hakari koto nite* | from Tawara Tōda's sword. |

The head gave a little hiss of mirth. People remarked to one another how terrifying it was that a head struck off in the 2nd month [of 940] and hung there in the 4th should have laughed on the 3rd day of the 5th month.

During the Hōgen conflict, only a year or two earlier, Yoshitomo had had Hadano Yoshimichi, a retainer, behead his own father, Tameyoshi. Now, after his recent defeat, he had fallen by the hand of another retainer, Tadamune. "He reaped in this very life the reward for his treachery," both high and low in the crowd muttered, "and no doubt he will spend the next one in the lowest pit of hell." Half the voices reviled him, and half pitied him.

In view of the current upheaval, it was decided on the 10th that the present era name would not do. A new era, Eiryaku, was therefore proclaimed. The era had been changed from Hōgen to Heiji in the 4th month of the previous year, but thoughtful people then remarked, "The characters of 'Heiji' suggest the meaning 'settle into a Taira peace.' The Genji are doomed." Then the current conflict arose, and, sure enough, most of the Genji were destroyed.

## 23. The Execution of Akugenda

Nanba no Saburō Tsunefusa learned that Akugenda lay gravely ill near Ishiyama-dera in Ōmi. He swooped down on the place, captured the man, and took him to Rokuhara.

Itō Kagetsuna was assigned to interrogate him. Akugenda said, "The late Yoshitomo announced that he would go down to the east, then bring his Musashi and Sagami retainers back with him up the Tōkaidō to attack the capital. He also ordered me to bring the men of Kai and Shinano with me up the Tōsandō, so I made my way through the mountains toward Hida, and some three thousand desperate men must have rallied to me. However, they scattered when they heard that Yoshitomo had been killed. It would have been all too easy to do away with myself, but instead I decided at least to go after a great Heike lord—not that success would win me lasting victory, but it would give me some satisfaction. I disguised myself as a servant and stood at the Rokuhara gate, holding a horse by the bridle or, shoes in hand, near where those entering remove their shoes. The place was too strictly guarded, though. I could only wander a while around the city and spy on Rokuhara from time to time. Then I began to attract suspicious looks, so I went down to the country, meaning eventually to go back. Now my has luck run out, and I have been captured."

Itō Kagetsuna said, "It is sad indeed that the scion of the main Genji line, and one so famous as a commander in battle, should have been taken so easily."

"Yes, it is," Akugenda replied. "I traveled the mountains for days through deep drifts, lashed by rain and driving snow, to the point of utter exhaustion. More recently, I have been at Rokuhara and in the city, with only one thin garment to keep Kamo River wind off me, and without enough to eat. I never rested, though, because I so wanted to kill an enemy. That ambition alone sustained me. Now, with time, I have fallen ill enough for Tsunefusa to capture me. Of course I might have been killed in the end, if this illness had not drained my strength, but I would have twisted the heads off two or three Tsunefusas before I died. Oh no, as a warrior I have nothing to be ashamed of. It is simply time for me to meet my fate." All present agreed that he was right.

On the 21st, at the hour of the horse [noon], Tsunefusa took him out to the Rokujō riverbank to execute him. Akugenda said, "The Heike, Kiyomori the first among them, are the most ignorant louts alive. Many men, both Genji and Heike, were executed at the time of the Hōgen conflict, but at least the executions were carried out at night. The man of bow and arrow aspires above all never to humiliate his foe. What brute would execute a man like me in broad daylight? Yes, my time is over, and, in this life, defeat in battle has burdened me with this cruel fate. Such is my shame. Once dead, however, I will become a mighty demon, or perhaps a thunderbolt. I will smash every one of the Heike, Kiyomori first, then all the way down to *you*. In Hōgen, Tameyoshi recommended a night attack on Takamatsu House; but no, his advice was rejected, and he lost. *This* time, Kiyomori was off on pilgrimage to Kumano, and I advised pursuing him, to keep him from getting beyond Yuasa or Shishi-no-se. 'We must capture every fool wearing pilgrim white and an upright *eboshi* hat,' I said. But no again: the idea was rejected as mere bluster. In Hōgen, and now in Heiji, what good did it do to reject a stern warrior's advice and follow instead the notions of scriveners and nobles? I have not said all this just to live that much longer. I speak the truth, and you know it. Now, do it!" He stretched out his neck, and his head fell.

## 24. Tadamune's Dissatisfaction

On the 23rd the two Osadas, father and son, received their reward. Tadamune became the governor of Iki and Kagemune an officer of the Watch.

"This is not enough," Tadamune complained. "If the reward is to be an office, then something like chief left equerry; if a province, then perhaps Harima as Yoshitomo's successor, or possibly Owari, since that is where I am from. That sort of thing would do. Yoshitomo might have turned out to be like Sadatō and Munetō if he had ever reached the north. There is no telling how many hundreds of thousands of warriors might have followed him. Instead I killed him here, without fuss, and presented his head. I call that outstanding service."

Iesada remarked on this subject to Kiyomori, "Confound it, I would gladly crucify the scoundrel on the Rokujō riverbank and make a spectacle of him for the whole city! He kills his hereditary lord and his son-in-law, and now he wants a bigger reward? There is no word for this! Just have him beheaded!"

"Who would ever kill an enemy of the court, if I did that?" Kiyomori replied.

"What will the Genji do to Tadamune and Kagemune if they ever come into their own again?" So wondered everyone in a spirit of bitter condemnation.

## 25. The Capture of Yoritomo

On the 9th of the 2nd month Yoshitomo's third son, Yoritomo, was taken alive by Yaheibyōe-no-jō Munekiyo, a man in the service of Yorimori, the governor of Owari. Munekiyo took him to Rokuhara.

On his way up to the capital, Munekiyo lodged in Ōi's establishment at the Aohaka post station in Mino. The next morning he noticed a fresh grave marker among the bamboo in the garden. Having already gathered what it might be, he dug it up and found a severed head buried with the body. Ōi told him the whole story and gladly gave him the head, which he took with him to the capital.

During the night of the 28th of the 12th month of the previous year, Yoritomo could not get through the deep snow in the mountains fast enough, and he had fallen behind his father. He then wandered here and there until the priest of Daikichiji, a small mountain temple in Ōmi, took pity on him and hid him. The temple was about to undergo repair, however, and the priest warned him that it would be dangerous for him to have that many people about.

Yoritomo left Daikichiji and wandered through the north of Asai county until an old couple pitied him and offered him a place to hide. In the 2nd month he decided to stay there no longer. Instead he would to go down to the east, confer with old allies of his house, and find out whether those close to him were still alive. He gave his host several *kosode* robes and an ochre *hitatare*, then set out in a single *kosode* of coarse cloth that had once belonged to his host's son, together with the son's dark blue *hitatare*. On his feet he wore straw sandals. Under his arm, wrapped in a straw mat, he carried in its scabbard an heirloom sword named Higekiri ["Cutbeard"].

In this guise he passed the Fuwa barrier and reached the spot known as Sekigahara. Seeing a large band of men approaching, he cautiously stepped off the path and stood hidden in a thicket. However, Munekiyo, who was on his way up from Owari, spotted him and wondered what he was doing there. Munekiyo's men captured the fellow, who turned out to be Yoritomo. Extremely pleased, Munekiyo mounted Yoritomo on a spare horse and took him up to the city. He had Yoritomo carry the head of Tomonaga, which he then gave to the chief of police. The police paraded it through the streets and exposed it. Yoritomo himself was given into the custody of Munekiyo, who was kind and took good care of him.

## 26. Tokiwa's Flight

Among Yoshitomo's many children, Akugenda had been beheaded; the head of Tomonaga, his second son, had been surrendered to the police, paraded through the streets, and hung in public view; and Yoritomo, his third, was now a prisoner whose life hung in the balance. Yoshitomo also had three children by Tokiwa, a maid in Kujō-in's service. They were very young, but all were sons, and no one expected them to be left in peace.

Tokiwa therefore made a decision. "I can manage having to mourn Yoshitomo," she reflected, "but not for an instant could I survive losing my boys. I will take them into hiding for as long as I can successfully remain undiscovered." She told her old mother nothing, and, because others' hearts are never to be trusted, she breathed no word, either, to the women in her service. She stole away under cover of darkness.

Imawaka, her eldest, was in his eighth year; Otowaka, her second, was in his sixth; and Ushiwaka, her youngest, was in his second. When she left, she had Imawaka walk ahead of her and carried Ushiwaka in her arms. Despite her intense anxiety, she had no idea where actually to go and so just followed her footsteps. They led her to Kiyomizu-dera, to which she had long been devoted.

She passed that night in vigil before Kannon with her two older boys on either side of her, under her skirts, and the youngest clasped inside her robe's front fold. All night she kept as quiet as she could so as not to wake them, but in her heart she said a great deal. Pilgrims from everywhere sat shoulder to shoulder and knee to knee, praying for all sorts of things. No one lives forever, but some still prayed for relief from their hard lot in life. Others, who enjoyed positions in the service of the great, prayed nonetheless to rise higher. Tokiwa, however, prayed to Kannon only to save her three sons. That was her only thought.

Tokiwa had been making monthly pilgrimages to Kiyomizu ever since her ninth year, and in her fifteenth she had begun chanting the thirty-three scrolls of the Kannon Sutra on the 18th day of every month.[68] She had profound faith that the compassionate Kannon of Kiyomizu would shed his light upon her. "I have heard," she prayed, "that, in the compassion and mercy of your Original Vow, you save even those whose karma is inexorable, and that, in your presence, flowers bloom and fruit ripens on ancient trees. Hail, Thousand-Armed, Thousand-Eyed Bodhisattva Kannon, oh save the lives of my three sons!" So she prayed, weeping, through the night, and surely Kannon did take pity on her.

It was nearly dawn when she went to the priests' quarters. They urged dried rice on her, soaked in hot water. She was too sick at heart even to look at it, but she managed to get her children to take some. On her earlier pilgrimages she had arrived in a splendid carriage, accompanied by an oxherd and attendants whose brilliant attire made imposingly visible the love that Yoshitomo showered upon her. This time, however, she had purposely dressed with great discretion to avoid attracting unwelcome attention.

Her weeping figure, with her three children around her, made an unbearably distressing sight, and the priests shed tears of their own. "Do stay here, as discreetly as you like, until it stops snowing," they said.

"That is kind of you," she replied, "but I cannot. This temple is too close to Rokuhara. I have no hope now but the grace of the buddhas and gods. Please pray to Kannon for me, as hard as you can." At the hour of the hare [6 A.M.] she left Kiyomizu-dera and started down the Yamato road, although not with any destination in mind. She simply walked south.

It was dawn on the 10th of the 2nd month[69] and still very cold. There was ice along the Otowa River, and a strong wind blew down from the mountains. Icicles hung all along the way, and once more the sky grew dark with snow. She could not even see where she was going. The children walked at first, urged on by their mother, but in time their feet swelled and bled. Sometimes they fell, and sometimes they just sat down in the snow, crying, "I'm cold, so cold, I don't know what to do!" There are no words to describe how this must have made their forlorn mother feel. Her courage failed her when they cried especially loudly, for fear that the enemy might hear; and when a passerby asked kindly after them, she trembled to think that there might be malice in the question. Such was her misery that she led her children under the gates of houses to rest.

She whispered to Imawaka while no one was near, "How *can* you not understand? The enemy is nearby, at the place called Rokuhara. If you cry, people will wonder why. As Yoshitomo's sons you will be taken prisoner and beheaded. If you want to live, don't cry! They say that a good son obeys his mother even in the womb, and *you* are in your seventh or eighth year! Why will you not listen to me?" Her reproach quieted the boy a little, and he paid attention. His tears flowed on, but not so that he cried aloud.

Her second son collapsed as before, crying, "Cold, I'm so cold!" Tokiwa could not possibly hold him, too, with the baby in her arms. Instead she held his hand as they walked. She was as thin as a wraith because she had not touched even water, hot or cold,[70] since learning of Yoshitomo's death, and her current plight taxed her so greatly that she could have fainted at any moment; but her love for her children banished from her thoughts even the length of the spring day. At last, to the booming of the sunset bell, she reached the village of Fushimi.

The sun went down and night came on, but she had nowhere to go. There were houses along the path, at the foot of the hills, but she feared the presence of the enemy there, since the inhabitants might easily be Rokuhara retainers. No, she decided, she could not ask for lodging at any of them. "The misfortune of my boys' father has brought this misery on me," she said to herself. She could only weep.

So it was that, despite the many and terrifying figures who—so she had heard—haunted these mountains, she and her three children sought shelter in a thorny thicket; and there, huddled hand in hand, they wept. Twilight passed, and traffic on the road stopped. She felt sure that this night would be their last. How she longed for the hut of some mountain villager who would not know who she was! If only he would hide them that night and save her children! Such were her thoughts when she saw a light ahead. She approached it and knocked at a woven bamboo door. A woman of mature years, apparently the owner, opened it and came forth. She stared at Tokiwa in surprise. "What is this?" she asked. "Where can you possibly be going, through the snow, with three small children and no trusty escort?"

Tokiwa answered, "My husband has been misbehaving, you see. I was so angry that I left him and took my children with me. Then, to make matters worse, it started snowing, and I got lost." She strove bravely to cover her misery with good cheer, but she failed, and her tears flowed onto her sleeves.

"I suspected you at first," the woman replied, "but obviously you are no ordinary person. What with all the turmoil these days, your husband is probably someone who matters. This old woman could never turn you away, no, not even if Rokuhara were to summon her, tie her up, humiliate her, and finally do her in for harboring a fugitive. We around here welcome any visitor. You must have been out in the open all the time, and you could hardly get through the night like that, as miserably cold as it has been lately. You could have gone to so many other houses, and knocked at so many other gates, that some bond from a past life must have brought you to mine. This is not much of a place, I am afraid, but do come in!"

She ushered them in and spread a new mat. She lit a fire to warm them and offered them food. Tokiwa was still too distressed to accept any, despite her tremendous relief, but she got her children to eat. She presented so painful a picture that the woman did all she could for her. As far as Tokiwa was concerned, she owed this respite to the grace of the Kannon of Kiyomizu. The future now looked brighter.

Otowaka was so exhausted from walking that he fell asleep on her lap. For Imawaka, still acutely aware of his father's fate and troubled by his mother's ceaseless weeping, no sleep was possible. Tokiwa lay with her face to the wall, overcome by tears of fond memory. The night wore on. Once all was quiet, she whispered in Imawaka's ear, "You poor dears! Some people, you know—those who do well in life—bring up ten or twenty children. Of course some in a family die before others, since that is the way of this sad world, but there certainly are many examples of parents who grow old together and then leave behind children to mourn them both. I have only you three boys, but, oh, I so hope I can keep at least one of you with me to the end! Who knows into whose hands we may fall tomorrow, or what fate may be yours? You may be drowned or buried alive. The way you depend on me, your mother, and the way I love you, my children—that may hardly outlast the coming dawn." She wept as she spoke.

Imawaka replied, "But, mother, what will become of you if I die?"

"If the three of you were to go before me," she answered, "I could not live a single day, a single moment longer. I would want to die with you."

The boy was very happy that his mother hated to leave them and preferred to die with them instead. "I won't mind dying," he said, "if only I can die with you." They lay cheek to cheek and hand in hand, and sleep never touched their eyes. No, they wept through a night—short, as spring nights always are—of restless misery. At last dawn came, eagerly awaited, to the crowing of cocks and the boom of temple bells.

Light was spreading across the sky when Tokiwa roused the children and prepared to leave. The woman hurried out and detained her, insisting that she stay there that day. "Give the children's feet a rest," she said, "and continue your journey when the snow has stopped." Tokiwa missed the capital, but that way lay a great menace for her boys, and she wanted only to put as much distance, as quickly as possible, between it and them. Nevertheless, the woman's kindness won her over, and she spent that day, too, at Fushimi.

The next dawn she again roused her children, bade her hostess farewell, and set out. The woman saw her off a good way and asked her in a low voice, "What connection forces you now into hiding? I did not feel that I could keep you any longer in this village, so close to the capital, and that is why today I have not done so. I am so worried about you, even though I do not know who you are! I am nobody, I know, but if things go better for you and you settle in the capital, please come and see me again!" She wept.

Tokiwa answered, "I cannot imagine such a bond forming between us unless in some past life we were mother and daughter. I will not forget your kindness for as long as I live." They parted in tears.

Travelers along the way looked upon her with pity and were sometimes kind, offering her a ride on horseback or carrying a child for her. So it was that after a surprisingly easy journey she reached Uda county in the province of Yamato. There she called upon a relative and explained that she had made her way there in the hope at least of saving her sons. At first her relatives hesitated to accept her, for fear of possible reprisals, but in the end they could not bring themselves to disappoint her hopes after so long and difficult a journey, and they welcomed her. Whatever the future might bring, for the time being, at least, she was safe.

# Book 3

## 27. Kiyomori Spares Yoritomo *with* The War Between Wu and Yue

Yoritomo's behavior in Munekiyo's custody resembled no ordinary boy's. Everyone who noted the maturity of his conduct wanted to save him. One such person suggested discreetly to Yoritomo that this could be accomplished if he were to ask Lady Ike to resolve the matter.[71] "Lady Ike," he explained, "is Lord Kiyomori's stepmother and the mother of Yorimori. She is the widow of Tadamori. People think very highly of her."

Yoritomo therefore approached Lady Ike privately on the subject. Having long felt pity for the suffering of others, Lady Ike considered his plea and decided that the sentence was too cruel. Now, in reward for his services Shigemori had recently been appointed to govern Iyo, and in the first month of the current year he had become the chief left equerry. Lady Ike called him to her and said, "It would be too cruel to behead Yoritomo, a boy in his twelfth or thirteenth year. Please urge Lord Kiyomori, from me, to make an exception in his case and spare him."

Shigemori accordingly raised the subject with Kiyomori. Kiyomori replied, "Lady Ike stands as high in my esteem as did my father himself, and her wish is my command. This, however, is an exceptionally troublesome matter. I might easily enough spare several dozen men on the order of Minamoto no Moronaka or Fujiwara no Narichika. This Yoritomo, however, is the scion of

Rokusonnō's line. No doubt it was being so obviously accomplished a warrior that got Yoshitomo, his father, promoted far beyond his brothers. He apparently did great things on the battlefield. No, I have no desire to commute Yoritomo's sentence to distant exile." He gave Shigemori no clear reply.

Shigemori reported this conversation to Lady Ike. She replied, "Kiyomori's might has quelled several rebellions and successfully protected our sovereign, meanwhile ensuring the prosperity of his house and the complete destruction of the Genji. What difference will it make if he spares Yoritomo? I feel so sorry for Yoritomo that I wonder whether perhaps he saved *my* life in a previous existence. I entrusted my appeal to you because I hoped that my messenger's stature would help to sway your father. He is not *my* son, of course, but for his superb stewardship of our house I love and value him far above even my own Yorimori. Surely he has noted over the years the strength of my feeling for him. I will find it difficult to forgive you if I gather that you care less for me because you are not my grandson." Tears sprang to her eyes.

Shigemori therefore approached his father again. "Lady Ike feels very strongly indeed on the subject," he explained. "When a foolish wish implants itself in a woman's mind, the consequences can be troublesome indeed. There is no telling what she may do if you persist in refusing her plea."

"She certainly knows how to make her voice heard," Kiyomori remarked. He took no further action.

Thus emboldened, Lady Ike renewed her tearful appeal repeatedly, now through Shigemori and now through Yorimori, her own son. Despite rumors that Yoritomo would be beheaded that very day or, if not, then undoubtedly the next, the execution was always delayed and in the end never carried out. "Great Bodhisattva Hachiman is with me," Yoritomo said to himself. "To achieve my goal, I need only stay alive." These precocious reflections were frightening indeed.

Yoritomo stated his wish, should he be granted a day more of life, to make memorial sotoba to his father. He had no wood, however, nor was he allowed any blade with which to carve it, so that his hope remained unrealized. Tanba no Tōzō Yorikane, a man in Lady Ike's service, pitied him in his disappointment and made a collection of small sotoba from cryptomeria and cypress. Yoritomo was very pleased. He wrote a rough approximation of Siddham characters on each, with, underneath, the invocation to Amida; bundled several hundred of them together; and said to Yorikane, "I should like to put these somewhere where rowdy boys will not scatter them, and where horses and oxen will not trample them."

"Allow me to do that for you," Yorikane replied. Now, there was at Rokuhara an old temple named Mankudoku-in. It had a pond with a small island in the middle. Yorikane stripped off his clothes in the cold of early spring, tied the sotoba to his topknot, and swam out to the island to place them there. Yoritomo saw that, ultimately, he owed Yorikane's success in doing so to Lady Ike's kindness.

In this connection people high and low criticized Yoritomo by telling the following story: "Mayuwa, the son of Prince Ōkusaka,[72] was in his seventh year when he slew Emperor Ankō, his stepfather and his father's enemy. Chiyo Dōji, the son of Kuriyagawa no Jirō Sadatō,[73] was in his thirteenth when he donned armor, thrust forth his shield, loosed an arrow, and slew his foe. Even a boy may follow the way of bow and arrow. That is what they were like, the men of old. Yoritomo should have taken his own life after his father was killed, but no, he let an old lady, a nun, know that he preferred to live. Just deplorable!"

Some, however, remarked, "The greatest commander, the bravest warrior would rather live than die. Besides, there is that Chinese story about Gou Jian, the king of Yue, and Fu Cha, the king of Wu. The two fought a battle. The king of Yue lost, and the king of Wu took him prisoner. Thereafter the king of Yue served the king of Wu more assiduously than any of the victor's old retainers. Impressed by his zeal, the king of Wu spared him. However, one of his ministers, Wu Zixu by name, warned him that to do so would mean the ruin of Wu. The king of Wu ignored this warning. When Wu Zixu insisted further, the king of Wu waxed wroth and executed him. Wu Zixu said before he died, 'Remove my eyes and fix them to the gate of Wu. I wish to see Yue rise up and destroy Wu.' Then he was executed. The king of Yue was on his way to his homeland, having been granted leave to go, when he saw a frog leap across his path. He dismounted and bowed to the frog. Those with him wondered why on earth he had done so. His minister, Fan Li, replied, 'Our lord was giving thanks for sound advice.' Men of courage then flocked to the king of Yue, who, years later, raised an army and attacked Wu. His victory over Wu at the mountain called Hui Qi is therefore referred to as 'cleansing the shame of Hui Qi.'"[74] No doubt it is in that spirit that Yoritomo wished to stay alive. Neither Lady Ike nor Kiyomori could have imagined what he had in mind. People remarked, "The very thought is terrifying!"

## 28. Tokiwa Goes to Rokuhara

Now, Tokiwa had given Yoshitomo three children. All were boys, and something had therefore to be done about them. The warriors sent out from Rokuhara failed to find her or her sons, but she had a mother, an old nun. Rokuhara summoned this old nun on the assumption that she must know where her daughter and grandsons had gone. She replied, "She took her children away with her on the very day she learned of Lord Yoshitomo's death. Where she went, I do not know."

"How could you possibly not know?" they insisted and tortured her in various ways. During a pause in the torture she said, "I am over sixty years old, and even in good health I have little enough life left me. None of my three grandsons has reached even his tenth year, and surely all, if no ill befalls them, have a long future ahead. How could I, for love of a dewdrop life that could end at any moment, cause the death of three boys who have their whole lives before them? I would not tell you where she has gone even if I knew. As it is, I have absolutely no idea."

In Yamato, Tokiwa heard what had happened and understood that her mother loved her just as much as she loved her own children. "But how," she asked herself, "can I allow her to suffer so without acting to save her? If evil karma from past lives has brought my boys to birth in this one as Yoshitomo's sons, there to die for their father's fault, there must be some reason for it. It is my fault alone, however, that such a misfortune should have fallen on my wholly innocent mother. If after this I still want children, I shall have to content myself with bringing up a relative. Never, through infinite kalpas and lives to come, will I have again the mother I have now. It will not help to mourn her loss after they have tortured her to death. As long as she is still alive, I must go and save her." In the company of her three sons she returned to the capital.

Finding her house closed and deserted, she asked the neighbors what had happened to her mother. They answered that the other day Rokuhara men had come for her and all the servants had fled, so that now she was in grave danger. Tokiwa had feared just this. She shed an unending stream of tears.

She called upon Kujō-in, to whom she said, "A woman is pitifully weak at best, I know that, but out of pity for my children I kept them always beside me and slipped away with them to a remote corner of the countryside. However, I gather that my mother, who has little enough time left as it is, has been summoned to Rokuhara and subjected there to harsh interrogation. Whatever the consequences for my children, I have brought them here with me to save my mother."

The lady herself, and all the gentlewomen present, wept. "Any ordinary woman, like us," the gentlewomen assured one another, "would have decided that her old mother was unlikely to live much longer and that, once her mother was gone, she could always pray for her in the next life, whereas a child has his whole life before him. How remarkable that she prefers to save her mother, even at the cost of losing her children! The buddhas and gods must surely have pity on her. Anyway, her children little resemble a warrior's sons. They are all very good boys and thoroughly appealing." Their mistress agreed. She had all four handsomely dressed; provided them with an ox, a carriage, and servants; and sent them off worthily equipped to Rokuhara. Tokiwa left her residence and crossed the Kamo River eastward. She felt as though she were crossing the River of Death, even though no one demanded her clothes.[75] Upon approaching Rokuhara she felt like a sheep bound for slaughter and today, at last, considered her own fate with sorrow.

Kagetsuna, the governor of Ise, took charge of her when she arrived. She said, weeping, "In the foolish weakness of a woman's heart I took my children down to the distant countryside, hoping to save them; but then I learned that my innocent mother had been summoned here, humiliated, and made to suffer pain. I decided that I had to save my mother, even at the cost of causing my children's death, and I have therefore brought with me the boys you have been seeking. Please let my mother go." Her filial piety impressed all who heard her, and they shed tears of their own.

Kagetsuna reported Tokiwa's words to Kiyomori. Her mother was released and went to Kagetsuna's quarters, where she fainted with anguish at the sight of her daughter and grandsons. Shortly she got up again, glared angrily at Tokiwa, and said, "Ah, you have done a terrible thing! I am old, and my next life approaches. How much longer do I have to live, then, even after surviving this? You might as well have stolen my grandchildren! What made you go off with them and put me through such misery? It is a delight to see you and them again, but agony to foresee that their presence here will mean their death." Hand in hand, cheek to cheek, they sank in anguish to the ground.

Kiyomori summoned Tokiwa. She went to his residence with her sons, the two older boys on either side of her and the youngest, Ushiwaka, in her arms.

Weeping, she said to Kiyomori, "Yoshitomo committed a great crime, and now that his children face execution, it would be wrong of me to beg for the life of a single one. Before they meet that fate, however, I trust that you will accept my plea to kill me first. Every mother, high or low, wanders in darkness for love of her children. I know that I could not live a moment longer without them. Take *my* life first, please, then do what you will with my sons. That is what I came to you to say, shaming as I did so Yoshitomo's memory and heedless of my own distressing appearance. What greater kindness could I ask of you in this life, and what greater merit could I offer you for the next?"

"Don't cry, mother," Otowaka said. "You sound more convincing when you don't cry."

At this Kiyomori, who so far had maintained a stern countenance, exclaimed, "Bravely said!" He turned aside and wept freely. The ranks of warriors attending him broke into sobs and stood there with downcast eyes. Not one lifted his gaze.

Tokiwa was in her twenty-third year. She was articulate, having served an empress, and the intensity of her feelings had given form, as such feelings must, to such eloquence as to move a fierce warrior to pity. Her eyebrow black[76] was smudged with tears, and her days of suffering had so wasted her that she was barely recognizable, but she was still more beautiful than any other woman. Everyone there felt sorry for her. "Never have I seen or heard of such a beauty," the men murmured among themselves.

"And no wonder," one remarked. "Lord Koremichi insisted on sending a beauty to the empress's residence. From among a thousand called to the palace for their reputed looks he chose a hundred, from a hundred ten, and from among that last ten he selected only Tokiwa. There could hardly be anything wrong with *her*!"

"Sure enough," another added, "her looks never cease to amaze me. Yang Guifei of Tang and Lady Li of Han, whose every smile flashed a hundred charms, can hardly have been lovelier than she!" So they bantered among themselves.

Tokiwa returned to Kagetsuna's quarters. She then heard loud footsteps approaching, and she almost fainted with fear that they were coming to execute her children. Weeping, she contemplated their faces, wondering how much longer she would see them. Her crying children looked up at her, holding her hands tight and trusting her, helpless as she was, to save them. Tears overflowed their sleeves in an endless stream.

Kiyomori said, "It is not up to me to decide on my own the matter of Yoshitomo's children. On the subject of reward or punishment, I can only await His Majesty's judgment. I shall inquire into his feelings on the matter."

The people of Rokuhara wondered what had put him in so mild a mood. "There is no telling what trouble these three boys may cause if they grow up," they objected. "You are doing your descendants no good."

"I see what you mean," Kiyomori replied, "but with Lady Ike insisting on sparing Yoritomo, an adult, it makes no sense for me to execute these young boys. Whatever you may say, their fate depends on whether Yoritomo lives or dies."

Tokiwa found it extraordinary that her boys should live a single day, a single moment longer, and she felt sure that she owed their doing so to the grace of the Kannon of Kiyomizu. She recited the Kannon Sutra and taught her sons to call the name of Kannon. As for Yoritomo, Lady Ike pleaded so persistently against the death sentence pronounced upon him that it was commuted to exile. The astonished Yoritomo took this development as evidence of Great Bodhisattva Hachiman's intentions for him, and his faith grew stronger than ever. It was decided that he should be banished to the eastern province of Izu. All agreed that Tokiwa's children, being so young, would be spared as well; and sure enough they were, on the grounds of their innocence.

## 29. The Exile and Recall of Tsunemune and Korekata

On the 20th of the 2nd month, Retired Emperor Go-Shirakawa made his usual progress to the viewing stand in front of Lord Akinaga's residence at Hachijō-Horikawa. He was enjoying the prospect of hills veiled by evening smoke when men claiming to be from the palace aggressively boarded up the stand where he was. Furious, he summoned Kiyomori. "His Majesty is too young to have thought this up," he said. "Tsunemune and Korekata must be behind it. I want them arrested and jailed."[77]

Kiyomori replied to the retired emperor's order, "I gave Your Eminence loyal support during the Hōgen conflict and risked my life again to do so during the troubles of last year, in an effort to restore peace. I am always at your disposal, to act as you wish." He sent warriors to the homes of Tsunemune and Korekata. At Tsunemune's house, they killed Michinobu and Nobuyasu.

Tsunemune and Korekata were seized and sat down forcefully before Kiyomori in the central courtyard at Rokuhara. They had already been sentenced to die when Lord Tadamichi expressed his view of the subject. "The death penalty had lapsed long ago, ever since the execution of Nakanari under Emperor Saga, when during the Hōgen conflict Shinzei, a man of enormous talent, committed the error of imposing it. Last year, only two years later, rebellion broke out once more, proving all too soon the truth of the saying that executions provoke endless armed troubles. What will come next, after the heads of senior nobles start to fall? As they say, 'There is no return from distant exile. It amounts to a sentence of death.' Better, then, to commute the death penalty to distant exile."

All who learned of this opinion praised it, saying, "Lord Tadamichi's advice is wise indeed. His ancestors have protected the throne ever since the days of Lord Kamatari, and his exclusive concern for virtuous government honors our age as well. His descendants are sure to flourish as greatly as he."

Shinzei's twelve sons, some clerics, some laymen, had been banished far and wide. All were now recalled. The feelings of Shinzei's wife, Ki-no-nii, are painful to imagine. Nobuyori, Shinzei's rival for power, had been executed. Ki-no-nii's husband would certainly have been recalled from his place of banishment, if only he had lived, and the news of her sons' recall only made her miss him more. Go-Shirakawa, who now had no one with whom to discuss state affairs, likewise regretted his loss.

Tsunemune was exiled to the province of Awa. Korekata, who had apparently renounced the world, was banished to Nagato. Minamoto no Moronaka had received a weighty sentence because of his collaboration with Nobuyori, but it was lightened because of the way he had saved the Sacred Mirror. Nonetheless, the nobles agreed that he should not remain in the capital. He was therefore exiled to Muro-no-yashima in Shimotsuke, thus replacing Shinzei's son Narinori, now recalled. He hummed this poem when he crossed the bridge at Yatsuhashi in Mikawa:

| | |
|---|---|
| *yume ni dani* | No, I never dreamed |
| *kakute mikawa no* | that like this I would one day, |
| *yatsuhashi o* | here in Mikawa, |
| *watarubeshi to wa* | see my path take me across |
| *omoi ya wa semashi* | the bridge at Yatsuhashi.[78] |

Go-Shirakawa recalled him as soon as the poem reached his ears.

Tsunemune was called back from Awa and rose in time to right minister. He therefore came to be known as the Awa minister. Lord Koremichi remarked, "Life turns up such curiosities! Long ago our realm apparently boasted a *kibi* minister. Now we have an *awa* minister. No doubt one day we will have a *hie* minister."[79] When Tsunemune planned the banquet to celebrate his appointment, he invited Koremichi to be the guest of honor. Koremichi gave the messenger who delivered the invitation this blunt response: "I have no intention of sharing the leftovers from the Awa minister's return journey to the capital."[80] This gibe was so typical of him that people just laughed.

As for Korekata, it appeared that the retired emperor was still too angry to recall him. This news must have distressed Korekata greatly, because he wrote at the end of a letter to a gentlewoman at his residence:

| | |
|---|---|
| *kono yo ni mo* | Now a new abyss |
| *shizumu to kikeba* | yawns, I hear, to swallow me— |
| *namidagawa* | O River of Tears!— |
| *nagareshi yori mo* | and more sorely drench my sleeves |
| *nururu sode kana* | than ever mere banishment. |

The gentlewoman talked about this poem so much that Go-Shirakawa took pity on the man after all and hastened to recall him.

## 30. The Banishment of Yoritomo *with* Moriyasu's Dream

As to the death sentence pronounced on Yoritomo, Lady Ike's repeated and varied appeals yielded instead banishment to Izu. She then summoned him. "Until just yesterday I was making every effort in my power on your behalf," she said, "and today success has crowned my efforts. I understand that you are to be exiled to Izu, or so I believe the province is called. Ever since the days of my prime, I have found every tale of misfortune that has reached me unbearable. I have saved the lives of many and ensured that their heads should remain on their shoulders. Now that I am merely an old nun, I assumed that Lord Kiyomori had heard by now too many such pleas from me to heed this one, but I nonetheless approached him on the subject; and although I doubted any possibility of success, he did indeed, in your case, commute death to exile. I expect no greater joy in what remains of my life."

Yoritomo replied, "Madam, I owe my life to your kindness. Not through all my future lives could I repay the debt I owe you. I shall blame no one for my fate, whatever misfortune may eventually overtake me in the province to which I am bound. However, so long a journey will be painful without a single servant to accompany me."

"I quite understand," Lady Ike replied. "Many have served your forefathers for generations, but fear has discouraged them from coming forward. Surely they will make their presence known, once the commutation of your sentence has been formally announced." Yoritomo accordingly arranged with Munekiyo to have the announcement made.

Housemen and servants then came forward, to the number of seventy or eighty. The thirty and more housemen among them declared their unanimous recommendation that Yoritomo should please Lady Ike by renouncing the world, painful as the thought might be, before going down to Izu. Kōketsu Gengo Moriyasu alone demurred, whispering in Yoritomo's ear that he should save his topknot by pretending not to have heard any such advice.

Moriyasu said again, "It is extraordinary that you, alone among a thousand, should have been spared." He then assumed a reverent attitude and continued, "The Great Bodhisattva Hachiman has desired it to be so."

Thereafter, Yoritomo never replied when urged to cut off his topknot. He remained equally silent when urged not to. His thoughts are frightening to surmise.

On the 20th of the 3rd month of Eiryaku 1 [1160], the news spread that Yoritomo would start down to Izu. Lady Ike had her blinds raised for a good look at him when he went to bid her farewell. "Now that I have saved you from the brink of death," she said, "I hope that in all things you will do as I ask. Never hold or even look at a bow, an arrow, a sword, or a dagger. Never hunt or fish, or even consider doing so. Evil-tongued as people are, gossip is bound to bring me, while I still live, news of any further trouble that may involve you; and I would be very sorry indeed if you were to encounter any renewed threat. I wonder what karma from past lives makes you this dear to me, when, after all, I am not your mother and you are not my son. The sufferings of others touch me so deeply!" She could not restrain her tears.

Yoritomo, in the spring of his fourteenth year and therefore still very young, grasped nonetheless the intensity of her concern for him and wept freely, with downcast gaze. After a moment he restrained his tears and replied, "I lost my mother on the 1st of the 3rd month of last year, and on the 3rd of the 1st month of *this* year my father was taken from me. That made me a true orphan. Unfortunately, no one pitied me for it. To *you*, however, my mother and father are no doubt profoundly and humbly grateful, for the way you have save my life." Again he burst into tears.

"So indeed they surely are," Lady Ike replied, renewing the flow of her own. "Filial devotion always calls down the favor of the gods and ensures length of days. You will do well to read the sutras and call the Name in order to give your parents a happier rebirth. I once had a son of my own, you know: the chief right equerry Iemori. It is always with a pang that I remember him as a boy. He served Retired Emperor Toba and was doing exceedingly well when Kiyomori, who at the time was an official in the Bureau of Central Affairs, provoked an incident at the Gion Shrine.[81] The monks of Mount Hiei lodged a complaint against him, demanding distant banishment. While His Majesty struggled to reach a decision on the matter, the monks concluded that his tardiness was due to intercession by Iemori on behalf of Kiyomori, his older brother. So they laid curses upon Iemori, and in his twenty-third year he died of Sannō's malediction. I did not believe at the time that I could survive his loss a moment longer, but that was already eleven years ago. Until yesterday your fate, too, weighed on my heart, but after today I shall weep no more. You have your whole life before you, and your recall to the capital will certainly come in its time. At my age, though, when any day could be my last, I can hardly expect to witness it myself. No, I know that I will never see you again, and for that I am very sorry." She wept afresh, and Yoritomo wrung more tears than ever from his sleeves.

At dawn on the 20th day of the 3rd month of Eiryaku 1, Yoritomo left Rokuhara and started out on his long journey to the east. Many saw him off, but most found that they had footwear yet to make, or a matter yet to discuss with someone or other, so that those who actually set out with him numbered no more than three or four. Of these, only Moriyasu was fully dressed for travel and went with him as far as Ōtsu.

"What happened to all those people?" Yoritomo exclaimed. "There seemed to be so many of them!"

"With a journey to so distant a region before them," Moriyasu replied, "some missed their wives and children, others their mothers and fathers, too acutely to come. No doubt they will join you later." In the end, not one turned up.

Every other exile lamented his lot, but not Yoritomo—and no wonder, banishment being far preferable to decapitation. Still, he could not help missing the capital. Now and again he halted his horse and gazed behind him. Having once been a chamberlain in service at the palace, he dwelled in memory on all those whom he had known there. Having served also in the empress's household, he found that he could not forget that time, either. "I was saved by Lady Ike," he reflected, "who to me is neither father nor mother. It is extraordinary to have encountered anyone that kind and generous." In this mood he missed even Rokuhara, the headquarters of his foe. The horse of the Hu barbarians neighs into a north wind; the bird from Yue nests on a southern branch.[82] Even dumb beasts have the wit to long for home. When King Dongpingsi[83] died far from home, the grasses and trees that grew on his tomb mound all leaned toward where he was born. Youzi became a deity and protected those passing on the road;[84] Du Yu became a bird and cried to travelers to turn back.[85] Each of these lost his life on a long journey and left his body in an alien land, even as his homesick spirit wandered, revealing its bitterness at being confined to remote wilds. That is just how poor Yoritomo felt.

The man sent to escort Yoritomo into exile was a police underling named Suemichi who began robbing those whom they met on the road from about Awataguchi on.[86] Yoritomo asked him to stop. "There will be trouble," he said, "if the authorities ever learn that my journey into exile was marred by misconduct."

Moriyasu accompanied Yoritomo as far as Seta. "I should properly go with you all the way," he said, "but my mother, now a nun, is over eighty. Any day could be her last, and the prospect of parting from me distresses her greatly. Once she has passed away, I will hasten to join you and serve you."

Yoritomo crossed the river at Seta by boat. While there he noticed a torii standing before a cryptomeria grove and asked Moriyasu what divinity it announced. "A very weighty one," Moriyasu replied, "since Seta is the capital of Ōmi. You would do well to worship there."

"And what is the shrine called?"

"The Takebe Shrine."

"I will spend tonight there," Yoritomo declared.

"Stay rather at a post station," Moriyasu urged him.

"No, I will spend the night in vigil before the sanctuary, to pray for a bright future."

Yoritomo accordingly repaired to the Takebe Shrine. Moriyasu whispered to him late that night, when the escort was asleep, "The words I spoke in the capital, when I urged you not to renounce the world, were not mine. No, they were an oracle from the Great Bodhisattva Hachiman. In the capital, you see, I had an extraordinary, sacred dream. You were on pilgrimage to Iwashimizu, dressed in pilgrim white and a tall *eboshi* hat, and I was with you. You, however, were in the main hall of the sanctuary, whereas I was below on the ground, at the foot of the sacred fence. A celestial youth in his twelfth or thirteenth year, carrying a bow and arrows, stood before you in the main hall. He said, 'I bring you the bow and quiver of Yoshitomo.' Then, from within the sanctuary itself, a mighty voice spoke, saying, 'Keep them stored safely here. Yoritomo shall have them from me in good time. For now, have Yoritomo swallow this.' The celestial youth went to the edge of the curtain and received from behind it something that he then placed before you. I saw that it was sixty-six thin strips of dried abalone.[87] The mighty voice then spoke again, saying, 'Eat, Yoritomo!' You then made three mouthfuls of the larger strips and tossed the smaller ones to me. I put them in the breast fold of my robe. I awoke to a mood of great elation. Reflecting upon what the dream might have meant, I concluded that Lord Yoshitomo, who had entrusted his bow and arrows to the security of Hachiman's sanctuary, might have suffered temporary destruction as an enemy of the court, but that your own future success was assured. The sixty-six strips of dried abalone, so it seemed to me, stood for the sixty-six provinces of Japan, which you were to hold in your grasp. That you had given me in my dream a few leftovers from them, and that I had placed them in the front fold of my robe, suggested to me that I, too, worthless though I may be, could look forward to a happy future."

To this speech Yoritomo made no reply. With a dazed air he said only, "Come, Moriyasu, stay with me at least as far as the Kagami post station."

Moriyasu replied, deeply moved, "Let my mother then suffer whatever fate awaits her. I shall be with you wherever you go."

"No," Yoritomo rejoined, "that cannot be. I deeply appreciate your devotion, but *I* would then be responsible for your mother's distress. By abandoning filial conduct you would offend the wishes of the buddhas and gods;

and if you were to do that, you would imperil the divine favor that I enjoy." He made sure that Moriyasu went no further.

Yoritomo passed the Fuwa barrier and went on to the Aohaka post station in Mino. He grieved as he rode by it, remembering that this was where his father, Yoshitomo, had beheaded Tomonaga. When he crossed the Kuize River—the one down which Genkō had steered his boat—the unknown boatmen riding its waters, and the very flow of the current, stirred nostalgic thoughts.

Upon reaching the Atsuta Shrine in Owari, he asked a local man, "Where is Noma, in the Utsumi district, where the late Lord Yoshitomo was struck down?"

"It is the mist-shrouded hill yonder, beyond the Narumi shore," the man replied, whereupon the tearful Yoritomo prayed in his heart, and no wonder: "Hail Great Bodhisattva Hachiman! Restore me to my rightful place in the world! Strike down Tadamune and Kagemune, and exhibit their remains to my father beneath the sod!"

Yoritomo's mother, a daughter of Suenori, the chief priest of the Atsuta Shrine, had borne three children: a girl and two boys. The girl, known as Bōmon-no-hime, had been adopted by Gotō Sanemoto and remained in the capital. As for the other boy, his maternal uncle Tomotada, the head of the Office of Carpentry, had seized him at Katsura, in Suruga, and delivered him to the Heike. Because it is not the practice to exile anyone lacking a name,[88] he was dubbed Mareyoshi and banished to Kira in the province of Tosa: hence "Kira no Kanja," the appellation by which he came to be known. So there was Mareyoshi in the south, in Tosa, while Yoritomo was in Izu, in the east. Separated by so great a distance, the brothers suffered from harsh karma indeed.

## 31. Kiyomori Renounces the World *and* He Visits the Nunobiki Waterfall *with* Akugenda Becomes a Thunderbolt

Now, Tameyoshi had been executed in Hōgen and Yoshitomo in Heiji; and the house of Taira had flourished exceedingly ever since. Kiyomori had risen to chancellor; his sons commanded in tandem the two corps of the Palace Guards; and his paternal relatives all rose in rank as they pleased, until more than sixty of them were senior nobles or privy gentlemen. In the 11th month of Nin'an 2 [1167], his fifty-first year, Kiyomori became ill, renounced the world, and took the religious name Jōkai. He built Sutra Island off the Hyōgo coast, thus facilitating shipping between the provinces, and at Fukuhara built himself a residence where he then spent most of his time.[89]

One day Kiyomori set out with several dozen retainers and members of his house on an excursion up to the Nunobiki Waterfall.[90] Nanba no Saburō Tsunefusa stayed at home, claiming that a bad dream had warned him against going. The others laughed. "For shame," they said, "that a man who wields bow and arrow should heed dreams and omens!" Perhaps he came to agree, because he eventually joined them, late.

They saw the waterfall and were at the foot of the hills, on their way back, when a fierce wind suddenly blew, clouds covered the sky, lightning flashed repeatedly, and thunder roared aloft. Tsunefusa paled and said to a man nearby, "This is exactly what I dreamed. At his execution Akugenda promised, with terrifyingly dark looks that I will never forget, to return as a thunderbolt and kill me. That must be why I dreamed of him last night. In my dream people were watching a shining object the size of a *kemari* ball fly off toward the southeast, and I recognized the spirit of Akugenda. It then turned back, and I felt sure that I was about to be killed. Thunderbolt he may be, but as long as there is life in me, he will feel the edge of my sword! Bear witness for me when I am gone!"

With this, Tsunefusa drew his sword. Sure enough, a black cloud came down over him with a crash of thunder. It seemed to threaten Kiyomori, too; but Kiyomori had with him, in a brocade bag hung around his neck, a copy of the *Rishu-kyō* copied with five brushes by Kōbō Daishi.[91] He waved it about, and the thundercloud lifted. The men then saw Tsunefusa lying there, dead, his body slashed to shreds. The sight was unbearable. His sword was shattered right up to the hilt. Kiyomori might well have died, too, if he had not been wearing the sutra copied by Kōbō Daishi.

Of old Kitano no Tenjin,[92] enraged by his exile, loosed a thunderbolt that killed the left minister Fujiwara no Tokihira. In that case, a deity manifested himself in our world to demonstrate a way of government that sweeps aside the slanderous official and rewards the loyal one. In Akugenda's case, a defeated commander's rage over being executed in broad daylight turned him into a thunderbolt that killed Tsunefusa. "What kind of a man does it take," people wondered in terror, "to vent his wrath even after death?"

## 32. Ushiwaka Goes Down to the North

Lord Kiyomori had a room prettily done up, installed Tokiwa in it, and visited her there often. From ancient times to this very day, they say, wise emperors and fierce warriors have frequently gone astray on the path of love, neglected matters of government, and ignored all advice. "Far better, then, never to taste the love of a beautiful woman": so wrote Bo Juyi, and rightly.

Tokiwa's three sons grew as the years went by. Imawaka, the eldest, studied at Daigoji and became a monk there under the religious name Zensai. A prodigious fighter, he was known to one and all as Akuzenji.[93] Otowaka, the middle one, served the Hachijō Prince[94] as a lay acolyte named Ensai. Ushiwaka, the youngest, was on Kurama, in the lodge presided over by Zenrin-bō Ajari Kakujitsu, a disciple of Tōkō-bō Ajari Rennin.[95] He was known there as Shanaō.

In Shanaō's eleventh year, knowledge of the genealogies of the great houses and perusal of records pertaining to the various professions opened his eyes. "I see that I stand in the tenth generation from Emperor Seiwa [r. 858–876]," he said to himself, "and that my forebears left the court nine generations ago. I am in the eighth generation from Rokusonnō and in the fourth from Hachimantarō Yoshiie, a descendant of Tada no Mitsunaka and the youngest son of Yoriyoshi. My grandfather was Tameyoshi, and I am the last son of Yoshitomo. Yoriyoshi, then the governor of Sagami, warred for nine years in Mutsu against Sadatō and Munetō. When final success eluded him, Yoshiie went down to Mutsu, won the Later Three Years War, and was appointed to govern Dewa. When I grow up, I will do the same and finish what my father, Yoshitomo, set out to achieve."

Shanaō asked Zenrin-bō, the senior resident of his lodge, to give him a sword like Bishamon's.[96] "I cannot do that," Zenrin-bō replied. "Bishamon's sword has long been his great treasure. There would be trouble if the abbot and the monks at large ever heard that I had done so."

Shanaō did not ask again. Instead he recruited the acolyte from the neighboring lodge to go with him again and again to places where the local youth gathered; and there, with short sword and dagger, he practiced attack and pursuit. At pursuit and flight he was very quick, leaping unerringly over earthen walls and board fences. Sōjō-ga-tani[97] was said to harbor tengu and ghosts, but he fearlessly went through it every night to Kibune. "This is no ordinary young fellow," the astonished temple priests assured one another.

Having attracted Kiyomori's attention, Tokiwa bore him a daughter. After he had lost interest in her, the daughter married Fujiwara no Naganari, the lord of the Treasury, and apparently gave him many children.[98] As for Shanaō, his teachers urged him to become a monk as soon as possible, but he insisted on first consulting his exiled brother, Yoritomo. "If *he* tells me to shave my head, I will," he said. If he says no, then no. Apart from that, I cannot think well of my two elder brothers for having become monks, and I have no intention of doing so myself. I will run through anyone who tries to force me into it."

"The fellow looks as though he really means it! Better stay away from him!" the monks murmured among themselves. Rennin and Zenrin-bō, Shanaō's senior and junior teachers, put up a pretense of disapproving, but they understood his feelings well enough and privately felt compassion for him.

In those days a merchant who traded in gold with the north often came on pilgrimage to Kurama, and his guide there was Zenrin-bō, the senior resident of Shanaō's lodge. Shanaō approached him. "Take me down with you to the north," he said. "I will ask a great man I know there, on your behalf, for twenty or thirty gold *ryō*." The merchant agreed to take him.

There was also, among the warriors from the east, one known as Shigeyori, the deputy director of Imperial Tombs. This man was another Kurama pilgrim. Shanaō approached him, too, and asked him where he was from.

"From Shimōsa," the man replied.

"Who is your father? What is your house? What is your name?"

"My father is Fukasu no Saburō Mitsushige, and I, all unworthy, am Shigeyori, the deputy director of Imperial Tombs. I am of the Genji."

"Then you are the man for me," Shanaō declared. "Who is your patron?"

"I am a close associate of Lord Yorimasa, the head of the Armory."

"I have my reasons for questioning you in this way," Shanaō continued. "You see, I am the youngest son of Lord Yoshitomo, who initiated the Heiji conflict and then was killed. My mother, Tokiwa, a maid in the service of Kujō-in, had three sons. My two older brothers have become monks, but not I, not Shanaō. No, I prefer to become a man. What worries me is what the Heike may think when I do. So take me away from the capital with you. We will have a good time shooting game."

Shigeyori replied, "If I did that, the monks here would accuse me of having abducted their acolyte."[99]

"But who would have anything more to say if I just died? Just think who I am! The rest should be easy." By now there were tears in his eyes.

"Very well," said Shigeyori.

Shanaō was in his sixteenth year when he left Kurama, at dawn on the 3rd of the 3rd month of Shōan 4 [1174]. Fearing how the world might interpret his departure, he claimed that a certain acolyte had it in for him; but such in fact was his nature that everyone at his lodge, monk or acolyte, was sorry to see him go.

Late that night, at the Kagami post station, he bound up his hair, thrust into his sash the dagger that he kept ready for when he could assume the role of a warrior, and took out the *eboshi* hat that he had affected in the past only in jest.

Shigeyori asked when they set out the next morning, "So you have come of age? What sponsor placed the *eboshi* on your head?"

"I did it myself."

"Then what is your name?"

"Genkurō Yoshitsune. I must have a bow and arrows."

"Very well," Shigeyori replied. He gave Yoshitsune a quiverful of arrows and a bow. Quiver at his hip and bow in hand, Yoshitsune rode on as he pleased, since Shigenori had given him free use of his mount. Wherever the footing was good he practiced galloping and shooting. And so they continued their journey toward the north.

They came to the Kisegawa post station in Suruga. Yoshitsune suggested that they go to Hōjō.[100]

"My father met Yoritomo," Shigeyori answered, "but not I, not yet. Let us first settle down in my home province and then contact him by letter." Yoshitsune agreed, and they passed on by. Shigeyori then wrote Yoritomo that he had Yoshitsune with him in Shimōsa. Yoritomo's reply urged him to look after Yoshitsune well.

Yoshitsune had spent a year or so hunting when the local men set out to capture a horse thief. The man was six feet tall, however, and from behind a large tree he defended himself so fiercely, his dagger drawn, that no one dared to approach him. Yoshitsune stole up beside him and kicked the blade out of his hand. It hit the ground with a clang. He then gripped the waistband of the man's *hakama*, lifted him up, dealt him a hard blow, and took him prisoner.

Another time, six robbers broke into a peasant's house near Shigeyori's. Armed only with a sword, Yoshitsune charged in among them, killed four, badly wounded two, and emerged from the fray without a scratch on him. News of this exploit spread through the province. "I just hope that the Heike never learn of it," the worried Shigeyori remarked.

In due course Yoshitsune met Yoritomo. "I am an adult now," he said, "and everyone in this and the neighboring provinces says that there will be trouble if the Heike hear about me. For me, the consequences hardly matter, but they could be damaging for *you*. I would rather go on to a province where no one knows me and keep an eye on the situation from there."

Yoritomo replied, "In Mutsu there is a woman whom I hold in high regard. You must go to her. Her father was Ōkubo Tarō, of Kōzuke. She was in her thirteenth year when he went on pilgrimage to Kumano and called upon Lord Yoshitomo. He told Yoshitomo that Yoritomo, among all possible candidates, was the one whom he would most gladly make his heir, and he respectfully requested Yoshitomo's approval. The girl declared after her father's death that she might as well marry a nobody, and she refused. 'No,' she said, 'I will marry Fujiwara no Hidehira, in the north.' One night she was on her way to Hidehira when Shinobu no Kotayū, one of Hidehira's retainers, waylaid her, married her, and had two children by her. She brought up both after his death, after receiving her widow's portion and his house. She is not poor. Go and find her. I will give you a letter for her."

Yoshitsune took the letter, went down to Mutsu, and delivered it. That night the lady (now a nun) received him and reminisced about Yoritomo as a boy. "To the girl I was then, the late Lord Yoshitomo, too, seemed very impressive," she said. "You do not quite measure up to either of them, but I am prepared to believe that you are Yoshitomo's son. You *are* Yoritomo's younger brother, are you not?"

"Yes, I am," Yoshitsune replied.

"I have two sons," the lady went on. "They are Satō Saburō Tsuginobu and Satō Shirō Tadanobu.[101] Tsuginobu is a great drinker and a rough character. When drunk, he has no notion of right or wrong. Tadanobu, his younger brother, is very serious and drinks little."

She called in Tadanobu. "This is a younger brother of Lord Yoritomo, who is now in Izu," she said. "Please see that he enjoys every attention." Tadanobu agreed to do so.

Yoshitsune went on to Taga, the Mutsu provincial capital, and found there the gold merchant whom he had met at Kurama. He said to the merchant,

"You can turn up, unannounced, anywhere you like. Nobody cares. Take me to see Hidehira."

So he crossed over to Hiraizumi. There he approached Hidehira through a gentlewoman who patronized this merchant particularly, buying bath robes,[102] incense, and so on from him whenever he came down from the capital. Hidehira received him.

"Who are you?" Hidehira asked.

"I am the youngest son of Lord Yoshitomo, who died in the Heiji conflict."

"So you must be that extravagant fellow who simply declared himself of age and announced his name as Genkurō Yoshitsune. There will be unfortunate talk if I take you in myself—talk that will do you no good, either. In Dewa and Mutsu I do as I please, aside from whatever the provincial governor and his deputy may be up to, so stay a while and seek any patron you like. You are a presentable young man—someone is bound to want you for a son-in-law; or somebody without a son will want to adopt you. I say this for your own good, because I understand what you have in mind. And what I say is strictly between you and me. Breathe no word of it to anyone, not even to a member of my household."

Yoshitsune was greatly reassured. "I apologize for making so abrupt a request," he said, "but I would like to give something to the gold merchant who has been assisting me."

"Of course," Hidehira replied. He gave Yoshitsune thirty *ryō* of gold dust.

Yoshitsune then went on to Shinobu.[103] From there he frequently visited the Kanto, where he approached the Chichibu, the Ashikaga, the Miura, the Kamakura, the Oyama, the Naganuma, the Take, and the Yoshida, staying ten days here and five days there.[104] Whenever he noted a large property owner he would say to himself, "I'd like to finish off that fellow, take his property, and gain more strength to achieve my goal." He would say to himself whenever he noted a particularly valiant warrior, "Ah, I'd like to get that fellow to rebel with me!"

He was spending a night at Matsuida in Kōzuke, in a household of no great standing, and he said to himself when he met his host, "I like the looks of this man. He has courage. I'll get him to be my standard-bearer when I attack the Heike." So he asked to stay longer.

"You young, barefoot wanderer," the man answered, "you don't look to me like just anyone. No, you must be a gambler or a thief, or perhaps you've come to murder me." He sent Yoshitsune away.

## 33. Yoritomo Raises Righteous Forces[105] *and* He Crushes the Heike

On the 17th of the 8th month of Jishō 4 [1180], seven years after Yoshitsune's departure from the capital, Yoritomo killed Kanetaka, the acting governor of Izu, in a night attack. Defeats at Ishibashiyama, Kotsubo, and Kinugasa followed. He then moved on to Awa and Kazusa, where Kazusa-no-suke Hirotsune joined him with all his men. Passing on to Shimōsa, Yoritomo also gathered that deputy governor, Tsunetane, to his forces and entered Musashi, where every single warrior declared allegiance to him.

When this news reached the capital, Akuzenji at Daigoji and Ensai at Hachijō clapped *oi*[106] on their backs and raced down to the east before the barriers should close. Their flight provoked the Heike to order Hasuike Iemitsu, of Tosa, to execute Mareyoshi, who was in exile there. Iemitsu told Mareyoshi, "Lord Yoritomo has raised rebellion in Izu, and the Heike therefore command me to execute you."

"Thank you for letting me know," Mareyoshi replied. "I read the Lotus Sutra daily for my father, but I have not yet done so today. Please give me a little more time." He went into his private chapel, quietly read the Lotus Sutra, slit his belly, and died.

Yoshitsune sought out Hidehira at Hiraizumi and sent in this message to him, "I have had news of Yoritomo's rebellion. I wish to bid you farewell and start for the Kanto."

Hidehira received him. "You will need these things," he said. He gave Yoshitsune a dark blue *hitatare*, armor with scarlet lacing darker in hue toward the bottom, and a gold-fitted sword. "I have plenty of horses and saddles," he added. "Take any you please." Yoshitsune chose the fourteen-hand Karasuguro ["Crow Black"] from among twelve presented to him, placed a gold-trimmed saddle on the horse's back, and mounted it. Satō Tsuginobu stayed behind in order, he said, to look after certain affairs both personal and official. Tadanobu rode with Yoshitsune. The Shirakawa barrier was guarded, but they passed through it safely by claiming that they were on their way to take the waters at the Nasu hot spring.

The gold merchant had started as a junior member of a courtier household, but then poverty had forced him to take up his present trade. Now he joined Yoshitsune's company and was made a warrior dubbed Kubo Yatarō.

Ise no Saburō, Yoshitsune's host at Matsuida, was originally from Ise. His household was wealthy. It was fear of the possible consequences that had made him turn Yoshitsune out, when Yoshitsune asked to stay longer with him. Yoshitsune said this time, upon arrival at Ise no Saburō's house, "You cannot have known who I was when I came here a few years ago. I am Genkurō Yoshitsune, a younger brother of Lord Yoritomo."

"I *thought* there was something about you," Ise no Saburō replied, "and I was right! I will join you." And he did.

Yoritomo was camped at Ōbano in Sagami with over a hundred thousand horse when Yoshitsune arrived with his eight hundred, white banners flying. "Who are *you*?" Yoritomo demanded to know. I do not recognize that brocade *hitatare*, nor have I ever seen white banners flown that way."

"I am Genkurō Yoshitsune!" the new arrival announced.

"You are so much older than when I last saw you!" Past memories returned to Yoritomo, and his eyes filled with tears. They say that he continued, "When Hachimantarō Yoshiie fought the Later Three Years War, Yoshimitsu, his younger brother, who was then an official in the Bureau of Justice, resigned his post, left his bowstring bag at the Palace Guards headquarters, and raced to the Kanazawa fortress in Mutsu. Yoshiie remarked, 'It is as though the late Lord Yoriie had returned to life,' and he moistened his armor sleeves with tears. I feel as though I were reliving my ancestor's past."

The Ichijō, Takeda, and Ogasawara[107] charged forth from the province of Kai and set out for Suruga to kill Hiromasa, the acting governor there. Hiromasa had few men of his own, and more than a thousand mounted warriors loyal to the Heike rushed to his aid. The Genji from Kai split their three thousand into three corps and surrounded them. Hiromasa was killed.

This news moved the Heike to dispatch an imperial army of over fifty thousand men under the command of Taira no Koremori. It camped at Kanbara, on the Fuji River. Yoritomo crossed over Ashigara and Hakone with over twenty thousand men and established his camp on the Kisegawa in Suruga. The night before the battle was to begin, the Heike mistook the noise of waterbird wings, rising from a marsh beside the river, for battle cries. They fled back toward the capital without shooting a single arrow.[108]

In the 3rd month of Yōwa 1 [1181] the Heike rushed to the Sunomata River in Mino. Although appointed head of the Genji in a decree from Prince Mochihito, Jūrō Kurando Yukiie had been robbed of authority by his two nephews, Yoritomo and Kiso Yoshinaka, and had stationed himself on the east bank of the Sunomata River[109] with only five hundred horse. Ensai said to him, "Life being so fragile, I may miss better rebirth in my next if I die tonight without attacking the Heike, my father's enemy, there across the river. So farewell." He and his fifty followers charged across the river and into the enemy camp. The Heike commanders were Shigehira and Noritsune. Surrounded by their men, Ensai was killed.

On the 25th of the 7th month of Juei 2 [1183] Kiso Yoshinaka burst into the capital, and the Heike fled. Taira no Yorimori received from Yoritomo a written, confidential oath stating, "The son of Lady Ike is to stay. I feel as though the late Lady Ike herself were before me."[110] Yorimori therefore stayed behind. Not only did he lose none of his original property, but he was actually granted more.

Osada no Shōji Tadamune and his son Kagemune did not join the Heike, but in time the wrath of heaven seems to have struck them for killing their hereditary lord. First, they raced with fifty men to Kamakura, where Yoritomo welcomed them and entrusted them to Doi no Jirō. Yoritomo then sent his brothers Noriyori and Yoshitsune up to the capital, to suppress Kiso Yoshinaka. This they did, then triumphed at Ichi-no-tani. Each time a messenger brought him a battle report from them, he asked, "And the Osadas—how did they fight?"

This was the answer: "Osada Tadamune is a superb fighter, and he performed wonders in both places." Yoritomo then ordered that neither father nor son be allowed to fight again. After the Heike were annihilated at Dan-no-ura, Osada presented himself at Kamakura. Yoritomo informed him that he had given certain instructions to Naritsuna[111] and ordered him to return in haste to his home province, where he was to pray for his late lord's enlightenment in the life to come.

Osada gladly set out to do so and was feeling quite safe when Nomi no Kojirō swept down on him and his son, seized them, and crucified them.[112] Nor was this done in any ordinary way. Their hands and feet were nailed with huge nails to boards laid before Yoshitomo's grave; the nails were torn from their fingers and toes; the skin was stripped from their cheeks; and four or five days later they were beaten to death. Perhaps they had imagined that assassinating their hereditary lord would assure their descendants prosperity, but they suffered in this very life the karmic reward for their crime, made their infamy known to all, and exposed their shame.

Lady Ike's man, Tanba Tōzō, went to Kamakura and presented himself unannounced from the open space before Yoritomo's residence. "I am Yorikane, who once served Lady Ike," he announced.

"Tōzō from Tanba, is it?" Yoritomo replied.

"Yes, sir."

"You are very welcome. I had been thinking of calling upon *you*." He invited Yorikane up into his guards' office.

"This man," Yoritomo explained to his men, "once showed me, in a manner that I will never forget, good will that far surpassed what I deserved; and he was also in the service of Lady Ike. For both reasons he is my honored guest. I wish him to have a gift." Those close to him brought forth from his storehouse armfuls of leopard skins, tiger skins, eagle feathers, hawk feathers, silk, and *kosode* robes, and piled them so high before and behind Yorikane that they hid him completely.

"Have you no formal request?" Yoritomo asked.

"The village of Hosono, in Tango, has belonged to my family for generations," Yorikane answered, "but powerful interests have taken it from me."

"A word on this subject to the retired emperor should settle the matter," said Yoritomo, and he issued the appropriate document. He then ordered that his gifts to Yorikane be conveyed for him, post station to post station, all the way to the capital.

Kajiwara's slander destroyed the relationship between Yoshitsune and Yoritomo. Yoshitsune went down to Mutsu and for years took refuge with Hidehira. After Hidehira's death, Yoritomo tricked his son, Yasuhira, and had Yoshitsune killed. Then he destroyed Yasuhira himself.[113] Thereafter he controlled all of Japan.

Yoritomo said to Chikayoshi when he entered Taga, the provincial capital, "There are two men in Japan who are always on my mind. The first is that grand counselor, Lady Ike's son, whose head I left on his shoulders. I would like to do more for him. The second is Kōketsu Gengo Moriyasu, to whom I have not yet shown sufficient gratitude."

Chikayoshi replied, "Moriyasu is an expert *sugoroku* player, and he is often called to the retired emperor's residence." Yoritomo concluded that he could not summon him on his own and refrained from doing so. Chikayoshi then seized an opportunity to let Go-Shirakawa know that Yoritomo wished to see Moriyasu. Go-Shirakawa allowed Moriyasu to go, but Moriyasu was too immersed day and night in *sugoroku* ever to do so.

Yoritomo first entered the capital on the 7th of the 11th month of Kenkyū 1 [1190]. On the way he stopped at Sen-no-matsubara in the province of Ōmi. There, an emaciated old couple forced their way to him through the crowd. Yoritomo's men demanded to know who they were and charged them with making a nuisance of themselves.

"We have every right to appear before Lord Yoritomo," they replied; and so they did.

"Who are you?" Yoritomo asked.

"Many years ago, sir, you stayed with us at Azai-no-kitagōri. We are still alive, and we came to pay our respects when we heard that you were on your way up to the capital."

"Too much has happened since then," Yoritomo replied, "and I have forgotten you, but you are welcome nonetheless. What are you carrying?"

"The *doburoku* that you drank then, sir."[114] They presented him with two earthenware jars.

Smiling, Yoritomo ignored the copious food and drink already before him to take three drinks of their *doburoku*. "You had a son," he said. "Bring him to me. I would like to do something for him."

"We have brought him with us," they said and had their son come forward. Yoritomo took him into his service under the name Ōmi no Kanja, known later as Adachi no Shinzaburō Kiyotsune. He also gave the old couple two white horses, saddled, and two chests filled with silk and *kosode* robes.

On arrival in the capital Yoritomo went to call on Retired Emperor Go-Shirakawa. His Eminence recalled with emotion the long-ago days when Yoritomo had been in service there. He then called for the sword Higekiri, which was placed before him in a brocade bag. "I gather that this sword is a great Genji treasure," he said. "Kiyomori treated it as a protective talisman while he had it in his possession, and he never allowed it out of his residence. No doubt it will mean a great deal to you, since your house so values it." He presented the sword to Yoritomo.

Yoritomo prostrated himself three times before the sovereign, received the sword, and withdrew. He then summoned Moriyasu, to whom he gave an abundance of horses, arms and armor, silk, and *kosode* robes. Yoritomo bestowed no land upon Moriyasu because he had never come to Kamakura.

On the 13th of the 3rd month of Kenkyū 3 [1192], Go-Shirakawa passed away. Only then did Moriyasu go to Kamakura. Yoritomo said to him, "If you had come earlier, I would have arranged for you to have a province and estates, but it is too late for that now. Take up a new life, then, as soon as a vacancy turns up. The place may be small, though." Yoritomo gave Moriyasu half of the Taki estate in Mino.

Moriyasu had married the widow of Genkō, of Washi-no-su, who had died in battle when Yoshitomo was killed at Noma in Owari. He married her a year or two after that. Since the couple were both in his service, Yoritomo gave them Ue-no-nakamura in the province of Mino. In the 12th month of Kenkyū 9 [1198] he went there and summoned Moriyasu. "Come to me next year, after the 15th of the 1st month," he said. "The whole of the Taki estate will then be yours."

On the 15th of the 1st month of Shōji 1 [1199] Yoritomo died, and Moriyasu never received this land. He said, "I once dreamed that the late Lord Yoritomo held the world in his hands." Chikayoshi remarked, "You would have had your grant of land if only you had eaten the abalone that he gave you in your dream; but you never did, since you put it instead in the front fold of your robe." Moriyasu was too embarrassed to say a word in reply.

When Yoshitsune was in his second year, Lord Kiyomori spared him because he was then still a babe in arms. Kiyomori never imagined him in time destroying the Taira house. Now, because of Yoshitsune, Kiyomori's whole line had perished. The orphan of Zhao hid under his mother's skirts and did not cry. Ison of Qin grew to adulthood in a jar. So it is with those whose lines are destined to endure.[115]

# An Account of the Jōkyū Years

# Summary and Note on the Text

YORITOMO'S LINE as shogun in Kamakura soon died out. Neither of his sons ever actually governed, and both were assassinated—the last one, Sanetomo, in 1219. Thereafter, boys from the high Kyoto nobility were brought in as mere figureheads. After Yoritomo, real authority in Kamakura belonged to Hōjō Tokimasa (1138–1215), the father of Yoritomo's formidable wife Masako (1157–1225). Tokimasa and his successors bore the title *shikken* ("adjutant"). In collaboration with Masako, Tokimasa's second son Yoshitoki (1163–1224) further consolidated the Kamakura regime; but he also aspired to govern Japan.

## Book 1

Yoshitoki continues to profit from land that Retired Emperor Go-Toba (1180–1239, r. 1183–1198) had given to Kamegiku, his favorite mistress. Go-Toba demands that this arrangement cease. When Yoshitoki refuses, Go-Toba's gentlewoman Kyō-no-nii urges chastising him. This disagreement leads to the Jōkyū conflict.

Ordered by Go-Toba to plan an attack, Fujiwara no Hideyasu approaches the powerful Kanto warrior Miura Taneyoshi, then present in Kyoto. Taneyoshi, who has a grudge against the Hōjō, recruits his elder brother Yoshimura.

Go-Toba first assembles warriors for the alleged purpose of guarding a Buddhist observance. Yin-yang divination predicts an unfavorable outcome, but the decision is nonetheless reached to kill Iga Mitsusue, a Yoshitoki relative charged with protecting the capital. Sasaki Hirotsuna, another relative of Mitsusue, invites him to his house, entertains him, and then joins the attackers. Mitsusue sets fire to his house and dies fighting.

Before dying, Mitsusue sends Kamakura an urgent message, while Taneyoshi sends another to Yoshimura. Kamakura receives from Go-Toba a decree (*inzen*) demanding Yoshitoki's death. Masako assembles key personnel, informs them, and requires them to declare their allegiance. All support Kamakura. Yoshimura sends Taneyoshi's messenger back without a reply and urges Yoshitoki to arrest Go-Toba's messenger. This is done.

A council of war decides to send 190,000 men against Kyoto from three directions: Tōkaidō, Tōsandō, and Hokurikudō. Yoshitoki sends Go-Toba a mocking reply.

## Book 2

Dismayed, Go-Toba likewise orders the forces under Hideyasu to be divided into three. He also prepares to defend Kyoto at Uji and Seta. However, he unwisely splits up an army of 120,000 horse to defend the city's many gates, and he rejects advice to counterattack forcefully. The killing of one Genban Tarō, who had escaped from Kamakura to join Go-Toba, sparks the outbreak of hostilities. Many on the Kyoto side mistake a flight of white cranes for white (Genji) banners and flee without a fight. Mineya Saburō, Minamoto Kakeru, and others fight well, but the Kyoto forces are defeated everywhere.

Go-Toba moves briefly to the foot of Hiei and then returns to the city. The defenders at Seta and Uji are overwhelmed. In the sixth month of 1221, Go-Toba commands Taneyoshi, poised to fight the deciding battle, to withdraw. Outraged, Taneyoshi takes his own life. The next day Hōjō Yasutoki (1183–1242), Yoshitoki's son, reaches Rokuhara and reports victory.

Yoshitoki orders the three retired emperors of the time into exile: Go-Toba to Oki, Tsuchimikado (1195–1231, r. 1198–1210) to Tosa on Shikoku, and Juntoku (1197–1242, r. 1210–1221) to Sado. Go-Toba renounces the world, as do his companions in exile. Go-Toba's two sons are exiled as well. Juntoku exchanges plaintive poems with the great Fujiwara lord Kujō Michiie. Nobles of all degrees who had joined Go-Toba are sent to Kamakura and murdered on the way. Most of the warriors who had fought for Kyoto, with their sons, are captured and killed. Go-Takakura (1179–1223), who had never actually reigned, ensures the continuity of the retired emperor's powers, and his son, Go-Horikawa (1212–1234, r. 1221–1232), assumes the throne.

## Note on the Text

Four versions of *Jōkyūki* survive. The first, the *Maeda-ke bon*, appears to be no earlier than 1274. The second, known as the *Rufu-bon*, is a version published in movable type about 1600. The third, entitled *Jōkyū no ikusa monogatari* (*Tale of the Jōkyū War*), seems to be the draft text for a now-lost picture scroll. These versions differ somewhat among themselves—some contain more material than others—but not radically so.

The fourth, the one translated here, is the *Jikyōji-bon*. Andō Tameakira (1659–1716), a scholar of Japanese literature, copied it in the winter of 1689 from a manuscript that he had found in a Kyoto bookshop. Tameakira is known especially for his *Shika shichiron* (*Seven Discourses on the Work of Murasaki Shikibu*, 1703), the first continuous essay (rather than footnote-like glosses on discrete items) ever written on *The Tale of Genji*.

The *Jikyōji-bon* text differs in many ways from the other three and shows signs of being older. For example, the passage on young Noritsugu, who died in 1240, ends with the assurance that he is still alive. However, the introductory section (here entitled "The Cosmic and Historical Background") is somewhat extravagant in character and could be later. It recalls the decorative passages found in the mid-fifteenth-century *Hōtoku-bon* text of *Hōgen*.

*Jōkyūki* manuscripts have no subheadings, unlike *Hōgen*, *Heiji*, or *Heike*. The ones here have been added by the modern editors.

# Book 1

## 1. The Cosmic and Historical Background

The buddhas manifest themselves in sensible form to benefit sentient beings in the *sahā* world.[1] Seen in broad perspective, they do so without beginning and without end. There will never be a time when they are not manifest.

More particularly, we hear of a thousand buddhas manifest in the past, a thousand in the present, and a thousand in the future: hence three thousand in the Three Ages. The past kalpa is that of Splendor, the present one that of Wisdom, and the one to come that of Star-Dwelling. Each of the Three Ages includes twenty lesser eras of waxing and waning. A thousand buddhas manifested themselves during the waxings and wanings of the past kalpa; a thousand more have done so during those of the present kalpa; and so it will be also during the kalpa to come.[2]

Then when did the Buddha Shakyamuni come into the world? He first did so during the ninth waning era of the present kalpa, that of Wisdom, when he bore the name Kuruson. Humans then lived for forty thousand years. In the time of the Buddha Kunagonmuni humans lived for thirty thousand years, and in that of the Buddha Kashō for twenty thousand. Shakyamuni was then born as a bodhisattva into the inner sanctum of the Tosotsu Heaven; and today, when the human life span is a hundred years, he is present among us. He renounced the world in his nineteenth year and achieved enlightenment in his thirtieth. In his eighty-eighth he entered Nirvana and was laid to rest on the west bank of the Batsudai River, northwest of Kushina, the capital, in a coffin shining with a golden, compassionate light. Since then more than two thousand springs and autumns have passed like a dream, yet his teaching flourishes still. Those who master it, laymen and clerics alike, understand both past and future.

Now, we learn that there are sixteen major lands on the southern continent of Jambudvīpa, five hundred median lands, ten thousand minor lands, and infinite lands like scattered millet grains. However, we here set aside lands other than our own. The fortunate realms where the Buddha's Way and the Sovereign's Way[3] now prevail are Tenjiku [India], Shindan [China], Kikai [the Ryukyus?], Kōrai [Korea], Keitan [the region of the Khitans?], and our own land of Japan. In these the Buddha's Way has been known widely ever since the kalpa began.

Minshu founded the royal line in India. It is said that 84,210 kings reigned between him and Shakyamuni's father, King Jōbon. In China the first king was named Pan Gu. It is said that 86,242 sovereigns reigned between him and Emperor Ming of the Later Han.[4]

In Japan, seven generations of celestial gods reigned first, then five generations of earthly gods. The first of the celestial gods was Kunitokotachi, and the last, seven reigns later, were the pair Izanagi and Izanami. Their reign ended the age of the celestial gods. The first earthly god was Amaterasu Ōmikami, who is now our great deity. Five reigns followed, up to that of Fukiaezu-no-mikoto. The age of the earthly gods then ended. It had lasted twelve reigns.

After the gods came the one hundred human emperors. The first was Emperor Jinmu, the fourth son of Fukiaezu-no-mikoto. Eighty-five emperors reigned between then and Jōkyū 3 [1221]. During that time there were twelve instances of armed rebellion against the sovereign. The first occurred under Emperor Suizei, Emperor Jinmu's third son. One hundred and eighty thousand mounted warriors crossed the sea to subdue our realm. They made war here, but they lost and returned whence they had come.[5]

The ninth reign after Emperor Jinmu was that of Emperor Kaika. Emperor Kaika seized the throne from his elder brother and thereafter governed the realm.

The fourteenth sovereign was Emperor Chūai. Jingū Kōgō, his empress, reigned after his death. She was the first woman emperor.[6] Because Emperor Chūai had died by a foreign hand,[7] she conceived the wish to seize Kikai,

Kōrai, and Keitan (the Three Koreas) and have them serve her own country.[8] To that end she led 180,000 mounted warriors to Hakata in Kyushu, where she assembled her fleet.

As it happened, she was then pregnant. She was soon to give birth to a son when, in the 10th month, she addressed the child in her womb, saying: "If you have the fortunate destiny, once born, to occupy the throne, then delay your birth until this military campaign is over." The child accordingly did so. In the *kanoto-no-mi* year, on the 2nd of the 10th month, Jingū Kōgō subdued the Three Koreas, and she returned to Hakata on the 28th of the 11th month of that year. On the 5th of the next month her son was born. She retained perfect health and vigor into her seventieth year. She reigned for seventy years and passed away in her hundredth. Her son was therefore in his seventieth year when he assumed the throne, and he reigned forty-three years. He was Emperor Ōjin, now the Great Bodhisattva Hachiman.

The thirty-second sovereign was Emperor Yōmei [r. 585–587]. Yōmei's second son, Prince Shōtoku, and the minister Mononobe Moriya disagreed over whether to diffuse the Buddha's teaching throughout the land, and their disagreement turned in the end to war. Moriya was killed. Prince Shōtoku then built Shitennōji in Naniwa, as he had vowed to do if he won. Shitennōji was the first Buddhist temple in Japan.

The thirty-eighth sovereign, Emperor Saimei [r. 655–661], killed the heir apparent. After reigning once, he stole the throne to reign a second time.[9]

The forty-second sovereign was Emperor Montoku. An evil man, he killed his brothers and proclaimed the first year-period, Taihō [701–703].[10]

Next, during the [Tenpyō] Hōji era [757–765], Emperor Shōmu, Montoku's eldest son, clashed in battle with the prince, his younger brother.[11]

## 2. The Taira-Minamoto Conflict

Emperor Toba was the seventy-third sovereign. In retirement he deposed his eldest son, Emperor Sutoku, and placed Emperor Konoe, the son of his current empress, on the throne. Konoe passed away in his seventeenth year. Being Toba's favorite son and a younger brother of Sutoku did not save him. Sutoku assumed that the throne would now either return to him or go to Prince Shigehito, his eldest son. To his astonishment, the imperial dignity went instead to his younger half-brother, Emperor Go-Shirakawa. This was a bitter blow. Toba had wanted it so, however, and he could do nothing to change it. He strove to be patient until, all too soon, Toba passed away. Then, during the first forty-nine days after his father's death, he raised rebellion. There ensued a battle between the reigning emperor, Go-Shirakawa, and the retired, Sutoku. This incident, known as the Hōgen conflict, involved the first armed clash to take place in the capital. Sutoku lost and was banished to the province of Sanuki.

The eightieth human emperor was Takakura, Go-Shirakawa's third son. His empress, Tokuko, a daughter of Taira no Kiyomori, acquired the title Kenreimon-in. Her son became Emperor Antoku, who acceded to the throne in his third year. Kiyomori, Antoku's maternal grandfather, wielded supreme power in the realm, and no Genji dared to raise his head. However, his good fortune then came to an end. His eldest son, the palace minister Shigemori, died, and the evil of his ways grew daily. Meanwhile, on the strength of a decree issued by Go-Shirakawa,[12] Minamoto no Yoritomo drove up toward the capital from the eastern provinces, while Kiso Yoshinaka did so from the north. Soon the Heike fled. At last, in the 1st month of Genryaku 2 [1185], Yoritomo's younger brothers Noriyori and Yoshitsune defeated the Heike at Yashima in Sanuki. Late in the 2nd month, the entire house of Taira drowned at Dan-no-ura, and the Taira supreme commander, the former palace minister Munemori and his two sons, were captured with many others. All were executed, and soon the world belonged to the Genji. Yoritomo then built himself a residence in Kamakura[13] and came to be known as Kamakura-dono.

So it is that, between the ancient reign of Emperor Suizei and the recent one of Emperor Antoku, there have been twelve instances of armed disorder that involved the sovereign.

## 3. The End of Yoritomo's Line

Lord Yoritomo went up to the capital repeatedly, displayed his military prowess, and won such matchless merit that he was promoted to the senior second rank and appointed commander of the Right Palace Guards. His sway extended over the whole realm, from Kyushu and the two islands of Iki and Tsushima in the west to Tsugaru and the Ebisu island in the east. His glory illumined all within the four seas.

Late in the 12th month of Kenkyū 9 [1198] he attended a dedication ceremony for a new bridge over the Sagami River. On his way back a water spirit possessed him. He became extremely ill and lay bedridden for half a month until the last of his strength left him. Visibly at death's door,[14] he said to his wife, Hōjō Masako, who was at his bedside, "I have been declining for half a month. Many years have passed since we married, and now the hour of my death approaches." He then summoned his eldest son, Yoriie,[15] and said to him, "My life is over. Take good care of Senman[16] after I am gone. The local lords and powerful landowners of the eight provinces of the Kanto must not foment plots against you. You and Hatakeyama[17] must keep the peace in this land of Japan." Alas, these were his final words.

Yoriie did not yet grasp what his position required of him. Despite widespread criticism, he ignored his father's last injunction and sought support instead from Kajiwara Kagetoki.[18] In his sixteenth year he was appointed intendant of the Left Gate Watch, and for six years the world was his.[19] However, there was nothing filial about his conduct. Intoxicated with his own glory, he made no effort to govern and ignored all advice from his mother and his uncle, Hōjō Yoshitoki. In the end, he was murdered in his bath at Shūzenji, in the province of Izu, on the 28th of the 7th month of Genkyū 1 [1204].

Perhaps his younger brother, Senman, enjoyed better karma. Senman came of age in his thirteenth year and received the name Sanetomo. He rose rapidly from the fourth to the third rank and from the post of captain in the Palace Guards to right minister. His virtue spread over the four seas, and his glory illumined the seven circuits of the land.

An imperial envoy came down from the capital on the 20th of the 1st month of Kenpō 7 [1219] to attend the banquet of thanks for Sanetomo's ministerial appointment. The banquet was held at the Tsurugaoka Hachiman Shrine in Kamakura; and there Akuzenji, the shrine's chief administrator and a son of Yoriie, Sanetomo's elder brother, assassinated him. Yes, one's karmic recompense in the Triple World is like a lamp flame in the wind; one's fated life is like a dream one night in spring. It exactly resembles the morning glory withered before the sun is high, the dewdrop trembling on the leaf, or the mayfly gone within a day.

At this point Hōjō Yoshitoki reflected, "The Genji are finished as protectors of the imperial court. Who, then, is to govern Japan? If I were to seize power over the realm, who would contest my having done so?"

In the summer of that year he sent Hōjō Tokifusa[20] up to the capital, to request from the emperor a figure suitable for appointment as shogun. On the 18th of the 6th month of Kenpō 7, the third son of the regent Kujō Michiie, and a maternal grandson of Saionji Kintsune, the commander of the Right Palace Guards, was sent down to Kamakura to ensure peace. The boy's childhood name was Mitora[21] because he had been born in the year, on the day, and at the hour of the tiger. Fujiwara no Sanemasa accompanied him as his adviser, and Hōjō Yoshitoki was named his protector. Since there was some doubt about the legitimacy of appointing as shogun a boy in only his second year, imperial rites for the first three days of the New Year were performed from the 18th to the 20th of that same 6th month. The new shōgun went on pilgrimage to the Seven Shrines and then resided in Kamakura.

## 4. Go-Toba Decides to Curb the Power of Kamakura

Retired Emperor Go-Toba now began to ponder the situation. As a reward for their triumph over the Heike, who had sown chaos in Japan, the Genji had been granted the right to appoint a steward to each estate.[22] Go-Toba therefore found it increasingly strange that it was Yoshitoki who governed as he pleased, despite having done nothing to deserve the privilege, and he feared that Yoshitoki might well ignore an imperial decree.

The world did not generally approve of Go-Toba's ways. From morning to evening he devoted himself not only to hunting small birds or racing horses, but also to swimming, acrobatics, sumō wrestling, archery, and, above all, the arts of war. He spent his time day and night readying weapons and planning an armed uprising. Irascible as he was, he visited instant, arbitrary punishment on anyone who crossed him. Whatever minister's or senior noble's home, or villa, struck his fancy, he had the place designated an imperial residence. There were six of these in the capital and many more in the countryside. Such was the scope of his amusements that he summoned *shirabyōshi* dancers from far and wide and favored them one after another. The way he invited them up into the headquarters of the Eight Bureaus, there to trample and soil the brocade cushions spread on the floor, suggested, to the observer's horror, the imminent collapse of the Sovereign's Way and of all imperial authority. He readily took over the hereditary property of senior nobles and privy gentlemen, appropriated shrine and temple paddy fields, merged ten holdings into five, and gave everything away to his *shirabyōshi* favorites. Perhaps it was the mounting distress of venerable shrine and temple priests, who had seen their institutional lands confiscated, that finally provoked Go-Toba to initiate the armed disturbance that led to his banishment. This was a terrible thing.

How did it all start? Apparently with a dancer named Kamegiku, who lived at the Sameushi and Nishi-no-tōin crossing. Go-Toba was so mad about her that he gave her father a post in the Bureau of Justice. Finding the compensation for the post insufficient, he then issued a decree granting Kamegiku, for as long as he himself should live, the more than three hundred *chō* of the Nagae estate in Settsu.[23] Kamegiku's father received this document, pressed it reverently to his forehead, and rushed down to the estate, where he announced that he was now in charge.

The Kamakura-appointed steward ignored him. "Lord Yoshitoki was granted this estate by the late Lord Yoritomo," he said, "and imperial decree or not, I will not have you claim it without a formal order ceding it to you and bearing Yoshitoki's seal." He sent the man away.

Kamegiku's father complained to Go-Toba, who was highly displeased. He summoned Fujiwara no Yoshimochi. "Go down to the Nagae estate," he commanded, "get rid of that steward, and deliver him to me." Yoshimochi hastened there and ordered the steward out, but the steward ignored him, too.

Yoshimochi returned to the capital and reported the outcome to Go-Toba. "If that is the way even the lowest of the low are talking," Go-Toba declared, "then naturally Yoshitoki would have only contempt for a retired emperor's decree."

When Go-Toba heard what Yoshitoki himself had to say on the subject, he issued another decree. It said, "Yoshitoki may well own a hundred or a thousand other estates, and if he does, he is welcome to them all. However, he is to give up the Nagae estate in Settsu."

Yoshitoki read it. "How can the retired emperor possibly issue such a decree?" he said. "Let him claim, if he wishes, a hundred or a thousand other estates. Nagae, however, was granted me in recognition of my services by the late Lord Yoritomo. He will have to execute me to get it." So it was that he rejected Go-Toba's decree for a third time.

This news naturally troubled Go-Toba more than ever. He called these senior nobles into council:

Konoe Motomichi
the regent Kujō Michiie
the Tokudaiji left minister Kintsugu
the Bōmon grand counselor Tadanobu
the Azechi counselor Mitsuchika
the Sasakino counselor Arimasa
the Naka-no-mikado counselor Muneyuki
the Kai consultant-captain Norimochi
the Ichijō consultant-captain Nobuyoshi
the prelate Gyōgo
the prelate Sonchō.

He then conveyed to them his dismay at Yoshitoki's repeated rejection of his command and asked them to consider carefully what action to take.

Lord Motomichi said, "Of old, the shogun Fujiwara no Toshihito was in his twenty-fifth year when he went down to the east, and there a devil got into him. He declared himself the greatest commander in all Japan and announced that he would attack Tang China. Daigen Myōō quelled and trampled him into submission, and he then entered the General's Barrow.[24] Toshihito is the last warrior from the capital I have ever heard of. Please, just persuade Yoshitoki to change his mind."

The gentlewoman Kyō-no-nii[25] now addressed the council from behind her blinds. She said, "Six provinces contributed to rebuilding the Great Hall of State:[26] Aki and Suō from the San'yōdō region, Tajima and Tango from the San'indō, and Echigo and Kaga from the Hokurikudō. The first four did so as a matter of provincial duty, in response to an order from Mitsuchika and Fujiwara no Hideyasu; but in Echigo and Kaga the stewards appointed by Kamakura apparently ignored the same order. Now, when you cut down a tree, you have to cut it *all* down, lest it regrow.[27] So cut down Yoshitoki, Your Eminence, and govern Japan as you see fit."

Retired Emperor Go-Toba demanded that Hideyasu be summoned. This was done. His formal order to Hideyasu said, "It is inadmissible that Yoshitoki should have ignored repeated imperial decrees. I have resolved to crush him. You will take whatever measures are required to achieve this end."

With profound respect Hideyasu replied, "Miura Taneyoshi, a younger brother of Miura Yoshimura,[28] the governor of Suruga, is currently in the capital. I will discuss the matter with him. We will easily dispose of Yoshitoki."

Hideyasu, the governor of Noto, lived just north of the storehouse compound of Kaya House. He invited Taneyoshi there, offered him wine and refreshments, and said, "Let us spend today drinking quietly together, you and I." Once both had relaxed he went on, "Now, Taneyoshi, why not give up Miura and Kamakura, come up to the capital, and serve Retired Emperor Go-Toba? You probably have some thoughts of your own on the subject. His Eminence, you see, is a very great sovereign, and I suspect that he has lately been pondering certain plans. You may be loyal to Kamakura, but will you not, nonetheless, follow this great lord? Come, Taneyoshi, what do you say?"

Taneyoshi replied, "An excellent idea, Hideyasu! To give up the Miura and Kamakura of my ancestors, to come up to the capital and serve Retired Emperor Go-Toba—why, that is just what I myself wish to do! You may wonder why. Well, do you know who my wife is? She is the daughter of the temple administrator Ichihō, a great figure in Kamakura. She came to serve the late Lord Yoriie's wife, who then gave birth to a son. Hōjō Tokimasa, the governor of Tōtōmi, killed Yoriie, and Yoshitoki, Tokimasa's son, killed the son. My wife wept day and night after we were married. It was pathetic. She would say, 'If I were a man, I would disappear far into the mountains and pray for him in the afterlife. Oh, if only I were not a woman!' Her tears were painful to see. The cosmos might be solid gold, and life would still be worth more. Yes, human life is priceless, but my own means nothing to me now that inexorable karma confronts me with this choice. I had already meant to come up to the capital, offer His Eminence my services, raise rebellion, loose a good arrow against Kamakura, and so console myself and my wife; but it is an honor indeed to receive an imperial order commanding me to do just that. Now I need only send a letter on the subject to Yoshimura, my elder brother. Disposing of Yoshitoki will then present no difficulty at all. This is what the letter will say:

> I intend to go up to the capital, raise rebellion in Retired Emperor Go-Toba's service, loose a good arrow against Kamakura, and never return there. Now, neither father nor son among the local lords and wealthy landowners of the eight provinces of the Kanto ever forgets the duty of arms he owes to Kamakura. Yoshitoki will therefore send a large force up to the capital. This force will surround the

> imperial palace with many circles of men and attack the rebels. For this reason you, my brother, must reach an agreement with Yoshitoki and, in his presence, behead the three children, in their ninth, seventh, and fifth years, that you have in Miura. Then you and Yoshitoki will be in perfect accord. You will stay behind when Yoshitoki's men go up to the capital, and you will then rouse the men of Miura to kill Yoshitoki. Once they have done so, you will no doubt have lost your children, but in exchange you and I will control all of Japan.

I need only send him that letter. He will then have no trouble disposing of Yoshitoki. There is no time to lose. You must quickly arrange to raise an army."

Hideyasu reported the plan to Go-Toba, who called it brilliant. He commanded Hideyasu to begin making the required arrangements.

Hideyasu published this announcement:

> "On the 28th of the coming 4th month a great ceremony is to be held at Jōnanji. You are to attend it in armor, to mount guard."
>
> Each of these gentlemen personally received Go-Toba's written command:
>
> Tadanobu
> Mitsuchika
> Arimasa
> Muneyuki
> Nobuyoshi
> Norimochi
> and the prelates Chōgon and Sonchō.
>
> A circular order conveyed his command to the following:
>
> Hideyasu, the governor of Noto
> Iwami-no-zenji
> Wakasa-no-zenji
> Ise-no-zenji
> Nagaie, the governor of Awa
> The governor of Shimotsuke
> The governor of Shimōsa
> The governor of Oki
> Sasaki Hirotsuna, the governor of Yamashiro
> Ōuchi Korenobu

Gotō Motokiyo
Ôe Yoshinori
Miura Taneyoshi
Fujiwara no Hidezumi
Kasuya Arinaga
Sasaki Takashige
Mano Munekage
Yata Tomonao
Ono Shigetoki
Heinaizaemon-no-jō
Fujiwara Yoshimochi
Kasuya Arihisa
Saitō Chikayori
Satsuma Saemon-no-jō
Adachihara Saemon-no-jō
Kumagae Saemon-no-jō
Shume no Saemon-no-jō
Miyazaki Sadanori
Tōta Saemon-no-jō
Taira no Arinori and his five sons
Nakatsukasa-no-nyūdō and his son.

The following were summoned from the provinces:

TANBA

Hegi no Gyōbu-no-jō
Tachi no Rokurō
Jō no Jirō
Ashida Tomoie
Kurimura Saemon-no-jō

TANGO

Tano Hyōe-no-jō

BOOK 1

TAJIMA

Asakura Nobutaka

HARIMA

Kusada Uma-no-jō

MINO

Yahi Hyōe-no-jō
Rokurōzaemon
Hachiya-no-nyūdō and his two sons
Tarumi Saemon-no-jō
Takakuwa
Kaiden no Tarō Shigekuni
Kakehashi
Ueda
Utsumi
Teramoto

OWARI

Yamada no Kojirō

MIKAWA

Suruga-no-nyūdō
Uma-no-suke
Mahira Shigezaemon-no-jō

SETTSU

Seki Masayasu
Watanabe Kakeru

KII

Tanabe no Hōin Kaijitsu
Tai Hyōe-no-jō

YAMATO

Uda Saemon-no-jō

ISE

Katō Kagenaga

IYO

Kōno Michinobu

ŌMI

The Sasaki League and Ōe Chikahiro, with one thousand horse.

JŌKYŪ 3, 4TH MONTH, 28TH DAY [1221]
SUBMITTED TO THEIR EMINENCES AND HIGHNESSES AT KAYA HOUSE

Senior Retired Emperor Go-Toba, Second Retired Emperor Tsuchimikado, Third Retired Emperor Juntoku, Prince Masanari, and Prince Yorihito[29] were all at Kaya House together. From that day on the warriors from the provinces were divided into distinct corps, and the gates on all four sides of the residence were secured.

Go-Toba had seven yin-yang masters divine the success or failure of the enterprise. They did so. The current heads of Abe no Seimei's line—Abe no Yasutada, the head of the Yin-Yang Bureau, and Abe no Yasumoto, the head of the Office of Music—reported: "The present outlook is poor. Success will be ensured if you set your plan aside for now, change the era name, and initiate your undertaking early in the 10th month."

Go-Toba was hesitating when Kyō-no-nii addressed him once more. "Your Eminence," she said, "A yin-yang master speaks only for a kami.[30]

Can Hōjō Yoshitoki's karma compare with the senior retired emperor's? Besides, once one person has heard such news as this, everyone soon knows it. It cannot possibly remain secret after being announced to a thousand warriors. Yoshitoki will only cause Your Eminence still worse trouble when the news reaches him. You must resolve to act without delay." Go-Toba therefore summoned Hideyasu and decreed that the police official Iga-no-hōgan Mitsusue, a relative of Yoshitoki, should forthwith be put to death.

## 5. The Attack on Mitsusue

The two great pillars of the realm were then Lord Motomichi, the Fugenji regent, and Lord Yorizane, the Nakayama chancellor. They remarked between themselves, "Alas, His Eminence has entered upon a rash undertaking. Yoshitoki has fought many battles since Yoritomo's time. He is a highly experienced warrior. This will not end well." Both foresaw the outcome, and neither joined in the court's further deliberations on the subject. Go-Toba, who knew their opinion, forbade that henceforth either should be informed or consulted.

After receiving Go-Toba's command, Hideyasu summoned Miura Taneyoshi to a council of war. "I have had from His Eminence an order to execute Iga-no-hōgan Mitsusue," he said. "But what day would be best? You grew up with him and must know him well. I want to understand better how to proceed."

Taneyoshi replied, "I appreciate your addressing me so frankly. The best day will be the 15th of the 5th month. Mitsusue is a warrior through and through, you see, mounted or on foot. He is a great fighter, peerless with his sword and very brave. No indiscriminate attack on him is likely to succeed. The better course would therefore be to have him summoned to His Eminence's residence and executed there, surrounded, in the open space before the house. If he ignores the summons, then luck will govern the success of any attack on him.

So the days passed, and the 14th of the month arrived. Sasaki Hirotsuna, the governor of Yamashiro, was the father-in-law of Mitsusue's son. He decided to let Mitsusue know of this plan when he heard of it. He invited Mitsusue to his house, offered him wine, and casually urged him to enjoy himself. Their meeting became quite relaxed. Hirotsuna had them served by a beautiful girl whose looks perfectly complemented the wine, and he pressed Mitsusue to drink again.

Mitsusue felt entirely at ease. "I gather that there have been many warriors in the capital lately," he said. "I wonder why. Last night I dreamed that three messengers came to me with an order from the police. They took my strung bow and cut its grip into seven pieces. I woke up so depressed that I will always remember your warm hospitality of today."

Hirotsuna reflected that, for a warrior, another's fate today may be his own tomorrow. He longed to tell Mitsusue what lay in store, but he knew all too well that the next day—the day of the execution—Go-Toba would learn that he had done so, realize that he had sided with Mitsusue, and demand his head. He decided nonetheless to let him know, but as though the matter did not necessarily concern him personally. He therefore said to Mitsusue, "I wonder what His Eminence has in mind. The capital is apparently in turmoil. The way the world is going these days, the turmoil may involve us or it may not. I will count on you if anything happens; and you, please count on me."

Sunset came, and Mitsusue returned home. There he called in the *shirabyōshi* dancer Kasuga no Kanaō and spent the night enjoying the pleasures that she and her companions offered.

The morning of the 15th arrived. Hideyasu summoned Mitsusue three times, in conformity with Go-Toba's decree. The summons struck Mitsusue as odd, and he did not hasten to respond. Instead he called in his foster brother, Jibu no Jirō Mitsutaka. He said, "I am summoned to the retired emperor's residence at the same time as turmoil reigns in the city. Apparently warriors from many provinces have entered the capital. Go to the palace and to the retired emperor's residence, and try from a safe distance to see what is going on."

Mitsutaka rushed to Kaya House. On the way, at the crossing of Sanjō and Higashi-no-tōin, he ran into the messenger bearing Go-Toba's decree, accompanied by a thousand mounted warriors. "What are all those men doing here?" he asked a local youth.

"Those? They are on their way to act on an imperial decree ordering the execution of Iga-no-hōgan Mitsusue."

Mitsutaka thought that he was dreaming. Astonished and greatly agitated, he raced back and called Mitsusue to the double doors into the guest wing of the house. "Why, you are under imperial ban!" he announced. "The thousand men charged by the retired emperor with executing you are even now on their way. They are nearly here. Never mind the decree, no matter which emperor it comes from, reigning or retired. At least shoot a good arrow back!"

Mitsusue remained calm. "Then whichever emperor it may be, just let him try to execute me," he said. "He will not find it easy. Now, I trust that no one will object if I let the ladies go before this messenger arrives." He told Mandokoro no Tarō to present them with their gifts.

Mandokoro no Tarō went inside, took out many things, and rewarded the entertainers amply. Mitsusue composed himself. "Let this wine remind you to pray for me after I am gone," he said, swallowing his tears. He started two parting cups going round, to his right and to his left. Then he sent the entertainers on their way.

To Mandokoro no Tarō he said again, "Imperial decree or not, I will loose a good arrow before I die. How many battle-ready men do I have here at the moment?"

Mandokoro no Tarō replied, "You have:

Jibu no Jirō Mitsutaka
Ōtsu Uma-no-jō
Satsuma no Ukon
Nieda no Saburō and his two sons
Ikara no Musha and his two sons
Ōma Tarō
Yosaburō
Katagiri Genda Nagayori
Enpeiji
Yajirō
Yamamura no Saburō
Kawachi no Tarō
Koyama Kotayū no Jirō
Ikenobe no Tarō
Seza no Shichirō
Kakihara
Ōi Matajirō
Kumaō,

for a total of eighty-five mounted men."

Mitsusue addressed these housemen and retainers as follows: "Whatever the threat, I do not doubt that with your support I could break through the attackers and escape to Kamakura. However, I would be shamed before Yoshitoki if he were to feel that merely in order to live a little longer I had ignored a messenger bearing an imperial command, and that by fleeing to Kamakura I had sullied the arms of the great lords and wealthy landowners of the eight provinces of the east. So I will *not* flee to Kamakura. No, I will fight until I am the only one left alive, and then I will die fighting. Those of you who acknowledge all that I have done for you over the years, stay with me to the last and come with me over the Mountain of Death. But let those who do not prize a fair name, those who prefer to live, escape now. Let them go anywhere they please, before the fighting begins. No one will hold it against them.

Who were they, then, who, ordinarily so anxious to please their lord, took him at his word and fled? The first were Ōtsu Uma-no-jō and Satsuma no Ukon; then others followed, one by one, until only twenty-nine remained. None of these, either, looked any too sure that they really wished to stay. Mitsutaka therefore hastened to lock the compound gates and said, "Listen to me, all of you! Many, once so eager to please their lord when he stood high in the world and to enjoy his favor, have now treacherously fled. If anyone among the few left is still thinking of flight, he will have to soar into the sky or smash his way through the earth. I have locked the gates! In any case, no one still meaning to flee would escape the enemy's notice, since he is almost upon us. No, let us resist fiercely here in our lord's compound and die fighting!" His speech settled the twenty-nine men's resolve.

Mandokoro no Tarō brought out a ranking commander's set of armor, profusely decorated with butterflies and chrysanthemums, and gave it to Mitsusue. Mitsusue said, "Would fighting in armor help me to win? My men are few and the attackers many. No, I will engage them without armor, loose a good arrow against them, and die: it is for *that* that my name will live on." He drew his silver-trimmed dagger and cut every cord that bound the parts of the armor together.[31] "This armor is an heirloom in my line," he said, "and I had always meant to die with it; but I have dismantled it because the enemy might get their hands on it after my death. It would be too galling to have them oohing and ahing over it." He tossed it into the mud.

From this gesture Mitsutaka gathered the strength of Mitsusue's resolve. He said, "Twenty-nine men seem to have stayed after the others fled. That makes thirty-one, including you, their commander, and your son. With this force you must break through the attackers, barricade yourself in the grounds of Kaya House, secure the compound's four gates, and fight to the death. If you are defeated, then slip between the blinds into the house, go to the retired emperor, rest your head in his lap, and kill yourself."

Mitsusue replied, "That might do for you, Mitsutaka, and for Mandokoro no Tarō. The others may well open a gate and flee, but as for me, I will fight until no one else is left and die fighting. When I run out of arrows I will fight on with my sword. If all seems lost, set fire to the house and prepare to kill yourselves."

For the battle that day Mitsusue wore, over a *kosode* robe displaying tie-dyed white circles, a white, unlined *katabira* shift and a wide-mouthed *hakama* trouser-skirt. His silver-trimmed dagger hung at his side, while two quivers, one holding sixteen arrows and the other a like number, rode at his back. So equipped, there at the double doors of his guest wing he untied the cords that bound the bundles of arrows, strung three closely rattan-wrapped bows, and awaited the foe's assault.

"Arm yourself, Juō, quickly!" he said. His son Juō, then in his fourteenth year, accordingly equipped himself for battle. Over a *kosode* decorated with round, coin-like motifs he wore a white *katabira*, a yellow *hakama*, and green-laced body armor. His gauntlets were of white-patterned purple leather. At his side he wore a seven-and-a-half-inch dagger, and the quiver at his back held sixteen arrows fletched with dyed feathers. Holding his tightly strung, rattan-wrapped bow and an open red fan, he awaited the enemy behind one of the building's interior pillars.

An attack force a thousand strong bore down on the compound from the Kyōgoku side, their banners just visible over the locked gate. Mitsusue said, "How much longer will that locked gate keep us alive? I hate to imagine what those men out there may be thinking of us. Open it!" Mitsutaka and Kumaōmaru did so, whereupon Taneyoshi, Kusada Uma-no-jō, Rokurōzaemon, Gyōbuzaemon, and Hirotsuna, in that order, burst in with two dozen of their men.

Mitsusue brushed off his left sleeve with his red fan, stepped down into the open space before the building, and advanced to within a bow-length of the muzzle of Taneyoshi's horse. He said, "So you are Taneyoshi? Yes, I have been in the capital lately, but I have done nothing here to offend His Eminence. Why am I under imperial ban?"

Taneyoshi replied, "This is the situation, Mitsusue. We grew up together, and I think highly of you. However, times change and now an imperial decree places me in command of a force charged with executing you."

Mitsusue retorted, "Oh yes, I know all about it. You and Hideyasu plan to eliminate Yoshitoki and share control of Japan between you. Your first step toward this goal is obviously to get rid of *me*, whose men are few. A man of bow and arrow looks one day to another and the next to himself. If Kamakura hears of this, the great warriors and wealthy landholders of the Kanto will not forget their old, martial allegiance. No, Yoshitoki will assemble a great host, drive on up to the capital, attack again and again those who have raised rebellion against him, and behead them all. *Then*, Taneyoshi, you will have good reason to regret ever having concocted this scheme of yours."

Kusada Uma-no-jō broke in, "How will you ever execute this man, Taneyoshi, if you give him so much time?"

Taneyoshi took an arrow from his quiver, drew the string back the full length of the shaft, and let fly. The arrow pierced Mitsusue's left sleeve and went more than half way through the frame of the double doors behind him. "I always held you and Mano Jirōzaemon to be the best archers in the capital," Mitsusue said, "but your first arrow has missed. I was sure that it would finish me, but no, in war the gods still smile on me, not you—no, not anymore. This is my forty-eighth year. See now, Taneyoshi, what I can do!" He took an arrow fletched with white feathers, drew to the full, and let fly. It split a strip a hand-breadth long from the grip of Taneyoshi's bow and sped straight on through the neck of Kusada, immediately behind him. Kusada collapsed.

Taneyoshi reflected, "It would greatly damage my reputation and Go-Toba's if, at the very start of Go-Toba's campaign, his senior commander were to be killed by an enemy arrow." He therefore withdrew outside the gate, to forestall any disparaging remarks.

Rokurōzaemon moved in to fight next, but he, too, lost and withdrew. Hirotsuna then advanced, with an arrow fitted to the string. He said, "Only yesterday you and I were still friends, but times change, and I am here to execute you in compliance with an imperial decree. I sponsored the coming-of-age of Juō, your son, who is also my son-in-law. The time has come for you and me to pit ourselves against each other."

Mitsusue replied, "Hirotsuna, you are no worthy opponent for me. Get out of the way! I will show you how a man fights. Challenge Juō, by all means, if you want to." He went inside. "Come out, Juō, right now!" he said. "Your father-in-law wants to see you."

Juō obediently stepped down into the open space before the house with those sixteen arrows, fletched with dyed feathers, on his back. "Is that you I see, Lord Hirotsuna? Do you know who I am? I am Jirō Mitsutsuna,[32] the second son of Iga-no-hōgan Mitsusue. This is my fourteenth year. I hereby return to you the arrow that you gave me when I came of age." He drew to the full and let fly. The arrow pierced the sleeve of Hirotsuna's armor and stopped, halfway through.

Hirotsuna, too, retreated outside the gate. "Look at this, gentlemen!" he cried. "Look at the power of Jirō Mitsutsuna's bow, in only his fourteenth year!" He broke the arrow and disposed of it.

Noma Munekage spoke next. "Meditations on transience ill become a warrior. As things stand, the next attack is mine." He stood at the south side of the gate, mounted on his dappled roan.

"You there at the south side of the gate," Mitsusue cried, "in scarlet-laced armor without a helmet: You are Noma Munekage, if I am not mistaken. If you are, then that is not the way you usually talk. Come here! I want a word with you!"

Noma Munekage replied, "How remarkable, Mitsusue, that, among all the men present you should address yourself to me! I am honored! Very well, here I come!" He untied his quiver and leaned it against the wall, drew his sword, attacked, and cut Mitsusue's bowstring. His bowstring cut, Mitsusue retreated into the house. Jibu no Jirō Mitsutaka advanced to fight in his stead but took a gash on the left side of his belly and fell from the veranda. Nieda no Saburō and his two sons came forward in turn, but they, too, fell to Munekage's sword. Next came Ikara no Musha, only to fall to the ground with a deep gash to his inner thigh.

"This fellow, at least, has some shame," Munekage remarked as he bent down to take the man's head, whereupon Mitsusue shot from within the house an arrow that pierced the center of Noma Munekage's forehead and went straight through to the back of his head, where a knot secured his *eboshi* hat. Munekage blacked out and was instantly gone. Meanwhile, Kagami no Saemon and Tanobe Jūrō attacked in turn. Kagami no Saemon turned back, defeated, and Tanobe Jūrō was slain.

Many died on both sides, including thirty-five attackers. Mitsusue himself was gravely wounded. Knowing his end to be near, he went back into the house and summoned Mandokoro no Tarō. "Do not let the enemy set fire to the place," he commanded. "Set fire to it yourself." Mandokoro no Tarō set fire to the main house. The flames rose into the sky.

Mitsusue then called Juō to him. "I am finished," he said. "Kill yourself." Juō rushed three times into the flames and three times retreated.

"If you can't do it, Juō, then come here," Mitsusue said. "I have some last words for you." Juō went to him. Mitsusue drew him down onto his lap. "When Retired Emperor Juntoku went on pilgrimage to Iwashimizu Hachiman," he said, "in the 11th month of last year [1220], I secured the end of the bridge across the Yodo River, and he said approvingly, 'This fellow looks sharp.' I was so pleased that I meant to put my name in for one of the offices to be announced this autumn, when the appointments list is published. But now my life is over now. Too bad."

Juō replied, "I am not up to taking my life, but, father, please let me die by your hand."

"I thought you would say that life means too much to you, and you hope to escape to Kamakura," Mitsusue answered. He pulled Juō close against him, drew his dagger, and was about to plunge it in when tears so blinded him that he could no longer see the spot. Nonetheless, he thrust the blade in three times and heaved the body into the flames. He next called the Name and prayed, "All hail to the Refuge! O Great Bodhisattva Hachiman, O Kamo and Kasuga, have pity on me! I who remained in the capital have done nothing to offend the retired emperor, yet a decree from him requires me to surrender my life. I leave my name to future generations." He prostrated himself three times toward Kamakura, praying that, once he was dead, Lord Yoshitoki should smite his enemies. Then, hand in hand with Mandokoro no Tarō, he collapsed into the fire, onto the body of his son.

## 6. Go-Toba Decrees the Dismissal of Hōjō Yoshitoki

Hideyasu went to report to Go-Toba on the outcome of the battle. Go-Toba asked how it had gone. "It was extremely violent," Hideyasu replied. "The imperial messenger, supported by a thousand men, fought Mitsusue's thirty-one from the start of the hour of the sheep [1 P.M.] to the end of that of the monkey [5 P.M.]. Thirty-five men on Your Eminence's side were killed and an uncounted number wounded. On the other side, a few men sensitive to shame were killed, and Mitsusue and his son took their own lives."

"Alas," Go-Toba answered, "I only wish that I could have won him over, spared his life, and appointed him to lead my army."

Go-Toba then ordered prison for the right commander Saionji Kintsune and his son, the counselor Saneuji, apparently because he suspected them of being in league with Kamakura. They resembled that man of Tang, in favor in the morning and, in the evening, condemned to death.

One of Mitsusue's servants started out for Kamakura on the 15th at the hour of the dog [8 P.M.]. Taneyoshi returned home, wrote precisely the letter that he had suggested earlier, and, also at the hour of the dog, dispatched it to Miura Yoshimura, his elder brother.

In addition, Go-Toba ordered Hideyasu to win over the following men to the imperial side:

Takeda
Ogasawara
Koyama Tomomasa
Utsunomiya Yoritsuna
Nakama Gorō
Musashi-no-zenji Yoshiuji
Hōjō Tokifusa
Miura Yoshimura.[33]

Hideyasu received this command, and the counselor Mitsuchika promulgated the retired emperor's decree, as follows:

Retired Emperor Go-Toba has issued the following decree:

> After the death of Minamoto no Sanetomo, the men of his house requested imperial guidance on how to proceed. Lord Yoshitoki appeared adequate to represent Us in Kamakura. It was observed, however, that in that case the three Minamoto shoguns would have no successor to continue their work. Various opinions suggested a remedy for this situation. It was decided that the office should revert to a son of the regent, endowed as he would be with exceptional merit. Unfortunately, this son was still too young to display such merit. Consequently, the ambitious Lord Yoshitoki usurped the authority of the court. His doing so

contravenes proper government, and for that reason he no longer represents Us. He is dismissed from office. All authority henceforth resides in imperial hands. Whoever ignores this decree and plots rebellion shall be executed forthwith. All who render loyal service to this end shall be rewarded. This decree is hereby promulgated. It must be obeyed.

JŌKYU 3, 5TH MONTH, 15TH DAY [1221]
RECORDED BY MITSUCHIKA.

## 7. The Reaction in Kamakura

Mitsuchika entrusted the decree to Oshimatsu, one of Go-Toba's servants. At the hour of the tiger [4 A.M.] on the 16th, Oshimatsu hurried off with it toward Kamakura, counting on returning laden with gifts from the great warriors and landowners there—the fair recompense for his faithful service. At a normal pace he would have reached his goal on the 20th, but as it was, he arrived on the 19th at the hour of the monkey [4 P.M.].

Mitsusue's servant arrived the same day at the hour of the bird [6 P.M.]. He went straight to Hōjō Masako and reported what had happened. She said, "I have never in my life esteemed anyone more than I did him. Let all of Kamakura know."

Kamakura was instantly in an uproar. Takeda, Ogasawara Nagakiyo, Utsunomiya Yoritsuna, Nakama Gorō, and Musashi-no-zenji Yoshiuji gathered to Masako at the news.

Masako said, "Hear me, gentlemen! I have never in my life thought more highly of anyone than I did of Mitsusue. First, I lost my daughters.[34] Next, I lost my husband, Lord Yoritomo. Then I lost Yoriie and, soon, Sanetomo. I recovered from those four losses, but a fifth afflicts me now that Mitsusue has been killed. Five griefs—one, so to speak, for each of the five obstacles that afflict a woman.[35] Gentlemen, you were called to the capital, to guard the palace there. For three years, rain or shine, you spread your mats before the emperor's residence, thought of home, and longed for your wives and children. It was my son, Sanetomo, who had you relieved one by one of this duty. If you were to back the capital, gentlemen, attack Kamakura, and trample the graves of Yoritomo and Sanetomo beneath your horses' hooves, how could you, who owe these two men so much, expect ever to enjoy divinely ordained good fortune in war? Will you not shrink from bringing tears to the eyes of the nun who now addresses you,[36] recluse that she is in the depths of the mountains? Since childhood I have always spoken plainly. So tell me equally plainly, gentlemen: Will you back the capital, or will you back Kamakura?"

Takeda Nobumitsu stepped forward. He said, "Long ago, forty-eight major warriors and wealthy landowners swore to protect the Genji for seven generations, and I cannot believe that a single one now would break that oath. My lady, you may count on them to fight for you." All present agreed. Not one man dissented.

Pleased, Lady Masako spoke again. "Very well, gentlemen," she said, "then it is time to hold a council of war in Lord Yoshitoki's guards' office." All present proceeded there without delay.

Meanwhile, Taneyoshi's messenger arrived on that same day, the 19th, also at the hour of the bird. He went to the home of Miura Yoshimura. Yoshimura noticed his younger brother's man and asked him his business. The man said that he had a letter for him.

Yoshimura unrolled the document and read it. "What an appalling letter for Taneyoshi to write, after three years in the capital!" he exclaimed. "This is far worse than Wada Yoshimori's rebellion some years ago.[37] I will not give it a second glance." He rolled the letter back up and asked the man whether he had come alone.

"I traveled with Oshimatsu, who serves Retired Emperor Go-Toba. He was carrying a decree ordering the execution of Yoshitoki. He and I parted once we entered Kamakura."

"Inspection at the barriers is strict," Yoshimura said. "I will not reply. Just tell Taneyoshi that his letter has been received." He sent the man back to the capital.

Rolled-up letter in hand, Yoshimura went to Yoshitoki. "This is Taneyoshi's third year in the capital," he said, "and I have just received this letter from him. Read it! When Wada Yoshimori rebelled a few years ago, I got into trouble for trying to mediate between him and you. I am telling you this now because I swore loyalty to you in my youth and stand by my oath. My brother's messenger says that one Oshimatsu, a servant of Go-Toba, came down with him from the capital bearing a decree that orders your execution. Apparently the two separated once they entered Kamakura. If the great warriors and landowners to the east were to learn what is in the decree, all would no doubt turn against you and me. Yoshitoki, you must have Kamakura searched thoroughly for Oshimatsu before they find out."

Yoshitoki agreed. He sent out six hellishly hardbitten lieutenants, each with his own search party, to scour the town. They found Oshimatsu at the home of Kasai Kiyoshige and rushed him back to Yoshitoki so fast that his feet hardly touched the ground.

Yoshitoki snatched the decree from Oshimatsu, looked it over, and informed his men. A horde of them saddled their horses and raced to his residence, with bearers behind them carrying their armor. Yoshitoki said, "If you wish to execute me, gentlemen, then do so now and send my head up to the capital for the retired emperor's inspection."

Shichijō no Jirōbyōe instantly replied, "Hear me, Lord Yoshitoki! Forty-eight great warriors and landowners swore long ago to protect the Genji for seven generations, and it is therefore *you* who are Lord Sanetomo's successor."[38]

Yoshitoki answered, "How are we then to take Go-Toba's decree, if today and hereafter those forty-eight are all agreed? I wish to hear each man's opinion." No one in the rows of men present said a word.

Nakatsukasa Kanesada, from Usukawa in the province of Suruga, announced that he had an idea how to reply. Everyone asked what it was.

"What do you say, gentlemen?" Kanesada answered. "Why not write this?" 'The retired emperor receives a vast quantity of tribute two or three times a year. That should satisfy him. What more does he want, that he should now issue this decree? Pity for Lady Masako's tears, shed in her mountain retreat, has moved the many warriors gathered here from the three circuits of the Tōsandō, Tōkaidō, and Hokurikudō to suggest to the retired emperor that he might wish to call in warriors from the western provinces and follow the ensuing battle from behind his blinds.' "

"Brilliant, Kanesada!" Takeda Nobumitsu exclaimed. "You have spoken for us all. And to whom should the letter be addressed?"

They decided on Go-Toba's private secretary. The reply was carefully committed to writing and given to Oshimatsu. Yoshitoki said, "Rather than have Oshimatsu deliver it, I would prefer to send some men in a show of force. If we have Oshimatsu go, the men from beyond Mount Utsu[39] will probably align themselves with the capital. See to it that Oshimatsu can neither escape nor die."

Takeda Nobumitsu agreed to do so. He entrusted Oshimatsu to Uma-no-nyūdō, who incarcerated him in shackles.

## 8. Kamakura Plans Its Campaign

Yoshitoki then began his council of war. He entrusted Kiyomi-ga-seki, on the Tōkaidō, to Yuyama Kojirō; Misaka-no-seki, on the Tōsandō, to Misaka Saburō; and Shioyama and Kurosaka, on the Hokurikudō, to Yamashiro Tarō.[40]

"Bring in any suspicious-looking characters, gentlemen," Yoshitoki said, "but avoid shaming them. I gather that in the late Lord Yoritomo's time Hatakeyama Shigetada[41] led the advance guard. Those days are over, though. Who could do so now? Nonetheless, Hōjō Tokifusa, the governor of Sagami, will command our force along the Tōkaidō, and these men will lead the twenty thousand under him:

Adachi Kagemori
Mōri Suemitsu
Ishido-no-nyūdō
Honma Tadaie
Itō Suketoki
Kajii
Tannai
Noji Hachirō
Kawara Gorō
Kowada Sakon
Ōkawa-dono
Ōmi Sanekage
Usami Sukemasa
Uchida Gorō
Kuge Saburō
Hōjō Tokimori.[42]

Hōjō Yasutoki,[43] the governor of Musashi, will command the second force, and these men will lead the twenty thousand under him:

Seki Masatsuna
Araida-dono
Mori Gorō
Koyama Tomomasa
Koyama Tomonaga

Miyoshi Yasutomo
Utsunomiya Yoritsuna
Nakama Gorō
Tōnai Saemon
Andō Tadaie
Takahashi Yoichi
Inden Ukon
Inden Gyōbu
Abo Sanmitsu
Ōmori Yajirō and his brother
Hoi Saemon
Hachikawa-dono
Sanuki Hidetsuna
Date-no-nyūdō
Date Heiji
Kaneko Heiji
Isa Yukimasa
Kotomo Rokurō
The head of the Tan League[44]
The head of the Kodama League
The head of the Inoda League
The head of the Kaneko League
Araki Jirō
The head of the Arita League
Yajirōbei
Miura Yasumura[45]
Hōjō Tokiuji.

Ashikaga Yoshiuji[46] will command the third corps.

The fourth corps will follow Sano Saemon Masakage and Nita Shirō.

Yamagara Yukikage and Chiba Jirō will follow along the Tōkaidō, leading the seventy thousand men of the fifth corps.

The supreme commanders on the Tōsandō will be Takeda Nobumitsu and Ogasawara Nagakiyo, with fifty thousand men. Their deputies will be:

Minamoto Tomomitsu
Minamoto Naganobu

Misaka Saburō
Ninomiya Yasuyori
Tomobe Rokurō
Takeda Nobunaga.

On the Hokurikudō the supreme commander will be Hōjō Tomotoki,[47] leading seventy thousand men.

By the Tōsandō, Tōkaidō, and Hokurikudō we will press up toward the capital with 190,000 horse.[48] I will remain here, but I know already where the crucial battles will be:

On the Hokurikudō:[49]

Mount Tonami
Miyazaki
Shioyama
Kurosaka;

on the Tōsandō:[50]

Ōido
Itabashi
Mushiroda
Kuisegawa;

on the Tōkaidō:

Ōmiko
Ichinose
Mamedo
Jiki-no-watari
Takakuwa
Sunomata.

These, gentlemen, will be the sites of the crucial battles. To win there, keep your saddle girths tightly cinched. Remain calm even if the enemy does not. If the enemy slackens, keep after him with everything you have.

Once the men on the Tōkaidō have passed the Fuwa barrier in Mino, and those on the Hokurikudō have passed Tsuruga harbor and Arachi-yama[51] in Echizen, then all three columns are to join. Take Uji and Seta, enter the capital, set fire to the city south of Gojō, rout out the rebels, cut off their heads, and present these heads to Go-Toba. Let me know by courier if the Musashi and Sagami men are not enough. I will send a force under Shigetoki and lead a hundred thousand men myself up to the capital. There I will fight on until I come before the retired emperor. If the battle is lost, I will leave the capital, dig deep trenches at Ashigara and Kiyomi-ga-seki, engage the enemy at Yui-no-hama, and fight fiercely on. If victory still eludes me, then, just as Shui Tarō, of old, received seven imperial decrees, barricaded himself at Moji-no-seki, and for seven years seized control of the nine provinces of Kyushu,[52] I, Yoshitoki, will set fire to Kamakura until the smoke of the whole town rises into the heavens; flee to the depths of the north; send no further rolls of dyed Hachijō silk or feather cloaks prized by the Ebisu[53] up to the capital; and make do with what this life has given me. Gentlemen, set out with all speed along the Tōkaidō behind your commander, Tokifusa, as soon as I have selected an auspicious day. Yes, the 21st of the 5th month is a day to begin a great undertaking. Go then, go!"

On the 21st, the men assigned to the Tōkaidō advance guard stood in the avenue leading to the Tsuruoka Hachiman Shrine. Each drew an arrow from his quiver and offered it to the three sanctuaries. They then set out along the Yui-no-hama shore and on past Koshigoe-yama, toward Mount Ashigara.

Oshimatsu had presumably heard everything that Yoshitoki had said about the disposition of the Kamakura forces. Yoshitoki therefore summoned him, sat him down in the open space before his residence, and said, "Go on up to the capital and tell Retired Emperor Go-Toba:

> Your Eminence, two or three times a year you receive in tribute rolls of Hachijō dyed silk; silver; gold; priceless Ebisu feather cloaks; and fine horses. Surely all this should satisfy you. What more could you possibly desire, that you should have placed Yoshitoki under imperial ban? He has mustered 190,000 spirited warriors who even now are on their way up to the capital along the San'yōdō, Tōkaidō, and Hokurikudō routes. By all means, then, summon the warriors of the western provinces, set the two forces against each other, and follow the battle from behind your blinds. If you find your men insufficient in number, then send such fleet-footed servants as myself against the foe, while Yoshitoki, for his part, comes up here with one hundred thousand horse, to gain victory at all costs and seek an audience with you. That is what Yoshitoki instructed me to say.

Now, give Oshimatsu provisions for his journey!"

They gave Oshimatsu six quarts of dried, cooked rice and threw him out of the gate. He set out as though toward the Mountain of Death, past Ōnami, Koshigoe, and Futokorojima-yama,[54] until he reached the Sagami River. There he bathed and felt so much better that he reflected, "Rather than eat this dried rice little by little, here and there, I will eat it all immediately and then continue quietly on my way." Accordingly, he washed and ate his rice. He then reflected further, "I hurried down to Kamakura and looked forward to a more leisurely return journey to the capital, honored by gifts from the great warriors and landowners there. Instead I was shackled and imprisoned, and I feared that every voice I heard might mean that my head was to come off. Well, I should be all right now for another ten years." He decided not to hurry. He reached the capital on the 5th day[55] at the hour of the bird [6 P.M.] and presented himself in the open space before Kaya House.

# Book 2

## 9. Go-Toba Launches His Campaign

Retired Emperor Go-Toba and, below him, every minister, senior noble, counselor, consultant, gentlewoman, and so on gathered together. "Look, Your Eminence!" they cried, "Oshimatsu has brought you the head of Yoshitoki!" They lifted Go-Toba's blinds to reveal an excited crowd.

Oshimatsu lay prostrate on the ground before the house. Fujiwara no Hideyasu called out, "What is the matter with you, Oshimatsu? Why, on so joyous an occasion, are you lying facedown like that? Get up and tell us about Kamakura! Tell us everything!"

Hailed repeatedly in this way, Oshimatsu at last sat up and replied, weeping, "They say that ours is now a world forever at war, a world destined soon to turn upside down. Indeed, this is what Yoshitoki ordered me to tell Retired Emperor Go-Toba:

> Your Eminence, two or three times a year you receive in tribute rolls of Hachijō dyed silk, silver, gold, priceless Ebisu feather cloaks, and fine horses. Surely all this should satisfy you. What more could you possibly desire, that you should have issued this decree? Yoshitoki has mustered 190,000 spirited warriors who even now are on their way up to the capital along the San'yōdō, Tōkaidō, and Hokurikudō routes. By all means, then, summon the warriors of the western provinces, set the two forces against each other, and follow the battle from behind your

> blinds. If you desire still more fighting, then send fleet-footed servants like myself against the foe, while Yoshitoki, for his part, comes up to the capital with one hundred thousand horse, to gain victory at all costs and seek an audience with you.

That is what Yoshitoki instructed me to say." All who heard him, high or low, lowered their gaze in consternation.

His Eminence declared, "Gentlemen, that is exceedingly unfortunate. You are the ones, are you not, who urged me to fight? Now there is no way back. Gather your armies as quickly as you can and confront the enemy!"

Hideyasu heeded his order, gathered his forces, and divided them into different corps. He said, "Seven thousand horse will proceed down the Tōkaidō, commanded by myself and by:

Kawachi-no-hōgan Hidezumi
Miura Taneyoshi
Fujiwara Hirotsuna
Yata Tomonao
Ono Naritoki
Ōuchi Koretada
Heinai Saemon
Heiza Saemon
Fujiwara Yoshimochi
Saitō Chikayori
Satsuma Saemon
Adachi Genzaemon
Kumagae Saemon
Awa-no-kami Nagaie
Shimōsa-no-kami
Kōzuke-no-kami
Shigehara Saemon
Minamoto Kakeru.

Five thousand will proceed down the Tōsandō, commanded by:

Hachiya-no-nyūdō and his two sons
Tarumi Saemo
Takakuwa-dono

Tarō Shigekuni
Kakehashi
Ueda-dono
Utsumi
Gorō
Teramoto-dono
Ōuchi Korenobu
Seki Masayasu
Ashikaga Tadahiro
Taira Arinori and his five sons
Kōzuke-no-nyūdō and his three sons.

Seven thousand will advance down the Hokurikudō, commanded by:

Ise-no-zenji
Iwami-no-zenji
Hachida-dono
Wakasa-no-zenji
Oki-no-kami
Hayai Hōgan
Ōe Yoshinori
Shume Saemon
Miyazaki Sadanori
Ueai Saemon
Shiraki Kurōdo
Nishiya Kurōdo
Yasuda Saemon
Yasuhara Sanetoshi
Narita Sukeyasu
Ishiguro-dono
Ōtani Saburō
Mori Jirō
Tokuda Jūrō
Noki Genda
Hazashi Hachirō
Nakamura Tarō
Uchikura-no-kami.

The roster shows that 19,326 horse will advance along the Tōsandō, the Tōkaidō, and the Hokurikudō. The rest are to secure Uji and Seta."

He sent Yamanokuchi, too, to defend Seta. The Mino, Harima, and Suō explicators,[56] as well as Chishō and Tango, led seven hundred men down there. Five hundred went to Mio-ga-saki,[57] and two hundred to the bridge at Seta. They stripped the planks from three spans of the bridge, drew nine stout ropes across it, planted randomly spaced stakes in the riverbed, laid abatis, and waited for the enemy to arrive.

The men sent to Uji followed Fujiwara no Norimochi, Fujiwara no Tomotoshi, and Kanba-no-nyūdō, and they acted under the direction of the Nara rock-fighters.[58]

Minamoto no Arimasa was posted to Maki-no-shima,[59]
Fujiwara no Muneyuki to Fushimi,
Fujiwara no Tadanobu to Imoarai,
the Yoshino administrator to Uoichi,
the prelate Sonchō to Ōwatari,
and Kōno Michinobu from Iyo to Shimo-no-se.

The rest, a thousand horse under Fujiwara no Mitsuchika, occupied Kaya House itself.

The commander on the Tōkaidō, Fujiwara no Hidezumi, reached a small moor in the locality of Tarumi in Mino. There he subdivided his corps for battle and assigned the following men to secure key locations:

Hachiya-no-nyūdō to Ai-no-watari,
Ōuchi Korenobu, Seki Saemon, and Ashikaga Tadahiro to Ōido,
Kōzuchi Yoritsune to Uruma-no-se,
Ogino Kagekazu and Yamada Shigetsugu to Itabashi,
Utsumi, Goryō, and Teramoto-dono to Hi-no-miko,
Sekida, Kakehashi, Ueda-dono to Igi-no-watari,
Hideyasu and Taneyoshi to Mamedo,
Koremune Takachika, Shimojō, and Katō Mitsusada to Jiki-no-watari with three thousand horse;
Shigehara Saemon and Minamoto Kakeru to Kami-no-se,
Yamada Shigesada to Sunomata.[60]

It was unfortunate of him to have dispersed his twelve thousand men into twelve[61] separate strongholds.

## 10. The Clash with Tsukui Takashige

Meanwhile Hōjō Tokifusa, leading the Kamakura advance guard along the Tōkaidō, reached the Hashimoto post station in Tōtōmi. Now, Tsukui Tarō Takashige, in the capital a retainer of Moritsuna, the governor of Shimotsuke, was from the province of Awa. He had been on his way to Kamakura, rowing a boat laden with tribute for the capital, when—such was then the fate of many a warrior—he fell into Tokifusa's hands and was forced to accompany him all the way to Hashimoto. He could not even take leave of his wife and children.

Tsukui Takashige reflected, "Warrior that I am, I feel that I will have upheld my honor if I manage to see my lord in the capital one last time." He therefore left Hashimoto one night with nineteen mounted men. He did not dismount before Tokifusa, nor did he salute him in any way.

Tokifusa noticed this and summoned Uchida Saburō, the head of the Uchida League. "Who was that?" he asked. "He must not get away with passing my lodging without even dismounting. Go and find out."

Uchida Saburō went for a look and returned to his lord. "That was Tsukui Takashige, sir, a retainer of Moritsuna, the governor of Shimotsuke."

Tokifusa replied. "Success in war descends from heaven and wells up from the earth.[62] "Our eastern warriors' horses are tired. Go after him with some Tōtōmi men."

Uchida Saburō obeyed. With a hundred men he passed Takase, Miyaji, Honnogawara, and Otowabara in Mikawa, and caught up with Takashige at last at Ishihaka. There he hailed him. "You are Tsukui Takashige, are you not?" he called. "If you are, you are the man Lord Tokifusa has sent me to find. I am Uchida Saburō. Turn back! I want a word with you!"

Takashige turned back and brought his horse up beside Uchida's. "Hear me, gentlemen!" he cried. "I am a warrior, and I am on my way to the capital to bid my lord farewell. Is anything wrong with that? So let us now slay one another, your men and mine."

Eleven of Takashige's nineteen men drew their swords, while the remaining eight each put an arrow to the string. A fierce clash followed. Thirty-five of the one hundred attackers were struck down and many wounded. Eleven of the nineteen defenders were killed, while the remaining eight took refuge in an innkeeper's house on the south side of the road. There they barred the gate, set the house on fire, slit their bellies, and died.

Uchida Saburō collected the eleven heads and attached them to a pole at Honnogawara. Then he went on to the Hashimoto post station, where Tokifusa was lodging, and to Tokifusa. Tokifusa saw that in this instance victory had been his. He drew an arrow from his quiver and dedicated it to the god of war.

## 11. Crossing the Rivers

Yamada Shigesada, then at Sunomata, learned that Sendō Tōtōmi no Isuke had reached the provincial capital of Owari. He called in Fujiwara Hidezumi and said, "I understand that Tokifusa and Sendō Tōtōmi no Isuke have reached the Owari capital. It makes no sense, Hidezumi, to have dispersed our twelve thousand men on the Tōsandō and Tōkaidō into twelve separate strongholds. Let us instead muster the whole force; cross the river at Sunomata; attack the Owari capital; take Isuke's head; go on past Takase, Miyaji, Honnogawara, and Otowabara in Mikawa; attack the Hashimoto post station; take the heads of Yasutoki and Tokifusa; from there attack Kamakura; take the head of Yoshitoki; set fire to Kamakura and send the whole town up in smoke; follow the Hokurikudō; take the head of Hōjō Tomotoki; and then make our way back up to the capital and report to Retired Emperor Go-Toba."

Hidezumi was fainthearted by nature. He replied to Shigesada, "This is what I think. Your proposal deserves consideration. However, if we were to unite our Tōsandō and Tōkaidō forces; cross at Sunomata; take the head of Isuke, said now to be in the Owari capital, then those of Yasutoki and Tokifusa; and continue on toward to Kamakura, then we would find ourselves surrounded by Tomotoki advancing up the Hokurikudō, and by Takeda Nobumitsu and Ogasawara Nagakiyo advancing up the various branches of the Tōsandō, and securing them along the way. The result would be needless humiliation. The journey here from the capital has exhausted our horses. Let us instead wait here, for as long as necessary, to exterminate the warriors from the east."

Yamada Shigesada reflected, "I do not at all like what Hidezumi says. If that is how it must be, I will take my men across at Sunomata myself." He then summoned Izuna no Gonpachi and Shimo no Tōgo. "I gather that Hōjō Tokifusa and Sendō Tōtōmi no Isuke have reached the capital of Owari," he said. "Go and look over the situation." He sent them on their way.

Meanwhile, Isuke summoned Chūgenji and Chūroku. He said, "Apparently the warriors from the capital have reached Sunomata. Go and see whether or not the situation favors us."

These two pairs of men ran into each other on the Ushio embankment. "Look there, Chūroku!" Chūgenji said. "Apparently the warriors from the capital have reached Sunomata, and those two look to me like forward scouts. Seize them and take their heads!"

Gonpachi heard him. "We are not scouts for the men from the capital," he said. "I am the post station keeper at Kayatsu in Owari."

"If that is really who you are," Chūgenji retorted, "then *we* are scouts for the forces of Lord Yoshitoki in Kamakura. These forces are now on their way up to the capital in violation of the decree issued by Retired Emperor Go-Toba; and meanwhile the men from the capital have apparently arrived at Sunomata. So let us examine the situation together."

"Very well, come along with me," Gonpachi replied. "Shimo no Tōgo, you too must accompany these gentlemen and look things over." They set off together.

They passed Motokiji-no-haka, then Ichi-no-miya. Gonpachi said to himself, "It is pointless to keep these men with us. I would rather seize them." He gripped his halberd short, knocked the two to the hard earth of high summer, tied their hands behind their backs, bound them securely, mounted them on a stolen enemy horse, and drove them ahead of him across the river at Sunomata. He took them to Yamada Shigesada.

Shigesada said, "Well done, gentlemen! Win the coming battle, and I will grant you land and make you wealthy." He offered them wine and gave them six quarts of dried, cooked rice. Knowing as he did how a warrior acts, he gave Chūroku to Hidezumi, the commander on duty that day; but, slack as Hidezumi was, he let Chūroku escape while he was eating a meal.

Shigesada summoned Chūgenji and asked him what people in Kamakura were saying. Chūgenji gave him a full report. Yamada then gave him into Gonpachi's custody. In the end Chūgenji was executed on the Mori embankment, where his head was hung on public view.

Meanwhile Hōjō Tokifusa, leading the advance along the Tōkaidō, left the post station at Hashimoto, passed Yahagi in Mikawa, then Yatsuhashi, Tarumi, and Ezaki, to arrive at the Atsuta Shrine in Owari. There he drew an arrow from his quiver and offered it to the divinity. He reached the Akaike post station that night. The next day he set up camp at Ichi-no-miya, also in Owari, and prepared his men for battle. "The task of securing the roads will be assigned in order of seniority," he announced. "Mamedo goes to Hōjō Yasutoki, and Takakuwa, Ōido, and Kawai to Amano Masakage."

Takeda Nobumitsu and Ogasawara Nagakiyo arrived at a Tōdaiji estate in the province of Mino. Ogasawara wondered aloud, "The *sahā* world is ruled by impermanence. Lord Takeda, what outcome do you foresee?"

Takeda answered, "Now, now, Lord Ogasawara. This is what really matters: If Kamakura wins, we rally to Kamakura, and if the capital wins, we rally to the capital. That, Lord Ogasawara, is what a warrior does."

Meanwhile Hōjō Tokifusa sent the following note by rapid courier: "To Lords Takeda and Ogasawara: Successfully cross the river at Ōido and Kawai, and the six provinces of Mino, Owari, Kai, Shinano, Hitachi, and Shimotsuke will be yours."

"Then let us cross, by all means!" the two men exclaimed. Takeda moved to do so at Kawai, Ogasawara at Ōido.

Ichikawa Shingorō, the first among Ogasawara's retainers, raised his fan and beckoned to the banner on the other side. "You, over there, the banner-bearer . . . !"[63] he called. "If you are worthy, let me cross so that we can meet. If you are not, then I will not trouble my horse to take me across."

Satsuma Saemon came forward to say, "Talk that way all you like, men, but you are Lord Yoshitoki's retainers. How could we possibly let you cross, when an imperial decree requires us to suppress the enemies of the throne! Just get across if you can!" He beckoned to Shingorō.

Enraged, Shingorō retorted, "Think before you speak! Who here could not claim imperial ancestry?[64] Takeda and Ogasawara, too, are descended from Emperor Seiwa. Yoshitoki's line goes back to Emperor Kanmu. Everyone here is descended from one emperor or another! If that is the way you want it, then here we come. Just watch!" He started his thousand and more riders across the river.

Takeda saw this and asked, "Who is he, that warrior who has started his men across?"

"Ichikawa Shingorō, Ogasawara's chief retainer," Satsuma Saemon replied.

"What does Shingorō mean by crossing now? Glory must be what he is after, since he is giving the enemy no glimpse of his men's neckplates[65] and seems hardly to care that the river may sweep their drowned bodies away. We have a strong young swimmer here. I want him to go and test the depth of the water. Come back!"

Satsuma Saemon summoned Arasaburō, then in his nineteenth year, and had him go and test the depth. Arasaburō removed his armor, took two arrows from his quiver, and, bow in hand, plunged with them into the river. He swam until he came up on the opposite bank. There he spotted Takakuwa. "Aha," he said to himself, "one of the enemy! I'll get him!" He realized that he himself would die on the spot if he missed, but he nonetheless put one of his wet arrows to the string, drew to the full, and let fly. The shaft went through Takakuwa's left side and planted itself in the edge of his saddle. Takakuwa fell headlong from his mount and died.

The capital force now raced to attack, while Arasaburō plunged again into the water. He swam some 150 yards and emerged on the bank where Ogasawara stood. Ogasawara said, "So you're the fellow who came up on the far bank and killed an enemy commander! Put your armor back on!"

Arasaburō did so, then reported to Hōjō Yasutoki. "Only about twenty yards of the riverbed could give a horse footing," he said. Then he turned to the men. "Gentlemen, do you know how to cross a river? Have the stronger horses cross upstream and the weaker ones downstream from them, so that the stronger one slow the current for the weaker. Tie up your armor sleeves, keep the upper tip of your bow even with your horse's head, and attach the reins to the pommel of your saddle. That, gentlemen, is the way to do it."

The first leader to ride into the river was Chido Rokurō. The second was Hiragōri Shirō. Nakajima Gorō and Takeda Nobumitsu came third. In all, as many as five thousand men crossed over.

Ōuchi Korenobu and Chido Rokurō engaged each other. Twenty-five men fell to Korenobu's arrows and were swept away by the river. Korenobu grappled with many others and took their heads.[66] When Koretada, his son, was killed he suspected that his rear was weak and fell back.

Ninomiya Yasuyori and Hachiya-no-nyūdō fought. Hachiya's arrows felled twenty-four of Ninomiya's men. Once the attackers were fully across, the two forces closed with each other. Hachiya-no-nyūdō took many heads but then sustained a grave wound and killed himself.

Ogasawara saw all this happen and started his three thousand across. Everyone reached the other side. Ichikawa Shingorō, who resented Satsuma no Saemon's earlier words,[67] singled him out for attack. He caught the top of Satsuma's helmet with his grappling hook, dragged him to the ground, and took his head.

Hachiya-no-kurōdo[68] saw this. "This is when a brave man retreats," he said to himself, "and that is what I will do." Whip raised high, he fled into the mountains. Hachiya Saburō galloped after him. "Where are you off to?" he shouted. "Do really imagine, the way things are going, that flight can save you? Come back! Let us take the head of our father's enemy!" However, Hachiya-no-kurōdo pretended not to hear him and kept going.

Saburō could do no more. He turned back and challenged Takeda. "If I am not mistaken," he said, "you are Takeda Nobumitsu." Do you know *me*? I am Hachiya Saburō, a son of Hachiya-no-nyūdō and a descendant of Rokusonnō. See now what I can do in battle!" He drew an arrow from his quiver, fitted it to the string of his rattan-wrapped bow, drew to the full, and let fly. The arrow pierced the breastplate of Takeda's chief retainer, stationed to Takeda's left. The man fell instantly from his saddle. Saburō's second arrow went straight through the neck of Takeda's page. The two men then grappled together. Both fell from their mounts. First one gained the upper hand, then the other, until Saburō drew his dagger and drove it in from the top of the helmet to the back of the armor. Takeda seemed done for. Just then, however, Takeda Hachirō[69] fell on them, dragged Nobumitsu out of the way, and took Saburō's head. Without him, Nobumitsu would have been finished.

The capital forces on the Tōsandō all fled. Takeda and Ogasawara took Ōido and Kawai, then pursued their attack down the Kiso River. At Unuma-no-se, Kōzuchi Yoritsune asked when he spotted them, "Those warriors heading down the river: Are they friend or foe?"

Ueda Gyōbu replied, "They are Takeda and Ogasawara, moving downstream after taking Ōido and Kawai."

"Then we must engage them with everything we have," said Yoritsune.

Ueda Gyōbu replied, "Life is the greatest of all treasures. Just being alive, they say, can find you the jellyfish's bone.[70] Escape, Lord Kōzuchi, rather than fight. Rejoin Amano Masakage, enter Hōjō Yasutoki's service, and prepare to rise high in the world."

Kōzuchi Yoritsune agreed that this was the better course. He rejoined Amano Masakage and declared submission to Yasutoki.

Hōjō Yasutoki called Kōzuchi Yoritsune into his presence. "Hear me, gentlemen!" he said. "Once a warrior has joined the capital side, that is where he should stay; once he has joined Kamakura, that, too, should be where he stays. But no: here is this man before me. I do not understand. Every warrior knows this, and so should *he*. Behead these traitors, gentlemen!" They cut off the heads of Yoritsune and his eight sons, and exposed them to view on iron poles.

At Itabashi,[71] Ogino Kagekazu and Yamada Shigetsugu charged forward to engage the enemy. They took many heads, but in the end their side weakened, and they fled.

At Igi-no-watari, Sekida, Kakehashi, and Ueda-dono exchanged opening arrows with the men from the east and took many heads, but then they, too, buckled and fled.

At Hi-no-miko, Uchimi, Goryō, and Teramoto-dono, cornered by the chief priest of the Atsuta Shrine,[72] were cut down on the Morokoshi River.

Hideyasu and Taneyoshi, who had secured Mamedo-no-watari, charged forward to engage. "Do you know me?" Taneyoshi cried. "I am Miura Taneyoshi, Miura Yoshimura's younger brother!" His arrows felled twenty-three enemy warriors, and the river swept their bodies away. They took many heads once the enemy had crossed, but at last they buckled and fled.

Koremune Takachika and Shimojō-dono, who had secured Jiki-no-watari, lay in wait. On the opposite bank, Seki Masatsune, Yamato-no-nyūdō, and Oshino-no-nyūdō surged forward, broke up a chapel that stood by the river, turned it into rafts, and on these rafts prepared to cross. Kanō-no-nyūdō said, "Not one in a thousand men has ever managed to cross at this spot. Cross upstream!"

Yamato-no-nyūdō responded, "No, no, cross *here*! Lord Yoshitoki charged me with reporting on the battle in council. Was there ever any decision, gentlemen, to cross upstream? I am over seventy now, and I do not mind dying." He started over with more than a hundred men and lost not a single one. Takachika and Shimojō, looking on, prepared to escape. They fled without loosing a single arrow.

Katō Mitsusada, from Ise, followed the example of the Heike. The Heike were on their way down to attack the provinces of the east when, at Fuji-no-numa in Suruga, the noise of wings from a flock of teal so alarmed them that they fled.[73] In Mitsusada's case, the men of the Narumi coast in Owari had set fires to gain better access to the mountains, whereupon countless birds flew up to escape the flames and passed over Kawanuma-no-ura in Ise. Among them were one hundred snowy herons. Mitsusada exclaimed at the sight, "Look, gentlemen! Seaborne warriors have raised their white banners and even now are bearing down on us! We are lost!" He set fire to the Nagae and Magari halls, built to stand side by side a thousand years, and, while their smoke rose to the heavens, led his three thousand mounted men in flight without shooting a single arrow.[74]

At Kami-no-se, Shigehara and Minamoto Kakeru Saemon engaged the enemy. Kakeru said, "Do you know me, you Kanto men? I am Minamoto Kakeru of the Watanabe League, famed throughout the fourteen counties of Settsu and a warrior known to be worth a thousand!" So he flung out his name. He was indeed a powerful warrior, and in a trice his arrows felled fifteen attackers; the river swept their bodies away. There followed a fierce, hand-to-hand clash. "I'm Kakeru! Kakeru, that's me!" he shouted as he raced about, taking many heads. He and his men held out until early the following morning, putting up a magnificent fight; but in the end they, too, fled.

Kawachi-no-hōgan Hidezumi, who had secured Sunomata, fled early in the night.

## 12. Go-Toba Learns of the Defeat

At dawn on the 8th of the 6th month of Jōkyū 3 [1221], Kazuya Hisasue and Chikugo Arinaka, both wounded, went to Retired Emperor Go-Toba and reported that the eastern warriors had attacked in numbers beyond counting and that on the 6th, at Sunomata, his forces had all fled after putting up initial resistance. This was bad news. Go-Toba was extremely upset. He took the two younger retired emperors and his two princes to the lodge of the great prelate Sonchō, near the Kamo River on Oshi-no-kōji. Senior nobles and privy gentlemen, young and old, accompanied him. Truly, one never knows the consequences of shooting a single arrow.

At the hour of the bird [6 P.M.] Go-Toba proceeded to Higashi-Sakamoto.[75] Alas, the small force with him appeared to count less than a thousand men. The capital was in turmoil. For some reason he then returned to the capital,[76] which reassured the people somewhat. The bridges at Uji and Seta were dismantled in preparation for battle. Every senior noble and privy gentleman with some knowledge of arms set out in that direction.

Meanwhile Yamada Shigesada fought on furiously and took many enemy heads. However, he noted that no one from his side was left on the Kiso River, either upstream or downstream. This was discouraging. "I had meant to die in battle here," he reflected, "but what is the point of fighting to the death all alone? The Tōsandō and the Tōkaidō meet at Kuisegawa, so that is where I will go."[77] He led three hundred riders there.

Three thousand men of the Kodama League advanced toward him when he arrived. "Who are these warriors? Are they friend or foe?" their leader asked. Andō Tadaie replied, "As far as I can tell, their leader is Yamada Shigesada, who fought so fiercely at Sunomata. Capture him, if that is really he."

The Kodama leader charged and engaged them. Shigesada said, "Hear me, gentlemen! Do you know me? I am Yamada Jirō Shigesada from the Mino-Owari border, a descendant of Rokusonnō!" He attacked furiously. A hundred Kodama men fell within range of his arrows. Forty-eight of Shigesada's men were killed.

Shigesada's fierce attack drove the Kodama men back. He said, "If they retreat, gentlemen, then do likewise. If they attack, then do the same. Fight without a thought for your lives!" So he rallied his men. Then he commanded, "This will be the order of attack:

First, Morowa Sakon Yōgen
Second, Konamita no Uma-no-jō
Third, Ōga Tarō
Fourth, Kokubu Tarō
Fifth, Yamaguchi Genta
Sixth, Yagen Jihei
Seventh, Gyōbu-bō
Eighth, Mino-o no Sakon Yōgen
Ninth, Enoki
Tenth, Kogorō Hyōe."

Kodama no Yoichi[78] charged them with three hundred men. "Go, Morowa!" Shigesada ordered. Morowa assumed an attack posture but fell back to Kogane-yama. Konamita engaged the enemy with his nineteen men and took thirty-five heads. Fifteen of his men were killed, and the remaining four retreated to Shigesada's side. Kitayama Saemon charged them with three hundred men. Ōga Tarō counterattacked and took many heads. Then he, too, retreated to rejoin Shigesada.

## 13. The Deaths of Taneyoshi and Shigesada

On the 14th of the 6th month, in the middle of the night, Minamoto Kakeru and Yamada Shigesada reached Go-Toba's Kaya House. Taneyoshi reported to Go-Toba, "My lord, your fight is lost. Order the gates thrown open! We will await the enemy in attendance upon you, put up fierce resistance, and die fighting before your eyes."

Go-Toba issued this fainthearted reply: "If you stay here, Kamakura warriors will surround this place and attack me. That would be extremely unfortunate. Flee now as fast as you can. Go anywhere you like."

Taneyoshi said to Kakeru and Shigesada, "What a craven attitude for His Eminence to take! I regret ever having allowed such a sovereign to talk me into rebelling. Where will I find refuge now? Properly, I should take my life here, but I gather that my elder brother, Miura Yoshimura, is on his way up from the Yodo road. Rather than rush out and fall by the hand of the first comer, I prefer to meet him a last time and explain myself to him. It is by Yoshimura's hand that I will die."

The three of them equipped themselves for war and set off down Ōmiya as far as Tōji; and there they lay in wait for the foe.[79] Nita Shirō challenged them. Kakeru responded. "Gentlemen," he said, "listen to me! Do you know me? I am Minamoto Kakeru, a key member of the Watanabe League in Settsu, west of the capital, and a member of His Eminence's West Guard!"[80] So he flung out his name, fought bravely, and took ten heads; but all his men had fled, and he, too, therefore fled toward Ōe-yama.

Yamagara Yukikage mounted his challenge. Shigesada advanced to answer it. "Do you know me?" he cried. "I am Yamada Shigesada!" He fought fiercely and took fifteen enemy heads. Many of his own men, too, were killed, and he fled toward Hannyaji-yama in Saga.

Next there appeared a flying, three-striped banner: gold above, then purple, then dark blue. Taneyoshi said, "*This* banner is Miura Yoshimura's!" He raced toward it.

"You there," he cried, "are you Miura Yoshimura? If you are, do you know *me*? I am Taneyoshi. An honorable life awaited me in Kamakura, but then, unfortunately, you turned against me. I went up to the capital, raised rebellion in the retired emperor's service, and trusted you enough to send you, in Kamakura, a letter on the subject. I wish I had not done so, however, because you were actually Yoshitoki's ally—you had betrayed and killed our uncle, Wada Saemon. I meant to take my life back there, like a man, but I wanted to see you first." He flung out bitter reproaches.

"There is nothing to be gained from tangling with a fool," Yoshimura replied. He returned to Yotsuzuka.[81]

Taneyoshi took a few enemy heads and then reflected, "My good fortune in war is over. Who would honor his father's memory, though, by taking the head of a brother destined to prosper for having triumphed over his sovereign?" He therefore rode north up Ōmiya to Ichijō and then fled westward. He continued on to Konoshima[82] after hanging the enemy heads before the western prison; and there, at the hour of the dragon [8 A.M.] on the 15th, he and his son took their lives. All lamented the death of so fine a warrior.

## 14. Yasutoki at Rokuhara; Yoshitoki Ordains the Rebels' Fates

On the 15th of the 6th month, at the hour of the serpent [10 A.M.], Hōjō Yasutoki arrived at Rokuhara. On the 17th, at the hour of the horse [noon], Hōjō Tomotoki, Yoshitoki's second son, arrived there as well. Yasutoki then sent a report in haste to Kamakura. It read: "Of the men who set out from the east to fight those from the capital, 13,620 died, swept away by the rivers or slain in battle. Those who, like myself, reached the capital and now desire their reward number 1,800. It therefore behooves you to provide suitably for them. What am I to do with Retired Emperor Go-Toba? Where am I to put the two princes? How am I to dispose of the senior nobles and privy gentlemen? I await your instructions on these matters."

Yoshitoki received the report. He said, "Look at this, gentlemen! I could ask for nothing more. My good fortune is greater than any monarch's! Yet such was my karma, once, that I was born the lowest of the low."

This was Yoshitoki's reply:

> Prince Morisada shall be appointed retired emperor.[83] The throne shall go to his third son.[84] Retired Emperor Go-Toba shall be sent into distant exile, although to

> a place still within the confines of the realm: the province of Oki.[85] The princes shall be exiled as you see fit. The senior nobles and privy gentlemen shall be sent down to the Kanto. There shall be no mercy for those below them: all are to be beheaded. Your first duty is therefore to restore order in the capital. No harm must come to the Konoe regent [Fujiwara no Iezane]; to the Kujō regent [Fujiwara no Michiie]; to Shichijō-in [Go-Toba's mother]; to Rokujō-in [unknown]; to the prince-abbot of Ninnaji [Cloistered Prince Dōjo, a son of Go-Toba]; to the Tokudaiji minister [Fujiwara no Kintsugu]; to the Nakayama chancellor [Fujiwara no Yorizane]; or to the Ōmiya captain [Saionji Kintsune]. Whoever violates this order, even a Kamakura ally, shall be arrested and beheaded. Hōjō Yasutoki and Hōjō Tomotoki are to report immediately to Kamakura. Considering the danger to the capital, Tomotoki is to secure the seven provinces of the Hokurikudō.[86]

So the letter read.

On the 2nd of the 7th month, Retired Emperor Go-Toba left Kaya House and proceeded to Izumi House on Oshi-no-kōji.[87] On the 4th, he continued on to Yotsutsuji House.[88] From there the members of his entourage returned to their own homes. On the 6th, he left Yotsutsuji House, accompanied by Chiba Tanetsuna, and proceeded to the Toba Mansion. Three familiar companions went with him as of old: Saionji Saneuji, Fujiwara no Nobunari, and Fujiwara no Yoshimochi.

On the 10th, Hōjō Tokiuji[89] repaired to the Toba Palace. He entered the main house fully armed and lifted the imperial blinds with the tip of his bow. He said, "Your Eminence, you are under sentence of exile. Come forth immediately." In voice and demeanor he resembled an envoy from Enma, the king of hell. Go-Toba said nothing. Tokiuji spoke again. "What orders have you given?" he demanded to know. "Are you sheltering still more rebels? Come forth this instant!"

This time Go-Toba answered him. "How, in my present situation, could I possibly shelter further rebels? If I am to leave to the capital, however, the thought of separation from the princes, my sons, is very painful. And Yoshimochi, the son of the chief priest of Gyōganji—I have had him in my service ever since he was a boy, and I am especially fond of him. Please allow me to see him again."

Tokiuji shed tears and sent this written message to Yasutoki: "I wonder what bond has so long united Yoshimochi and His Eminence. His Eminence asked to be allowed to see Yoshimochi again. Here in the capital he has asked for nothing else. It seems to me that you might send Yoshimochi to him immediately."

Yasutoki said, "Gentlemen, look at this letter from Tokiuji! This year is his seventeenth, and see how kind he can be! It is so touching!" He then ordered Yoshimochi to renounce the world and sent him in that guise to Go-Toba.

"So," Go-Toba said when he saw him, "you have renounced the world. It is time for me to do the same." He received the precepts from the prince-abbot of Ninnaji and became a monk. The prince-abbot himself, and every witness high or low, even to the bravest warrior, shed tears and wrung out wet sleeves. His mother, Shichijō-in, received his hair, feeling as though she were dreaming. Wailing, she collapsed amid bitter, pathetic tears of grief.

Go-Toba must have wished to see himself in his new guise, because he summoned Fujiwara no Nobuzane and had him paint his portrait. The result was not an image in a mirror, but in it he saw his long decline. As things stood, he would never again exercise governing authority. Very early the next morning he therefore set out with the reigning emperor for Kujō House.[90]

Emperor Go-Horikawa assumed the throne. The Jewel and the Sword,[91] abandoned amid the prevailing bitterness, were brought to his residence amid scenes of indescribable public rejoicing. The regent's reappointment[92] no doubt completed this fortunate event. Such is the natural way of the world, of course, but no one ever imagined such an outcome.

## 15. The Retired Emperors Are Banished

On the 13th of the 7th month Itō Suketoki took custody of Go-Toba, who then left the Toba Palace with Yoshimochi in a palanquin carried backwards.[93] He was accompanied by such gentlewomen as Nishi-no-onkata[94] and by female household officials. He also insisted on the company of a holy man, since he did not know where he might breathe his last. "I should like to see Hirose House again," he said; but he was not allowed to do so. On his way to Akashi, Minase House, too, remained hidden beyond distant clouds. He was now in Harima, where Ebina Suetsuna took charge of him for that part of the route. In the province of Hōki, custody of him passed to Kanamochi no Hyōe. On the 14th he reached Ōhama-no-ura in Izumo. He sailed on from there to Oki once the wind was favorable. Illness afflicted him throughout the journey, and his thoughts must have been black indeed. The physician Nakanari had renounced the world to accompany him.

Alas, in the capital he had never even heard of such wind and waves, and he felt utterly miserable. Wringing the tears from his sleeves, he made this poem:

| | |
|---|---|
| *miyako yori* | From the capital |
| *fukikuru kaze mo* | not a single breath of wind |
| *naki mono o* | ever blows my way, |
| *oki utsu nami zo* | and yet I have visitors: |
| *tsune ni toikeru* | the forever pounding waves. |

Then Yoshimochi:

| | |
|---|---|
| *suzugamo no* | I, just as I am, |
| *mi to mo ware koso* | must have changed into a duck— |
| *narinurame* | so it seems to me— |
| *nami no ue nite* | for now I spend all my life |
| *yo e sugosu kana* | tossing on the ocean waves. |

Go-Toba sent these poems to his mother, Shichijō-in, who replied:

| | |
|---|---|
| *kamikaze ya* | O wind of the gods, |
| *ima hitotabi wa* | I beg you: just one more time |
| *fukikaese* | blow him back to me: |
| *mimosusogawa no* | the Mimosuso River |
| *nagare taezu wa* | surely has not ceased to run.[95] |

On the 10th of the 10th month the second retired emperor, Tsuchimikado, was banished to Hata in the province of Tosa. The grand counselor Minamoto no Sadamichi saw him off. Four gentlewomen accompanied him, together with the privy gentlemen Minamoto no Masatoshi, a lieutenant, and Minamoto no Toshihira, a consultant. All this was too dreadful to describe. The eventual accession of Tsuchimikado's son[96] may suggest how deeply it affected the divinities Amaterasu and Hachiman.

The third retired emperor, Juntoku, was exiled to Sado. He started his journey there on the 20th of the 7th month. During the night he entered Okazaki House. Two gentlewomen traveled with him, together with the Kasan-no-in captain Fujiwara no Nobutsune and Fujiwara no Noritsune, an officer of the Watch. Juntoku lost nearly his last companion when Nobutsune became ill and returned home. Envious of the season's first wild geese, crying as they passed aloft on their way to the capital, Juntoku entrusted him with this message for the reigning emperor:

| | |
|---|---|
| *Ōsaka to* | We are on our way |
| *kiku mo urameshi* | past Ōsaka, the geese cry, |
| *nakanaka ni* | and I seethe within. |
| *michi shirazu tote* | If only they would turn back, |
| *kaerikine koso* | realizing that they are lost! |

Noritsune, too, became ill and returned home. He promised to come back, but, alas, he never did, and for Retired Emperor Juntoku life became a heavier and heavier burden. Weeds choked his door, and through the walls passed every blast of wind. Not for an instant did he forget the capital. He sent messages to his mother and to his empress; and he also sent this, in a letter to the former chancellor, Michiie:[97]

No cloud blemishes
the moon and the sun
coursing over Heaven's high plain;
wherefore I never doubted
the purity of my own heart.
Yet the geese rose from the fields
crying, and I wept
to leave the lovely capital,
trusting all the while
to be back at very least
when autumn winds blow;
but the day of my return
remains quite unknown,
like the fluttering of a leaf,
a kudzu leaf in the Northern Marches.

Still more my dewdrop life
resembles the wayside grasses
stretching on, as I, today,
yet survive, like an old pine
standing on the sandy shore
of a rough sea, uttering
with dying voice pathetic sighs,
weeping onto tear-soaked sleeves,
sleepless through the endless nights,
gazing on the moon aloft.
Those autumns above the clouds,
long ago, return to mind,
barring sleep, and the present
seems to be only a dream,
while burning pangs of longing
rise like smoke from evening fires
to fill the empty sky.
Yes, every thought of mine
goes to those I knew at home—
thoughts in great profusion,
like the ferns fringing these eaves,
like the wind-driven waves
pounding this shore, like the sorrows
birth in this sad world brings,
in accordance with past deeds:
that I know full well,
but such is the human heart
that the knowledge brings no comfort.
Autumn here is as it was,
in times gone by, at Akashi:
colored leaves of every hue,
yet no shelter anywhere
from the season's chilly rain,
while, alone, I fade away,
yet untouched by bitter frosts,
and in infamy my name
runs on as a mountain stream

tumbles on, its waters
ferrying undying foam;
so even now, here I am,
before me a dark future.

(*envoy*)

| | |
|---|---|
| *nagaraete* | Should I linger on |
| *tatoeba sue ni* | long enough to see again |
| *kaeru to mo* | where my life began, |
| *uki wa kono yo no* | this world's endless misery |
| *miyako narikeri* | would still be my only home. |

So great was his sorrow that his health declined daily, and no doubt this brought physicians from the city to his side. In the capital there were people who looked forward eagerly to every letter from him and who were gladdened simply by the sight of his handwriting. No words can convey the trouble in their hearts.

The former chancellor replied:

Widening wastes of time,
month by month, day by day,
keep me far from you, my lord,
as clouds hide the sky
 [a phrase missing]
at so great a distance
I cannot even guess
when we two may meet again.
With all my heart, morning and night,
my lord, in your noble abode,
I served you once upon a time—
you whom now, invisible,
I address only in letters,
each one carrying my thoughts
to where you are, far away;
nor have I, to comfort me,
anything but flowing tears—
an Asuka River
where tomorrow I may drown,

for the spring of yesterday
swiftly brought on present grief.
Where there runs in Ōmi
the Isaya River,
down the Toko Mountain road,
so they say, the patterned mat
spread in vain inspires no poems
  [a phrase missing]
the inlet, the mountain's rim,
in the blue heavens above
the face of the sun
shines down upon my robe
while autumn draws to a close
and visitors no longer come,
grasses wither under wintry rains,
and the very sky above
  [a phrase missing]
glowers on Mount Arachi,
snow blankets the road,
and all through the frosty nights
plovers beside the water
lift their plaintive cries,
briny drops sprinkle sleeves,
and, at evening, smoke
rises from each village
where the seafolk dwell—
smoke and waves, rising, rising
high above the clouds,
where floats the moon of dawn,
the moon I so admire.
Autumn meanwhile shrouds the heart
here in the capital,
through the blackness of long nights,
nights of early frost,
white chrysanthemums wither to brown.
From the pallor of these nights
I wake to an unsleeping dream,

one that surely is unreal,
yet leads me to wander, lost.

(*envoy*)

| | |
|---|---|
| *itoedomo* | Hateful as it is, |
| *nao nagaraete* | must I, in this world of ours, |
| *yo no naka ni* | linger on and on, |
| *uki o shirade ya* | nursing a faint hope of spring |
| *haru o matsubeki* | while ignoring misery? |

## 16. Banishments and Executions

On the 24th, Prince Masanari was exiled to Muro-no-asakura in Tajima. Go-Toba had been especially fond of this son, whom he had given into the care of his daughter, Sen'yōmon-in. The prince set off accompanied, most distressingly, by only three or four gentlewomen and privy gentlemen.

On the 25th, Prince Yorihito was banished to Kojima in Bizen. Brought together from their separate residences by the recent troubles, all Go-Toba's sons had now scattered again to live among the Ebisu[98]—the unhappy consequence of karma from past lives.

The senior nobles and privy gentlemen were sent down to the Kanto. Takeda Nobumitsu was charged with taking Fujiwara no Mitsuchika there, and Ogasawara Nagakiyo was entrusted with Fujiwara no Muneyuki. Adachi Kagemori took Fujiwara no Tadanobu; Itō Suketoki took Minamoto no Arimasa; Hōjō Tomotoki took Fujiwara no Norimochi; and Kuge Saburō took Fujiwara no Yoshitsugu. Yoshitsugu was banished to Ashida in Tango, but then slander led to his execution.

Muneyuki was executed at the Kikugawa ["Chrysanthemum River"] post station in Tōtōmi. In a local resident's house, which he had entered in order to wash his hands, he wrote:[99]

Of old, chrysanthemum water flowed in the district of Nanyang,
and he who drew of it, downstream, lived a long, long life.
Now, along the Tōkaidō, there is a Chrysanthemum River,
and he who stands on its west bank finds that his life is over.

Mitsuchika was beheaded at Ukishima-ga-hara in Suruga. He chanted scripture beforehand and gave voice also to this poem:

| | |
|---|---|
| *ima suguru* | The length of my days |
| *mi o ukishima ga* | culminates in misery |
| *hara ni mite* | at Ukishima, |
| *tsuyu no inichi zo* | where this dewdrop life of mine |
| *koko ni kienuru* | any moment now will end. |

Norimochi was drowned in a fast-running river. He summoned Hōjō Tomotoki and said, "Since those who die by the sword fall into the ashura realm, please drown me instead." They built a large basket, put him in it, and plunged it into the river. He left behind this message for his wife:

| | |
|---|---|
| *haruka naru* | Now that I must plunge |
| *chihiro no soko ni* | down into the watery deep, |
| *iru toki wa* | a thousand fathoms, |
| *akade wakareshi* | my last, fondly longing thoughts |
| *tsuma zo koishiki* | go to you, my wife at home. |

Arimasa, too, was beheaded.

Being the brother-in-law of the late Lord Minamoto no Sanetomo,[100] Tadanobu had a connection powerful enough to save his life when he applied to be spared. He returned to the capital from the bridge at Hamana and then, in his own good time, renounced the world. However, for some reason he was later banished to Echigo.

Chōgen was banished to Mutsu. They say that in time he achieved rebirth in paradise.

Lower-ranking figures were all beheaded.

Koyama Tomomasa executed an order to bring forth Yosōzaemon from Kiyomizu-yama and behead him.

Nakahara Suetoki executed an order to bring Chikayori forth from the Northern Hills and behead him.

Itō Suketoki executed an order to bring Uchikura-no-kami forth from Yawata-yama and behead him.

Sasaki Nobutsuna executed an order to bring Sasaki Hirotsuna, his elder brother, forth from the province of Ōmi and behead him.

Gotō Mototsuna executed an order to bring Gotō Motokiyo forth from Katsura-no-sato and, alas, behead him—his father.

Heizaemon executed an order to bring the brothers Fujiwara no Hideyasu and Suezumi forth from the province of Kawachi and behead them.

Sagano Saemon executed an order to bring the head of Yamada Shigesada, who had taken his own life, forth from Hannyaji-yama and present it for inspection.

Miura Yasumura, Yoshimura's younger brother, executed an order to bring the head of Miura Taneyoshi, who had taken his own life, forth from Konoshima for inspection.

Every one of these men, down to Kumano no Bettō and Yoshino-no-shugyō, was beheaded without mercy.

## 17. Noritsugu and Seitaka

These men's sons, too, were brought forth one by one and beheaded. Two particularly moving cases were those of Noritsugu, Norimochi's son,[101] and of Seitaka, the son of Hirotsuna.

Noritsugu, in his sixteenth year, was summoned to the main house at Rokuhara. Hōjō Yasutoki received him. "So you are the son of the famous Fujiwara no Norimochi!" he said. "What a handsome boy! I like your looks and manner very much. I worried a great deal about my own son, Musashi no Tarō, when he fought at Uji, Seta, and Makishima. Very well, then, I will spare your life, which I can afford to do as long as the gods are still with me. Executing you would not help me if they withdrew their favor. I therefore order you released immediately. You may go home."

Those present said in praise, "What a wonderful gesture, under the present circumstances!" Young Noritsugu, too, enjoyed divine favor, and apparently he does so still, in good health.

Seitaka, the son of Sasaki Hirotsuna, was a treasured acolyte of the prince-abbot of Ninnaji. Yasutoki learned where he was and sent a large force of warriors to demand that he be surrendered. The prince-abbot begged to keep him, but his entreaties fell on deaf ears. He said, "It is a great disappointment that there should be no pardon for Seitaka, despite my pleas. I gather that his mother is at Takao. She must be informed."

Seitaka's mother arrived at Ninnaji with a single gentlewoman. In principle no woman was to enter the abbot's quarters, but there is a time and place for everything. She was led to the west wing of his residence, and Seitaka was summoned. He could not stop crying.

"Never in my life has anyone caused me as much sorrow as this child," Seitaka's mother said. "A few years ago there was that smallpox epidemic, and then I despaired over the loss of my husband, Hirotsuna. And now the enemy has my son. It is too hard! You may as well kill me here and now, and let my son take his own life, rather than drag me to Rokuhara and torment me there. I do not want to see anything so awful." Her words ended in a storm of weeping. All present wrung the tears from their sleeves.

The prince-abbot nonetheless refused to honor her request. "I cannot grant what you ask," he said, "however intensely you may desire it. He must go immediately to Rokuhara." A carriage was brought up, and the boy was put on board. The other young acolytes, for years his companions day in and day out, clung to the shafts to keep the carriage from moving, fearing what might be in store for him. However, there was nothing they could do.

Two monks accompanied the carriage: Ōkurakyō-no-hōin and Dobashi-no-igishi. The prince-abbot had distressing words for them. "This," he said, "is my message to Rokuhara: 'If you behead him, as you may well feel you must do, please at least return his body. I should like to see it one last time and pray for him in the hereafter.' "

So Seitaka went to Rokuhara. His mother, reluctant though she was to witness his fate, still could not refrain from following him, weeping, all the way there on foot.

Yasutoki summoned Seitaka. "So you are the son of the famous Sasaki Hirotsuna, are you?" he said. "I like your looks very much. No wonder the prince-abbot of Ninnaji had you with him."

The two monks accompanying the boy said, in tears, "The prince-abbot requests that, if it is necessary to take this boy's head, his body at least be sent back to Ninnaji, so that our master can pray for him in the hereafter."

Yasutoki straightened his posture and replied, "Gracious, repeated appeals from the prince-abbot have decided me: I will release Seitaka immediately. Now, I understand that Seitaka's mother has come for him and even now stands at my gate. It is a great shame that the wife of Sasaki Hirotsuna should have had to walk here barefoot this way. Mother and son are both free to go."

Seitaka's mother heard him. She and the two monks happily pressed their palms together, wished Yasutoki ever greater divine favor in war, boarded the carriage together, and set off back to Ninnaji.

They were passing the east end of the bridge at Kiyomizu[102] when they encountered Seitaka's uncle, Sasaki Nobutsuna. Nobutsuna went straight to Rokuhara and said to Yasutoki,[103] "If you mean to spare Seitaka, then I will take my life before your eyes."

Yasutoki exclaimed in horror and surprise, "But you left Kamakura with me, stayed with me during a journey of fifteen hundred leagues,[104] fought beside me without regard for your life, and managed to come through all that alive. Why on earth should you kill yourself because of Seitaka? Bring the carriage back, if the matter is that serious!"

So it was that Yasutoki recalled Seitaka. Those accompanying him said, nodding to one another, "Lord Yasutoki is a good man. Nobutsuna's demand is just too cruel."

Seitaka's mother realized that this was the end. "Unless this life is a dream or a vision," she reflected, "I will never see him again." She got down from the carriage, blind with weeping, and made her way back to where she lived. Yasutoki called Seitaka back and gave him into the custody of Nobutsuna. Messengers kept arriving at Rokuhara to find out what had happened, and the acolytes who had long been Seitaka's constant companions came to make their own inquiries. Seitaka said, "Please go home, all of you. I long to see the prince-abbot a last time, and that makes me very sad; but, you see, there is simply nothing to be done." He pressed his sleeve to his face and wept.

Yasutoki summoned his housemen and retainers. "Who among you will cut off Seitaka's head?" he asked. None volunteered to do so. "Then give him to Nobutsuna, since he is Nobutsuna's particular enemy."

Nobutsuna took charge of Seitaka and beheaded him on the riverbank at Rokujō. He said before he did so, "Do not condemn me for this. I must kill him because his father most unfortunately attacked me, and his obnoxious men then came at me across the river. That is why I must do it."

Weeping and lamenting, Seitaka's mother came to see him die. Seitaka faced the west and prayed, "Hail, Amida, Lord of the Western Paradise, O be true to your original, compassionate Vow and bring me to rebirth in your Land of Bliss!" His head fell before he had even finished speaking. His mother clung to his body, wailing without restraint. All who witnessed the moment, high or low, shed tears.

Now, of old Minamoto no Yoriyoshi fought for twelve years in Mutsu to destroy Sadatō and Munetō. The present conflict between Retired Emperor Go-Toba and Hōjō Yoshitoki lasted only three months. Yoshitoki enjoyed pleasure and glory for having pacified the realm. Surely no like example can be found in either China or Japan.

After that the prelate Sonchō disappeared. Years later he stole into the capital with the intention of raising rebellion. However, Rokuhara discovered his presence there, and he fell into the hands of Suge Chikanori. He was summoned to Rokuhara and beheaded. Ōuchi Korenobu donned monkish robes, renounced the world, and took up residence on Mount Hiei. In the end, however, Rokuhara learned of his presence there, summoned him, and banished him to the western provinces.

The old world was now so utterly changed that many new and happy events occurred. An appointments list was announced,[105] and the three provinces of Mino, Tanba, and Tango were awarded to Prince Morisada. Fujiwara no Sanemasa received the province of Sanuki, while Fujiwara no Motoyasu became the head of the imperial Treasury.

On the 16th of the 8th month of Jōkyū 3 [1221], Prince Morisada became Retired Emperor Go-Takakura and undertook to govern the realm as he wished. He received this title because he had already renounced the world as a junior prince.[106] His receiving it made a happier moment than that of his renunciation.

On the 23rd, the new retired emperor's first progress took him to Ōi House. Since his Jimyōin residence was by now overgrown with weeds and *shinobu* ferns, he enjoyed the beautiful landscaping, the cool breeze, the green pines, and all the colors of the garden. The destiny that had led him at last to rise so high appeared to be the very one that had plunged the world into chaos. On the whole, it is no surprise that he should have come to govern the realm. As Emperor Takakura's second son, he should have succeeded Emperor Antoku. This outcome, however, was unforeseen.

A further appointments list was announced.[107] Fujiwara no Ienobu and Minamoto no Tomozane became consultants; Fujiwara no Korehira the left captain, and Fujiwara no Suketsune, the right controller, became head chamberlains; and governors were appointed to over twenty provinces.

On the night of the 9th of the 9th month Ōi House burned down. Unhappily, every trace of Retired Emperor Juntoku's dwelling was thus obliterated. Retired Emperor Go-Takakura, who had not inhabited it long, moved immediately to Kaya House. The same fire destroyed many gentlemen's homes. The Ichijō residence of Fujiwara no Kintsune, the right commander, the residence of Fujiwara no Iezane, Nishi-no-tōin House, and countless homes of other great nobles burned down.

On the 10th of the 10th month Fujiwara no Kintsune became palace minister. The event was felicitously celebrated. That night Kintsune presented his formal thanks. All this was most pleasing. A great banquet was held in the Ichijō residence of Fujiwara no Michiie. All the senior nobles were present. An informal concert followed. The performers were as follows:

| | |
|---|---|
| Rhythm clapper | Fujiwara no Takanaka |
| Flute | Fujiwara no Kin'yori |
| Shō | Fujiwara no Iehira |
| Biwa | Fujiwara no Mitsutoshi |
| Sō-no-koto | Fujiwara no Iesada |
| Wagon | — |
| Hichiriki | — |

Each man displayed his skill to delightful effect.

The 11th month then arrived, and with it the Gosechi ceremonies. They began on the evening of the 22nd. The senior nobles who provided a dancer each were Saionji Saneuji, the Ōmiya counselor, and Fujiwara no Ienobu, the left controller; the provincial governors who did the same were Fujiwara no Morotsune (Mimasaka) and Fujiwara no Kunimichi (Nagato). Their participation ensured the success of the event.

The enthronement of Emperor Go-Horikawa took place on the 1st of the 12th month.[108] Before dawn that day the new emperor repaired to the Office of Shrines. The scene on the great avenue and the grandeur of the Great Hall of State did indeed evoke a new beginning. The new emperor's elder sister, Princess Kuniko, took the role of his mother and was known thereafter, at once felicitously and touchingly, as the empress-mother.

And so the world continued on its way.

Copied by Andō Tameakira from an old<br>*Jōkyūki* manuscript, winter 1689

# Significant Figures Mentioned

THIS LIST OF FIGURES named in *Hōgen monogatari*, *Heiji monogatari*, and *Jōkyūki* is chosen from the complete list of names mentioned in these three works and included, with biographical notes, in Tochigi Yoshitada, Kusaka Tsutomu, et al., eds., *Hōgen monogatari, Heiji monogatari, Jōkyūki*, Shin Nihon koten bungaku taikei 43 (Tokyo: Iwanami, 1992), 409–458 (*Hōgen* and *Heiji* names listed together) and 459–480 (*Jōkyūki* names). In following text, all three texts are indicated together for each name, since some names appear in all three. The numbers that follow each text title indicate the number of the relevant subdivision of the corresponding work. The asterisk that precedes a name mentioned in an entry means that that name has its own entry in the list.

The biographical sketch given for each name includes, where relevant, a brief mention of the subject's achievement in music and poetry. It is impossible to overstate the esteem in which these accomplishments were held in medieval times.

AKINAGA. Fujiwara. 1117–1167. A mid-level court official, close to *Shirakawa. He reached the office of provisional middle counselor (*gonchūnagon*) in 1164.

*Heiji* 22, 29

AKITOKI. Fujiwara. 1110–1167. A mid-level court official and provincial governor, married to a daughter of Taira no *Tadamori. His daughter became

*Antoku's nurse (*menoto*). Akitoki reached the office of provisional middle counselor (*gon-chūnagon*) in 1160. He held the fifth court rank during Hōgen, and in 1167 achieved second rank and renounced the world (*shukke*).

*Hōgen* 25

*Heiji* 9

AKUGENDA. Yoshihira. See Yoshihira.

ANTOKU. 1178–1185. Emperor. The eldest son of *Takakura, by Taira no *Kiyomori's daughter Kenreimon-in. Drowned at Dannoura in 1185.

*Jōkyūki* 2

ARIMASA. Minamoto. 1176–1221. A mid-level court official who rose to the office of *gon-chūnagon* (provisional middle counselor). He renounced the world after the Jōkyū conflict and then was captured and executed.

*Jōkyūki* 4, 9, 16

BIFUKUMON-IN. Fujiwara no Tokuko. 1117–1260. *Go-Toba's empress.

*Hōgen* 1, 3, 4, 19, 22

*Heiji* 19

BŌMON-NO-HIME. Minamoto. 1155?–1190. A daughter of Minamoto no *Yoshitomo.

*Heiji* 14, 30

CHIKAYORI. Saitō. ?–1221. A minor court official who fought on *Go-Toba's side. Executed by Nakahara *Suetoki.

*Jōkyūki* 3, 9, 16

CHŌGON. 1152–1228. Ninnaji priest and personal chaplain (*gojisō*) of *Go-Toba.

*Jōkyūki* 3, 16

GENJITSU. Minamoto. ?–? A monk of Kōfukuji in Nara.

*Hōgen* 12, 20

GENKEN. Fujiwara. ?–? A Kōfukuji monk related to *Yorinaga. Involvement in the Hōgen conflict led to confiscation of his property.

*Hōgen* 21

GO-SHIRAKAWA. 1129–1192. Emperor, then Retired Emperor. Fourth son of *Go-Toba and younger brother of *Sutoku; father of *Nijō, *Takakura, Prince *Mochihito, and the distinguished poet Princess Shokushi; and grandfather of *Antoku and *Go-Toba. In 1155 he succeeded to *Konoe, with the backing of *Bifukumon-in and Fujiwara no *Tadamichi. Opposition to this succession by Sutoku's supporters sparked the Hōgen conflict.

Aided by Fujiwara no *Shinzei, Go-Shirakawa initiated personal rule by the reigning emperor (*shinsei*). After abdicating, he then ruled throughout five reigns as a retired emperor (*insei*). This was one cause of the Heiji conflict.

*Hōgen* 1, 4, 5, 14, 17, 31, 35, 36

*Heiji* 1, 2, 3, 4, 5, 6, 7, 8, 11, 13, 18, 22, 29, 33

*Jōkyūki* 2

GO-TOBA. 1180–1239. Emperor. Fourth son of *Takakura. Enthroned by *Shirakawa in 1183, after *Antoku's flight from Kyoto. He continued Shirakawa's *insei*. Go-Toba plotted the failed Jōkyū conflict and died in exile on the island of Oki. He was a major *Shinkokinshū* poet.

*Jōkyūki* 4 (with his four sons: *Tsuchimikado, *Juntoku, Prince Masanari, Prince Yorihito), 5, 6, 7, 9, 12, 13, 14, 15

HIDEHIRA. Fujiwara. ?–1187. Son of Fujiwara no Motohira, a major military official (*Dewa no ōryōshi*) in northern Japan; married to the daughter of Motonari, Fujiwara no *Nobuyori's younger brother. In 1170 he was named commander of the court's military outpost in the north (*Chinjufu shōgun*). On his deathbed he had his sons swear allegiance to *Yoshitsune rather than to *Yoritomo.

*Heiji* 32, 33

HIDEYASU. Fujiwara. ?–1221. A Hokumen (retired emperor's) guard for *Go-Toba, and a provincial governor. Commanded troops for Go-Toba in the Jōkyū conflict, then was captured and executed.

*Jōkyūki* 3, 6, 16

HIROTSUNA. Sasaki. ?–1221. Protector (*shugo*) of Ōmi and Nagato, then Hokumen guard for *Go-Toba and provincial governor. Fought for *Go-Toba in Jōkyū, then was captured and executed.

*Jōkyūki* 3, 5, 16

HIROTSUNE. Kazusa. ?–1283. Allied with Minamoto no *Yoshitomo in Hōgen and Heiji, he responded to *Yoritomo's later call for troops. Too proud to dismount even for Yoritomo, he also criticized Yoritomo's subservience to the court in Kyoto.

*Heiji* 14, 16, 17, 21

IEHIRO. Taira. ?–1156. Served *Sutoku and *Yorinaga, and was appointed a magistrate (*hōgandai*) together with Minamoto no *Tameyoshi. Killed in Hōgen by Ashikaga *Yoshiyasu.

*Hōgen* 6, 8, 15, 16, 18, 25, 35

IENAGA. Fujiwara. ?–? A provincial-governor-level courtier and household official of *Toba. Also served Fujiwara no *Tadazane and *Yorinaga.

*Hōgen* 7, 10, 22

IESADA. Taira. 1084–1167. A leading warrior under *Tadamori, rewarded for his effective suppression of pirates in cooperation with *Kiyomori.

*Hōgen* 34

*Heiji* 8, 16, 24

IESUE, Sudō Kurō. ?–? A foster brother of Minamoto no *Tametomo.

*Hōgen* 10, 13, 14

IKE, Lady. Ike no Zenni. Fujiwara. ?–? Taira no *Tadamori's second wife and *Kiyomori's stepmother. At Tadamori's death became a nun. After the Heiji conflict she persuaded Kiyomori, through his eldest son *Shigemori, to exile rather than execute the young Minamoto no *Yoritomo.

*Heiji* 27, 30, 33

IMAWAKA, OTOWAKA, USHIWAKA. Minamoto. The sons (with *Yoritomo) of *Yoshitomo, *Tameyoshi's eldest son. Ushiwaka, the youngest, became the famous Minamoto no *Yoshitsune.

*Heiji* 20, 21, 26, 28 (Imawaka not in 28), 32, 33 (Yoshitsune)

*Jōkyūki* 2

JUNTOKU. 1197–1242. Emperor. *Go-Toba's third son. Enthroned in 1210, he abdicated in 1221. Exiled to Sado after supporting Go-Toba's Jōkyū conflict. Juntoku left a personal poetry collection, as well as the valued poetry treatises *Yakumo mishō* and *Kinpishō*.

*Jōkyūki* 4, 15

KAGEMORI. Adachi. ?–1248. A Kamakura warrior and official. Renounced the world after *Sanetomo, the last Minamoto shogun, was assassinated in 1219.

*Jōkyūki* 8, 9, 16

KAGESHIGE. Katagiri. ?–1159. A houseman of Minamoto no *Tameyoshi.

*Heiji* 14, 16, 17

KAKERU. Minamoto. ?–1221. Known only as a fierce fighter.

*Jōkyūki* 9, 11, 13

KANENAGA. Fujiwara. 1138–1158. *Yorinaga's eldest son, adopted by *Tadamichi.

*Hōgen* 20, 30

KINCHIKA. Fujiwara. 1131–1159. A son of the left minister (*sadaijin*) Taira no *Saneyoshi.

*Hōgen* 12, 17

KINNORI. Fujiwara. 1103–1160. A high-ranking court noble, the eldest son of the chancellor (*daijōdaijin*) Fujiwara no Saneyuki. In Hōgen he held the second rank and the offices of provisional major counselor (*gon-dainagon*) and commander of the Left (rather than Right, as in *Hōgen* 9) Gate Watch (*saemon no kami*). Appointed palace minister (*naidaijin*) in 1157.

*Hōgen* 9, 11

KI-NO-NII. Fujiwara Tomoko. ?–1166. Fujiwara no *Shinzei's wife and the nurse of *Go-Shirakawa. A highly influential figure.

*Heiji* 7, 12, 29

KINTSUGU. Tokudaiji. 1175–1227. Appointed left minister (*sadaijin*) in 1224. A poet and *biwa* musician.

*Jōkyūki* 3, 14,

KINTSUNE. Saionji. 1171–1244. A son of palace minister Saionji *Kinmune, married to a niece of *Yoritomo, and the grandfather of the shogun Fujiwara no Yoritsune (1219–1256). In 1221, he warned Kamakura of *Go-Toba's plot against it, which led to the imprisonment of his son, *Saneuji. Appointed chancellor (*daijōdaijin*) in 1222.

*Jōkyūki* 3, 6, 14, 16

KIYOMORI. Taira. 1118–1181. Eldest son of *Tadamori and a dominant figure throughout this period, especially in *Heike*. He became head of the Heike in 1153.

*Hōgen* 5, 9, 12, 13, 14, 17, 20, 23, 24, 25, 26, 31, 35

*Heiji* 2, 4, 8, 9, 12, 16, 23, 24, 27, 28, 29, 30, 31, 32

*Jōkyūki* 2

KONOE. 1139–1155. Emperor. *Toba's ninth son, by *Bifukumon-in. His reign coincided with the *insei* dominance of his father, which caused him much distress. One empress (*kōgōgū*) was Tashi, an adopted daughter of *Yorinaga; a second (*chūgū*) was Teishi (*Kujō-in), an adopted daughter of *Tadamichi, forced on him to counter the influence of Tashi and Yorinaga.

*Hōgen* 1, 3, 4, 22

*Jōkyūki* 2

KON'ŌMARU. 1141–? Sent by Minamoto no *Yoritomo to assassinate *Yoshitsune, Yoritomo's brother.

*Heiji* 20, 21

KOREKATA. Fujiwara. 1125–? A younger brother of *Mitsuyori. His mother was *Nijō's nurse. *Toba, at his death, begged him to keep *Sutoku from the throne.

*Hōgen* 9

*Heiji* 2, 6, 11, 12, 13, 20, 29

KOREMICHI. Fujiwara. 1093–1165. A high-ranking courtier. His sister married Fujiwara no *Tadamichi. He was the father of *Kujō-in Teishi, *Konoe's empress. Koremichi was appointed palace minister (*naidaijin*) in 1156, left minister (*sadaijin*) in 1157, and chancellor (*daijōdaijin*) in 1160. Poems by him appear in *Kin'yōshū* and *Shikashū*.

*Hōgen* 5, 6

*Heiji* 4, 5, 10, 13, 18, 28, 29

KORENOBU. Ōuchi. ?–? Fought for *Go-Toba in Jōkyū.

*Jōkyūki* 3, 9, 16

KORENORI. Fujiwara. ?–? Fujiwara no *Shinzei's third son.

*Heiji* 4, 10

KUJŌ-IN. Fujiwara Teishi. 1131–1176. A daughter of chancellor Fujiwara no *Koremichi (1093–1165), subsequently adopted by *Bifukumon-in, then by Fujiwara no *Tadamichi. *Konoe was obliged to accept her as a second empress to counter the influence of his first empress, Tashi, an adopted daughter of *Yorinaga.

*Heiji* 20, 26, 28

MAREYOSHI ("Kira no Kanja"). Minamoto. 1152–1182. A son of Minamoto no *Yoshitomo and a half-brother of *Yoritomo. Exiled to Tosa in the aftermath of the Heiji conflict.

*Heiji* 29, 33

MASAIE. Kamada. 1123?–1160. A foster brother of *Yoshitomo. Masaie changed his name to Fujiwara when named to a guards post during the Heiji conflict.

*Hōgen* 13, 14, 24, 26, 34

*Heiji* 5, 14, 15, 16, 19, 21

MASAKO. Hōjō. 1157–1225. Daughter of Hōjō Tokimasa (1139–1215), the first adjutant (*shikken*) of the Kamakura Bakufu, and the formidable wife of Minamoto no *Yoritomo.

*Jōkyūki* 7

MASAYORI. Minamoto. 1127–1190.

*Hōgen* 6, 12, 17

MICHIIE. Kujō. 1193–1252. Eldest son of regent and chancellor Fujiwara no *Yoshitsune and husband of Rinshi, a daughter of Saionji *Kintsune. His mother was a niece of Minamoto no *Yoshitomo.

*Jōkyūki* 3, 14, 15, 16

MITSUCHIKA, Azechi counselor. 1176–1221. A mid-level courtier whose wife was *Juntoku's nurse (*menoto*). He collaborated with *Go-Toba in planning the Jōkyū conflict, after which he was captured and executed.

*Jōkyūki* 3, 7, 9, 16

MITSUHIRO. Taira. ?–1156. A son of *Iehiro.

*Hōgen* 15, 18, 25

MITSUYASU. Minamoto. ?–1160. A provincial governor whose daughter became *Toba's favorite and *Nijō's nurse. Joined Nijō's forces in Heiji, then changed sides. Eventually exiled and executed.

*Heiji* 2, 5, 6, 14, 15

MITSUYORI. Fujiwara. 1124–1173. *Korekata's elder brother.

*Heiji* 9, 11

MOCHIHITO. 1151–1180. Prince. The third son of Go-Shirakawa and full brother of the distinguished poet Princess Shokushi (1149–1201). In 1180, he and *Yorimasa attempted a failed rebellion against *Kiyomori. While fleeing toward Nara he was killed in Uji, at the Byōdōin.

*Jōkyūki* 33

MORINORI. Fujiwara. ?–? A mid-level courtier, a brother of *Norichika, *Tsunenori, and the monk *Genken. Close to *Sutoku. After Hōgen conflict he renounced the world but was banished to Sado, then later recalled. An aunt, married to Fujiwara no *Tadazane, was the mother of *Yorinaga.

*Hōgen* 8, 15, 22

MORIYASU. Kōketsu Gengo. ?–1173? Fought under Minamoto no *Tameyoshi, then *Yoshitomo.

*Heiji* 30, 33

MOROKATA (another name for Fujiwara no Munesuke). 1077–1162. Became chancellor (*daijōdaijin*) in 1157. An expert flute player, he also loved peonies and kept bees.

*Heiji* 4, 10

MORONAGA. Fujiwara. 1138–1192. A high-ranking courtier and son of *Yorinaga; adopted by *Tadazane. Dismissed from office and exiled to Tosa after the Hōgen conflict, then pardoned in 1164. Became chancellor (*daijōdaijin*) in 1177, then was dismissed in 1180 and exiled to Owari. Pardoned and returned to Kyoto in 1182, after which he retired and renounced the world. A musical genius, Moronaga is responsible for the preservation of the corpus of Heian music.

*Hōgen* 20, 30, 32

MORONAKA. Minamoto. 1116–1172. A mid-level courtier, exiled in connection with the Heiji confict, then recalled in 1166 but not reinstated. Said to have hidden the Naishidokoro (the Sacred Mirror, one of the imperial regalia) during the Heiji conflict and to have started a fight in *Go-Toba's residence. His sister was the poet Kojijū.

*Heiji* 1, 18, 19

MOTOKIYO. Gotō. 1155–1221. A Hokumen guard for *Go-Shirakawa and *Go-Toba.

*Jōkyūki* 3, 16

MOTOMICHI. Konoe. 1160–1233. A son-in-law of Taira no *Kiyomori and close to *Go-Shirakawa. He held the office of regent most of the time between 1179 and 1186, and in 1196.

*Jōkyūki* 3, 5

MOTOMORI. Taira. 1139–1162. *Kiyomori's second son.

*Heiji* 5

MOTOZANE. Fujiwara. 1143–1166. *Tadazane's first son and a high-ranking courtier. During the Heiji conflict he married Fujiwara no *Nobuyori's daughter and in 1158 gained the office of regent for Nijō.

*Hōgen* 12

*Heiji* 4, 10, 18

MUNEKIYO. Taira. ?–? Nephew of Taira no *Iesada. A Hokumen guard for *Go-Shirakawa, he was a houseman of Taira no *Yorimori. His kindness to the young *Yoritomo, when Yoritomo was held in confinement, eventually got him and Yorimori invited to Kamakura.

*Heiji* 25, 27, 30

MUNEMORI. Taira. 1147–1185. *Kiyomori's third son and the lackluster head of the Heike after his father's death.

*Heiji* 16, 19

*Jōkyūki* 2

MUNEYOSHI. Fujiwara. 1084–1170. A ranking courtier, appointed palace minister (*naidaijin*) in 1164.

*Hōgen* 5, 6

MUNEYUKI. Fujiwara. 1174–1221. A mid-level courtier. Renounced the world after the Jōkyū conflict and was sent to the Kanto. He was executed.

*Jōkyūki* 3, 8, 16

NAGAKIYO. Ogasawara. 1162–1242. A major commander in the Tōsandō region during the Jōkyū conflict, after which he was appointed protector (*shugo*) of Awa. His wife was the daughter of Wada Yoshimori (1147–1213).

*Jōkyūki* 7, 8, 11, 16

NAGAMORI. Taira. ?–1156. A cousin of *Kiyomori and a Hokumen guard for *Sutoku.

*Hōgen* 8, 25

NAGANORI. Fujiwara. 1143–? Fujiwara no *Shinzei's fifth son.

*Heiji* 4, 10

NAOZANE. Kumagai. 1181–1208. Mentioned in a list of men commanded by Minamoto no *Yoshitomo as being from Musashi. Famous because of the Atsumori episode during the battle of Ichinotani (1184), recounted in *Heike*.

*Hōgen* 12

NARICHIKA. Fujiwara. 1138–1177. A ranking Fujiwara noble, appointed governor of Echigo already in his 7th year. Brother-in-law of Taira no *Shigemori and *Fujiwara no Nobuyori; father-in-law of Koremori (1157–1184?), Shigemori's son. Dismissed from office after the Heiji conflict, then reinstated, in a pattern later repeated. Intensely favored by Go-Shirakawa, probably as a lover. After joining the anti-Heike Shishigatani plot (1177), Narichika was exiled to Bizen and killed.

*Hōgen* 35

*Heiji* 2, 13, 18

NARIMASA. Minamoto. ?–? A mid-level courtier whose sister married Fujiwara no *Yorinaga and gave birth to *Moronaga. He supported *Sutoku during the Hōgen conflict, then renounced the world and was exiled to Echigo.

*Hōgen* 8, 10, 22, 32

NARITAKA. Fujiwara. ?–? A houseman of *Yorinaga. He backed *Sutoku during Hōgen, then renounced the world and was exiled to Awa.

*Hōgen* 8, 15, 22, 32

NARIYORI. Fujiwara. 1136–1202. A full brother of *Mitsuyori and *Korekata.

*Heiji* 4, 11

NIJŌ. 1143–1165. Emperor. *Go-Shirakawa's eldest son, brought up by *Bifukumon-in. Although meant to become a monk at Ninnaji, he succeeded to the throne after Go-Shirakawa's abdication.

HŌGEN 35

HEIJI 1, 12

NOBUCHIKA. Fujiwara. 1155–? A son of *Nobuyori, and Taira no *Kiyomori's son-in-law.

*Hōgen* 2

*Heiji* 19

NOBUMITSU. Takeda. 1162–1248. Took part in Minamoto no *Yoritomo's campaigns to suppress his cousin *Yoshinaka (1184) and to conquer the north (1189). During Jōkyū commanded forces in the Tōsandō region.

*Jōkyūki* 7, 8, 11, 16

NOBUYORI. Fujiwara. 1133–1159. Began his career at roughly the provincial governor level, but then gained *Go-Shirakawa's unreasoning favor and rose with unusual speed. What he offered Go-Shirakawa is unclear, since his only talents seem to have been imposing looks and arrogance. Ambition brought him into murderous rivalry with Fujiwara no *Shinzei, Go-Shirakawa's principal adviser. In the end he was beheaded.

*Hōgen* 15, 35

*Heiji* 1, 2, 3, 6, 9, 13, 14, 15, 17, 18

NORICHIKA. Fujiwara. ?–? A brother of *Morinori, *Tsunenori, and the monk *Genken, and a houseman of *Yorinaga.

*Hōgen* 8, 32

NORIMOCHI. Fujiwara. 1185–1221. Fought for *Go-Toba in Jōkyū. After defeat at Uji he renounced the world, then drowned himself.

*Jōkyūki* 3, 8, 16

NORIMORI. Taira. 1128–1187. *Tadamori's fourth son, hence a younger brother of Kiyomori. Distinguished himself in both Hōgen and Heiji. *Naritsune, his son-in-law, was implicated in the anti-Heike Shishigatani plot, which then compromised Norimori as well. Lost two sons (Narimori, Michimori) in the battle of Ichinotani (1184).

*Hōgen* 12, 23

*Heiji* 12, 14, 22

NORINAGA. Fujiwara. 1109–? An upper-level courtier who fought for *Sutoku in Hōgen, then renounced the world and was exiled to Hitachi. Once pardoned, he retired to Mount Kōya. Norinaga has thirty-seven poems (a large number) in imperial collections (*chokusenshū*).

*Hōgen* 6, 8, 10, 18, 22, 32

NORIYORI. Minamoto. ?–1193? A half-brother of *Yoritomo and *Yoshitsune. Yoritomo eventually had him executed.

*Heiji* 33

*Jōkyūki* 2

OSHIMATSU. ?–? In 1221, Oshimatsu delivered Retired Emperor *Go-Toba's decree (*inzen*) to the Kanto, ordering the suppression of Hōjō *Yoshitoki.

*Jōkyūki* 7, 8, 9

OTOWAKA. The childhood name of *Yoshitsune. It simply means "youngest son."

SADANORI. Fujiwara. ?–? *Shinzei's second son. Rose swiftly after the Hōgen conflict but after Heiji was dismissed, renounced the world and retired to Mount Kōya. He is the father of the important Kōfukuji monk Gedatsubō Jōkei (1155–1213).

*Hōgen* 12

*Heiji* 4, 10

SADAYASU. Tate. ?–1183? During the Heiji conflict he delivered Fujiwara no *Nobuchika, *Nobuyori's son, to the enemy and was praised by *Yoshitomo.

*Heiji* 8, 12, 14

SAIKŌ. Fujiwara. ?–1177. Nominally, a monk. A sister of his grandfather (Tadamitsu) was Fujiwara no *Shinzei's wife, and Saikō's mother was Shinzei's nurse (*menoto*). He was in *Go-Shirakawa's intimate service. Saikō joined *Narichika in the anti-Heike Shishigatani plot (1177). *Heike*, Book 2, describes his torture and execution.

*Hōgen* 35

*Heiji* 6

SANEKIYO. Fujiwara. ?–? Dismissed as head of *Sutoku's household after the Hōgen conflict and exiled to Tosa.

*Hōgen* 6, 8

SANEMORI. Saitō (Nagai no Saitō Bettō). 1126–1183. A houseman (*gokenin*) of Minamoto no *Tameyoshi. Joined the Heike after the Heiji conflict. His two sons served Koremori (1157–1184?), *Shigemori's son. Took part as an old man in the Heike northern campaign.

*Heiji* 14, 16, 17

SANETOMO. Minamoto. 1192–1219. Second son of *Yoritomo and *Masako, and the last Minamoto shogun. Assassinated by Kugyō, his nephew, in 1219. His well-known personal poetry collection is entitled *Kinkai wakashū*.

*Jōkyūki* 3 (Senman, his childhood name), 6

SANEUJI. Saionji. 1194–1269. Son of chancellor (*daijōdaijin*) Saionji *Kintsune. In 1219 Saneuji went to Kamakura for the ceremony marking *Sanetomo's appointment as right minister (*udaijin*) and witnessed Sanetomo's assassination. Supported *Go-Toba in Jōkyū and was imprisoned for a time. Appointed palace minister (*naidaijin*) in 1231 and in 1246 chancellor, although he immediately resigned. Also served as court representative to Kamakura (*Kantō mōshitsugi*). His daughter was Go-Daigo's empress.

*Jōkyūki* 6, 14

SANEYOSHI. Taira. 1097–1157. During his career held all three ministerial (*daijin*) offices. He became left minister (*sadaijin*) in 1156, after the fall of Fujiwara no Yorinaga, then renounced the world (*shukke*) and died. The great poet Saigyō (1118–1190) had been one of his retainers before becoming a monk.

*Hōgen* 6, 12, 23, 25

SHIGEHITO. 1140–1152. Prince. *Sutoku's first son. After Hōgen renounced the world at Ninnaji.

*Hōgen* 1, 4, 9, 23, 31

*Jōkyūki* 2

SHIGEMORI. Taira. 1138–1179. *Kiyomori's eldest son, extremely prominent in *Heike*.

*Hōgen* 12, 13

*Heiji* 2, 18, 19, 27

*Jōkyūki* 2

SHIGENARI. Minamoto. ?–1159. Protected *Sutoku at Ninnaji during the Hōgen conflict, then saw him off on his way to exile on Shikoku. During the Heiji conflict he sacrificed his life for *Yoshitomo.

*Hōgen* 9, 17, 19, 31

*Heiji* 3, 5, 19, 21

SHIGENORI. Fujiwara. 1135–1187. *Shinzei's fourth son by *Ki no Nii. Married to a daughter of *Kiyomori, he rose swiftly in rank and office after Hōgen. Resigned as middle counselor (*chūnagon*) when the Heike fled the capital (1183). Suspected of sympathy with *Yoritomo and *Yoshitsune. His daughter Kogō (1157–?) was loved by *Takakura.

*Heiji* 4, 8, 10, 20

SHIGESADA. Yamada. ?–1221. Served *Go-Toba, fought as a leading warrior in Jōkyū, and killed himself after the defeat. His son, taken alive, was executed.

*Jōkyūki* 9, 11, 12, 13, 16

SHINJITSU. Minamoto. ?–? A Kōfukuji monk. Once jailed for violent behavior and described in one document as "the most defiant, warlike monk in Japan," Shinjitsu led the Kōfukuji attack on Kinpusen in 1345. Nonetheless, he reached the highest rank at Kōfukuji. After Hōgen his property was confiscated.

*Hōgen* 10, 12, 20

SHINZEI. Fujiwara no Michinori. 1106–1159. A mid-level courtier and son of Fujiwara no Sanekane (1084–1112). Married to *Ki-no-Nii. Served *Toba and was close to *Kiyomori. A brilliant scholar with no hope of promotion commensurate with his talent, he became a monk in 1144; Shinzei was his name in religion. He taught *Yorinaga the art of divination. His wife had been *Go-Shirakawa's nurse (*menoto*), which brought him close to that emperor, under whom he engaged in a major reform project. He left such learned works as *Honchō seiki* and a commentary on *Nihongi*. *Heiji* describes his unusual death.

*Hōgen* 5, 12, 14, 20, 25, 33, 35

*Heiji* 3, 4, 5, 6, 8, 10

SONCHŌ. Fujiwara. ?–1227. An Enryakuji monk and a key figure on *Go-Toba's side in Jōkyū. Said to have tried to kill Saionji *Kintsune, his brother-in-law, for being in sympathy with Kamakura.

*Jōkyūki* 3, 9, 12, 16

SUESHIGE. Hirayama. ?–? A Musashi warrior who fought for *Yoritomo. In rivalry with Kumagai *Naozane to lead the Genji attack at Ichinotani.

*Heiji* 14, 16

SUETOKI. Nakahara. ?–1136. One of the Kamakura elders during Jōkyū.

*Jōkyūki* 14, 16

SUEZANE. Minamoto. ?–1159. A mid-level courtier and provincial governor in *Toba's service. Supported the emperor in the Hōgen conflict, and in Heiji was allied with *Nobuyori. He and his son Suemori were executed.

*Hōgen* 5, 9, 20, 25, 26, 34

*Heiji* 2, 19

SUKETSUNE. Minamoto. ?–? A Hokumen guard and houseman (*gokenin*) of *Yorinaga.

*Hōgen* 5, 9

SUTOKU. 1119–1164. Emperor. *Toba's eldest son, enthroned in 1123. In 1141, at Toba's insistence, he abdicated in favor of *Konoe. Despite Sutoku's wish to have *Shigehito, his eldest son, succeed Konoe, *Go-Shirakawa instead came to the throne. After Toba's death he allied himself with Yorinaga. *After defeat in the Hōgen conflict he renounced the world at Ninnaji and was exiled to Sanuki, on Shikoku. In 1177 it was felt necessary to hold a ceremony to pacify his angry ghost. Eighty poems by Sutoku appear in imperial anthologies.

*Hōgen* 1, 3, 4, 5, 6, 7, 8, 9, 10, 11, 12, 13, 14, 15, 16, 17, 18, 19, 20 31, 32, 34, 35
*Heiji* 3, 11
*Jōkyūki* 2

TADAIE. Andō. ?–1221. Fought under Hōjō *Yoshitoki. In Jōkyū he drowned in the Uji River, at the time of the battle there.

*Jōkyūki* 8, 12

TADAMASA. Fujiwara. 1124–1193. An upper-level courtier and a cousin of *Narichika. He married Narichika's sister, and their son, Kanemasa, married a daughter of *Kiyomori. Tadamasa also brought up Kiyomori's daughter by Tokiwa. In Hōgen a middle counselor (*chūnagon*), he rose to palace minister (*naidaijin*) in 1167. In 1168 he followed Kiyomori as chancellor (*daijodaijin*).

*Hōgen* 8, 10, 14, 15, 17, 24, 25, 35
*Heiji* 4, 18, 19

TADAMICHI. Fujiwara. 1097–1164. Eldest son of *Tadazane and father of the great monk, poet, and historian Jien (1155–1225), the author of *Gukanshō*. Appointed chancellor (*daijōdaijin*) in 1128, he served as regent for *Toba, *Sutoku, *Konoe, and *Go-Shirakawa. In 1180 *Tadazane, his father, stripped him of the title of head of the Fujiwara house (*uji no chōja*) in favor of *Yorinaga, his younger brother. After *Konoe's death, he and *Bifukumon-in ensured the succession for Go-Shirakawa, rather than Sutoku's son *Shigehito. After the Hōgen conflict he regained the title of *uji no chōja*, and in 1158 he ceded the office of regent to *Motozane, his eldest son. Tadamichi was versed in both Chinese and Japanese learning, and he was an expert musician. Sixty of his poems appear in imperial collections (*chokusenshū*).

*Hōgen* 4, 5, 6, 12, 15, 20, 33
*Heiji* 4, 10, 12, 18, 20, 29

TADAMORI. Taira. 1096–1153. The father of *Kiyomori. Under *Shirakawa and *Toba, Tadamori fought bandits and the belligerant (*gōso*) monks of Enryakuji, and also distinguished himself fighting pirates. He was rewarded with various court appointments, and in 1132, over many objections, was granted direct access (*shōden*) to the palace (*Heike*, Book 1). He took part in the enthronement of *Konoe in 1150. A very wealthy and powerful figure.

*Hōgen* 23

*Heiji* 27

TADAMUNE. Osada. ?–1185. A warrior from Owari. He killed *Yoshitomo and Yoshitomo's son-in-law, Kamada *Masakiyo.

*Heiji* 21, 22, 24, 33

TADANOBU. Fujiwara, the "Bōmon grand counselor." 1187–? Fought for *Go-Toba in Jōkyū, then was captured and sent to Kamakura, where his younger sister, the wife of Minamoto no *Sanetomo, pleaded successfully for his life. He returned to Kyoto, renounced the world, was exiled to Echigo, and was later pardoned. Poems by him appear in several imperial collections.

*Jōkyūki* 3, 8

TADATSUNA. Taira. ?–1156. A house official for *Yorinaga.

*Hōgen* 8, 25

TADAZANE. Fujiwara. 1078–1162. The eldest son of the regent Moromichi (1062–1099), but adopted by his grandfather Morozane (1042–1101) when Moromichi died prematurely. In his fourteenth year he received the junior third rank. Appointed *kanpaku* (regent) in 1105 and *sesshō* (also translated "regent") in 1107, and in 1112 became chancellor (*daijōdaijin*). In 1130 he fell out with *Shirakawa and was briefly stripped of the important post of *nairan*. In 1140 he renounced the world (*shukke*). Tadazane took the office of regent from *Tadamichi, his first son, and offered it to *Yorinaga, his second. When Yorinaga refused it, Tadazane instead dismissed Tadamichi as head of the Fujiwara house (*uji no chōja*) and appointed Yorinaga. In the Hōgen conflict Tadazane supported Yorinaga, whose death devastated him. He then retired from the world. Slender and graceful, Tadazane played the *sō no koto* expertly and also had a beautiful singing voice. He left a major *kanbun* diary (*Denryaku*) and other works.

*Hōgen* 4, 10, 20, 21, 30, 32, 33

TAKAKURA. 1161–1181. Emperor. *Go-Shirakawa's fifth son and the father of *Antoku, in whose favor he abdicated.

*Jōkyūki* 2

TAKANAGA. Fujiwara. 1141–? The third son of *Yorinaga. He ended up exiled to Izu.

*Hōgen* 20, 30, 32

TAKASUE. Fujiwara. 1127–1185. A half-brother of *Narichika. Close to *Toba, and a household official of *Go-Shirakawa and *Takakura. He probably was a lover of *Yorinaga.

*Hōgen* 20

*Heiji* 18

TAMENAKA. Minamoto. ?–1156. Seventh son of *Tameyoshi.

*Hōgen* 8

*Heiji* 5

TAMETOMO. Minamoto. 1139–? *Tameyoshi's eighth son; his mother was a singing girl (*yūjo*) from the harbor town of Eguchi. Grew up in Kyushu. Physically, Tametomo was exceptionally powerful, drew a huge bow, and shot extraordinarily long arrows. He was also uncontrollable. In 1154 his father dismissed him from office because of his behavior, but to no avail. Captured in Ōmi in 1155 and exiled to Izu, where he seized control of the "Seven Izu Islands" (*Izu shichitō*). When pursued he killed himself. His children in Kyushu were executed.

*Hōgen* 7, 8, 10, 11, 13, 14, 36

TAMEYOSHI. Minamoto. ?–1156. Father of *Tametomo. Adopted as a child by his grandfather Hachimantarō Yoshiie (1039–1106). A junior officer in the imperial guards and police, he held a few provincial governor posts and eventually reached the fifth rank. Tameyoshi served *Tadazane, then *Yorinaga. In 1154 he was dismissed from office because of Tametomo's outrageous behavior. In the Hōgen conflict he was persuaded to support *Sutoku. After the defeat he was cut down by *Yoshitomo, his son.

*Hōgen* 7, 8, 12, 13, 15, 16, 17, 24, 32, 35

TANEYOSHI. Miura. ?–1221. A nephew of *Yoritomo. A respected Kamakura houseman who moved to Kyoto and joined Toba's plan to overthrow Kamakura Bakufu. A senior commander in Jōkyū, he killed himself after the defeat.

*Jōkyūki* 3, 5, 7, 9, 11, 13, 16

TOBA. 1103–1156. Emperor. Eldest son of Emperor Horikawa (1079–1107, r. 1086–1107). He remained powerless under the *insei* rule of *Shirakawa, but then wielded power for twenty-eight years under the reigns of *Sutoku,

*Konoe, and *Go-Shirakawa. Favored the Heike. Toba retired from the world (*shukke*) in 1141 and had himself succeeded by Konoe, his son by *Bifukumon-in. This provoked a clash with Sutoku and, after his death, the Hōgen conflict. Particularly devout, Toba made twenty-three pilgrimages to Kumano. He was also known as a fine flute player. Eight of his poems appear in imperial collections (*chokusenshū*).

*Hōgen* 1, 2, 3, 4, 5

*Heiji* 5

*Jōkyūki* 2

TOKIFUSA. Hōjō. 1175–1240. A son of Hōjō Tokimasa (1138–1215, the first adjutant [*shikken*] of the Kamakura shogunate) and a younger brother of *Yoshitoki. Tokifusa took part in the pacification of northern Japan (Mutsu). In Jōkyū he and his nephew *Yasutoki led an army into the capital. Later he was appointed the Kamakura representative in Kyoto (*Rokuhara tandai*).

*Jōkyūki* 3, 6, 8, 10, 11

TOKIWA. 1138–? Parentage. One of *Yoshitomo's wives and the mother of Zenjō, Enjō, and *Yoshitsune (in childhood Imawaka, Otowaka, Ushiwaka). Tokiwa was a servant of *Kujō-in. After Yoshitomo's death she married Fujiwara no Naganari (?–?) and Taira no *Kiyomori, for each of whom she bore a daughter.

*Heiji* 20, 21, 26, 28, 30, 32

TOMOMASA. Koyama. 1155–1238. A mid-level court official and provincial governor, charged in Jōkyū by *Go-Toba, with many others, with suppressing Hōjō *Yoshitoki. He renounced the world in 1234.

*Jōkyūki* 6, 8, 16

TOMONAGA. Minamoto. 1144–1159. The second son of *Yoshitomo.

*Heiji* 14, 19, 21, 25

TOSHINARI. Takashina. ?–? A house official of *Tadamichi.

*Hōgen* 6, 21?

TOSHINORI. Fujiwara. 1122–1167. *Shinzei's fourth son.

*Hōgen* 12

*Heiji* 4, 10

TOSHITSUNA. Yamanouchi Sudō Takiguchi. ?–1159. Fought under *Yoshitomo.

*Hōgen* 13

*Heiji* 14, 15

TSUCHIMIKADO. 1195–1231, r. 1198–1210. Emperor. Eldest son of *Go-Toba. Took no part in the Jōkyū conflict, but afterwards was exiled by his own wish to Tosa (Shikoku). He left a personal poetry collection.

*Jōkyūki* 4, 16

TSUNEFUSA. Naniwa Saburō. ?–? On an excursion with *Kiyomori he was killed by *Yoshihira (Akugenda Yoshihira) in thunderbolt form.

*Heiji* 8, 23, 31

TSUNEMORI. Taira. 1124–1185. A younger brother of *Kiyomori, and the father of Tsunemasa and Atsumori.

*Hōgen* 12

*Heiji* 18

TSUNEMUNE. Fujiwara. 1119–1187. A pillar of the court. His daughter took part in the enthronement ritual for *Nijō in 1159. Exiled in 1160, after the Heiji conflict, he was recalled in 1162 and reinstated in 1164, the year he was appointed palace minister (*naidaijin*). In 1166 he became left minister (*sadaijin*). *Yorinaga praised him as "incomparable." Tsunemune adopted Munezane, *Shigemori's last son.

*Heiji* 2, 11, 12, 20, 29

TSUNENORI. Fujiwara. ?–? The elder brother of *Morinori, *Norichika, and *Genken. His aunt was *Yorinaga's mother. A houseman of Yorinaga, he also served *Sutoku. After the Hōgen conflict he renounced the world and was exiled to Sanuki.

*Hōgen* 8, 15, 21, 22

YASUHIRO. Taira. ?–1156. Fought for *Sutoku in Hōgen and was killed by Ashikaga *Yoshiyasu at Ōeyama.

*Hōgen* 7, 8, 12, 25

YASUTOKI. Hōjō. 1183–1242. Eldest son of *Yoshitoki. After the Jōkyū conflict Yasutoki served with *Tokifusa as the Kamakura representative in Kyoto (*Rokuhara tandai*). In 1224, the two established the governing council of elders (*hyōjōshū*) headed by the shogunal adjutant (*shikken*). In 1232 Yasutoki established the seminal *Goseibai shikimoku* ("Formulary of Adjudication"), concerning rights to hold and to dispose of land. Renounced the world in 1242. That same year, the sudden death of Emperor *Shijō led to his supporting Go-Saga for the succession. In Jōkyū, Yasutoki attacked Kyoto on the order of Yoshitoki and gained victory for Kamakura.

*Jōkyūki* 7, 8, 14

YORIKATA. Minamoto. ?–1156. The fourth son of *Tameyoshi.

*Hōgen* 7, 8, 13, 24

YORIMASA. Minamoto. 1104–1180. A mid-level warrior and official, based in the province of Settsu, who backed *Go-Shirakawa in the Hōgen conflict. In 1158 he was granted direct access (*shōden*) to the retired emperor's residence and, in 1166, to the imperial palace. After fighting in Hōgen and Heiji, Yorimasa was old when, in 1180, he drew Prince *Mochihito into a failed rebellion (1180) against the Heike and killed himself at the Byōdōin in Uji. His daughter, the poet Sanuki, served *Nijō. Twenty poems by him appear in imperial collections.

*Hōgen* 9, 12, 14

*Heiji* 15, 16, 32

YORIMORI. Taira. 1132?–1186. The fifth son of *Tadamori (by *Lady Ike), a half-brother of *Kiyomori, and initially a provincial governor-level court official. He fought in Hōgen, and in Heiji he sufficiently distinguished himself to be awarded the third court rank. Close to *Toba, he accompanied him on a pilgrimage to Kumano. In 1176 he fell out with Kiyomori and in 1179 was relieved of office. He trusted *Yoritomo, who had saved his mother's life, and did not flee the capital with the rest of the Heike in 1183; instead he went to Kamakura. Yoritomo had his property restored, and he was appointed *gon-dainagon* (provisional grand counselor). Shunkan, whose banishment by Kiyomori became famous in song and story, was his brother-in-law.

*Heiji* 12, 14, 18, 19, 27, 33

YORINAGA. Fujiwara. 1120–1156. *Tadazane's second son, adopted by *Tadamichi. In his seventeenth year he was named palace minister (*naidaijin*), and in his thirtieth reached the first rank, the post of left minister (*sadaijin*), and that of head of the Fujiwara house (*uji no chōja*). Rumored to have killed Emperor *Konoe by means of magic, Yorinaga lost *Toba's trust and failed to gain that of *Go-Shirakawa, whom Tadamichi supported. Yorinaga's support of *Sutoku for the succession, after Toba's death, provoked the Hōgen conflict, during which Yorinaga was killed by a stray arrow. An irascible man, he was posthumously named chancellor (*daijōdaijin*) in 1177, in order to pacify his angry ghost. *Shinzei called him a genius beyond any in Japan. *Daiki*, Yorinaga's diary, is a valuable historical source.

*Hōgen* 5, 6, 8, 10, 11, 12, 15, 20, 21, 30, 32

YORINAKA. Minamoto. ?–1156. *Tameyoshi's fifth son.

*Hōgen* 7, 8, 24, 27

YORINORI. Minamoto ?–1156. A house official for *Yorinaga. Ordered by Yorinaga in 1151 to burn down *Tameyoshi's travel lodging in Settsu. In Hōgen he hastened to raise troops and was punished, but *Heike* has him taking part in the Heiji conflict.

*Hōgen* 20

*Heiji* 5

YORISUKE. Fujiwara. 1112–1186. In Hōgen, a supporter of *Sutoku.

*Hōgen* 6, 10

YORITOMO. Minamoto. 1147–1199. Founded the Kamakura shogunate. He was the third son of *Yoshitomo, a half-brother of *Noriyori and *Yoshitsune, and a cousin of *Yoshinaka. His mother was the daughter of Suenori, the chief priest of the Atsuta Shrine. In his youth he held various junior court offices and reached the fifth rank. After the Heiji conflict he was exiled to Izu rather than executed, thanks to the intercession of *Lady Ike. In 1183, after the Heike fled the capital, he became a provisional grand counselor (*gon-Dainagon*), and in 1192 he was named *seiitaishōgun*, the supreme military title. Yoritomo's wife was Hōjō *Masako, the daughter of Hōjō Tokimasa (1138–1215, the first shogunal adjutant [*shikken*] of the Kamakura Bakufu).

*Heiji* 5, 14, 19, 21, 25, 27, 30, 33

*Jōkyūki* 2, 3

YOSHIHIRA (Akugenda Yoshihira). Minamoto. 1141–1160. A son of *Yoshitomo. Reputed to have killed *Tsunefusa in the form of a thunderbolt.

*Heiji* 8, 14, 16, 21, 23, 31

YOSHIMICHI. Hadano. 1108–1169. His wife's sister married Minamoto no *Yoshitomo and bore *Tomonaga. After fighting under Yoshitomo in the Hōgen conflict, he was charged with executing *Tameyoshi and his sons.

*Hōgen* 26, 28

YOSHIMOCHI. Fujiwara. 1205–1268. Much favored as a boy by *Go-Toba, Yoshimochi became one of the retired emperor's Hokumen guards. Commanded troops in the campaign to suppress *Yoshitoki, then renounced the world (*shukke*) after the Jōkyū conflict. He accompanied Go-Toba to Sado and brought his ashes back to the capital.

*Jōkyūki* 3, 9, 14

YOSHINAKA. Kiso (Minamoto). 1154–1184. A cousin of *Yoritomo and *Yoshitsune. Although first to take the capital after the Heike flight in 1183, he was later killed by Yoritomo's men.

*Heiji* 33

*Jōkyūki* 2

YOSHITOKI. Hōjō. 1163–1224. Son and successor of Tokimasa, the first shogunal adjutant (*shikken*) to the shogun in Kamakura, and the effective head of the shogunate. After the Jōkyū conflict he ordered *Go-Toba into exile on Oki and appointed a *Rokuhara tandai* (the shogunal representative to the court in Kyoto). Renounced the world just before his death from a chronic illness.

*Jōkyūki* 3, 5, 6, 9

YOSHITOMO. Minamoto. 1123–1160. Eldest son of *Tameyoshi and father of *Yoritomo and *Yoshitsune. Yoshitomo grew up in the east. Wishing to expand his horizons, in 1143 he invaded land belonging to the Ise Shrine and ended up controlling fifteen provinces along the Tōkaidō. Lost his father and brothers in the aftermath of the Hōgen conflict. In 1159 he donated his holding in the province of Ise to ensure promotion for Yoritomo, who then longed to avenge his death.

*Hōgen* 4, 6, 7, 9, 10, 12, 13, 14, 15, 17, 20, 24, 25, 26, 27, 28, 31, 32, 34, 35,

*Heiji* 2, 3, 4, 5, 6, 8, 11, 13, 14, 15, 16, 17, 18, 19, 20, 21, 22, 23, 24, 25, 26, 27, 28, 30, 31, 32, 33

YOSHITSUNA. Minamoto. ?–1134. Second son of Yoriyoshi and younger brother of Hachimantarō Yoshiie.

*Hōgen* 7, 24

YOSHIUJI (Musashi-no-zenji). Ashikaga. 1189–1254. A grandson of Hōjō Tokimasa (1138–1215), married to the daughter of *Yasutoki. One of the Kanto's chief commanders, he distinguished himself in the Jōkyū conflict. He renounced the world in 1241.

*Jōkyūki* 6, 7, 8

YOSHIYASU. Ashikaga (Minamoto). 1127–1157. A descendant of Hachimantarō Yoshiie, and a Hokumen guard for Toba. In the Hōgen conflict he supported *Go-Shirakawa with one hundred mounted warriors. Killed *Iehiro, *Yasuhiro, *Mitsuhiro, *Yasuhiro, and several other Taira men, but died shortly after being promoted for his service.

*Hōgen* 9, 20, 25

# Maps

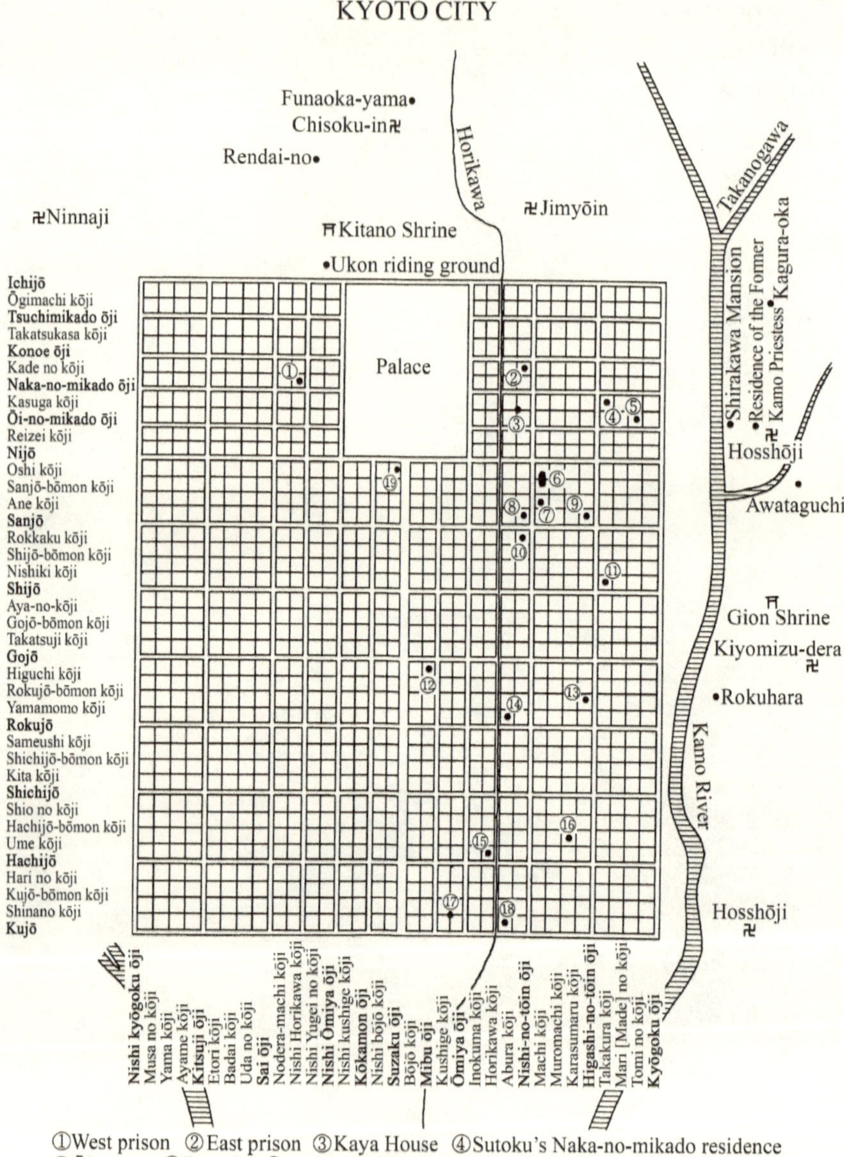


FIGURE M.1 Map of Kyoto city.

KYOTO AREA

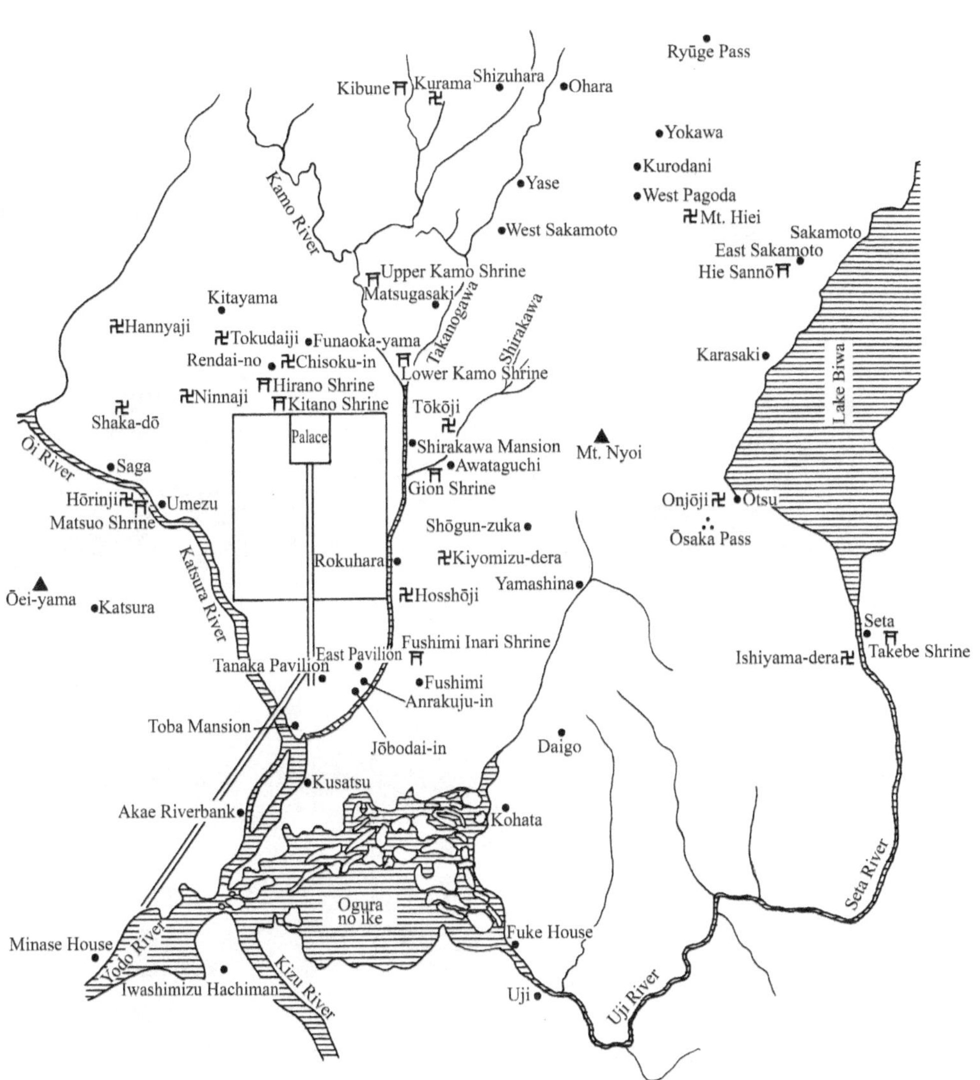


FIGURE M.2 Map of Kyoto area.

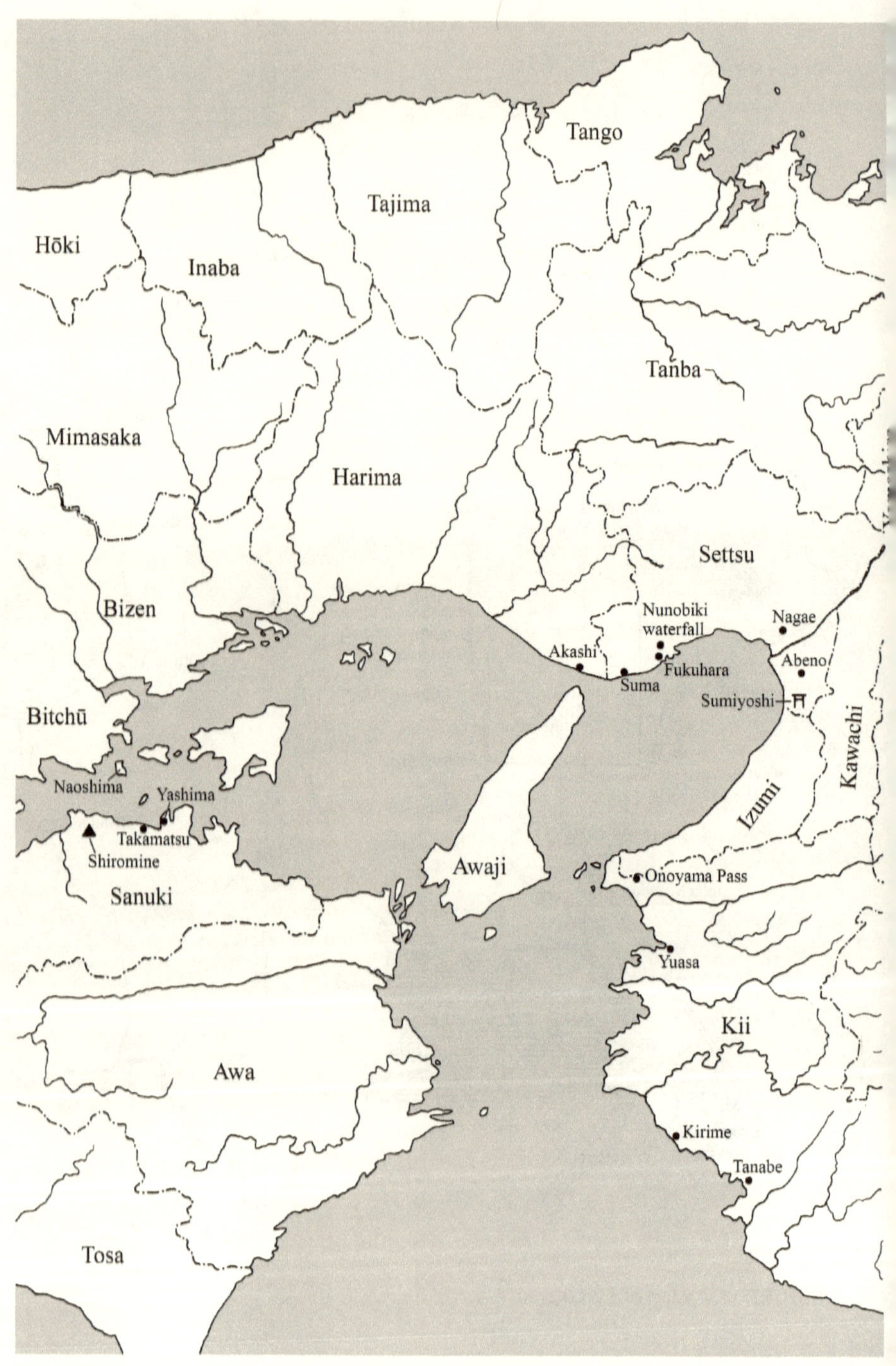


FIGURE M.3 Map of Central Japan east.

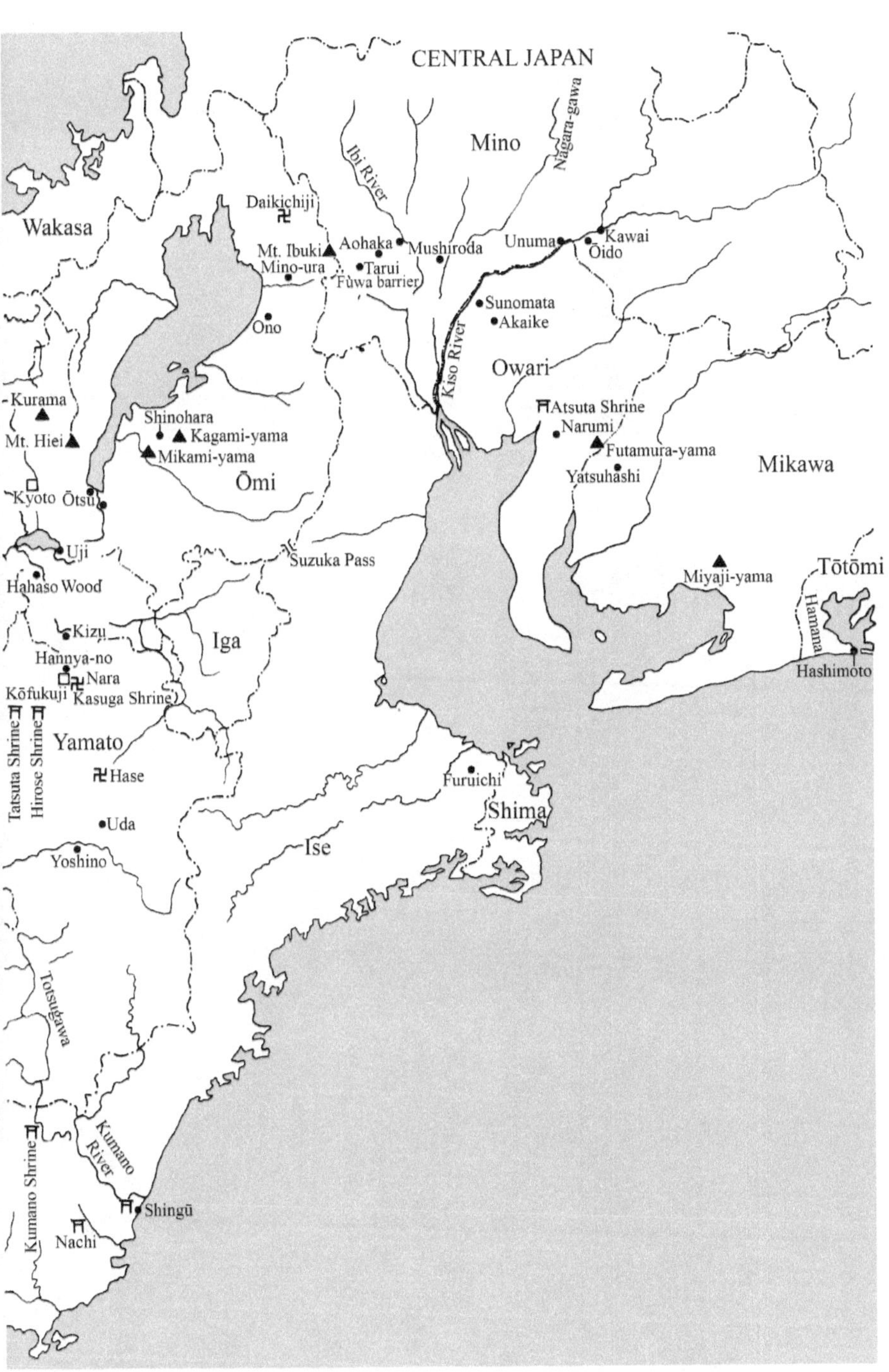


FIGURE M.4 Map of Central Japan west.

# Genealogical Charts

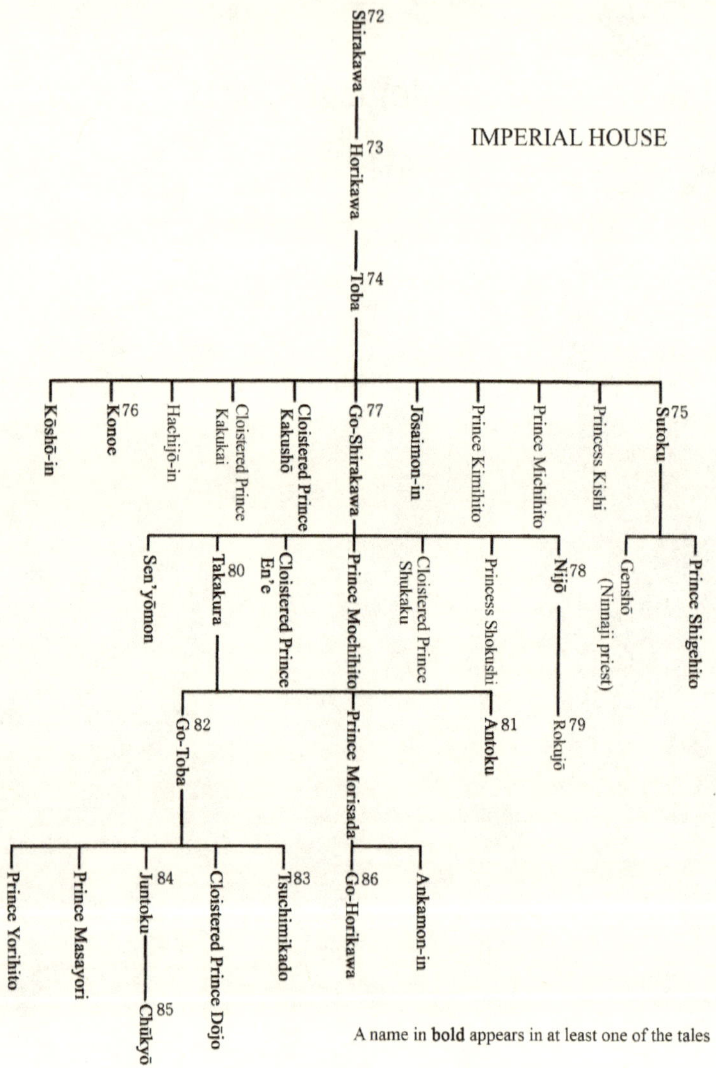


FIGURE G.1 Genealogy of Imperial House.

## OTHER EMPERORS MENTIONED

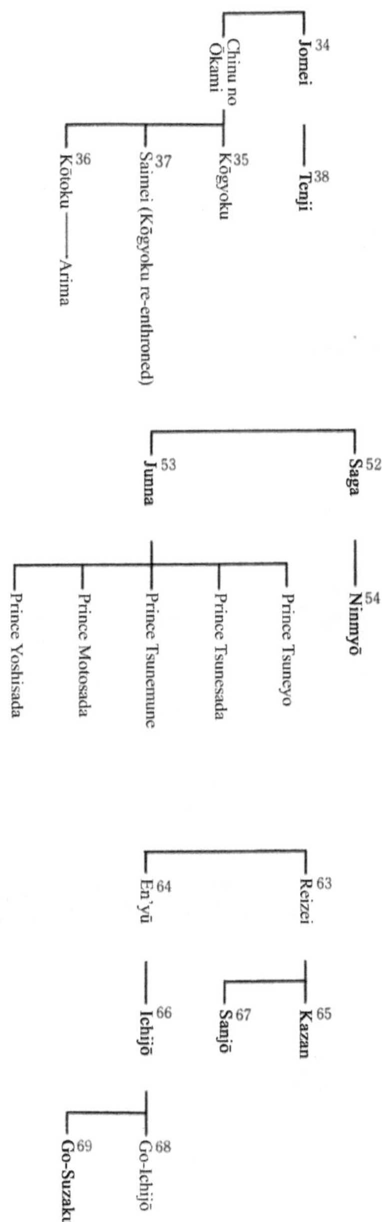


FIGURE G.2 Genealogy of other emperors mentioned.

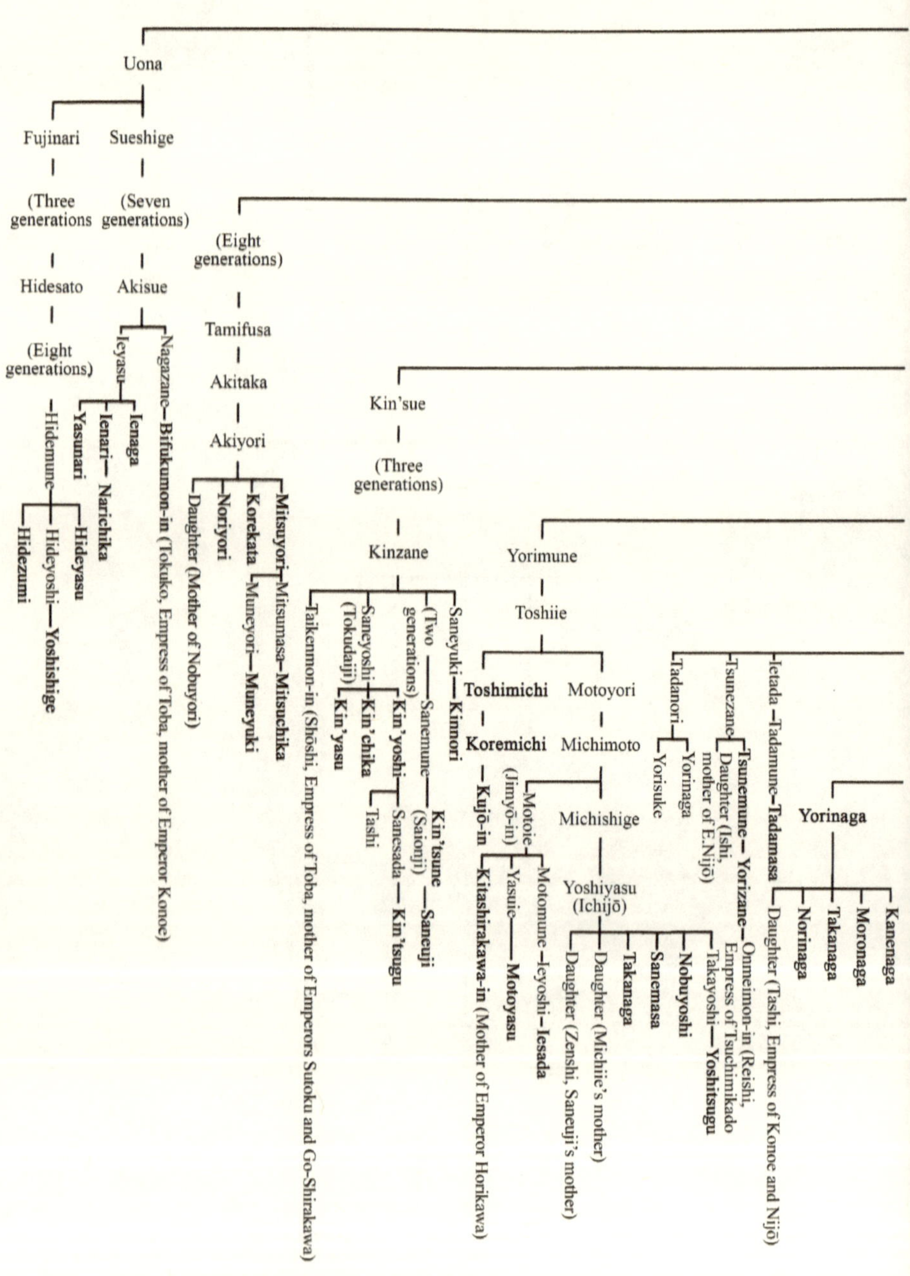


FIGURE G.3 Genealogy of Fujiwara.

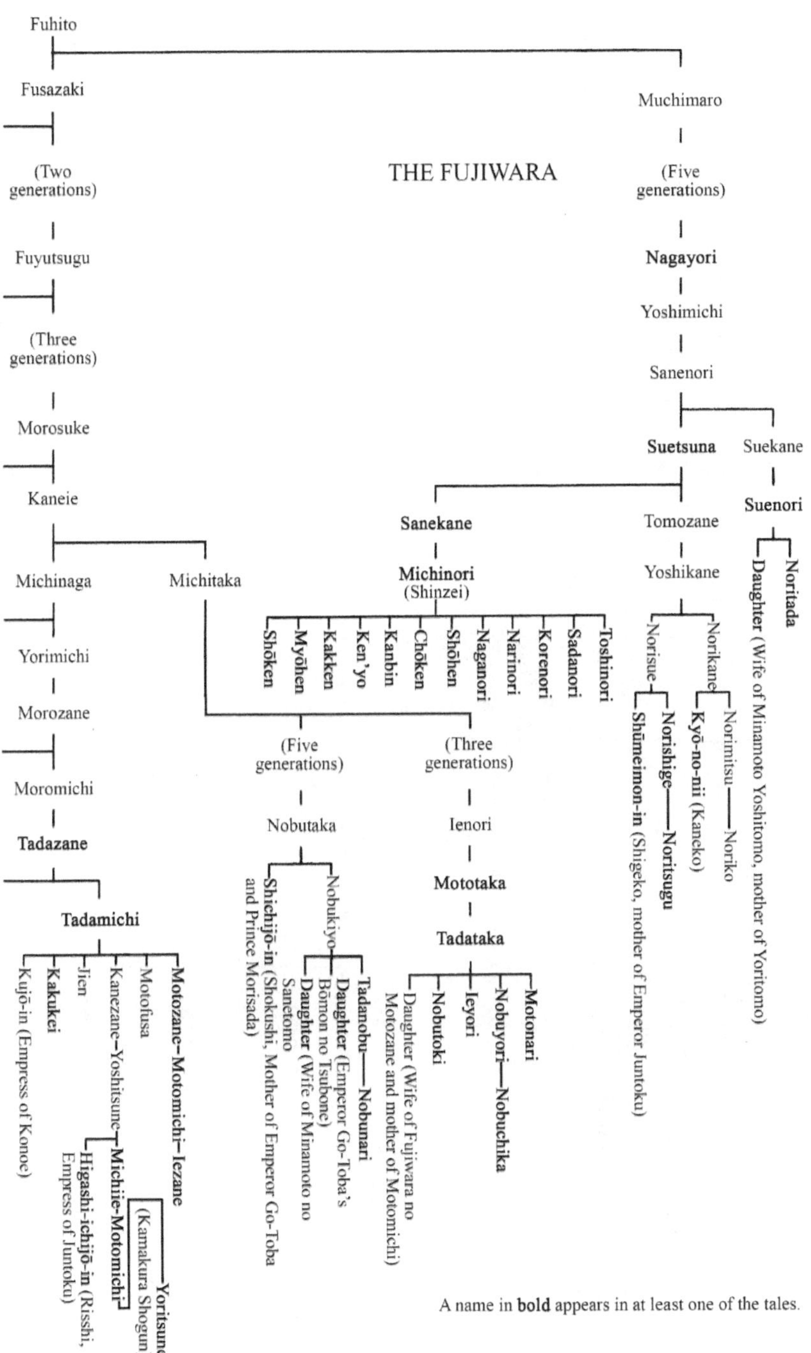


FIGURE G.4 Genealogy of Fujiwara (*continued*).

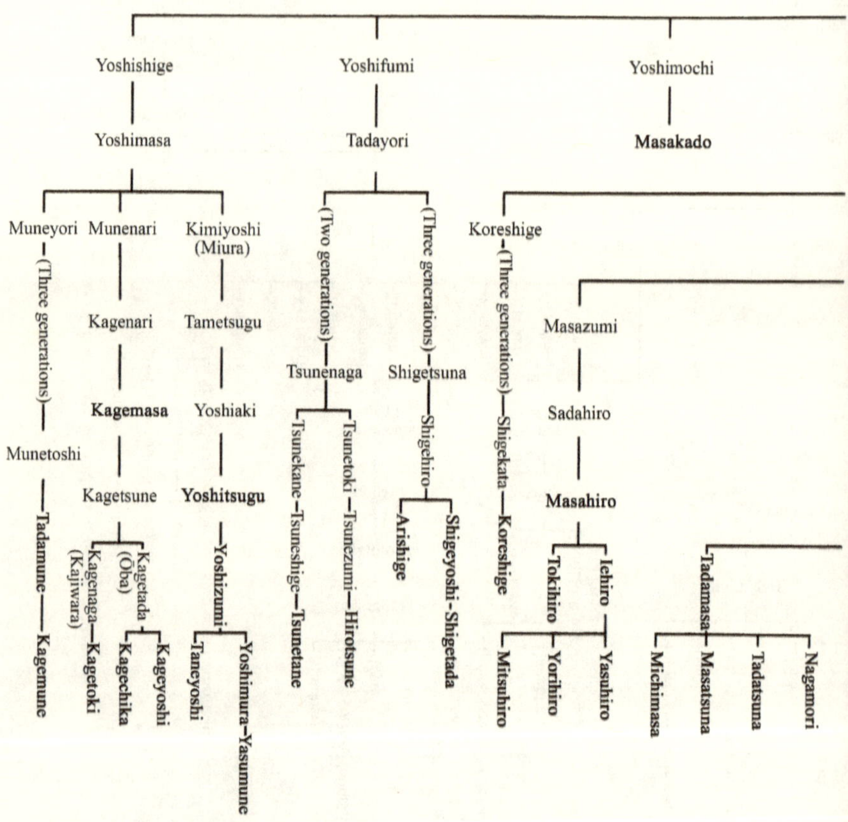


FIGURE G.5 Genealogy of Kanmu Heiji.

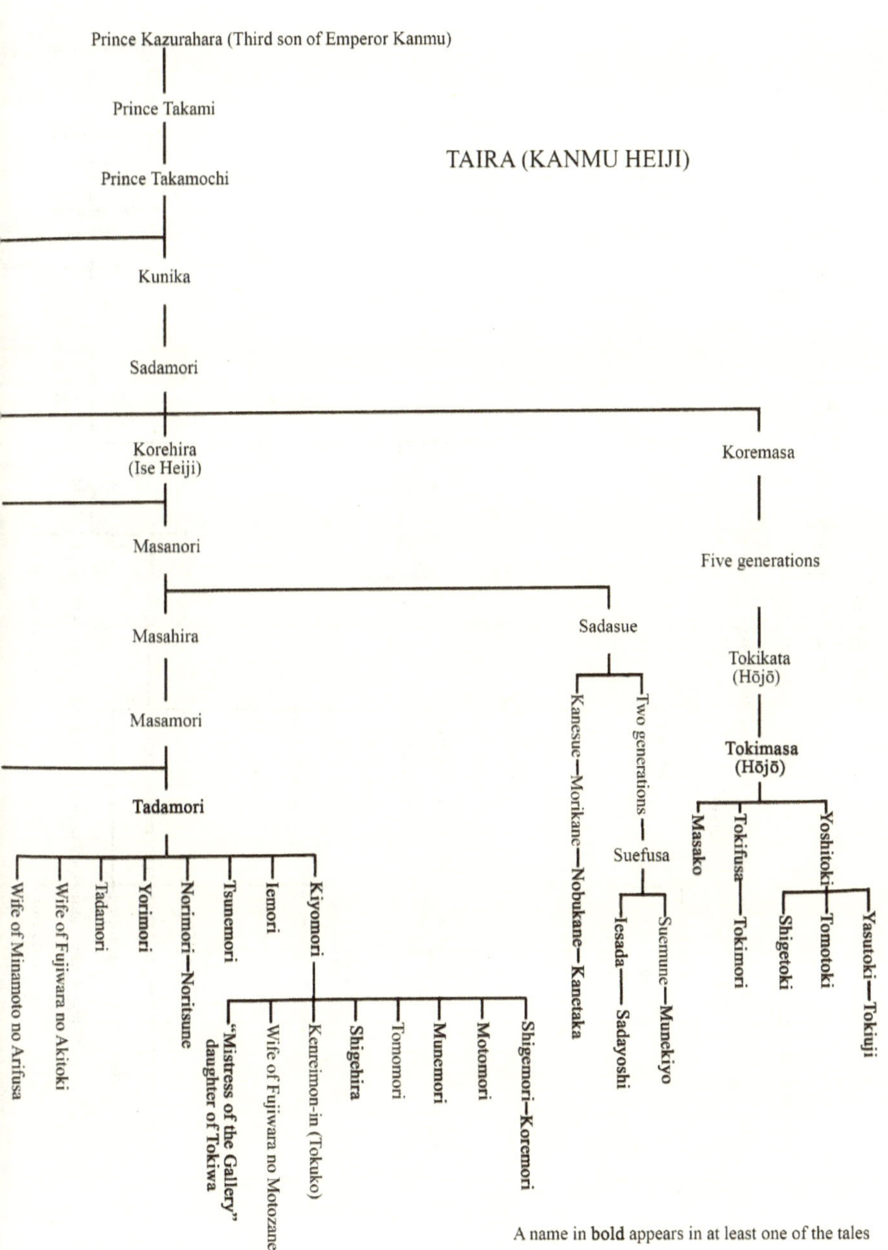


FIGURE G.6 Genealogy of Kanmu Heiji (*continued*).

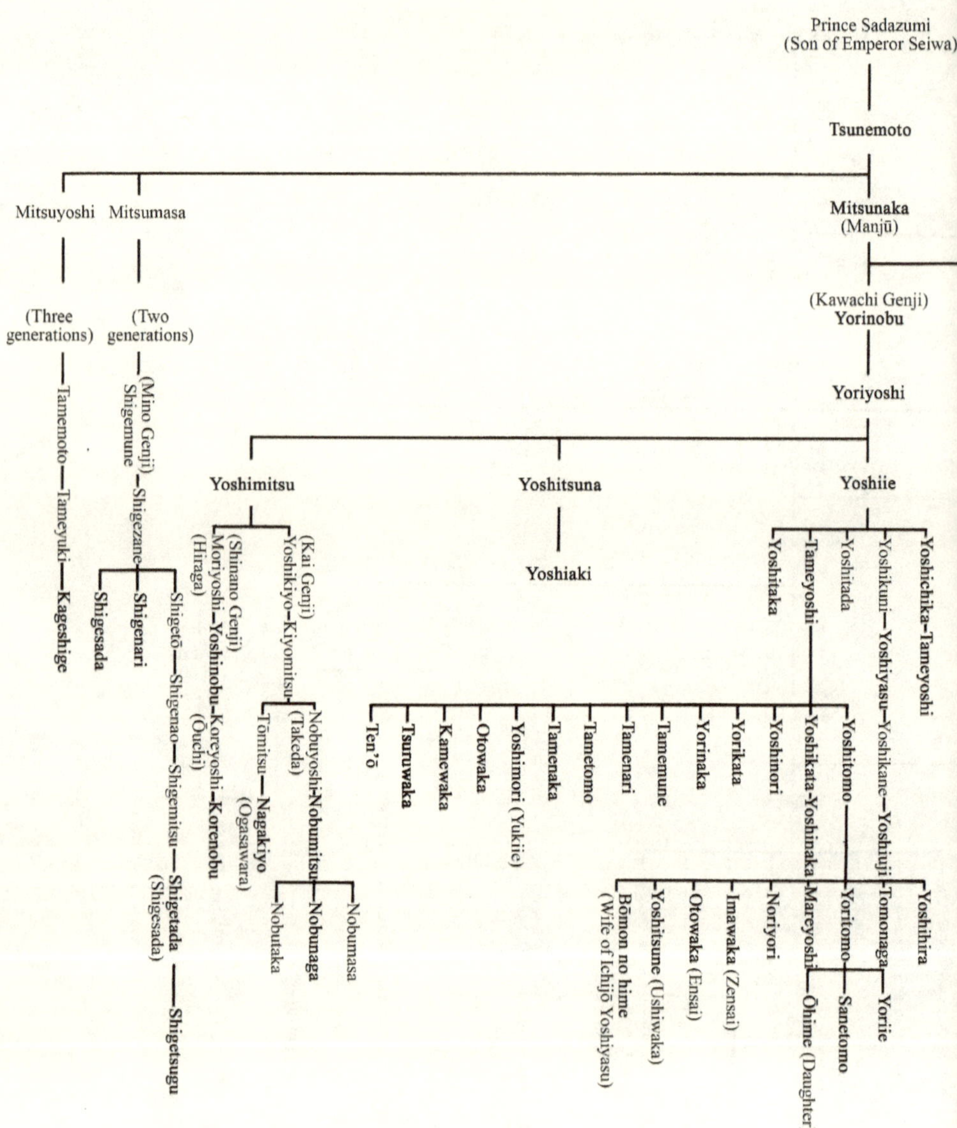


FIGURE G.7 Genealogy of Seiwa Genji.

MINAMOTO (SEIWA GENJI)

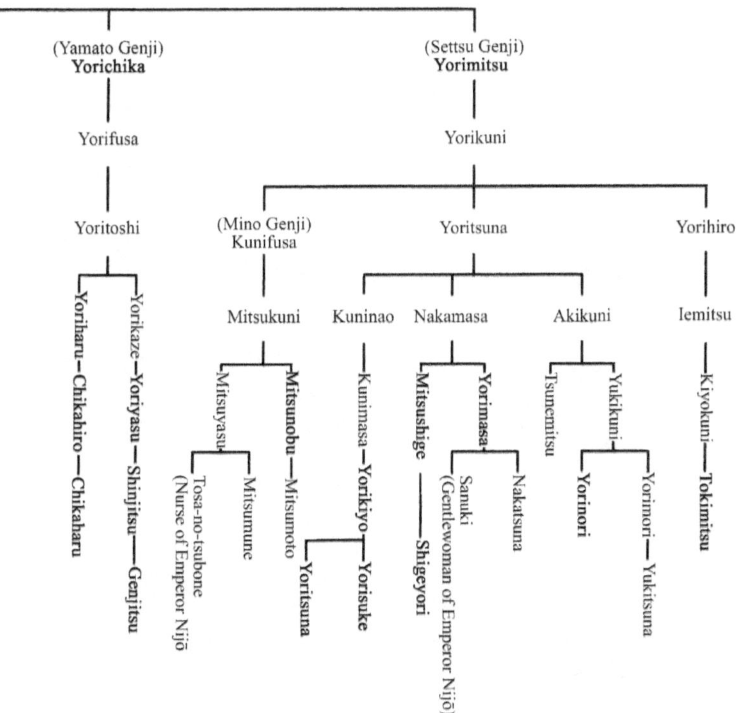


A name in **bold** appears in at least one of the tales.

FIGURE G.8 Genealogy of Seiwa Genji (*continued*).

# Notes

## Introduction

1. Hiroshi Kitagawa and Bruce T. Tsuchida, trans., *The Tale of the Heike*, 2 vols. (Tokyo: University of Tokyo Press, 1975–1977); Helen Craig McCullough, trans., *The Tale of the Heike* (Stanford, CA: Stanford University Press, 1990); Burton Watson and Haruo Shirane, trans., *The Tales of the Heike*, Translations from the Asian Classics (New York: Columbia University Press, 2008); and Royall Tyler, trans., *The Tale of the Heike* (New York: Penguin, 2012).
2. Delmer M. Brown and Ichirō Ishida, trans., *The Future and the Past: A Translation and Study of the* Gukanshō, *an Interpretative History of Japan Written in 1219* (Berkeley: University of California Press, 1979), 89.
3. Genji and Heike are collective names derived from alternate readings (*gen* and *hei*) for the characters for *minamoto* and *taira*. "Heike" literally means "house of Taira," and "Genji," "Minamoto lineage." "Heiji" (mentioned in following paragraph) means "Taira lineage." The year-period name Heiji is written with different characters.
4. Tsunemoto began as a junior government official in the province of Musashi, and from there he first reported to the court the rebellion of Taira no Masakado (?–940), a cousin of Kiyomori's ancestor Sadamori. Eventually he took part in suppressing this rebellion and the slightly later one of Fujiwara no Sumitomo (?–941). The names Masakado and Sumitomo therefore both recur in Genji boasts, although non-Genji men were actually more prominently involved.
5. In the ideal, ceremonial pattern adopted from the continent, the sovereign faced south, with his two senior ministers to his left and right. The left outranked the right.

6. The *nairan*'s original function was to fill in temporarily when a regent was ill or had died. He inspected all documents submitted to or issued by the emperor. In time, however, the post became functionally equivalent to the office of regent.
7. Earlier English translations of these works include Marisa Chalitpatanangune, "Heiji Monogatari: A Study and Annotated Translation of the Oldest Text" (PhD diss., University of California, Berkeley, 1987) (the first two of the three books); William H. McCullough, "Shōkyū ki: An Account of the Shōkyū War of 1221," *Monumenta Nipponica* 19, no. 1–2 (1964); Edwin O. Reischauer and Joseph K. Yamagiwa, *Translations from Early Japanese Literature* (Cambridge, MA: Harvard University Press, 1951) (the first two books of *Heiji*, with selections from the third); and William R. Wilson, *Hōgen monogatari: Tale of the Disorder in Hōgen*, Monumenta Nipponica Monograph (Tokyo: Sophia University Press, 1971).

## The Tale of the Hōgen Years

1. Sutoku did not formally receive this name (Sutoku Tennō) until 1871.
2. The honorary title (*ingō*) awarded to Fujiwara no Nariko (1117–1160), who eventually became Toba's empress. She was not actually appointed a consort (*nyōgo*) until 1140, and she received the title of Bifukumon-in only in 1149.
3. In his diary (*Daiki* for Kyūju 2/8/27 [1155]), Fujiwara no Yorinaga described a report that the spirit of the late Emperor Konoe, speaking through a medium, had said that someone had cursed him the previous year by driving nails into the eyes of a doll, and that he had then gone blind and died. Bifukumon-in (Konoe's mother) and Tadamichi suspected Tadazane and Yorinaga. Yorinaga called the idea preposterous but conceded that it was on everyone's lips.
4. Taikenmon-in (mother of Sutoku and Go-Shirakawa) and Bifukumon-in (mother of Konoe).
5. He would have spoken to them only from behind blinds.
6. The "dragon visage" (*ryūgan*) is the emperor's face and the "jade presence" (*gyokutai*) his physical body. "Golden floor" is a similar rhetorical flourish.
7. In short, death comes to both. "Tathāgata" (J. Nyorai) is a title of the Buddha. A shrāvaka is one of the Buddha's direct disciples.
8. Tōsanjō ("East Sanjō," also read Higashi Sanjō) was an exceptionally large residence that figures repeatedly in Heian history. Built originally by Fujiwara no Yoshifusa (804–872), it passed down in the line of Fujiwara regents and at times was inhabited also by emperors. It burned down in 1166 and was not rebuilt.
9. Takamatsu House was next to Tōsanjō, to the south. It dated back (allowing for repeated rebuilding after fires) to the early eleventh century and had belonged now to great Fujiwara nobles (men or women), now to retired emperors. Cloistered Emperor Toba had lived there with Bifukumon-in. Go-Shirakawa moved there when he became emperor in 1155.
10. Tadazane was closely associated with Chisoku-in, a Tendai temple mentioned several times in following text. It was located south of Funaoka-yama, in the north of the city.

11. Regarding "private inspector," see the section "The Hōgen Conflict" in the introduction. "Practical" suggests that Yorinaga's authority was de facto rather than de jure.
12. *Junso*, a virtue associated with the exemplary rulers of Chinese antiquity.
13. Tadazane had had Tadamichi (b. 1097) adopt the much younger Yorinaga (b. 1120) as his son.
14. The Tanaka Pavilion was built by Fujiwara no Tsunetaka in 1152, in the north sector of the Toba Mansion compound. Sutoku moved there in the 6th month of that year. Cloistered Emperor Toba died there, and Sutoku remained there during the first seven days of mourning, before setting out for the capital. The Toba Mansion was a magnificent residence complex built by Emperor Shirakawa in 1085–1088 for his retirement. It was located in Toba, a short distance south of the capital.
15. Ise and Iwashimizu Hachiman.
16. The stars are the officers of the court, the waves the people.
17. The protector deities of Tōsanjō.
18. Uzusama and Kongō Dōji are wrathful Buddhist deities, surrounded by flames. They were invoked to ward off disaster and suppress enemies. The deity Shōdengu (also known as Kangiten) was invoked to prevent such misfortunes as sickness and robbery.
19. The spirit of the departed was believed to wander the "intermediate realm" (*chūin* or *chūu*) for forty-nine days before entering a new incarnation. Prayers were said every seventh of these days to ensure a good rebirth.
20. This priestess was Sutoku's full younger sister.
21. These were men of fourth and fifth rank, higher than those in the Lower North Guards. The North Guards protected the retired emperor.
22. Daigo lies well east of the easternmost outskirts of the capital. Yorinaga follows a circuitous route.
23. The discrepancy between palanquin and carriage, *koshi* and *kuruma*, is puzzling. Perhaps the passage from "Sugawara" to the end of the paragraph is an interpolation from another manuscript, now lost.
24. Liu Bang, the founder of the Han Dynasty.
25. The translation of this sentence conceals a recurring ambiguity in the original. In principle, the word *dairi* should mean the imperial palace proper. Here, however, it designates whatever dwelling the emperor currently inhabits. The original does not distinguish between *dairi* and *sato-dairi*, the more strictly correct term for an imperial residence "in town." In *Heiji*, Rokuhara likewise becomes the *dairi* when Emperor Nijō moves there. In this case, Go-Shirakawa is living in Takamatsu House.
26. As a child Shigehito had been given into the care of Tadamori, Kiyomori's father.
27. Another name for the North Pavilion (Kita-dono), already mentioned, of the Shirakawa Mansion.
28. Despite the way reference maps are drawn, streets like Ōi-no-mikado or Kasuga-kōji clearly extended across the Kamo River for some distance onto its east bank.

29. Bamboo planted in the 5th month and cut in the 8th month of its fourth year.
30. The General's Barrow (Shōgun-zuka) is at the summit of Mount Kachō, immediately east of Kyoto. Its legendary origin and purpose are explained in *Heike* 5:1.
31. A generalized notion, originally Chinese, of the generations of emperors past and to come.
32. The so-called Kusuko Incident (810). It involved a clash, encouraged by Heizei's mistress of staff Fujiwara no Kusuko, between Retired Emperor Heizei and Emperor Saga.
33. The shrine complex associated with the great Buddhist establishment on Mount Hiei. Mount Hiei as a whole protects the capital from the evil influences thought to come from the northeast (the "demon gate"). Otoko-yama is the location of the Iwashimizu Hachiman shrine, southwest of the city.
34. Immediately north of Takamatsu House.
35. *Yōyo* (also *tagoshi*): a very light, simple palanquin for use over short distances.
36. Two of the imperial regalia. The third is the Sacred Mirror. The Sword was lost during the sea battle of Dan-no-ura in 1185.
37. An *eboshi hikidate*: a soft *eboshi* hat worn under the helmet, then straightened up to the tall *eboshi* shape when the helmet was removed.
38. *Wakidate*, an element of a full suit of armor.
39. Fuke House (Fuke-dono), a villa belonging to Fujiwara no Tadazane, was near Uji. The mountainous region south of Yoshino, south of Nara, included the remote Totsugawa gorge. It was famous for its population of fierce ascetic monks.
40. An heirloom weapon passed down in the regental house from the time of Fujiwara no Morosuke (908–960).
41. *Happuri*, a minor, seldom-mentioned item of armor that was presumably put on last.
42. On the 1st, 11th, and 21st day of the lunar month a yin-yang deity known as Daihakusei (the planet Venus) was immobile in the east, blocking that direction and making it unlucky to move that way.
43. Presumably Emperor Kanmu (r. 781–806), the "Kashihara Emperor." Prince Kazurahara (see *Heike* 1:1) was Kanmu's son.
44. *Mitokorodō no yumi*: a bow made of laminated wood and bamboo and tightly wrapped with rattan in three places (*mitokoro*) to keep these elements from separating.
45. He had received no land from Kiyomori as a reward for services rendered.
46. *Uma no toki naru ni*. This time makes no sense. The expression has no counterpart in the *Hotoku-bon* or the *Rufu-bon* texts.
47. The two joins between the shaft and the feathers and between the shaft and the arrowhead.
48. The horse is four "feet" (*shaku*), seven "inches" (*ki*) tall. If these units really equaled their customary English equivalents, it would be 13.75 hands, the size of a large pony. The Japanese horses of the time seem to have been relatively small, but one this size could hardly have carried the mighty Tametomo.
49. Beating his horse's flanks. Japanese riders did not use spurs.

50. This *kaburaya* ("humming arrow") turns below, in effect, into a *hikime*, a related but, in principle, distinct arrow type. A *kaburaya* humming bulb normally had eight holes, but Tametomo's has nine. The extended passage also mentions *soya* ("battle arrow") and *togariya* ("killer arrow"), said to be more powerful than a *soya*.
51. The normal length was twelve handbreadths.
52. The easier, "bow hand" side.
53. A warrior normally held two arrows (*moroya*) in hand at once.
54. An uncle (?–1156) of Kiyomori.
55. The oddly worded original here makes little sense, since the narrative says that Yorinaga was behind Sutoku. The passage has no counterpart in the *Rufu-bon* or *Hōtoku-bon* texts.
56. One of the peaks in the Eastern Hills, southeast of the Shirakawa North Pavilion.
57. "Sovereign Complete in Virtue" translates *jūzen no kimi*, a common expression for the emperor in these texts, but in this book seldom translated literally. It means that the emperor owes his lofty station to virtue, and consequent good karma, sustained through countless past lives.
58. Sannō, the generalized divinity of Mount Hiei, was honored above all in the Hiyoshi Shrine. Enryakuji, mentioned in following text, was the great Buddhist temple on the mountain.
59. Sōji-in, a subtemple on Mount Hiei, was founded in 850, under imperial sponsorship, at the request of the great monk Ennin. It was dedicated especially to rites for the emperor's health and longevity.
60. The province of Harima was wealthier and more prestigious.
61. They have gone down the Katsura River to its junction with the Kamo, where both become the Yodo River; gone on to the western end of the now-drained Ogura-no-ike; and turned up the Kizu River toward Nara. Hahaso Wood is on the west bank of the Kizu River.
62. Hannya-no is present-day Hannyaji-chō, northwest of Tōdaiji; Gozanmai is a graveyard.
63. Katsuragi no Tsubura, killed shortly after the assassination of Emperor Ankō (r. mid-5th century); and Emi no Oshikatsu, a minister under Junnin (r. 758–764), killed in 764.
64. The tutelary deity of the Fujiwara. The Kasuga Shrine is in Nara.
65. On Hōgen 1/5/22 warriors had burned down Tokudaiji, a temple within the grounds of a villa owned by Fujiwara no Saneyoshi, the palace minister.
66. Nothing in the text indicates what it is.
67. Suzuka was between Ōmi and Ise, Fuwa between Ōmi and Mino.
68. In the mountains east of Yase, below the West Pagoda of Mount Hiei.
69. Between Nara and Uji. This happened in 1113, when the Nara (Kōfukuji) monks were on their way to lodge a complaint in the capital.
70. Between Echigo and Dewa. Masakado had called himself the "new emperor."
71. Fujiwara no Motohira (?–?), the father of Hidehira.
72. A son of Tameyoshi, like the others named in following text.
73. All these allusions to Chinese poetry and other classics evoke longing for home.

74. *Koshi-guruma*, a sort of palanquin on two wheels, moved by porters.
75. Urge him to call ten times the sacred name of the Buddha Amida. These "ten callings" were conventionally felt to ensure Amida's welcome into his paradise.
76. Fujiwara no Korechika (974–1010), who shot Retired Emperor Kazan.
77. Another name for Iwashimizu Hachiman.
78. The Chinese Pure Land patriarch Dao Chuo (562–648) gave this figure in one of his works.
79. Warriors stationed at the Takiguchi guard post, northeast of the emperor's personal residence, the Seiryōden.
80. Presumably out of minimum respect for the remains.
81. They are half-brothers. Kanenaga was born in the 5th month of 1138 and Moronaga in the 2nd month of the same year, three months earlier. Perhaps Moronaga counted as junior because his mother ranked lower than Kanenaga's.
82. A son (704–765) of Fujiwara no Muchimaro. He was dismissed from his post in 757 and restored to it in 764.
83. The Fifth Prince, Kakushō (1129–1169), a younger brother of Sutoku.
84. Kangyō, a son of Emperor Horikawa.
85. A kind of carriage used only by persons of the very highest rank.
86. Apparently the carriage was drawn into the Toba Mansion compound by men, after the ox had been unhitched. Anrakuju-in was a sanctuary dedicated by Retired Emperor Toba in 1137 and located within the East Pavilion of the Toba Mansion.
87. The following lines, which come after this sentence, are omitted because in context they make little sense. They have no counterpart in the *Rufu-bon* or *Hōtoku-bon* texts.

    A certain Sadamune was present there. Shigenari ordered him to accompany Sutoku to Sanuki, give him into the care of the province, and return immediately to the capital. A servant named Yoshinaga was there. "I should like to accompany him to Sanuki," he said eagerly. The Sanuki governor Sueyuki asked, "How many men do you have?" "Three hundred," Yoshinaga replied. "Then no," Sueyuki answered. He had Yoshinaga stay where he was.

88. East of the Toba Mansion, near the confluence of the Kamo and Katsura rivers.
89. Presumably he receives Sutoku on board the boat.
90. Naoshima is off Okayama-ken, across the Inland Sea from Takamatsu. It is actually a mile or two from the mainland. The text's "two hundred yards" (two *chō*) may be an error for two "hours"—the time to get there from the mainland.
91. In other words, tears of blood—tears of bitter anguish.
92. Exiled to Suma for an unknown offence, Ariwara no Yukihira (818–893) left a poem that made his exile immortal. His stay there inspired Genji's exile to Suma in *The Tale of Genji*.
93. 733–765, r. 758–764. A grandson of Tenmu, Junnin was born in 733; elevated to heir apparent in 757; enthroned in 758; and exiled to Awaji in 764. He died there the following year. He did not receive the posthumous title of Junnin Tennō until 1871.

94. The first, on Sanjō, was south of Takamatsu House. Sutoku had lived there. The connection between Sutoku and the second is unclear.
95. If Sutoku really kept such a record of significant dreams, he was not alone in doing so. Surviving dream records include those of Jien (1155–1225), the author of *Gukanshō*, and the great monk Myōe (1173–1232). In *Genji* (early 11th century), the Akashi Novice has analogous dreams on the theme of reviving the fortunes of his house; and he, too, keeps a record of the sacred vows he had made to ensure their realization.
96. Saimei (594–661, r. 655–661) had reigned previously as Kōgyoku (642–645). Shōtoku (718–770, r. 764–770) had reigned previously as Kōken (749–758).
97. Suzaku reigned 930–946 and Shirakawa 1072–1086. Murakami reigned 946–967.
98. Tenmu (?–686) reigned 673–686.
99. The meaning of this expression is unclear.
100. A grandson of the Han emperor Xiaowu.
101. In the aftermath of the Tang-period An Lushan rebellion, which brought a tragic end to his love for the beautiful Yang Guifei.
102. A fifth-century emperor, the son of Emperor Ingyō.
103. In present-day Sakaide-shi, Kagawa-ken. The seaward side of the area appears now to be reclaimed land.
104. A locality in Ōmi.
105. An island about twenty miles off the east coast of the Izu Peninsula.
106. *Gobu daijōkyō*, the five major Mahāyana sutras defined by Tendai doctrine: *Kegon-kyō* (Flower Garland Sutra), *Daijikkyō*, *Daibon hannyakyō* (Greater Wisdom Sutra), *Nehan-gyō* (Nirvana Sutra), and *Hokekyō* (Lotus Sutra).
107. Far from any temple.
108. Yoshida Tsunefusa (1142–1200) noted in his diary (*Kikki*) under the date Juei 2/7/16 (1183), that Sutoku had copied the Five Mahâyana Sutras in his own blood and written at the end, "I have done this so that in an unjust reign my merit for the life to come should destroy the realm."
109. See the previous section entitled "The Execution of Yoshitomo's Child Brothers."
110. Other *Hōgen* texts identify this man in various other ways. He appears to be a monk, a former musician, also mentioned in Kamo no Chōmei's *Hosshinshū*.
111. The "log house" of Asakura figures in a hallowed poem by Emperor Tenchi (r. 668–671): "It is I who inhabit the log house of Asakura; whose son, then, are you, who call out your name to me as you pass by?"
112. Also "hand-palanquin," a conveyance permitted only very great nobles, clerical or lay.
113. The monk Saigyō (1118–1190) is one of classical Japan's greatest poets, and his visit to Shiromine (also read Shiramine) is well known. The dramatization of it by Ueda Akinari (1734–1809) in "Shiramine" (the opening story in his *Ugetsu monogatari*) is especially famous. In it, Saigyō encounters Sutoku's raging ghost.
114. The *Hōtoku-bon* and *Kotohira-bon* texts of *Hōgen* lack this closing account of Tametomo in the Izu islands.

115. The text actually names eight islands. Some of the Izu islands now have different names.
116. A warrior's sword hung at his left side.
117. Probably Aoshima, a small, extremely remote island south of Hachijō-jima.
118. Raikō is Minamoto no Yorimitsu (948–1021), the first son of Mitsunaka (Manjū). In legend Raikō killed rebels and bandits with the aid of his four chief lieutenants, the "Four Heavenly Kings."

## The Tale of the Heiji Years

1. Amatsukoyane (*-no-mikoto* is an honorific title) is the tutelary deity of the Fujiwara. It was understood in medieval Japan that the Sun Goddess (Amaterasu, the origin of the imperial line) and Amatsukoyane had concluded a pact, to the effect that for all time to come Amatsukoyane's descendants (the Fujiwara) would help the emperors to govern the realm. This pact explained and justified the standing of generations of Fujiwara regents.
2. Actually, Nobuyori's grandfather was Mototaka and his father Tadataka.
3. Mi Zixia (J. Bishika), a favorite of a Chinese ruler in the Warring States period, once enjoyed a peach so much that he gave his lord an uneaten half. This excessive familiarity offended his lord.
4. Fujiwara no Michinori (1106–1159). Shinzei is his name in religion and the one by which he is particularly well known.
5. Legendary Chinese emperors always cited as models of virtue in government.
6. The reigns of Emperors Daigo (897–930) and Murakami (946–967).
7. Fujiwara no Yoshichika and Fujiwara no Koreshige, who administered the realm during the three-year reign of Emperor Kazan (984–986).
8. During Hōgen, Go-Shirakawa had lived in Takamatsu House.
9. The *naien* was held late in the 1st month, and the *sumai no sechi* late in the 7th.
10. Left minister, right minister, and chancellor.
11. The generalized term used, *tenki*, presumably refers at least as much to Retired Emperor Go-Shirakawa as to the reigning Emperor Nijō.
12. *Kagami kura*, a saddle trimmed with mirror-polished metal.
13. On the northwest corner of Sanjō and Higashi-no-tōin. Retired Emperor Toba had occupied it before him.
14. The fabulous Afang Palace of the First Emperor of Qin, described in *Heike* 5:6.
15. "Go-Shirakawa" translates the term *innai*, although glosses in both SNKBT (p. 157, n. 39) and SNKBZ (p. 420, n. 12) read *innai* to mean "the retired [*in*] and reigning [*nai*] emperors." Where this translation has "he had gone," the original does indeed have two words: *gokō* (a progress by a retired emperor) and *gyōgō* (one by a reigning emperor). In reality, however, only Go-Shirakawa was confined in the imperial library, and the narrative (in agreement with *Gukanshō*) explicitly mentions only his presence in the Sanjō Palace. Nothing except *innai* and *gokō/gyōgō* suggests that Emperor Nijō is anywhere but in the imperial palace, from where, on the 25th, he is spirited away to Rokuhara. Moreover, the

corresponding *Rufu-bon* passage, which lacks the term *innai*, explicitly places Nijō in the palace proper and Go-Shirakawa in the library.

In truth, the term *innai* is ambiguous. For example, in *Shōyūki* for Chōtoku 3/4/17 (997) and *Chūyūki* for Kahō 2/9/24 (1096) it means "within the *in*" (the retired emperor's residence), hence the retired emperor himself. The presence of both *gokō* and *gyōgō* in the *Heiji* text probably results from this confusion. The SNKBT and SNKBZ texts here have both, but later passages on the same subject in the original manuscript, to which SNKBZ adheres, have only *gokō*, while the SNKBT editor felt obliged to add *gyōgō* from another manuscript. In context, *gyōgō* does not make sense. In following text, *innai* will continue to be taken as referring to Go-Shirakawa alone.

16. That is to say, descended from Muchimaro (680–737), a son of Fujiwara no Fuhito (659–720). The dominant Northern House supplied regents and other appointees to the very highest posts in the court hierarchy.
17. The Takashina had prospered by providing generations of provincial governors.
18. This was in Kōji 3 (1144), probably the 1st month. Shinzei renounced the world in the 7th month of that year.
19. Then in his thirteenth year.
20. A foster brother (?–1160) of Yoshitomo, and Yoshitomo's chief lieutenant. In following text, he continues to be named Kamada Masakiyo.
21. The passage between quotation marks reads as though taken (although perhaps garbled in the process) from an astrological manual. If it is, the manual may be the Tang Chinese astrological classic *Tianwen yaolu* ("Astrological Digest"; J. *Tenmon yōroku)* mentioned in *Heike* 6:12. (I have not seen it.) The translation of the first sentence is speculative. SNKBZ (p. 424, n. 13) calls the portent unknown and the passage unintelligible. SNKBT (p. 162, n. 1), too, calls the portent unknown but cites a *Gyokuyō* passage from 1177 (Angen 3/2/10) that refers to a celestial portent during Heiji. The shorter, counterpart passage in *Gukanshō* likewise mentions Jupiter (*mokusei*).
22. Narikage had served Retired Emperor Shirakawa and now served Toba.
23. Between the capital and Uji.
24. The explicit mention of both emperors (*shushō*, the reigning one, and *shōkō*, the retired) probably issues from the confusion over *innai*. In the *Rufu-bon*, Shinzei sees his reading of the celestial portent as confirmed: the loyal subject takes the place of his lord (*kimi*, a common word in *Heike* for Go-Shirakawa alone and rendered in following text, as in my *Heike*, as "sovereign").
25. Presumably they also roofed it and covered it with earth. *Gukanshō* reports Shinzei calling the Name in the pit. From that evidence SNKBT (p. 162, n. 22) concludes that his aim in having himself buried alive was to achieve rebirth in Amida's paradise. This interpretation apparently prompted, in turn, an assumption that Shinzei hides in the pit to escape being killed by his attackers. (The *Rufu-bon* text adds the touch that, once sealed in the pit, he breathes through a straw.) This idea ignores Shinzei's resolve, however mysteriously motivated and however magical in nature, to die for his *kimi* (Go-Shirakawa). To this end he surely meant to die undetected in the pit, presumably of starvation.

26. *Sai* ("west") is a specifically Buddhist reading of the character read *zei* (or *sei*) in Shinzei's name.
27. This Saikō is dramatically executed in *Heike* 2:3 for conspiring against Kiyomori.
28. *Sendatsu*, the Kumano monks who acted as guides for pilgrims.
29. The text specifies both types of imperial decree: *senji* (from a reigning emperor) and *inzen* (from a retired emperor).
30. A ceremonial baton held by a courtier in a formal setting.
31. Yorimitsu (948–1021) was a great warrior in the Minamoto lineage. Mitsuyori (1124–1173), however, was a Fujiwara descended from Fuyutsugu (774–826).
32. The boards on which one stood before mounting the steps up to the privy chamber. They were arranged so that the emperor could hear any approaching footsteps.
33. Korekata was the chief of the imperial police (*kebiishi no bettō*). It is not clear why the text speaks of a commander of the Palace Guards (*Konoe-daishō*), since Nobuyori was actually the intendant of the Right Gate Watch (*Uemon no kami*).
34. Kuroto-no-gosho, a long gallery extending from the north aisle of the Seiryōden to the Kōkiden.
35. A window near the north end of the west wall of the privy chamber—one could see through it into the *oni-no-ma* and the *hiru-no-omashi*.
36. There were twenty classes of death sentence. The first was by strangulation, the second by decapitation.
37. The northernmost gate on the west side of the greater palace compound.
38. Of the inner palace compound: the Sakuhei Gate.
39. Genjō was a *biwa* and Suzuka a *wagon* (musical instruments). The emperor had a special sort of throne (*daishōji*) to sit on and keys to all government offices. The "slips to announce the hours" (*toki no fuda*) were meant to be hung near the privy chamber.
40. *Kashiwabasami*. This was done in an emergency situation requiring decisive action.
41. The meaning of this gibe is unclear.
42. On the east side of the open area immediately in front of the Shishinden.
43. Shinzei had rebuilt the palace in Hōgen 2 (1157).
44. Unlike those of Shigemori's men, who are a fresh contingent.
45. A younger, full sister of Yoritomo.
46. Later texts of *Heiji* have Kiyomori so panicked by the war cries that he puts his helmet on backwards and Shigemori scolds him—a farcical touch that makes little sense, considering how these texts and *Heike* treat Kiyomori otherwise.
47. *Kurohoro* fletching, rare and impressive. A full quiver usually held twenty-four arrows.
48. Motomori was then in his twenty-first year, Munemori in his thirteenth.
49. Yorimasa's title means "The Genji [Minamoto] who is the head of the Armory." "Ise Heiji" means "Heike [Taira] from the province of Ise."
50. *Ishiyumi harite*: they had balanced boulders on the edge of the drop-off, secured with ropes. A boulder was meant to fall when its rope was cut.
51. The Heike had dismantled it to keep the Genji from the east away from the capital.

52. Part of Murasakino, west of Funaoka-yama. It was a burning ground.
53. "Seashore" is a textile print pattern. The hat is an *ori-eboshi* ("folded *eboshi*"), straightened because of the formality of the occasion.
54. The expression seems to mean "suffer a big loss while you're off somewhere having a good time." *Sarugaku* was a form of popular entertainment.
55. This list, in which several names are wrong, is so complicated that I have abbreviated it.
56. Fujiwara no Shimeko (1131–1176), Emperor Konoe's empress and a daughter of Fujiwara no Koremichi. This title (*ingō*) was awarded her only in 1168.
57. The "inner" teaching is Buddhism, while the "outer" teachings are Shinto, Confucianism, and Taoism.
58. A place celebrated in the poetic canon but otherwise unknown.
59. Muro-no-yashima was just north of Taga, the provincial capital, near present-day Tochigi-shi. The spot was near an Ōmiwa shrine, also known as Muro-no-yashima Myōjin. *Shūchūshō* (ca. 1190) describes a spring there—presumably a hot spring—from which rose a smokelike plume of vapor.
60. A conventionally emotive rather than realistically descriptive expression.
61. The Hachijō-Karasumaru temporary palace (*sato dairi*).
62. In Tengyō 3 (940), palace New Year events were canceled because of the rebellion of Masakado and Sumitomo.
63. The *nurigome*, the walled inner room of a Heian dwelling.
64. Under such painful circumstances the language often refers to children as "keepsakes left behind" (*wasuregatami*).
65. At Konoe and Nishi-no-tōin.
66. Yoshitomo had been the governor of Shimotsuke but never of Kii, which merely allows a word play on *ki no kami*, "governor of Kii" and "up a tree." The second play is on *yoshitomo*, the name and "[does] not [look] good"; while the third, on *age-tsukasa*, suggests "hung" and "promotion."
67. Probably Fujiwara no Sukemi, whose poetry collection (*Tōroku shū*) survives. The poem relies on word plays impossible to translate and all but hopeless to explain. I have tried to convey their spirit instead. Tawara Tōda is Fujiwara no Hidesato, who, together with Taira no Sadamori, put down Taira no Masakado's rebellion in 940.
68. The 18th of the month was the day dedicated to Kannon.
69. In the lunar calendar this date counts as early spring.
70. "Hot" water includes any hot drink or medicinal infusion.
71. Ike-dono (?–?, also Ike-no-zenni) was a daughter of Fujiwara no Munekane. She had been the wet nurse of Shigehito, Sutoku's son. She lived in the Ike-dono ("Pond Pavilion") at Rokuhara. Tadamori spent his later years with her there. The pavilion later passed to Taira no Yorimori (1131–1186), a younger brother of Kiyomori.
72. The fifth son of Nintoku, the half-legendary sixteenth emperor. Ankō (see following text) was the twentieth emperor.
73. The second son of Abe no Yoritoki (?–1057), who started the Earlier Nine Years War.
74. The narrative has the outcome backwards. Hui Qi (J. Kaikei) is where the king of Yue (J. Etsu) was defeated. He triumphed at Gusu-shan (J. Koso-san).

75. On the bank of Sanzu no Kawa (the River of Death), a hag known as Datsueba stripped the dead of their clothes.
76. *Aoki mayuzumi*, drawn on with the dried froth from the indigo dye vat.
77. *Gukanshō* reports Go-Shirakawa seating himself in this viewing stand (*sajiki*) and there summoning "menials" (*gesu*)—presumably singers, entertainers, and so on. The incident narrated here follows. The account says that the planks used came from the stack of lumber on Horikawa. The Tsunemune and Korekata mentioned were allies of Emperor Nijō, hence enemies of Go-Shirakawa. The viewing stand seems to have been a permanent, roofed structure, perhaps built for viewing the festival procession of the nearby Inari shrine.
78. Moronaka's poem looks back to Ariwara no Narihira's visit to Yatsuhashi in *Ise monogatari* 23.
79. The "kibi minister" was Kibi no Mabi, who, in the eighth-century reign of Emperor Shōtoku, served as right minister and ambassador to China. *Kibi* means common millet (*Panicum miliaceum*), *awa* foxtail millet (*Setaria italica*), and *hie* Japanese millet (*Echinochloa utilis*).
80. He declines to attend the *hatago furumai*, a party held at the end of a journey. Provisions left over from the journey were consumed.
81. *Honchō seiki* for Kyūan 3/6/15 (1147) records that when Kiyomori commissioned *dengaku* at Gion, to fulfill a vow, some of the men sent to guard the performance were armed, and men from the shrine sought to keep them out of the shrine grounds. A clash ensued, and men on both sides were wounded.
82. A passage from a Chinese poem, almost proverbial in medieval Japan. The "Hu barbarians" live in the north, and the land of Yue is in the south.
83. Liu Yuzhou, the fourth son of Emperor Xuan of Han. Given the land of Dongping, he died there, still longing to go home. The line seems to be from a poem in Chinese (*kanshi*) by Fujiwara no Hironari.
84. A son of the mythical (Chinese) Yellow Emperor. The name also just means "traveler."
85. The name of Emperor Wang of Shu, but also simply a literary name for the *hototogisu* (cuckoo). According to legend, Du Yu left his state after abdicating but so greatly missed home that after death he became a *hototogisu* that cried *Bu ru gui qu*, "The best of all is to go home."
86. The east end of Sanjō and the gateway to the Tōkaidō and Tōsandō.
87. *Noshi-awabi*, a felicitous gift.
88. The boy presumably had only his boyhood name at the time. He was probably then in his ninth year.
89. *Heike* 5:1 and 6:8 describe the move of the capital to Fukuhara and the building of Sutra Island.
90. In the hills behind what is now Kobe. It had long been a famous sight.
91. The *Rishu-kyō*, a sutra central to Shingon (Esoteric) Buddhism, is chanted morning and evening. "Copied with five brushes" means that Kōbō Daishi held brushes in both hands, with both feet, and in his mouth.
92. Sugawara no Michizane (845–903), enshrined at Kitano (a district of the capital) as the deity Tenjin.

93. *Zenji* is a common title for a low-ranking monk. The *aku* ("bad") is the one affected by tough warriors like Akugenda or, elsewhere in the history of these years, Akushichibyōe Kagekiyo.
94. Cloistered Prince Enkei, a son of Go-Shirakawa.
95. Kurama is a mountain temple a short distance north of Kyoto. According to later legend, Yoshitsune (Shanaō) learned swordsmanship there from a tengu.
96. The wrathful Buddhist guardian of the north and the principal deity at Kurama.
97. A valley or ravine that runs northwest from Kurama to Kibune. It was a site of mountain ascetic practice.
98. This daughter, adopted by Fujiwara no Kanemasa, is the "Mistress of the Gallery" mentioned in *Heike* 1:5.
99. "Acolyte" translates *chigo*, which also suggests something like "temple pet."
100. Yoritomo is at Hōjō, about six miles from Kisegawa.
101. Satō Tsuginobu was killed in a famous scene of the battle of Yashima (*Heike* 11:3). Satō Tadanobu fled the capital with Yoshitsune, eventually returned there, and in 1186 killed himself under attack. A fox disguised as Tadanobu is a key figure in the legend of Yoshitsune's beloved Shizuka and the drum Hatsune.
102. *Yumaki*, a white silk garment worn by a maid while bathing her mistress.
103. The home of the Satō brothers, now within the city limits of Fukushima.
104. These localities identify warrior groups descended from Fujiwara no Hidesato.
105. *Gihei*, warriors construed as acting on behalf of the emperor.
106. A sort of backpack chest worn by monkish travelers.
107. Genji warrior leagues.
108. *Heike* 5:11 describes this disaster in the 10th month of Jishō 4 (1180).
109. Now the Nagara River.
110. *Heike* 7:19 mentions this oath.
111. The head of a Genji warrior league in Musashi.
112. *Haritsuke*, the word used to translate "crucifixion." However, the punishment here is not crucifixion proper. The two men are apparently nailed to boards laid on the ground.
113. Hidehira died on Bunji 3/10/29 (1187), and Yoshitsune on Bunji 5/intercalary 4/30 (1189). Yasuhira was destroyed on Bunji 5/9/3.
114. *Doburoku* is raw, home-brew sake.
115. Zhao Wu, a minister of Jin in the Spring and Autumn period, was born immediately after his father was assassinated. He evaded the enemy by hiding under his mother's skirts and not crying. Eventually, he revived the house of Zhao. Ison of Qin is unidentified.

## An Account of the Jōkyū Years

1. The profane world of the cycle of transmigration.
2. These kalpa names appear to be fanciful. The past buddhas mentioned in following text (Kuruson, Kunagonmuni, Kashō) are the fourth, fifth, and sixth in the canonical list of the Seven Buddhas of the Past.

3. The complementary pair formed by the "Buddha's Way" and the "Sovereign's Way" (*buppō ōbō*) was fundamental to the medieval Japanese concept of a civilized state. It summed up the ideal complementarity between the "way" (or "law," or "teaching") of the Sovereign (government) and that of the Buddha (the ideals and protection of religion).
4. The second emperor of the Later Han Dynasty. Buddhism reached China during his reign, in AD 65.
5. No authority is known for this statement about the reign of Suizei or for the one in following text about Kaika.
6. Jingū Kōgō is not now seen as having reigned in her own right. However, many medieval or earlier documents refer to her unambiguously as an emperor. The terms for "emperor" are rarely gender-specific, but this one, *jotei*, means explicitly "woman emperor."
7. One of two fourteenth-century documents entitled *Hachiman gudō kun* claims that Chūai was killed by a "stray arrow" (*nagareya*) in a battle with a foreign monster. See Hagiwara Tatsuo, ed., *Hachiman gudōkun [jō]*, in Sakurai Tokutarō et al., eds., *Jisha engi shū*, Nihon koten bungaku taikei 20 (Tokyo: Iwanami, 1975), 171. The *Nihon shoki* account of Chūai's death is different.
8. This notion of the "Three Koreas" (*sankan*) is unintelligible unless one imagines that the notion of "Korea" covers all of northeast Asia.
9. Saimei, originally Emperor Jomei's (r. 629–641) empress, had reigned previously (642–645) as Kōgyoku. No source for this claim is known.
10. There is no known source for this claim, either. Japan's first year-period (*nengō*) was Taika (645) rather than Taihō.
11. Another claim that makes little sense.
12. The one delivered to Yoritomo by Mongaku in *Heike* 5:10.
13. Actually, he had first done so in 1180. His father had grown up in Kamakura.
14. *Azuma kagami* (Kenryaku 2/2/28 [1212]) records that he fell from his horse on the way back from the bridge dedication. However, *Hōryakukanki* (mid-14th century) claims that he fell ill upon returning to Kamakura, after looking into eyes of the ghosts of Yoshitsune and Yukiie and hearing the ghost of Antoku calling to him from the sea.
15. Yoriie (1182–1204) succeeded Yoritomo as shogun. When the Hōjō forced him to cede the post to his younger brother, Sanetomo, he moved in concert with Hiki Yoshikazu to overthrow him. He was defeated and killed.
16. The childhood name of Minamoto Sanetomo.
17. Hatakeyama Shigetada, destroyed by Hōjō Tokimasa in 1205.
18. A major commander under Yoritomo, and in *Heike* the destructive rival of Yoshitsune.
19. Actually, he received his Left Gate Watch appointment in his nineteenth year. Properly speaking, he held the title of shogun only in 1202–1203.
20. Hōjō Yoshitoki's younger brother.
21. "Triple Tiger." He is Fujiwara no Yoritsune (1218–1256), the fourth Kamakura shogun. He came of age in 1225 and was formally appointed shogun only in 1226, but all *Jōkyūki* versions make him shogun immediately.

22. In Bunji 1 (1185) Yoritomo had been granted the right to appoint constables (*shugo*) and stewards (*jitō*) throughout Japan.
23. According to *Azuma kagami* for Kenpō 7/3/9 (1219), Go-Toba responded to a request from Kamegiku by formally asking Hōjō Yoshitoki to cede him title to the Nagae and Kurahashi estates. Go-Toba's representative to the funeral of Sanetomo, assassinated some six weeks earlier, took this request to Kamakura. Six days later, Yoshitoki sent a thousand men to the capital, under his son Tokifusa, to deliver his refusal. Tokifusa also delivered Kamakura's request for Yoritsune, a son of Kujō Michiie, to succeed Sanetomo as shogun.
24. Daigen Myōō, or Daigensui, is a terrifying esoteric Buddhist protector deity. Fujiwara no Toshihito (?–?) became Chinjufu Shōgun in 915, Chinjufu being the government outpost at Taga in far northern Japan. According to *Konjaku monogatari shū* 14/45 and the very brief *Kojidan* 3/14, he proposed to attack Shiragi (Silla), not Tang. Shiragi appealed to certain great monks then studying in China, including the Japanese Enchin, to quell him, which they did. Toshihito died after slashing furiously at an invisible enemy attacking him from above. For the General's Barrow, see *Heike* 5:1.
25. Fujiwara no Kaneko, a daughter of Fujiwara no Norikane. Her elder sister was Go-Toba's nurse, hence her great influence with him.
26. Perhaps after the burning of the palace on Jōkyū 1/7/13 (1219), following the killing of Minamoto no Yorimochi on orders from Go-Toba. The rebuilding began on Jōkyū 2/3/22.
27. Presumably a saying then current, but the meaning of the original is uncertain.
28. Miura Yoshimura (?–1239), from Sagami, was a major retainer of Minamoto no Yoritomo and his successors. Taneyoshi (?–1221) was his younger brother.
29. Go-Toba and four of his sons.
30. Kyō-no-nii presumably means that a yin-yang master can convey the views only of a non-Buddhist deity (or deities) and that the law of karma, which brought Go-Toba to his present, peerless eminence in the first place, overrides the view of any such low-level power.
31. The original lists these parts in detail: *yoroi no takahimo, kusazuri, kukkei, shōji no ita, tsurubashiri, sendan no ita, wakidate.*
32. Mitsutsuna became Juō's adult name once he had come of age.
33. The end of this list may be corrupt, since the final words speak of winning over "these two or three men."
34. The first, who was married to Kiso Yoshinaka's son Shimizu no Kanja, wasted away after his death. The second was to become an imperial consort, but she died in her fourteenth year.
35. According to the Lotus Sutra, a woman cannot become five different kinds of sovereign beings, including a buddha.
36. Masako is nominally a nun. In the original she refers to herself repeatedly as "this nun."
37. In Kenryaku 3 (1213) Wada Yoshimori (a son of Yoshimune and a nephew of Yoshimura and Taneyoshi), provoked by Hōjō Yoshitoki, attacked Yoshitoki and his Kamakura headquarters. Sanetomo, the shogun, barely escaped when his

residence burned. Yoshimori was defeated and killed the next day. Yoshimura and Taneyoshi had at first promised him their support, but then they backed Yoshitoki.

38. The speaker calls Yoshitoki "the minister," referring to Sanetomo's nominal office of right minister in the court hierarchy. No doubt he really means that Yoshitoki is Sanetomo's true successor as shogun.
39. In other words, Suruga.
40. Kiyomi-ga-seki was a checkpoint (barrier) at Okitsu on the coast of Suruga (Shizuoka-ken); Shioyama was on the border between Noto, Kaga, and Etchū; and Kurosaka was on the way up Mount Tonami, toward the Kurikara ravine (*Heike* 7:6).
41. Destroyed by Hōjō Tokimasa in 1205.
42. A son of Hōjō Tokifusa and a grandson of Yoshitoki.
43. Yoshitoki's eldest son.
44. A warrior league from Musashi. The Kodama League (see following text) was also from Musashi. *Azuma kagami* mentions the Kaneko League as well. The others named are unknown.
45. A son of Yoshimura.
46. A great-great-grandson of Minamoto no Yoshiie.
47. The second son of Hōjō Yoshitoki.
48. This figure, like much in the rest of Yoshitoki's speech, is colossally exaggerated.
49. These Hokurikudō locations are in the provinces Etchū and Kaga.
50. All the locations mentioned in following text, from Ōido to Sunomata, are in the province of Mino.
51. Just south of Tsuruga.
52. It is unclear who Shui Tarō was, how his name is to be read, or where this story is from.
53. These items, mentioned again in following text, make no demonstrable sense.
54. These are in the province of Sagami (Kanagawa-ken).
55. The 1st of the 5th month of 1221.
56. The "explicator" (*rissha*) answered the questions posed by the "questioner" (*monja*) during a formal, scholastic debate at a great Buddhist temple.
57. A promontory on the west side of Lake Biwa.
58. *Inji*: rough characters, undoubtedly low-ranking monks, who fought with stones.
59. Within the modern city of Uji.
60. Sunomata figures especially prominently in the following narrative. Then in Mino, it is now Sunomata-chō in Anpachi-gun, Gifu-ken, between the Nagara River to the east and the Ibi River to the west. The former is the main issue. "Sunomata River" is an old name for the Nagara River.
61. The text lists only ten.
62. Presumably this means that success comes from exploiting whatever resources are naturally available.
63. The expression in the original is unintelligible.
64. The relevance of this issue is unclear. As for Takeda and Ogasawara, they are indeed Seiwa Genji, while Yoshitoki is a Kanmu Heiji.

65. His men are riding with their heads held high, rather than lowered to make their faces less vulnerable to enemy arrows and to expose instead the plates that hang from the back of the helmet and protect a warrior's neck.
66. Here, as in similar passages elsewhere (for example, immediately in following text), it not clear whether the narrative is attributing all these deaths to Korenobu alone, or to him and the men under his direct command.
67. "You are Lord Yoshitoki's retainers."
68. Hachiya-no-nyūdō's son. Hachiya Saburō, in following text, must be his younger brother.
69. A younger brother of Takeda Nobumitsu (Rokurō).
70. A saying: "You never know what marvels you may encounter in life."
71. Along the Kiso River in Mino, near Unuma; now within Kakamigahara-shi, Gifu-ken. Igi-no-watari, Mamedo-no-watari, and Jiki-no-watari (see following text) are fords across the Kiso River. "Hi-no-miko" and "Morokoshi River" are unknown.
72. Yoritomo's mother was the daughter of an earlier chief priest of the Atsuta Shrine.
73. *Heike* 5:11 tells the story.
74. It is unclear when this happened, if it did, and what the two "halls" (*tate*) were. Other *Jōkyūki* texts lack the incident.
75. According to *Azuma kagami*, the three retired emperors, together with the (very briefly) reigning Emperor Chūkyō, went first to the summit of Hiei and then to the Kajii Residence at West Sakamoto. Chūkyō reigned only from the 4th to the 7th month of 1221.
76. On the 10th of the 6th month.
77. Kuisegawa was a post station in present-day Ōgaki-shi, Gifu-ken; the river corresponds to the present-day Ibi River.
78. Presumably the Kodama leader.
79. They are at the northwest corner of the intersection of Ōmiya and Kujō.
80. The West Guard was added to the retired emperor's guard in Go-Toba's time.
81. The crossing of Suzaku and Kujō, near the famous Rajō Gate (Rashōmon). At the time it constituted a sort of gateway to the city.
82. The area of Konoshima Shrine, which still exists in modern Kyoto (Ukyō-ku).
83. Prince Morisada, the "Jimyōin Prince," was the second son of Emperor Takakura, hence Go-Toba's full brother, one year older. He was appointed retired emperor, under the name Go-Takakura, without ever having reigned.
84. Prince Yutahito, enthroned as Emperor Go-Horikawa (1212–1234; r. 1221–1232).
85. An island in the Japan Sea.
86. Wakasa, Echizen, Kaga, Noto, Etchū, Echigo, Sado.
87. The residence of the prelate Sonchō.
88. At the crossing of Ichijō and Made-no-kōji.
89. Yasutoki's eldest son.
90. The residence of Kujō (Fujiwara no) Michiie, south of Kujōbōmon and west of Muromachi-kōji. The "reigning emperor," the child emperor Chūkyō, received this posthumous name only in the Meiji period.
91. Two of the imperial regalia. The sword was a replacement, the original having been lost at Dan-no-ura (*Heike* 11).

92. Konoe (Fujiwara no) Iezane, appointed on 8th of 7th month; he had briefly been regent earlier.
93. A criminal was carried this way.
94. The mother of Prince Yorihito and a daughter of Fujiwara no Nobukiyo.
95. The Mimosuso River runs past the Inner Shrine at Ise, the sanctuary of the Sun Goddess. Its constant flow stands for the unbroken Japanese imperial line.
96. Emperor Go-Saga (1220–1272; r. 1242–1246).
97. This poem, like Michiie's reply, is a *chōka* ("long poem"), a form rare in medieval Japan. An "envoy" (a short poem in the standard thirty-one-syllable form) completes both. The envoys, like the other short poems (*waka*) in these texts, are translated into the 5-7-5-7-7 syllable meter of the original. While the *chōka* follow the same 5-7-5 pattern, little would be gained by responding to the challenge of translating them that way. They (especially Michiie's) are highly ornamented, according to long-established poetic tropes and conventions, and they have little narrative content, their purpose being rather to convey mood. In short, they often resist intelligible translation. That is why these versions, however free, may still be hard to follow.
98. A figure of speech: barbarian rustics. Properly speaking, the Ebisu were the people now known as the Ainu.
99. His poem is in Chinese.
100. Sanetomo's wife was a daughter of the palace minister Fujiwara no Nobukiyo.
101. His mother was a daughter of Taira no Tomomori, a dramatic figure in *Heike*.
102. A bridge across the Kamo River, west-northwest of Rokuhara, at approximately the location of the present-day Matsubara-bashi.
103. I have speculatively added "went straight to Rokuhara," since the passage is hard to follow otherwise.
104. Actually, about 115 leagues.
105. On the 28th of the 7th month of 1221.
106. The eldest son of Go-Takakura's father was Emperor Takakura (1161–1181, r. 1168–1180). Go-Takakura had renounced the world in 1212.
107. On the 29th of the 8th month.
108. The text has the 11th month, but court usage makes the 12th month, attested elsewhere, far more likely.

# Index

GPSR Authorized Representative: Easy Access System Europe, Mustamäe tee 50, 10621 Tallinn, Estonia, gpsr.requests@easproject.com

www.ingramcontent.com/pod-product-compliance
Lightning Source LLC
Chambersburg PA
CBHW021100110726
47900CB00007B/1957

* 9 7 8 0 2 3 1 2 1 4 6 7 4 *